U0069378

The Diamond Sutra Explained

Master Nan Huai-Chin

Translated by Pia Giammasi

All rights reserved. No part of this publication may be reproduced, stored in a retrieval system, or transmitted, in any form, or by any means, electronic, mechanical, photocopying, recording, or otherwise, without the prior permission of the author.

The Diamond Sutra Explained / Master Nan Huai-Chin ;translated by Pia Giammasi
Chinese title: 金剛經說甚麼（南懷瑾文化,2019）
Published by Nan Huai Chin Culture Enterprise Limited
www.nhjce.com
Translation Copyright © 2022 by Pia Giammasi
First Edition, First Printing

ISBN: 978-986-06130-7-0
Suggested Price: NT$600

TABLE OF CONTENTS

Master Nan Huai-Chin

INTRODUCTION TO MASTER NAN

This book, originally published in Chinese, was derived from a series of lectures given by Master Nan Huai-Chin in Taipei at the Shi Fang Institute. As Master Nan is less well known in the West, I would like to briefly introduce him.

Master Nan was born in 1918 in Leqing township of Zhejiang Province in China. As a youth, he received a classical Chinese education and then entered the Zhejiang Martial Arts School. He went on to study Political Science at the Central Military School and Social Welfare at Jinling University.

During World War II, Master Nan went to the South-west part of China and trained local forces in strategies of fighting against the Japanese invasion. He subsequently went to Sichuan to teach in the Officers' Education Department of the Central Military School there.

It was in Sichuan that Master Nan met the enlightened Zen Master, Yuan Huan-hsien. Seeing his potential, the Elder Yuan convinced Master Nan to attend a week of silent meditation by asking him to be the time keeper for the meditation sessions. During this retreat, Master Nan had an awakening which was confirmed by Elder Yuan. Master Nan resigned from his military duties and attended to Elder Yuan for some time. Thereafter, he went to the O'Mei mountains for a three year solitary retreat during which he meditated and read the entire Chinese Tripitaka (the Buddhist Canon).

By the time Master Nan came out of the retreat, the war had ended. As a reward for the contribution he made in defending the country, Master Nan was offered a key government position. He turned down the offer on principle and set off with two friends to Qing Hai, Tibet to seek out well and lesser known masters of the different Buddhist and Taoist schools.

During this journey, Master Nan and his two friends got seriously ill. They stayed in a small town to recuperate. Master Nan, being the least sick of them, had to go out to seek a job as they had no money. He took a menial job at a local newspaper while at the same time caring for the two sick friends. The editor-in-chief noticed that this man was no ordinary floor sweeper. Master Nan was soon editing and writing columns for the paper.

Master Nan is not only a master of Zen and Taoism, but he was also deemed a master of Esoteric Buddhism by Gonka Rinpoche. Master Nan embodies the true spirit and essence of Buddhism, that which goes beyond religion. He has spent a lifetime verifying cultivation claims, supporting social and cultural works, writing books and teaching students.

Master Nan is the author of over forty books which span the range of Buddhism, Taoism, Confucianism and classical Chinese philosophy and history. He has taught in Universities and private institutions in China, Taiwan, Hong Kong, the United States and Europe. As well, Master Nan supported many projects, both social and cultural, which revitalized Chinese culture and alleviated poverty in Mainland China.

In Master Nan's books, one has access to his extraordinary breadth and depth of knowledge and his penetrating wisdom which flows through all of his stories and anecdotes. He provides practical tools for spiritual practitioners of all levels, the purpose of which are all clearly delineated. Master Nan wields the sword of wisdom not only in regards to the intellectual and historical framework of Buddhism but also in regards to the efficacy of spiritual cultivation practices. Through his humorous, colloquial style of lecturing, one can easily absorb and digest the material he presents, and each reading will provide new insight. One would be foolish not to take the opportunity to think deeply about, meditate on and practice what has been presented. Master Nan's teachings are given in hopes that the listeners and readers will experience and realize the teachings, the Dharma, for themselves.

Personal Note

I first met Master Nan in March of 1989 in Hong Kong. It was my great fortune to be living on the same street as he was and a Buddhist nun, Ven. Hong Ren, arranged for me to meet him.. Master Nan can be described as a distinguished looking Chinese gentleman with a petite frame and strong features. He usually wears a dark blue, traditional long Chinese long gown or "chang pao" for men, and on his feet you can usually find a pair of cloth kung fu slippers. There is always a cup of hot Oolong tea, bowl of salted peanuts and a tiny folded wet towel for finger wiping on the table next to his chair – the chair in which only Master Nan sits! As to the quality of Master Nan's voice, it is something very special. It has many moods - sometimes calm and smooth like a lake, sometimes like a babbling stream and sometimes like the roaring ocean. In any case, the sound of his voice is deep and sonorous.

In my first conversation with Master Nan, he asked me if I was having any difficulty in my meditation practice. I told him that thoughts would often disturb my mental quiet. Master Nan then asked me where the thoughts came from and I looked and saw that thoughts come out of nowhere. I told this to Master Nan and he asked me where the thoughts went after they left. Again I looked inside and saw that they simply disappeared back into nowhere. After reporting this finding, Master Nan looked me straight in the eye and said, "Right, so don't worry about them."

After meeting him, during that period of time, I would go every evening to his house where he would give teachings. At that time my Chinese was very poor, but somehow he was able to communicate much to me and the other students did their best to help me understand his teachings. Over the weeks and months, Master Nan gently poked holes into my ideas of what Buddhism, spiritual cultivation and enlightenment were all about, and pushed open my mental walls of limitations. He taught me to stop grasping at thoughts. It is difficult to put into words all that I have learned from Master Nan. The wisdom of his teachings continually unfolds within my life. For example, he taught me to see things for what they are - to unwrap things from their cultural packaging or from my preconceived notions and prejudices and most importantly, to distinguish the appearance of something from its essence and function.

Master Nan always encouraged his students to be clear on the role that they play in life. Many problems occur because people are not clear about the role that they ought to be playing. If one wants to be a lay practitioner, then one must balance one's responsibility to work and family with one's commitment to practice. One must learn how to include one's work and family in one's spiritual practice. If one has a calling to live a monastic life and one's conditions allow for one to do so, then one should put all their effort into living the true spirit of a monastic. Since I have played many roles, this teaching has been important and helpful in aligning my energy in relation to the priorities each role demands.

Master Nan sets an incredible example having played each of the roles in his life with great wisdom and compassion. He has gone from riches to rags to riches many times in his life and whether he be rich or poor, Master Nan is always generous to the extent of his means. He has a magnanimous heart and spends all of his time, energy and money helping people any way he can. Master Nan treats his students like his own children, caring for their health and well being as well as their spiritual progress. Although Master Nan plays all roles to his best, he is not attached to any of them and so there is always a light, playfulness in all of his actions. Thus he teaches us to be serious about what we do but to not take ourselves too seriously.

Over the years, I have had the opportunity to listen to many of Master Nan's lectures and teachings and to read his books. Master Nan always placed great importance on the Diamond Sutra, as did many Chan/Zen masters throughout the ages. At the time I decided to translate this commentary, there were not many translations of the Diamond Sutra in English. The ones that were available had many discrepancies among them and I thought that by translating Master Nan's commentary on the Diamond Sutra, it would help to bring about a more insightful translation of the original text.

I do not expect that my work will in any way be the final translation of the Diamond Sutra but I do hope that this commentary will provide a useful tool which will help future generations in their spiritual cultivation. It is up to these generations to achieve higher levels of spiritual attainment and verify the quality of this translation based on their personal experience. Having been a student of Master Nan for many years, I did my best to retain the flavor and the feeling of his teaching in the translation and to balance cultural originality with 'understandability'. I hope that the reader will forgive me for any faults in the translation and I must take consolation in knowing that no matter how hard you try, nothing will ever be perfect!

Pia Giammasi

Master Nan and Pia Giammasi
(During her time as a monastic)
January 2001 Hong Kong

Forward

Master Nan is least interested in theory. He teaches with the main purpose of providing a framework for verifying and extending one's understanding or personal practice. In this role, he acts like a great Bodhisattva capable of re-constructing instantaneously all known esoteric literature into an intelligible and contemporary framework of knowledge that can be used at the level of cultivation practice. For Master Nan, all understandings and all classifications must ultimately be transcended, and as such, dispensed with. Master Nan often reminds his students that all teachings are ultimately knots that must be untied, but without a clear and detailed understanding of these knots, one does not even know how to begin to deal with them. Thus, in his moving discourses, all the fine points (or knots) from the various schools of practice are analyzed and compared to the nth degree of detail, and one can clearly sense that Master Nan speaks with undisputed spiritual authority built on a lifetime of personal experience and realization. It would appear that, unlike most previous or contemporary teachers, Master Nan has truly embodied wisdom through practice, and practice through wisdom. True nirvana for Master Nan does not reside in quietude or for that matter in anything whatsoever. Watching Master Nan teach night after night in his informal gatherings at his guest house is to witness wisdom in action, which simply engulfs all else. Those who understand, understand it well, and are treated like fellow friends, with the Master making sure of dispensing with the customary teacher-student types of relationships. Those who don't are challenged with a sharp sword of wisdom that can often be found intimidating. For such is Master Nan's style: cutting through all garbage and leaving absolutely nothing whatsoever behind. One cannot help but feel blessed with an interpretation of the Dharma that is uniquely different and uniquely refreshing. Through Master Nan, one essentially lives an unbroken lineage that dates to primordial times.

Master Nan's work can not be translated as a literary piece. I have personally found all the previous translations of his work less than satisfying. This is no translator's fault. When presented in Chinese, there is a rhythm, a primordial music so to speak, that permeates his words through and through. This is the same cadence of a Confucius or the twist of a Shakespeare, deeply experiential, deeply poetic, and bared nude of any traits or adjectives. When transliterated into another language, this aspect of the original work is lost. I have therefore found Pia's translation uniquely different in that she appears to have some profound experiences of her own and gives an interpretation of the Master's words that is less verbatim and much more personable. Pia Giammasi understandably spent hours meditating on the more difficult passages trying to capture the flavor and the gist of the original teachings.

She started on the translation in 1993 but made little

progress because of work. In 1996, she quit her job and went into a retreat on Lantau Island for a year to do the translation. She meticulously listened to the tapes of the original teachings, compared them with the Chinese book version, and later consulted directly with Master Nan on any passages that she felt needed clarifications. Master Nan in turn very patiently gave classes on an almost weekly basis for Pia's benefit in order to further expound on some of the more subtle and hidden meanings behind the Sutra.

Pia modestly attributes the lively quality of her translation to "having spent so much time with Master Nan and having interpreted his teachings so many times in public, that I feel I know his way of speaking and joking, and his rhythm..." For many of us, the translation almost reads like Master Nan speaking in English!

Because this work represents countless hours of perseverance for Pia, I can only extend the most heartfelt thanks to her for courage and determination to take it to fruition. Thanks are also due to Tom Ormand for his detailed editorial assistance and to Ken Pang and Robert Wang for their input and help throughout.

John Ding-E Young, M.D., Ph.D.

Acknowledgements

First Edition

There are several people who deserve much credit and thanks for this book to come into being. Firstly, I wish to thank Bill Bodri for planting in me the seed of inspiration for doing the translation, for reading over the manuscript and giving me encouragement along the way. I wish to thank Tom Ormand for the gracious donation of his time and effort in doing such a thorough and meticulous editing of the manuscript. I want to thank John Young – you have honored and blessed me for offering to publish the book and giving me so much support and encouragement. Many thanks to Ken Pang, Peter Senge and Rebekah Ingalls for the wonderful advice, encouragement and help that you gave. Most of all, I wish to thank Master Nan for letting me translate his book, for all of his time and patience in helping me to understand the difficult parts, and for showering me with his wisdom and compassion throughout the years.

Second Edition

I would like to thank Andrew Nan and TH Lee for supporting the publication of the second edition. Beyond the financial support, you both give me invaluable moral support, advice, and encouragement. One couldn't ask for better Dharma brothers!

As well, great thanks to the Nan Huaijin Culture Foundation in Hong Kong, to the Heng Nan Institute in Shanghai and the many devoted individuals of the Heng Nan's team who work tirelessly behind the scenes to help carry Master Nan's vision forward. Heng Nan Institute's magnificent buildings and grounds are home to the largest collection of Master Nan's original calligraphy, and hold classes, meditation retreats, conferences, and other special events. In commemoration of the tenth anniversary of Master Nan's passing, the Nan Huaijin Memorial Hall will be inaugurated at the Heng Nan Institute. The founder of the Heng Nan Institute, TH Lee, felt that, in addition to the inauguration of the Nan Huaijin Memorial Hall, it would be propitious to have some English translations of Master Nan's books come to print. Thus, this second edition of The Diamond Sutra Explained as well as other translations are being published.

Heng Nan Institute in Shanghai

Mr. TH Lee Founder of Heng Nan Institute

The translator, Pia Giammasi, next to the statue of Master Nan created by Chan Wen-Kuei, which was unveiled at Heng Nan Institute in Shanghai on Master Nan's hundredth anniversary in 2018.

THE GREAT WISDOM ABOVE AND BEYOND ALL RELIGION

Today happens to be Tomb-Sweeping Day and it is also the start of our class on the *Diamond Sutra*. I would like to dedicate these merits to the ancestors and parents of all those sitting here, to those not sitting here, and to all beings. The *Diamond Sutra* has had an unusually large influence on Chinese culture. These past thousand or more years, who knows how many people have studied or recited the *Diamond Sutra*, and because of this sutra have received blessings or even reached enlightenment.

Among the sutras, the *Diamond Sutra* is extraordinary because it goes beyond the essence of all religions and yet encompasses the essence of all religions. Studying the *Diamond Sutra* should not be like an ordinary study of religion simply looking at the contents of the sutra in the context of Buddhism. The Buddha says within the sutra, *"All the saints and sages vary only in mastery of this."* This is to say that the Buddha sees all the saints and sages from the ancient times up to the present, all the founders of religions, every one of them as having realized Tao. It is merely due to different levels or depths of realization that, in different places and at different times, the resulting ways of teaching or transmitting the Tao, of educating, and of helping sentient beings have taken on diverse characteristics of expression.

21

This point within the *Diamond Sutra* completely goes beyond the boundaries of all religions. The *Avatamaksa Sutra* states the same message. It not only recognizes that the basic instruction of all religions is to admonish people to avoid bad and to do good, but also acknowledges that there is only one absolute truth or ultimate Tao. It is merely the methods of expression through which religions are preached and passed on that are different. Even though each person sitting here probably has his or her own religious belief, first understand this essence, then put your ideas, concepts, religious views and methods aside. In this way, the study of the *Diamond Sutra* can be extremely beneficial to each of you.

Within the Buddhist sutras, the *Diamond Sutra* falls within the *prajna* category, so its original title is the *Diamond Prajnaparamita Sutra*. What exactly is prajna? Loosely translated, prajna is great wisdom. So, why wasn't the title directly translated as the *Diamond Great Wisdom Achieving Enlightenment Sutra*? Why still keep the original Sanskrit term? Because in the past, those who translated Buddhist scriptures had five principles, one being that if there was not a word in Chinese which exactly represented the concept embodied in the Sanskrit term, it would not be translated. They instead transliterated the pronunciation of the original term and added an explanation. It is comparable to the present-day exchange of knowledge between Eastern and Western cultures. For example, the word *chi* 氣 To use (as in *ch'i-kung*, 氣功, which is the cultivation of ch'i) just doesn't translate into English. It does not represent gas, nor is it equivalent to air. Foreign languages have specific words for the different kinds of ch'i, but in Chinese the ch'i character has different meanings when used in combination with other characters. For example, air (空氣 k'ung ch'i), gas (煤氣 mei ch'i), anger (生氣 sheng ch'i) and electrical power (電氣 tien ch'i) all use the character 氣 ch'i together with other characters to make new but related words. So for the singular word 氣 ch'i, it is best to transliterate the Chinese pronunciation and add an explanation. At the time of translating the sutra into Chinese, *prajna* was not translated into "great wisdom" because of the same principle. The spirit of these translation principles within translating is quite outstanding. Prajna wisdom is not ordinary wisdom. The word *wisdom* in Chinese (智慧 *chih hui*) often gets linked up conceptually with intelligence. If one has intelligence one then also, of course, must have wisdom. But, in actuality, there are many kinds of wisdom. Prajna wisdom indicates understanding Tao, realizing Tao, cultivating the self, releasing one from the bondage of birth and death and leap over the mundane. This is not common intelligence. It is the wisdom which is the root and origin of the body of Tao. The "so-called" original, or primal, wisdom is merely a name. In contemporary understanding; it's that which goes above and beyond average intelligence and common wisdom, that which can understand the essence and origin of life, the original nature. This cannot be the result of cognition. Rather, it is the great wisdom achieved through complete engagement in the cultivation of one's body and mind. It is this level of wisdom which is prajna. The word *wisdom,* which we commonly use, cannot express the full extent of the meaning of the word *prajna.* Therefore, it is not translated.

In Buddhism, the entire scope of the meaning of *prajna* can be divided into five groups or kinds. These five kinds are just a form of categorization. The first is true form prajna; the second is alambana prajna; the third, the prajna of literature; the fourth, the prajna of expedient means and the fifth, the family of prajna. The collective substance of these five categories is the "prajna" of Diamond Prajnaparamita.

Now, let's discuss these in turn, starting with the question, "What is true form prajna?"

True Form Prajna

True form is the essential substance of Tao, or *dharmakaya*, and is exactly the true essence of enlightenment. It is the Tao to which one awakens. And just what is this Tao? Is it found in emptiness or in phenomena? That which is called true form is just the dharmakaya, the original source of being.

Did humankind originate from a man or woman? At the creation of the universe, was there an egg or was there a chicken? And was it a chicken or was it a rooster? I'm just joking! The idea is to find the original source of being and diligently pursue the fountainhead of the universe, the original form of the dharmakaya.

Enlightenment is awakening to the dharmakaya. In Buddhist terminology, enlightenment is awakening to the empty nature of the dharmakaya. This is what is called true form prajna. It is wisdom as opposed to mere intelligence, which is conceptual in nature. Intelligence is limited to previous knowledge, experience, feelings or images; whereas, the true dharmakaya is inconceivable.

Those who study the sutras will often encounter the expression *inconceivable* (不可思議 lit. the meaning cannot be pondered), and through the literati, this expression has been brought into common usage. [In Chinese, the modern usage of 不可思議 has become synonymous with *incredible*] The common use of this word, however, is fraught with misunderstanding. Its original meaning was exclusively used to describe a method of realizing the dharmakaya. We cannot reach it through common knowledge or ideas, or through thinking about it, discussing it or researching it; therefore, *"the meaning cannot be pondered."* But, take notice! This is not to say that we are not able to think about it.

This "cannot" means that one cannot use the conceptual mind. If one uses ordinary knowledge or thinking to construct a logical idea of the Tao, this is completely wrong. If the Dharmakaya can be attained through conceptualizing, this still falls within the boundaries of illusory thinking. Therefore, it is said that it cannot be reached through thought, but that is not to say that one can't think about it. It must be verified through realization and not merely through thinking about it.

By the later period of Ch'an Buddhism, the meaning of the word *Tao* was very difficult to express. For instance, if one says the word *Buddha*, one has an impression or an idea in mind. Even though in Buddhism the word *Buddha* can sometimes mean the dharmakaya, most people who hear it automatically think of a big shining Buddha statue in a temple, which is once again clinging to form. Therefore, after the T'ang and Sung Dynasty, the Ch'an school did not use the word *Tao* or the word *Buddha*. It was just "this!" "This" is just That and that is just "this!" They are all just names anyway. In the *Avatamaksa Sutra*, it says, *"Call it Tao, call it Heaven and Earth, call it God, calling it a Sage will do, Buddha will do, Tathagata will do, Nirvana will also do..."* and continues to list over a hundred names. They are all just representative of true form prajna, the dharmakaya. Actually many people are searching for "this," and it is only after they find "this" that they understand the origin of life. So within the five categories of prajna, true form prajna is the most basic.

Alambana Prajna

As to alambana prajna, within recent years, many foreign students have discussed with me how to translate the Chinese words for *alambana* (境界 *ching-chieh*). I have told them, "You absolutely must not translate them." Stretching it, one could use the word *phenomena* or *state of being*, but this comes with the idea of being in the natural world. *Alambana* can only be transliterated as *alambana*, with an explanation added. It is very difficult to translate. It is even hard to explain or to express its full flavor. For example, the alambana of a "man of Tao" is expressed in the following two quotes. As Ch'an Master Yao-shan said, *"Clouds are in the clear sky, water is in a vase."* This is very natural: Clouds float in the sky; water is in a vase on the table. One is very high and far away; one is very shallow and near. This is simply an alambana. A T'ang Dynasty poem, which describes another alambana reads, *"A thousand rivers have water, a thousand rivers' moons; ten thousand cloudless miles, the ten thousand mile sky."*

When we speak of enlightenment or prajna, we usually employ the two sentences above. There is one moon in the sky. When it shines down upon a thousand rivers, every river has the moon's reflection. This is the meaning of *"A thousand rivers have water, a thousand rivers' moons."* If for ten thousand miles there is not a speck of cloud, then it's just unobstructed clear sky. This is a wonderful alambana. Many Ch'an Masters have gained enlightenment because of such alambana.

There was a monk who lived in a hut and who wrote the following alambana couplet: *"Ten thousand miles of clear sky opens its mouth to laugh, three empty white rooms raise their fists."*

"Ten thousand miles of clear sky opens its mouth to laugh." It is the same as Maitreya Buddha, who always heartily laughs, "Ha! Ha!" When the beloved smiling Buddha with the big belly became enlightened, everything appeared in its empty nature—everything appeared joyous. The three white rooms are just three empty

rooms endlessly vast. Such verse describes one kind of alambana, but doesn't necessarily represent the alambana of enlightenment. We constantly experience different alambana in our lives. Going through a painful experience, or without there being an actual painful situation but a fantasy of suffering, or worrying about suffering, all can be called a suffering alambana. After a happy experience has gone by, the more we muse about it, the more satisfying it becomes. This is especially true with older people. They don't like to muse about the future as they're losing their strength to walk that uncertain road. Rather, they'll think back on their younger days, shake their head and laugh to themselves, once again recollecting the flavor of those experiences. These are all alambana. One can see that they can be recognizable experiences, but they can't be put into words.

A person who is on the path of Tao, or an intellectual, will experience different alambana with each step that person takes. Just like one who is an artist, today he gets some new insight, or paints a painting and from it gains insight or inspiration difficult to put into words. This result is his alambana. Laborers also will have alambana specific to them. If a bricklayer, when he today lays the bricks and applies the mortar, produces an especially even wall, he will feel very satisfied. "Ahh! This is bricklaying!" This is an alambana that comes from laying bricks. This term *alambana* includes every different kind of state. When followers of the Tao make a little improvement or accomplish a small achievement, their alambana is just a little bit different. If they make a big improvement or advance, then there will be a big difference in their alambana. To put it another way, when one, through cultivation, reaches a certain alambana, life's alambana—in the larger sense of the word—opens up to a certain degree.

For us who are not yet walking the path of Tao, what alambana is there? There is the alambana of suffering common to all sentient beings. There is an old poem that reads, *"One hundred years, thirty-six thousand days; if not in the midst of worry, then in the throws of sickness."*

If one lives to be a hundred, that's one hundred years, day by day, three hundred and sixty days in a year. If one lives to be a hundred, it's but thirty-six thousand days. This is the alambana of humans. During the course of a day, if it's not frustration, then it's worry, or else maybe coming down with a cold, or a sore back perhaps. Even the perfectly healthy still get old—the eyesight goes, the hearing goes, the hair goes white, not a day goes by without some malady. This is the average human alambana. So it is said that the human experience is one of suffering as opposed to the majestic experience of *"Ten thousand miles of clear sky opens its mouth to laugh, three empty white rooms raise their fists."* The deportment of such a person is quite different.

There is an old saying, *"To be a true Buddhist is the work of a great man, but not necessarily the work of emperors, generals and statesman."* To be a Buddhist and walk the path of Tao takes a great man. Emperors, generals and statesman, although they may have an impressive manner, great ambitions, magnanimity and gifted abilities, still may not have the capacity to become enlightened or be true Buddhists. Why is this? Because the impressive manner, great ambitions, magnanimity, etc. of a true Buddhist are still different from those of great worldly men. Where does this different kind of alambana come from? It comes from true form prajna, arising naturally from the dharmakaya. For those who have realized true emptiness, the development of great wisdom is boundless. In Buddhist terminology, it's called "untaught wisdom" or "natural wisdom." At the moment of enlightenment, one's own treasury of wisdom opens up. It is not transmitted by a teacher; rather, one's original wisdom bursts forth. Above and below the heavens, there is not a thing unknown. This highest alambana of prajna cannot be attained through mental effort. It comes forth naturally. One does not need to think about it; it flows out naturally. This is the alambana of prajna wisdom itself.

Literary Prajna

We all know that literature embodies wisdom. Literature is also language because it takes spoken words and records them, changing them into written language. The symbols which represent Chinese language and thought are called Chinese characters and produce Chinese literature. The symbols which represent spoken English are called English words and produce English literature. French, German, and Russian all serve as symbols for their thoughts and spoken languages. Literature has its own realm. We have all been to school and can read, but how many people actually become true littérateurs? We know all the words, but still are not within the realm of the literati. For most, the wonderful sentences don't come out. There is no literary prajna. Yet some people's spoken language is like verse, where every sentence is poetic. Such a person has reached a scholarly alambana and has literary prajna.

Why is the *Diamond Sutra* so popular in China? One reason is because it is the product of Kumarajiva's literary prajna. He translated many sutras of which the *Diamond Sutra* and the *Lotus Sutra* have had an enormous influence on Chinese culture. The style of his writing created a special kind of elegant verse within Chinese literature—very moving Buddhist literature. By the way, his translation of the *Vimalakirti-Nirdesa Sutra* is also very special. It formed virtually its own literary realm. So later, when Dharma Master Hsuan-tsang and others did translations, there was no way for them to outdo Kumarajiva simply because of the difference in their levels of literary prajna.

Even though all may have the same amount of education, not everyone will become a true scholar. It's the same with those who cultivate the Tao. Some, although they may be diligent cultivators, may not reach the goal of enlightenment. This has a definite connection with literary prajna.

In the Ch'ing Dynasty, there was a historian named Chao-i, who was also a great scholar and poet. In his later years, he wrote three famous poems. One of them reads as follows:

In youth learning to wield language seems a bitter study, difficult to complete;
The presumption is made that one's effort is insufficient.
Not 'til one's golden age does one know it's not the effort;
Three parts are human striving, the remaining seven determined by heaven.

The poem says that as a youth while studying the subtleties of using language, one cannot fully express one's self, and one often feels awkward or unskillful while wielding this tool. It always seems as though one's effort is not enough. It is only after one gets old that one realizes one could kill oneself trying, but the effort is useless because only thirty percent is in the effort. The other seventy percent comes from natural ability. But, this refers just to the ordinary case. I know of and have personally met several great monks, who, although completely illiterate, after enlightenment wrote wonderful poetry, prose, etc. It seems almost unbelievable. When did they do all that studying? On which day? They hadn't received any formal education and they ordinarily didn't read any books.

Eighty years ago, my teacher met a monk one day who had originally been a barber. Unlike the hair stylists of today who are very sophisticated, the barbers of those days had a very low position in society. A barber would wander throughout the countryside "carrying his shop on his shoulder," so to speak. With a small stove on the front of the carrying pole and a bucket of water on the back, he would stop and set up shop whenever someone called to him. At that time, the children of barbers were not even permitted to attend the national examinations as the entrance qualifications were very strict. However, this barber became an enlightened Ch'an Master, an omniscient being. Upon passing away, an abbot left his temple to him. After he became the new abbot, some called him Abbot Yang, while others called him Barber Yang. Many scholars came to test him asking, "Abbot Yang, there's a sentence about which I'm unclear... Which book is it from?" He'd answer that it's on such and such page from such and such book. My teacher was very mischievous in his youth and went to ask the abbot about a sentence from *Dream of the Red Chamber*. Strangely enough, the abbot answered without mistake.

There was a rich opium addict who wished to quit, but couldn't do so on his own. He decided to ask Barber Yang to use some supernatural method to help him break this opium addiction. He went to see Abbot Yang and said, "Venerable Yang, please shave my head." (*Note: It was the style at the time for Chinese men to shave the front half of their heads and form a long braid of the hair on the back half.) While being shaved, the man started to have withdrawal symptoms—his nose ran and eyes watered profusely. Incidentally, he forgot to state his reason for coming.

As he was in great pain, this "Barber Yang" knowingly gave him a light slap on the back saying, "Leave it!" meaning escape. After this shave, the man never again smoked opium.

Upon enlightenment, literary prajna flows forth naturally. It is not the product of intelligence, which is merely superficial. Enlightened persons have incredible powers of memory. Just how powerful? Not only back to the memories of early childhood, but even the events of past lives can be clearly recalled. You may find this to be very strange, but there actually is such a thing. This is why the poet Su Tung-p'o wrote, *"To begin one's studies in this lifetime is already too late."* If we really wish to study, we must start early. This lifetime's efforts are in preparation for the next life.

Upon enlightenment, the knowledge learned throughout thousands of lives is at one's fingertips. This is the result of the functioning of prajna wisdom. Great cultivators have good memories. At a glance, they can take in ten lines. Those unskilled at study must plod along word by word. For the few, a page goes by at a glance, ten lines at a time, a thousand lines a day are not forgotten even when old. The older this person gets, the stronger his or her power of memory becomes. Of course, this person has great samadhi and prajna wisdom. This is literary prajna.

We have discussed these three different aspects of prajna so as to understand what the prajna of the *Diamond Prajnaparamita Sutra* means. The remaining two aspects of prajna are even more subtle and difficult to achieve. They deal with mental processes and moral behavior. The fourth aspect of prajna is prajna of skillful means.

Prajna of Skillful Means

Buddhist scriptures always mention skillful means. Within Chinese literature, there is a famous insult which goes, *"Without erudition, one is unskilled."* This is not an ordinary insult. In the book *History of the Han Dynasty,* it is used to insult Huo Kuang, one of the greatest generals of the Western Han Dynasty. During the Western Han period of Chinese history, he was a high-ranking general who was also a great leader and could be said to have been the stabilizing force behind that dynasty. But later historians criticized him saying, "Without erudition, one is unskilled." They were of the opinion that he did not have enough education. Therefore, in handling matters of national importance, he lacked intellectual sophistication and used inappropriate methods. So, we can see that this was no light insult. The average person is not even worthy of such an insult. It is an insult that has gone down in the annals of history, an incredibly skillful and sophisticated insult.

Skillfulness is not merely having means and ways. If one who has erudition and moral values wishes to educate another person, he naturally will be able to accomplish this task without anyone telling him how to be an educator. Simply being a good person and handling affairs well can reach the height of a sophisticated art without training, just naturally. For example, if one who teaches the sutras is able to make use of some special method to help others immediately grasp the meaning of difficult concepts, this can be said to be prajna of skillful means. This is the behavior of realized beings who use all kinds of expedient means to help society, to help mankind.

We have all seen images of the thousand-armed, thousand-eyed Kuan Yin Bodhisattva (Avalokiteshvara in Sanskrit)—one thousand arms, each with an eye in the middle of the palm and three more eyes on the head. We must kneel down and bow our heads in respect, great merciful thousand-armed, thousand-eyed Kuan Yin Bodhisattva. We must bow our heads to the ground; but, if when you lifted your head up, standing there in front of you were a person with a thousand arms and eyes, you'd probably jump out of your skin. Right? Of course you would. You've never seen anything like that before. You bow down your head and pray to the Bodhisattva, but if the Bodhisattva really comes, you may not be able to handle it.

There is a Chinese historical figure called "Duke of Ye, Lover of Dragons" from the Spring and Autumn Warring States Period. Ye was a place name and the Duke of Ye was the feudal prince of this small place. People today like to keep pet dogs. The Duke of Ye, however, throughout his whole life was interested only in having a pet dragon. Unfortunately, he had never seen a real one. Still, he had dragons carved on the pillars of the main hall, the paintings were all of dragons, in the bedrooms there were dragons, the furniture was decorated with dragons, and so forth. This whole thing really touched the heart of a real dragon who decided to go see the good duke. When the duke caught sight of it, he dropped dead out of fright.

Such is the case with many who search for the Tao; when they finally have some realization, it is the same story. So, if Kuan Yin Bodhisattva stood in front of you—we won't even mention the thousand eyes in each of the palms looking at you—just the eye in the middle of the forehead would be enough to make one faint. Right?

What does all this mean? Just think, if a person had the ability of a thousand arms and the wisdom behind a thousand eyes what s/he would be capable of doing! If one is to truly achieve great compassion and sympathy, one must have all the expedient methods and abilities of the Buddha with a thousand arms and eyes. This is the multifarious functioning of conduct and wisdom. To put it literally, *"Randomly picking up an object, each reveals the highest truth."* Any object randomly chosen can be used to express the highest wisdom. Like a magician who can grab any item and create magical illusions, those with prajna of skillful means can use any common thing to illustrate the highest wisdom.

Family of Prajna

The family of prajna follows from the wisdom that pours out from enlightenment. To use Buddhist terminology, it can be called virtuous conduct in accordance with resolution; or in modern language, behavior which is naturally moral. Virtuosity effortlessly comes forth in all situations.

What then is the family of prajna? We have all heard of the six *paramitas,* which are generosity (*dana*), discipline (*sila*), patience (*ksanti*), enthusiasm or effort (*virya*), meditative concentration (*dhyana*) and prajna. The first five make up the family of prajna which show us how to practice generosity, how to practice discipline, how to be patient, how to practice dhyana, in order to reach the highest enlightenment and become a Buddha. These can also be seen as five categories of virtuous conduct in accordance with resolution, all of which make up the family of prajna. I will not go into these further at this point since the content of the *Diamond Sutra* explains these five actions.

Now we can see that the concept of prajna includes all of these different aspects. Therefore, it cannot merely be translated as *wisdom.* There is really no appropriate translation and so we use the original Sanskrit term. Prajna includes the origin of enlightenment, and from the origin of enlightenment springs forth all these different aspects of prajna.

Nothing Undestroyable

Now we all have in our hands this *Diamond Prajnaparamita Sutra.* Why, before the *Prajna,* is the word *Diamond* added? Diamond amongst all materials is the hardest. The sutra, like a diamond drill, can penetrate all dharmas and also can be said to establish all dharmas. As only diamonds can cut diamonds, there is nothing which cannot be penetrated by it. So this sutra is called the *Diamond Prajna Paramita Sutra*. There are five or six different translations of the *Diamond Sutra*, but the one which is most commonly used is that translated by Kumarajiva. The other translations sometimes add "The Severer" to the beginning of the title, so it becomes, *The Severer Diamond Prajna Paramita Sutra*. The meaning being to sever the root of all pain and suffering and to become a saint, become a Buddha. Perhaps Kumarajiva felt that the sutra already clearly expressed this meaning within its text and so there was no need to put these extra words in the title.

If we were to name the sutra by its function, it could be called: *Severer of All Dharmas, Destroyer of All Sufferings, the Great Prajna Wisdom which Perfects All Buddhas, the Sutra Which Enables Escape from the Sea of Suffering by Leaping to the Other Shore.* (*Paramita* means to arrive at the other shore).

If I were to use the traditional method of lecturing and lectured two hours every day for a month straight, I still wouldn't be able to get through the title of the sutra. The traditional method, which entails word by word explanation, is actually an excellent way of teaching. It's very thorough. The word *sutra* alone sometimes could take a week to explain, and the next week would be spent explaining *diamond*. A month could be spent on the title alone, leaving one wondering where the title ends and the sutra begins. We will not employ this method as this kind of lecturing doesn't suit my personality. Rather, we'll just use a clear and simple, straightforward explanation.

Kumarajiva and the Empress Wu Tse-t'ien

Now I'd like to speak about the translator who was Kumarajiva, the famous Tripitaka Master of Yao-ch'in. His father was the prime minister of an Indian state who left his position to become a monk. His mother was a princess who forced the monk to disrobe and marry her. After the birth of their son, Kumarajiva, the princess herself decided she wished to become a Buddhist nun, but her husband wouldn't allow this. After all, he'd been very content living a monk's life until the princess forced him to marry her, and now she wanted to become a nun! Their story alone would make a good novel.

When Kumarajiva was eleven or twelve years old, he could be said to have already become enlightened. When he was in his thirties, he came to mainland China during the Southern and Northern Period. In order to invite this scholar to come, three Chinese countries were overthrown. (At that time, China was divided into separate countries.) In the history of mankind, from ancient times up to the present, never has there been such shocking events as in this historical period. It is very interesting to study.

Kumarajiva's scholarship was so highly prized that each of the countries vied for him, and economics and politics both took a back seat to this quest. One country destroyed another country, and the third country then destroyed this country. The whole history of it is actually quite long, and it would take at least two weeks of lectures to get through, so I'll just leave it at this brief explanation.

There are a few verses preceding the Chinese version of the *Diamond Sutra.* Today, especially since so many female seekers have come, I'll say a few words on the following *gatha*:

Nothing can be higher than the deepest subtle Dharma,
Throughout hundreds of thousands of eons most difficult to encounter,
I now see, hear, receive, retain, study and observe,
Desirous to realize the Tathagatha's true meaning.

These lines were written by the Empress Wu Tse-t'ien. The Empress herself had studied in depth the *Diamond Sutra* and is also reported to be the one who wrote the "How to" verses.

How to attain immortality,
the indestructible vajrasattva?
What conditions must come together
in order to gain indestructible strength?
How is it possible through this sutra
finally to reach the other shore?
May the Buddhas unlock the subtle mysteries

and proclaim them widely to all sentient beings.

Within Buddhist literature, these verses are a masterpiece. Buddhist verse must avoid sounding frivolous or humorous. It must be very carefully composed like this.

"How to attain immortality, the indestructible vajrasattva?" How can one gain peace, long life, immortality? Everyone wishes to live a long life, but just how does one truly achieve this? And exactly just how long is "long?" How does one get a body that doesn't ever get sick, doesn't die, the diamond indestructible body? Through what methods is it attained? This sutra tells how to reach the permanent, indestructible origin of all life.

"What conditions must come together in order to gain indestructible strength?" Indestructible strength is another thing for which humans wish, but what method, what culmination of circumstances can result in indestructible strength? Within our world there is nothing which is truly reliable or indestructible. Life is certainly not very reliable or indestructible. At the most, we have one hundred or two hundred years. Families, parents, children, spouses live together for a time but are also unreliable, and at last, all must separate. There is a saying frequently seen in Buddhist sutras, *"All gatherings will break apart."* When the circumstances bringing gatherings together are finished, all must separate. After money rolls in, then come the bills. There will be one day when one's fortune runs out and following it, the money goes. After one comes to power, there will come the day when one

will lose it. Buildings constructed will one day crumble. Is there anything on this earth indestructible and unchanging? Is there truly such a thing as indestructible strength? You must search for the answer.

"How is it possible through this sutra, finally to reach the other shore?" After studying the *Diamond Sutra*, how can one use the methods within it to escape from the sea of samsaric sufferings here, to the culmination of permanent joy and purity in nirvana over there? What are the methods? In relation to these questions, we hope that the Buddhas will reveal the most subtle, mysterious methods to us, to all sentient beings.

The *Diamond Sutra* which we use now is divided into thirty-two sections; whereas, the original translation had no divisions. The later period of education was different, as were literary customs, and so, required chapters and paragraphs. Originally, sutras were just one continuous paragraph, without punctuation even. Divisions were a later creation. The thirty-two sections of the *Diamond Sutra* were edited during the reign of Liang Wu-ti (A. D. 502-549). Who was the one actually doing the editing? It was the eldest son of Emperor Wu, Prince Chao-ming. (Prince Chao-ming also produced the *Chao-ming Wen Hsuan*, a collection of Chinese literary masterpieces, which he edited and which is mandatory reading when studying Chinese literature.)

Dividing the *Diamond Sutra* into sections and adding titles to each of these sections was the outstanding work of Prince Chao-ming. The titles were really very well chosen as they point directly to the main idea in each part. For instance, the first section of the sutra explains the reason for the teaching, or rather the reason behind the teaching. Examining it, one finds that the teaching in every sutra had its reason for being given. This lecture today also has its reasons behind it: Mr. Hsiao, Mr. Ts'ui and about five other true seekers left me no choice but to start this class!

The *Diamond Sutra* evokes powerful responses in those who read, recite and study it. In my own experience, I know one can actually get to the point of receiving whatever is truly sought. I'll tell everyone a secret. When I was in middle school, every morning I woke up at four. After exercising and practicing kung fu, I'd recite the *Diamond Sutra* once. Why would I recite it? Well, I didn't understand any of it, but people told me that it was very good to recite it, so I did. Because I lived at school, I didn't dare to use the wooden fish (beaten in time with recitation in temples) while reciting. I was afraid that people would think I was crazy. So I'd sneak into the reception room and recite the whole sutra as fast as I could. Once, at the part which reads "no notion of self, person, being and life," suddenly, I felt that I had disappeared. Where I disappeared to, I'm not sure, but after that I stopped reciting for some time. Later on, I came to understand the meaning of what happened. Reciting the sutra resulted in that unexpected experience. In historical accounts, there are many incidents like this.

During the Japanese-Chinese war, I was away from my hometown for eight years. Being far away from home and family, not being able to correspond and not knowing whether they were alive or dead, I kept only one vow. Without fail, every night before sleeping, I'd recite the *Diamond Sutra* and the *Heart Sutra* for my parents. Because of my experience, I knew in my heart very deeply that the power of reciting was very great. However, I kept this vow a secret and didn't tell others. I'll leave it at this. Those of you who wish for scientific proof of the power of this sutra, I could tell you a bunch of theories, but this is a class on Buddhism and not a science class. For now, we won't discuss science.

SECTION 1

REASON FOR THE TEACHING

Thus have I heard. At one time the Buddha was sojourning in the Kingdom of Sravasti, staying at Anathapindika's Park in the Grove of Jeta together with an assembly of twelve hundred and fifty bhiksus. As it was time to eat, the World-Honored One put on His robe, picked up His bowl and made His way into the great city of Sravasti where He begged for His food from door to door. This done, He returned to His retreat and took His meal. When He had finished, He put away His robe and bowl, washed His feet, arranged His seat and sat down.

Perfectly Ordinary

If we were to recite the *Diamond Sutra* according to the traditional way of reciting Buddhist scriptures, we would need to beat the wooden fish in time with each word—du, du, du—and just recite it through to the end. The wooden fish is not meant to be banged upon arbitrarily! Why must we beat the wooden fish? The wood is carved into the shape of a fish so as to remind us that in seeking the Tao, walking amongst men or in any situation of learning, we must be as diligent as fish. Fish have their eyes open day and night. For them, to stop and remain motionless for a while is considered sleeping. In the temples, we beat the wooden fish so as to remind ourselves to be diligent in our cultivation night and day, like fish, which are always alert.

The teaching of every sutra had different causes and conditions precipitating it. When the Buddha taught the *Surangama Sutra*, for example, the opening was different. After the Buddha had eaten, he saw that his cousin Ananda was having trouble in the city. Once again problems come up after eating, people start eating and all these problems arise—maybe people shouldn't eat. The Buddha immediately displays super powers to help Ananda. From the crown of his head, out shoots beams of light, big beams of light! Then a transformation body emanates forth and calls on Manjushri, to whom is transmitted a special mantra which enables him to quickly rescue Ananda and bring him back. If this was turned into a movie, it would be very exciting but hard to make. Each sutra has such an opening, but the *Diamond Sutra* is unique in that there is no beaming forth of light from the crown, or from the point between the eyebrows or from the infinity symbol on the Buddha's chest, and so forth. The *Diamond Sutra* simply begins with the Buddha taking his meal; but, we must realize that eating is actually not such an easy affair. In Beijing's White Cloud Taoist Temple, there hangs a famous couplet written during the Ming Dynasty, *"In this world, nothing compares to seeking the Tao; Under the heavens, nothing's more difficult than eating one's fill."* In this world, the best thing to do is seek the Tao;

under the heavens, nothing is more difficult than eating. Filling the stomach is the most difficult task in the world.

Ordinarily, we tend to think that Buddhas must walk along elevated three inches above the ground, stepping on lotus pads after which they then go soaring off into the sky. But the Buddha of this sutra is actually the same as us, eating, wearing clothes, begging, walking barefoot with the soles of his feet making contact with the mud. So, when Buddha returned from the city, He would wash his feet, eat His food and sit down to meditate. This tells us that the ordinary is Tao and the most mundane is the most exalted. In other words, true reality is found within the commonplace and the real heavenly realm of the Buddhas and saints is found within ordinary life. When one has truly perfected human wisdom, then simultaneously, the supramundane or heavenly wisdom is also perfected.

I hope the young people here will take to heart the spirit and the example set by the Buddha in the opening of the *Diamond Sutra*.

The Buddha Spoke in This Way

"Thus have I heard. At one time the Buddha was sojourning in the Kingdom of Sravasti, staying at Anathapindika's Park in the Grove of Jeta."

Every sutra starts with these words: "Thus have I heard." This is the Buddha's stipulation. In the *Parinirvana Sutra*, it says that as the Buddha was about to enter nirvana, Ananda said to him, "As you are about to leave us and I will take on the work of recording your words, how can others believe my work and not think that I have fabricated it?" The Buddha told Ananda at the start of a sutra to open with the words "Thus have I heard." The "I" represents Ananda, and so the sutra is a record of what "I" heard the Buddha say. You have to remember that Ananda's mind was better than today's tape recorders. He remembered everything the Buddha said, not leaving out a single word. To write the words "Thus have I heard," therefore expresses the fact that Ananda took personal responsibility for the accuracy of the sutras.

In the traditional method of teaching sutras, the simple phrase, "Thus have I heard" could be expounded upon for over a month with much elaboration. We, however, will not stray so far from the material at hand.

Now, Buddhism speaks of selflessness. How is it that an "I" suddenly pops up here? This raises a big question. Everywhere else the Buddha teaches us selflessness, but it is recorded in the sutras that the Buddha upon being born into the world, pointed to the heavens with one hand, to the earth with the other, took seven steps and then said, *"In heaven and on earth, I alone am the honored one."* So, Buddha at the beginning of his mission spoke of the self, "I alone am the honored one." Following this, all the way up to age eighty-one and throughout all those years in between, he spoke of selflessness. Then at age eighty-one when the Buddha was about to enter into nirvana, he spoke of "permanence, bliss, self and purity," once again bringing up the "self." For everyone who wishes to practice Ch'an meditation and look into a *hua tou*, this is a big *hua tou*. Ultimately, is there selflessness or is there a self? This self is what? This is a BIG question!

At One Time

The use of the words *"At one time"* also raises a big question. No sutra records an exact time or year; it's always "at one time." When was that time? That time is just that time; time is just time. To use the phrase "at one time" is wonderfully subtle. Similarly, in the sutras, we find here an eighty-four thousand, there an eighty-four thousand, everywhere it's eighty-four thousand! The phrase is used to describe something to which it is difficult to affix an exact number or measurement. Indians used eighty-four thousand to mean, "tons and tons of," or countless.

A realized being just does not have a concept of time. In the *Diamond Sutra*, it says, *"Past mind cannot be obtained, present mind cannot be obtained, future mind cannot be obtained."* The ordinary concept of time is merely relative. In truth, time has no ancient, no modern, no past, no future. Ten thousand years go by in just a flash; a flash of thought sweeps through ten thousand years. This meaning is encapsulated in the ancient poem which reads:

"The wind and moon, neither ancient nor modern,
Feelings and emotions, of themselves shallow or profound."

This moon, this sun, this wind, these mountains and rivers are always as they are. The beautiful blue sky and clouds seen by those in ancient times are also the beautiful sky and clouds seen by us today and which will be seen by those in the future. It's the same world. Therefore, the wind and moon are neither ancient nor modern. Feelings and emotions, however, can be shallow or deep. For some people, beautiful scenery inspires happiness, but for others who are suffering, to look at the same scenery incites depression and thoughts of death. So the wind and moon are neither ancient nor modern; feelings and emotions of themselves are shallow or profound. All of these are the making of the individual's mind.

Modern science also understands that time is merely relative, and in Buddhism, time is mind only. To a person in great pain, one minute, even one second, seems to last ten thousand years; but during times of great fortune and happiness, a hundred or even ten thousand years seem only to last but an instant, and therefore, time is not absolute. The past and the present are simply one time. The Buddha Dharma points to a huge issue, "one time"; no such ancient, no such present, and no such future as well! This is the theory behind "one time." If one wishes to *ts'an hua tou*, then this is a pretty big *hua tou*.

The Lecture Hall at Sravasti

At one time the Buddha was sojourning in the Kingdom of Sravasti, staying at Anathapindika's Park in the Grove of Jeta.

So, the first point of this sutra is to establish who recorded the discussion. "Thus have I heard"—"I," the Buddha's disciple, at that time, heard the Buddha speak thus. That time being "one time." The place also is recorded, "the kingdom of Sravasti," where the Buddha gave most of his teachings.

The Buddha spoke on the Dharma starting at age thirty-one and continued until his eightieth year. During these forty-nine years, most of his teaching work was done in Sravasti. Sravasti is located in central India and was a thriving center both culturally and economically. The king of Sravasti was King Prasenajit, a student of the Buddha also mentioned in the *Surangama Sutra*. There was a very moral elder named Anathapindika, who was one of the wealthiest men in Sravasti and, at the time, was a senior Zoroastrian. During a trip to Varanasi for the purpose of arranging a marriage for his son, he happened to meet the Buddha and developed a deep faith in Him. He entreated the Buddha to give teachings at Varanasi. (Varanasi was the capital city of the state called, at the time, Sravasti. It is now called Uttar Pradesh.) The

Buddha replied, "If you set up a place for teachings, I will come, fortune permitting."

Anathapindika upon arrival home sought out the best possible grounds, but alas, they belonged to Prince Jeta. The prince was in no need of money, but Anathapindika felt that only these grounds were worthy of being the place where the Buddha would teach. Anathapindika met with one of Prince Jeta's ministers, who then reported back to the prince. The prince laughed, "Is he crazy? Why does he want to buy this place?" The minister explained that he wanted to invite a great monk called Buddha to come and give teachings. The Prince exclaimed, "He is crazy! Tell him I won't sell even if he has a lot of money." The prince then set the terms; if the elder could use gold leaf to cover the 800,000 square meters of ground, it was his.

Anathapindika loved to give to charities. If the lonely and helpless cried out to him, he would help each and every one. He was a true philanthropist, and so he was called Anathapindika, meaning "benefactor to the friendless." He really did go and piece by piece cover the ground of Prince Jeta's park with gold leaf. When he had covered about half of the grounds, people started to report to the prince. The prince was shocked and personally went to ask Anathapindika why he was doing this. Anathapindika told him that it was for one who was truly a Buddha, truly a living saint. Prince Jeta said, "I believe your words. You don't need to continue doing this. We'll set up the place for teachings together." Thus, the place where the Buddha gave most of his teachings was called

"Anathapindika's Park in the Grove of Jeta." So now the time and place of this teaching has been established.

Twelve Hundred and Fifty People

"...together with an assembly of twelve hundred and fifty bhiksus."

Virtually every sutra will mention the above phrase. No matter where the Buddha went, it was always together with an assembly of twelve hundred and fifty bhiksus. Although we always see this written in the sutras, was it actually the case that whenever the Buddha gave teachings, it was just monks who went to listen? The sutras mention only monks, but how about lay people? How many men, how many women? Some sutras speak of hundreds of thousands of *nagas*, uncountable heavenly beings, the number of listeners at the time of the teaching being staggering and inconceivable. Ordinarily, however, there were these twelve hundred and fifty disciples, and wherever the Buddha went, they followed. They were his basic group of students and all were monks.

Why speak only of these twelve hundred and fifty? When the Buddha entered into His teaching period, the first group of students were these twelve hundred and fifty most difficult to tame. Amongst them was Sariputra, who, before becoming a monk, was a famous teacher. He had his own following of one hundred students. Of the three Kasyapa brothers, two of them had two hundred and fifty students and the other had five hundred. All together they numbered about one thousand.

They all had a great influence on the major theologians of their society. In addition, Maudgalyayana, who was older than the Buddha and had super powers, had one hundred students of his own. Narendrayasas had a clique of fifty. When these teachers converted to Buddhism, so did their students. This was the origin of the twelve hundred and fifty who followed the Buddha and heard all his teachings. Now don't forget the fact that among these followers were many who were decades older than Buddha. The Buddha was only about thirty-one or thirty-two when he started to teach. Sariputra, for instance, was older by twenty or thirty years, as was Maudgalyayana.

Bhiksu is the term for a monk. It literally translates as "a noble beggar," meaning one who begs for food. This doesn't mean ordinary food, but rather the sustenance of nirvana, that which is external and beyond birth and death. They beg the Dharma from Buddha and beg alms from sentient beings; thus, they are called bhiksus. In the deepest sense of the word, *bhiksu* means to be able to destroy the root of all suffering, leap over all life and death and succeed in attaining true realization.

A World and a Great-Thousand World

"As it was time to eat, the World-Honored One put on His robe, picked up His bowl."

"World-Honored One" is another name for the Buddha. The term *World-Honored One* commonly seen in the sutras refers to the one in this "world" who is the most worthy of respect. Take notice though, the "world" spoken of here is referring not just to the world of humans. Within Buddhist studies, there are two views of the world, one being the three-world view and the other being the four-world view. The three-world view includes: the material world, the world of countries and the sentient world.

To start with, the material world is speaking of the physical world. To put it into present-day context, it simply means planets. There are many planets out in space on which life exists. These planets make up the physical world, the material world. The world of countries, however, is the collection of all the different countries on a planet, like China, America, Europe, and so on. Hence, this world is limited to the range of the idea of a world made up of a collection of countries. Finally, the sentient world refers to those with sentience, who are called in Buddhist terminology "sentient beings". It's the idea of the world made up of living beings of all kinds who have a spirit, or soul, and intelligence.

The idea of four worlds includes the above three and in addition speaks of the world of saints and sages. The fourth world is the realm of those who have attained the Tao. Within Buddhism, the Western Paradise of Amitabha Buddha is an example of such a realm. A place where the Noble Ones of Tao and the saintly live together is called the world of saints and sages. The heavens that other religions talk of are also worlds of saints and sages, places where the virtuous live together.

We all know that within Buddhism there is the concept of the pureland and its opposite, the filthy world. This samsaric world is the filthy world, while Amitabha's Western Paradise is the pureland. This word *land* has two different concepts. One is of a land of infinite peace and light. This land, however, is not made of earth. It is not a physical place. Rather, it refers to the alambana of Buddhas, which is forever blissful and pure. The other concept of land speaks of our world here, this world where ordinary beings and saints exist together. This world can be said to include the four kinds of worlds and all the different kinds of lands.

I've mentioned all this in order to explain the term *World-Honored One*. In this world, the one most worthy of honor is a Buddha, so in the sutras the Buddha is usually called "World-Honored." The "world" spoken of in the sutras includes this world we know, and it extends to all the other worlds . That is how great a Buddha is.

There is another meaning which is that Shakyamuni Buddha, in this life, is the Buddha of our "three thousand great-thousand worlds." For those beginners who are studying Buddhism, I will briefly explain this idea of three thousand great-thousand worlds. This is the Buddhist concept of the universe. A few thousand years ago, almost no one believed this concept. When I was little, someone of the older generation asked me, "Do you know who the biggest boaster in the world is?" He said, "It's Shakyamuni

Buddha!" "How's that?" I asked. "He talks about three thousand great-thousand worlds being immeasurable and infinite. Who can believe this?"

The universe is immeasurable and infinite. It's all really unfathomable; it's too huge. At the time, I was young and so I'd just laugh along. Slowly, I realized that the older generation didn't really believe any of this. Now through advances in astronomy, there is much more proof of the validity of the Buddha's words. The transcendental wisdom of the Buddha is brought to light through modern science and is shown to be just awesome.

The Buddha's idea of a world is that of a solar system, which constitutes one world unit. So our solar system consisting of a sun, nine planets and their moons (the middle planet being the earth) makes up one world unit. In the past, physicists and astronomers thought the sun to be a stationary star. Now the talk has gone in the opposite direction. There is no fixed scientific theory on it. In the solar system, the earth is one of the smallest planets in comparison with the other planets, but to us it seems very large.

The Buddha said that the people of this earth have a life span of sixty to one hundred years and, to most people, a day and a night seem remarkably long. On the moon, however, daytime lasts for half a month (earth time) as does a lunar night. He gave formulas for figuring out other planetary time scales as well. This was all spoken of a few thousand years ago. Now that humans have gone into space, they've discovered the same phenomena that the Buddha spoke of more than two thousand years ago. He also told his disciples that, in space, there are solar system "worlds" like this one too numerous to compute, infinite like the number of grains of sand in the Ganges River. It's also comparable to the number of grains of sand in the Yellow River of China, which are beyond computation.

A solar system is called a single-world unit. A unit of a thousand "solar system worlds" is called a small-world. One thousand small-world units make up a middle-world unit. One thousand middle-world units then make up a great-world unit. The Buddha conveniently spoke in terms of space containing three thousand great-thousand worlds, but actually, there are unfathomable, uncountable, infinite numbers of worlds. A few thousand years ago, no one could believe this theory. Not only the macroscopic view could not be believed, but also the microscopic view could not be accepted as true.

Eating Food and Wearing Clothes

At the time of the Buddha in India, there were no filter machines for water. The Buddha, within the *vinaya*, had a set of procedures for the disciples to drink water. They must first pour the water through a gauze cloth and then place the cloth back in the water before drinking. Why was this? *"The Buddha beheld in a bowl of water, eighty-four thousand organisms."* The eyes of the Buddha could see that one bowl of water held eighty-four thousand lives, which we now call microorganisms. In light of this, we can see that we are really so extraordinary. When we swallow a mouthful of water, or, better yet, ten in rapid succession, innumerable and uncountable small lives all can be engulfed into our big stomachs. A few thousand years ago when the Buddha spoke like this, almost no one believed it and they all felt He was very trifling and picky. Now that science has advanced, everyone can believe this.

The Buddha was also the first to promote brushing one's teeth. Within the vinaya, the disciples followed the rule of brushing their teeth after having taken their meal. As there were no toothbrushes, they used a small branch of the willow tree. That's probably why Kuan-Yin Bodhisattva keeps a small willow branch soaking in her bottle of ambrosia, on one hand to sprinkle the nectar and on the other to brush her teeth. The willow branch, after being cut down, is soaked in water for a while; then, the thick end is pounded by a rock to make it splayed so it can be used to brush the teeth. This may even be better than today's toothbrushes for it's both soft and fragrant. Whether or not they used toothpaste back then, that I don't know!

These are all part of the rules for living which collectively are called the vinaya. The vinaya outlines a strict etiquette, and to look at it in modern terms, the Buddha promoted many good habits of hygiene and sanitation. In the sutras, it says that one who has attained enlightenment and become a Buddha will educate sentient beings in His Buddha land. This is the most valuable kind of education and these kinds of teachers are therefore called "World Honored."

"As it was time to eat." Time to eat. We must say a few words about this affair of eating. The Buddha's precept on eating was to take one meal a day at noon. Ordinarily, in Buddhist studies, the common human eating pattern of three meals per day is called "divided food" or "rolled food." The term *rolled food* comes from the Indian custom of eating with the hands and rolling the rice and food into small balls to put in the mouth. Indians use their hands, the Chinese use chopsticks, Westerners use forks—it's all basically using the hand anyway, so it can still be called "rolled food."

The morning is when heavenly beings take their meal, noon is when humans eat and evening is when those of the spirit world feed. Buddha therefore made this precept for humans specifically, with the one meal being at noontime. After the time of the Buddha, monks wouldn't eat after one in the afternoon to be in accordance with the Buddha's stipulation. This stipulation is difficult because of the differences in cultural customs all over the world. In some societies, breakfast is most important, and in others, it's lunch or dinner. All are different. This is what's called "divided food." This is the general human pattern of eating.

In truth, eating is not just limited to this. In addition to divided food, there is also "thought food." This refers to mental food or spiritual food. If those who feel extremely stifled or depressed lack this mental and spiritual food for too long, they may die. Another kind of food is "contact food." For example, if we are inside a room and are wearing too much clothing, we feel suffocated; or if we get buried under dirt or sand, we feel stifled and choked. This is a problem of the skin not getting enough oxygen to eat. Further, there is the food of consciousness, the working of the *alaya-vijnana*, which sustains life's existence. So, divided food, contact food, thought food and consciousness food can all be called man's sustenance.

The daily meal spoken of here in the sutra is the one meal at noon. This practice of taking one meal is the Buddha's own precept. Although the Buddha had been a prince before entering into the spiritual life, he was the living example of his vinaya. When it was time to eat, he would first put on his saffron robe, the robe which identified him and his disciples. Actually, the Buddha's clothes consisted of just saffron robes. The clothes which monks and nuns of the Chinese tradition wear now are in the style of commoner's clothes of the Ming Dynasty. The difference being that the ordained would wear plain colors and would shave their heads, thus being identifiable from the lay people. The Buddha's clothing was his saffron robe, which is also called the "field of blessings" robe. It was originally just a patched-up piece of saffron cloth, but now the numbers and patterns of the hems on one's robe are indicative of which vows one has taken. All these hems crisscross each other and look like an expanse of neatly demarcated fields. It is the symbol of one who cultivates blessings on behalf of all beings, and thus it is called the "field of blessings" robe.

From this sutra, we can tell that in his leisure time, the Buddha didn't necessarily wear his saffron robe. He usually wore just inner robes. Especially in India when it was hot, men had the custom of baring their arms. We now can see that Shakyamuni Buddha in His leisure time was a little more casual. When it came time to eat, however, he would wear his saffron robe and take his bowl. By the time this bowl came to China, there were pottery versions and there were copper versions but, all the same, it was just a bowl out of which to eat. Into this one bowl is put everything—rice, soup, vegetables, and so forth. Now looking at it, the Buddha invented individual meals two thousand years ago. He also made a rule that his disciples were to eat with a spoon as opposed to the traditional Indian way of eating with one's hands. Each person was to keep his own bowl and eat his own meal.

The Buddha has put on his robe and has picked up his bowl and then *"made His way into the great city of Sravasti."* He went to the capital city, *"where He begged for His food from door to door."* Within the Buddha's rules of discipline, his disciples not only weren't allowed to cook food, but they also weren't allowed to raise any crops. The rules of discipline at the time were very strict. They weren't allowed to plant crops because as soon as the hoe goes into the ground, who knows how many small creatures will be killed. Out of the same respect for life, during the summertime, the disciples all must enter the "rains retreat." They go to a cool place on high ground, where they engage in cultivation practice and meditation, and for the duration of the retreat, it is forbidden to go out. During the summer rainy season in India, the ground is so covered with insects that wherever one plants one's foot, many small lives get cut short. This is the reason behind the summer rains retreat. Before the summer, all the food supplies must be arranged. Not until autumn could they go out to beg again. The disciples of the Buddha could not plant crops in order to live. These were the rules during that time period. Take notice, "during that time period." Later, as time went on, changes came about slowly.

The Majestic Demeanor of a Noble Beggar's Life

As a second point on begging, the Buddha ruled that when doing so, disciples could not give rise to discrimination; the door of a poor man and that of a rich man are the same when begging. They must go one house after another without changing direction in order to avoid going to the indigent or to the wealthy in particular. Mahakasyapa, for example, came from a very well-to-do, influential family, but he felt a very special kinship with the poor. Thus, he would go to the impoverished areas to beg and would sometimes teach them or from their midst would take on new disciples. Another of Buddha's disciples, Subhuti, was the opposite. He preferred to go to affluent areas to beg and educate.

The Buddha called the two together to rebuke them. He said, "Both of you lack a sense of equality. Whether or not one has money, whether or not one has status, when begging one must look upon them equally. The heart should not discriminate. In addition, however much one family gives, they give. If it's not enough, then go on to the next house." In present times, when we see a monk standing at the door hitting a small chime, he is following the precept of Shakyamuni Buddha.

With regard to the rules of eating, the Buddhist families of Thailand still hold to them. Before the monks have come to beg, the cover of the rice pot is not to be opened. The moment they come, the pot is opened and the best portion of rice from the middle is scooped out and the rest of their bowl gets filled with vegetables. After the monks have left, then the family eats. These are the guidelines passed down within Buddhism.

"...made his way into the great city of Sravasti, where He begged for His food from door to door. This done, He returned to His retreat and took His meal. When He had finished, He put away His robe and bowl, washed His feet, arranged His seat and sat down."

This section speaks of begging and of eating the daily meal. When we look into this sutra, we discover that throughout the day and the night, the Buddha is always in the state of samadhi, the Tathagata's great samadhi. Only at noontime does He take a meal, meditate and rest awhile. From, probably one or two o'clock, our time, until five or six o'clock when it started to get dark, He would give teachings. After this, everyone would close their eyes and enter into samadhi. From reading this sutra, I believe that the situation at that time and the Buddha's practices were as such.

In Sravasti, the great capital city, He went from door to door begging, and after this, *"He returned to His retreat..."* It didn't say that He ate along the way back unlike us who buy a bunch of bananas and start in on them as we walk along the road, looking rather undignified as a result. The Buddha brought the bowl of food back to His own lecture hall and at His regular spot took His meal. When He had finished, He put away His robe and begging bowl. Then after this, there was another action, *"washed His feet."* He got some water and washed His feet.

This is why I say that this sutra is the most ordinary and truthful of the sutras. In the other sutras when the Buddha comes out, He will display super powers. Light will stream from the crown of His head, then lotuses will appear under His feet with each step, and the ground will be covered by white clouds... It's all so unbelievable! Only this sutra is so plain and telling. The Buddha is the same as any common man. He walks barefoot, His feet get muddy and He must wash them—very routine, very ordinary, very honest, just being a person.

"...arranged His seat and sat down." After washing His feet, He fluffed up his cushion Himself, arranged His seat and made it all neat and orderly. He didn't ask His students to wait on Him, nor did He have a servant who cleaned up for Him. He did everything for Himself. Life was just this disciplined, this mundane and this orderly. This beginning of the *Diamond Sutra* is completely different from other sutras, taking place amidst the common people. Other sutras first show the side of the Buddha which is too high to be reached, that which we can only try to imagine and which we prostrate to in awe and respect. How can we students of Buddhism ever become like Him who is like this? After reading

the *Diamond Sutra*, ahh! He was actually quite ordinary, just like us. The ways He lived and the ways in which He conducted His affairs are the same as ours.

In addition, before He became a monk, the Buddha had been a prince. Even so, He lived life the same way the common citizens did. For His disciples, who were many, He set up a code of discipline called the vinaya which functioned as their law. After He had set up this code and taught it to them, He needed someone to be in charge of discipline. At the time, India's caste system was strictly set, and amongst the disciples many were of the wealthy, or Brahman, class. Yet, the Buddha chose a disciple originally of the lowest social caste, named Upali, to enforce discipline. No matter who it was that broke the precepts, he had to deal with them equally.

If we look at the spirit of the Buddha and its expression within the practical aspects of life, we see that within the ordinary is the extraordinary. This is exactly the Buddha. Within the most mundane is set up the most extraordinary. This is the alambana of the Buddha.

SECTION 2

VIRTUOUS MANIFESTATION OPENS THE
QUESTION

Now in the midst of the assembly was the Elder Subhuti. Forthwith, he arose from his seat, bared his right shoulder, knelt upon his right knee and with palms joined respectfully, addressed the Buddha thus,

"Most rare World- Honored One! The Tathagata is skillfully mindful, perfectly instructing and entrusting the Bodhisattvas. World-Honored One, when virtuous men and virtuous women initiate the mind of anuttara-samyak sambodhi, how should their minds dwell? How should their minds be pacified?"

The Buddha spoke, "Excellent, excellent Subhuti, it is as you say. The Tathagata is skillfully mindful, perfectly instructing and entrusting the Bodhisattvas. Now, listen well to what I say. Virtuous men and virtuous women who initiate the mind of anuttara-samyak sambodhi should thus dwell and pacify their minds."

"I assure you, World-Honored One, we joyfully await your answer."

Virtuous Manifestation Subhuti

"Virtuous Manifestation" is the actual meaning of the name Subhuti. Subhuti, this name, represents his life's alambana, which was an expression of the highest virtue, manifesting in long life. Amongst the Buddha's disciples, Subhuti, Sariputra, and others were much older than the Buddha. Subhuti was not only an elder but also because of his morality, wisdom and disciplined lifestyle, a leader and role model for the Buddha's disciples at that time. He was of a venerable age and respectable character. His spirit and dignified demeanor amongst the Buddha's top ten disciples was very well-known.

Subhuti was the foremost among the disciples in realizing emptiness and so was sometimes called, "The Foremost in Emptiness." In this sutra, the Buddha goes on to discuss emptiness and phenomena deeply with Subhuti. In the later period of Buddhism, Subhuti came to be addressed as "Venerable Subhuti." Even in the vernacular Chinese culture, he is very well-known. How is this? He is known through the story of *Journey to the West,* a very popular Chinese classic. In the book, Subhuti was the teacher of Sun Wu-k'ung. The story of how Sun Wu-k'ung was searching for Tao and met his teacher, Subhuti, was actually a play on the story of the Sixth Patriarch meeting the Fifth Patriarch. The two chapters "Sun Wu-k'ung Stirs Big Trouble in Heaven" and "Seventy-two Transformations" depict the aftereffects of having studied with Subhuti. These portions of *Journey to the West* were depicted especially well. Due to this, Venerable Subhuti's name has remained very familiar amongst the Chinese peoples.

Now in the midst of the assembly was the Elder, Subhuti. Forthwith, he arose from his seat, bared his right shoulder, knelt upon his right knee and with palms joined respectfully, addressed the Buddha thusly,

> *"Most rare World-Honored One! The Tathagata is skillfully mindful, perfectly instructs and entrusts the Bodhisattvas."*

This section was written as if to give us a scenario to describe the setting. "Now" was just after the Buddha had eaten—His feet were washed, His meditation seat arranged just right and He had sat down crossed His legs and was ready to rest and relax. However, our elder disciple Subhuti wasn't so ready to let Him have that rest and says, "Not so fast, Honored One, I have a question to ask on behalf of the rest of the disciples." In the aforementioned *Heart Sutra,* it was Sariputra, who was also one of the Buddha's ten main disciples, whose question initiated the teaching. The lesson of the *Diamond Sutra* was initiated by Subhuti, and the *Surangama Sutra's* teaching was due to Ananda. Each one's question was different as was the method by which the Buddha replied to them and taught them. So the *Diamond Sutra* started with Subhuti asking a question. It was Subhuti who stood up and asked on behalf of the others, because, amongst them, he was the best in speaking on emptiness.

Nowadays, when we ask a question, we first raise our hand. During the Buddha's time, the rule was to stand up and uncover one's right shoulder. So, as all the disciples were sitting, Subhuti then stood up and removed his robe from his right shoulder. As to the question of why the right shoulder, there are many theories. The first is that when uncovered, it's more convenient for working. In addition, when walking with the Buddha, teachers or elders, one could offer this shoulder to support them, which is a traditional kind of Indian courtesy. The second theory is that the right hand is the propitious hand, while the left is inauspicious. Therefore, the robe must cover the left arm, and the right arm is used to offer incense. Then, there is also the contrary theory which states that it is the right hand which carries out bad actions, such as killing, and so one must use the left hand to offer incense in front of the Buddha. Those of ancient times had their intricate courtesies, which held meaning in their particular place and time. Later historians then placed various explanations on the same customs. As it was basically just a custom, for the time being, we won't bother to discuss it further.

So now, Subhuti has fixed his robe so as to reveal his right shoulder. He *"bared his right shoulder"* and then *"knelt upon his right knee and with palms joined respectfully,..."* To join the palms together was part of the etiquette of those times in ancient India. The Chinese also have this custom as well as bowing with hands folded in front. Indians have the method of joining the palms together with the fingers spread apart, but there are many other

71

ways of showing respect, such as cupping the hands together or holding both hands completely flat against each other. In the same spirit as we today raise our hand to ask a question of the teacher, Subhuti joined his palms together and *"addressed the Buddha thus, Most rare World-Honored One."*

Within the decorum of the sutras, and within Indian convention (There were a lot of rules!), when asking for advice from an elder, one must first present a whole package of laudatory preamble. The same as we Chinese would greet an elder person saying, "The venerable one is really so kind to me! I received so much inspiration from the guidance and advice that the venerable one gave me last time!" A lot of young people give me the same rap. I say to them, "I don't have time. What's your question? Ask quickly, get to the point. All of that talk—the teacher's good, the teacher's great, we must all venerate—is unwanted. I don't want to hear it." But of course, young people must still say all this in order to be polite.

"Most rare World-Honored One!" In the *Diamond Sutra,* the veneration has been concentrated into these few words. In other sutras, when the disciples stand up to ask a question, they first compose a whole symphony of praise. The Buddha really has great strength of imperturbability. He closes his eyes, waits for them to finish and then opens his eyes and says, "Please, go ahead and ask." The words of praise used in the *Diamond Sutra* are the work of Kumarajiva. He used only five words "Most rare World-Honored One!" Throughout the ages, seldom to appear, seldom to

be seen and most difficult to attain is the World-Honored One. Before it was mentioned that Dharma master Hsuan-tsang as well as some others also translated the *Diamond Sutra*. It is my personal opinion that Kumarajiva's version is the most simple and to the point, subtle beyond description.

In ancient times, translations of Buddhist sutras were required to be accurate, clear and graceful. No matter what subject material is being translated, the first requirement is to be accurate. One must in good faith not change the meaning of the original words. Still, the meaning must come across clearly, without ambiguity. Furthermore, the expression must be refined, having a high level of literary skill. Accuracy, clarity and grace are very important. We see many sutras that have been translated very accurately, exactly according to the original, and very clearly, but the words are just not very graceful. Translations such as Kumarajiva's, which achieve all three, are most exceptional indeed, and so I enjoy this version of the sutra very much.

This version of the sutra does not add explanation. It just directly follows the text: *"The Tathagata is skillfully mindful, perfectly instructs and entrusts the Bodhisattvas."* From the perspective of accuracy and clarity, the above line seems at first glance to miss the mark. Just what exactly is being said? There doesn't seem to be any connection for this line. However, after reading other versions, one gets the feeling that actually, Kumarajiva really captured the true essence in his form of expression. Looking back on his translation, one feels that it is wonderfully subtle.

Tathagatas and Bodhisattvas

So now we'll give some explanation of the two Buddhist terms *Tathagata* and *Bodhisattva*. Tathagata is another name for the Buddha. There are actually about ten different names for the Buddha, such as Tathagata and World-Honored One. The term *Tathagata* is the common title for anyone who has realized the Tao and attained Buddhahood. So Shakyamuni Buddha can also be called "The Tathagata Shakyamuni," and Amitabha Buddha could be entitled as "The Tathagata Amitabha." The words Shakyamuni and Amitabha in their titles are the specific names of certain personages. It's the same as the term *sage*. For example, Confucius, the Duke of Chou, King Wen, Yao and Shun are all names of famous sages in Chinese history. The word *Tathagata* functions in the same way as the word *sage*.

I often talk to people of other religions, encouraging them to retranslate their scriptures, since religion cannot be separated from literature. If one wishes to propagate a religious culture, the quality of the religious translations must be very high. The translations of the Buddhist sutras are of a very high literary alambana, and so have deeply influenced Chinese culture. For example, the translation of the term *Tathagata*, 如來 (lit. as if to come), is really very brilliant. Notice that it wasn't translated in the opposite way, "as if to go." If this had been the case, then no one would want to study Buddhism because the Buddha just skips out on them. By having used "as if to come," then it's always coming in, and this idea seems to strike a good chord in most people.

What is a Tathagata actually? Why are enlightened beings called a Tathagata? The Buddha gives an explanation of the term in the *Diamond Sutra* saying, *"Neither whence to come nor whither to go and so is called the Tathagata."* Neither coming nor going, neither created nor destroyed, neither moving nor still, neither joyful nor sad, neither high nor low; all are in equanimity and always existing. This is the logic behind the term *Tathagata*, as if to come. In the present-day way of thinking, it can be understood as the Buddha always being here with you, always by your side. One only needs to have one thought of earnest belief and the Buddha is right here.

During later periods, a poem was written which describes this very well. It reads:

> *Buddha is in the very heart of one's own mind,*
> *No need to go rashly seeking;*
> *Vulture Peak is at the seat of one's own heart.*
> *Each and all have the stupa of Rajagriha,*
> *It's just a matter of getting to the bottom,*
> *of the Vulture Peak Stupa to observe.*

There is no need to go to Vulture Peak in Rajagriha, India, to seek the Buddha. No need to travel so far when the Vulture Peak is at the heart of one's mind. Each and every being has his or her own Rajagriha Stupa, and it's just a matter of getting to the bottom of it to observe. There is also another version of the last line which reads, *"One need not search outside of the Vulture Peak Stupa."* But the point of it all is that Buddha and the Tao are within the heart and mind of each and every being. This is why the Ch'an masters say, *"The mind is Buddha; the Buddha is just mind. The Dharma cannot be found outside the mind."* To search for the Dharma outside the *mind* is not the Buddhist path.

Another Buddhist term is Bodhisattva, which is taken directly from Sanskrit. Bodhi means "to be awakened" and Sattva means "having sentiment." Therefore, to directly translate the meaning as a name would be "the awakened having sentiment," but this is really lacking in flavor. Young people may jump to the conclusion that it's from the "Sutra de Romance," which would definitely not be Buddhist. When one hears the term *Bodhisattva*, one is not exactly sure what it means and so one naturally feels a sense of respect. In this case, after careful consideration, the translators decided not to translate the meaning but rather keep the Sanskrit word.

"To be awakened." To what is a Bodhisattva awakened? To the alambana of a Buddha, or to put it into other words, to the will to improve one's self for the benefit of others. A third understanding is to become enlightened for the purpose of awakening others. We can also borrow a quotation from the Confucian scholar Mencius: *"It's for the earlier generation who've learned and awakened to thus awaken the later generation."* or *"The first to know must then awaken those to follow."* This is to say that those people who first come into knowledge or awaken to some truth must then teach and direct those who later follow on the same path. There are some who awaken to some truth and have no more longing for or attachment to fame and fortune. Thus, they may completely disengage from all worldly affairs, skip out on everyone and enjoy their own nirvanic existence. These are called arhats.

A Bodhisattva, having awakened himself and escaped from the sea of samsaric suffering, also has transcended the bounds of this physical existence. In the *ching-chieh* of a Bodhisattva, however, he will see all the different kinds of sentient beings of the world still bound by suffering and hardships and will want to return to the world to free all of them. To make this kind of sacrifice for the benefit of others, this is what is called "having sentiment," this is the great path of the Bodhisattva, the Mahayana.

Another meaning of "having sentiment" is as follows: Each and every being has a spirit, consciousness and sentiments; therefore, they have life. This is what is called "having sentiments." An ancient couplet reads, *"Extraordinary are the bones of an immortal; Extremely sentimental is the heart of a Buddha."* Not to be ordinary but to be truly extraordinary is very difficult. To be truly extraordinary is to have reached the state of a heavenly immortal. Bodhisattvas sacrifice their ego for the benefit of all sentient beings. Therefore, it is said that Buddhas and Bodhisattvas are the most sentimental of all, and hence the name "the awakened having sentiment". *Bodhisattva* is a general term for those amongst Buddha's disciples who follow the Mahayana path.

The Buddha's disciples who leave the worldly life—leave children, parents and home—are called bhiksus. In the sutras, the ordained Buddhist clergy are generally classified as Hinayana, but this is not always the case. The ones who leave worldly concerns and put all their heart's effort into self-cultivation, or in other words, the ones who discard all the empty illusions of the world, empty out everything and culminate their own individual Tao are at the alambana of Hinayana arhats. They are only concerned with their own achievement and not with anything else. In the Ch'an sect, these are called "board-bearing arhats." They walk along hefting a board on their shoulder, thus seeing only this half of things and not the other. In other words, they grasp firmly the empty, peaceful, serene side and, as to the troubled, suffering side, well the board blocks it from sight. "You guys go on in your chaos; I just won't look."

In Buddhism, the expression of true form (as discussed in the section on true form prajna) is called "indication" and is simply an outward or physical expression. The Bodhisattva-mahasattvas' outward expression is, for the most part, in the form of lay practitioners. For example, Avalokiteshvara, Manjushri and

Samantabhadra, are all Bodhisattvas and are all seen in the form of lay practitioners. Kshitigarbha-Bodhisattva, however, is one exception who appears as a monk. The ordained absolutely cannot wear brightly printed fancy clothes, nor can they wear make-up. But take a look at the Bodhisattvas—they all are made-up! They wear earrings, necklaces and bracelets, even lipstick and powder—decked to the nines! This is the appearance of the Bodhisattvas. What is the meaning behind this? It is to show that the Bodhisattvas enter the mundane world and, even though their outer appearance is worldly, their minds are in fact supramundane. Thus, the alambana of a Bodhisattva is called the Mahayana. The arhats stay in the alambana of emptiness, not daring to enter the world. They don't want to touch it, and so what they don't see won't upset them. This is the Hinayana alambana.

The Bodhisattva's path, however, is extremely difficult. For the most part, there are only a few ways to go. In the *Surangama Sutra* it says: "*To free others before one's own liberation is the heart of the Bodhisattva's mind. After their own complete enlightenment, Tathagatas are able to enlighten others, thus responding to the needs of the world.*"

The first sentence above is saying that there are those who have not yet attained Tao themselves but who have religious enthusiasm and wish to first help others, teach others to do good. Every religion has these kinds of people. They themselves have not attained enlightenment or even liberation, yet their enthusiasm to help others is just as great as, if not greater than, those with Tao. This is the stuff of which Bodhisattvas are made.

As to the second half of the quote, *"After their own complete enlightenment, Tathagatas are able to enlighten others, thus responding to the needs of the world,"* the meaning is as follows: After one has awakened and has completed the path of spiritual cultivation, this person then educates others. This is the Buddha of the present age, the living Buddha. Bodhisattvas are the preceding cause of Tathagatas; Tathagatas are the resultant fruition of Bodhisattvas. So now after this very simple explanation, we'll put the topic of Buddhas and Bodhisattvas to the side and return to the actual sutra. Let's not forget that Subhuti is still kneeling there asking on our behalf and the longer we discuss this, the longer he has to kneel.

The Sixth Patriarch and the *Diamond Sutra*

Subhuti is kneeling there saying *"Most rare, World-Honored One!"* In this world, the most precious teacher is our Buddha. *"The Tathagata is skillfully mindful, perfectly instructs and entrusts the Bodhisattvas."* One could explain this as Subhuti suggesting that the Buddha take good care of and look after the Bodhisattvas sitting there at the time. You, the Buddha, ought to instruct them well about how to practice and how to cultivate the Bodhisattva Tao. This is one way of explaining the meaning of the words.

At the time, Subhuti was kneeling there on behalf of everyone, on behalf of all the disciples, especially those Bodhisattvas on the Mahayana path who would enter the world. This category also includes those ordained (literally—leavers of home) who have resolved to enter the world. We know that there are many lay-practitioners who are Bodhisattvas, just as there are Bodhisattvas amongst the ordained as well. Even though they wear the outer garments that identify them as leavers of home, their desires, resolutions and deeds are all in accord with the Mahayana path. According to the words used, Subhuti seems to be saying on their behalf: "Excuse me, Buddha! Might the Venerable One hang on just a second before closing his eyes and going into meditation. There being so many of your disciples who are Bodhisattvas following the Mahayana path, you ought to take really good care of them. Point them in the right direction as to practice and cultivation!" At a glance, this is what the text seems to be saying.

Later on, in the Ch'an sect, the Fifth Patriarch would say that if one wished to realize the Tao and become a Buddha, simply reciting the *Diamond Sutra* with a concentrated mind would do. Even one who was illiterate need only recite "mahaprajnaparamita," and whatever one wished for, one would receive. The power is that great. This word mahaprajnaparamita encapsulates the meaning—culmination of great wisdom arriving at the other shore. The Sixth Patriarch, due to the *Diamond Sutra*, gained realization and, therefore, later generations called the Ch'an sect, the Prajna sect. Through the Fifth and Sixth Patriarch came the transmission of the essence of the *Diamond Sutra*, and the resultant promotion of reciting the *Diamond Sutra*.

"Is skillfully mindful" Kumarajiva's translation of this particular section is just indescribably subtle. Who knows how much wisdom went into it! When doing a translation, one must be accurate. One must not contradict the Buddha's meaning. For instance, after the tide of Ch'an Buddhism, there was an erudite layman who wished to write a commentary on the *Vimalakirti-Nirdesa Sutra.* He went to see the eminent monk Hui-chung, the emperor's spiritual guide, who told him: "Very well! You excel in scholarship and so may comment on the sutra." After this, he called for his disciple to give him a bowl of clear water, put into it several grains of rice and then placed a set of chopsticks across the top of the bowl. He then asked of the layman, "Do you know what I'm doing?" He answered that he didn't understand. The Venerable Hui-chung then said: "You don't even understand my meaning. Is it possible that you understand the Buddha's? Will you so presumptuously translate and comment on the sutras?"

Many people also believe that their own Buddhist studies are complete and that they can just start writing. However, upon research into Kumarajiva's biography, we find that he had already awakened and was at the alambana of a Mahasattva. Thus his translation of "is skillfully mindful" was so incredible.

Is Skillfully Mindful

Whether it's Confucianism, Buddhism, Taoism, or any other religion, no matter what kind of cultivation method people use, all are centered around being "skillfully mindful." One must very carefully look after one's thought world, the stirring mind of ideas. Some people's thoughts are unscrupulous, and they study Buddhism in hopes of attaining supernatural powers, such as being able to produce money from thin air. To study with this kind of motivation is not even worth mentioning. Others may just be curious about spectacular phenomena, such as seeing Bodhisattvas appear or, in the same way, may wish to go to the moon in one leap. To study Buddhism with such ideas and motivations is absolutely wrong. Take a look at the Buddha! How very ordinary—eating meals, wearing clothes, washing His feet and meditating—nothing particularly remarkable. Absolutely no wild imaginings, nor crazy behavior, and not in the least are there any religious overtones. The alambana of the Buddha is just so ordinary. The important point on which he tries to educate people is simply being *"skillfully mindful."*

This is keeping well, taking care of your sentiments, thoughts and ideas in the best way possible. The pureland method of reciting *Namo Amitabha*, for example, if done to the point of single-minded concentration is a method of being "skillfully mindful." When we do sitting meditation in which we do not allow the mind to wander, this is also being skillfully mindful. All religious methods of cultivation are but perfectly protecting the mind. What then is the main method of practice and cultivation prescribed in the *Diamond Sutra*? It is simply being skillfully mindful. Everyone should take special notice of this!

In the Buddhist sutras, there are the teachings on the Bodhipaksika dharma, the thirty-seven conditions leading to bodhi or Buddhahood which contain the four objects of mindfulness. These four are as follows: mindfulness of body, mindfulness of sensations, mindfulness of mind and mindfulness of Dharma. Of the four situations of mindfulness, mindfulness of body and mindfulness of mind are extremely important. Our body is impermanent. Our thoughts and ideas rise up and then fall to rest. They are unreliable, flitting around for a split second and then disappearing. If we take them to be the real mind, then we are making a mistake.

What is a "moment of mind"? The time between the breath in and the breath out is called a moment. According to the Buddhist explanation, during the time of one moment there are eighty-four thousand frustrations. Frustration is not necessarily suffering. Let's say there is a person sitting there, holding the *Diamond Sutra* in his hands being skillfully mindful. What kind of mind is he keeping? His mind is holding on to a thought or feeling of frustration and unhappiness. What's there to be unhappy about? He can't put his finger on it. One doesn't even know oneself, much less would a doctor or anyone else know. The average human alambana is in the midst of frustration.

Looking for Worry, Seeking Resentment

What's there to be frustrated about? A line from *Dream of the Red Chamber* describing the condition of a lady's heart reads, *"Without reason looking for worry, seeking resentment."* Actually everyone's mind is in this same situation. "Without reason" just out of the blue, "looking for worry, seeking resentment." Having no way to describe what is in one's heart and feeling frustrated—this is worry. "Seeking resentment" means whomever one looks at, one can't stand them. Those young ladies of well-to-do families after having eaten, go to look at the flowers, take an excursion, sit around and relax with no cares, but then suddenly they jump up, tear the flowers off the bush or hit someone. Why? Frustration! Why all this frustration? "Without reason," there is just no reason behind it, "sometimes seeming foolish, as if mad." Actually, it is not just these well-to-do ladies who are like this; humans for the most part are always absorbed in this alambana. This is the human experience described to a tee and it is the reason why it's said that within the time of a thought there are eighty-four thousand frustrations. From this, one can see why the book *Dream of the Red Chamber*'s literary value is so highly rated.

The Chinese drama *The West Chamber* also has some lines which describe the condition of the human mind very well. *"On the water, fallen flowers are a flow of red; during one's leisure, ten thousand worries; nothing to say but complain of the easterly wind."* The peach blossoms fall down and cover the water with their color—how lovely!   Originally, it had been a very beautiful alambana but then along came a person who saw it. Not having anything to complain about nor anything to detest, he just complained about the east wind "Oh, how I hate this east wind. It has blown down all the flowers. You heartless wind!" This person then goes and writes an essay berating the wind. He doesn't realize that he himself has a wind in his head.

This is a description of the human alambana: "On the water, fallen flowers are a flow of red; during one's leisure, ten thousand worries."   What are these worries?   No genuine matters of concern—one is just tense. One finally has some leisure time and all these anxieties come up. Just how many? There are ten thousand, ten thousand difficult-to-describe anxieties. And so, all day long one murmurs against heaven and begrudges man. When there's nothing to complain about, then one even complains about the easterly wind. This literary description of humankind is very astute.

This all came up when we started to discuss the word *moment*. The time between the breath in and the breath out measures a moment and contains eighty-four thousand frustrations. This is the life of a person. To escape from all frustrations and empty out the "moment" is to become a Buddha. It's as simple as that, but one must in all one's behavior keep well THIS moment.

Studying the *Diamond Sutra*, we can see what an exceptional teacher the Buddha was and how deep Subhuti's questions were.

Unlike some of the students here—"Teacher, may I disturb you for two minutes." I say, "You know very well it's going to take quite a few minutes, so just be on the level and say you want to ask a question." So then he goes on for half an hour and I listen for the question. After all that, I can't figure out what he's asking and end up with nothing to say, but complain of the easterly wind!

Diamond Eyes and Initiative

Subhuti is really quite good at asking questions. Actually, within his question itself, the answer is there, and there in the answer is the essence of the sutra. If one continues reading along, the Buddha then picks up this central point and says, "Ah, yes! Good answer!" Therefore, this sutra is different from all the others. The essence is in this sentence. They are like the eyes of a portrait. The Patriarchs of Ch'an hold this sutra in particularly high esteem because of the way in which it is written and because its essence is so exceptional. For anyone who wishes to practice Buddhism, this sentence tells everything one needs to know as to the method. The question and answer are contained in this sentence, *"The Tathagata is skillfully mindful, perfectly instructs and entrusts the Bodhisattvas."* This sentence spells out how to cultivate and practice.

Many students ask, "Teacher, how does one cultivate and practice? At present, I'm doing *ch'i-kung*, concentration on the breath and using the pureland method. Please, please teach me!"

There are others who go all over searching for methods to practice the Dharma and end up just spending a whole lot of time and money. Can the Dharma be solicited? Is there a Dharma which can be solicited? All are just fantasies of a mind of desire. All are merely frustrations. Where is the Dharma? The Dharma is in the heart of your mind. It is just being skillfully mindful. The beginning steps of any cultivation and also the culmination and perfection of Buddhahood are but being "skillfully mindful." This most important issue is exactly the *Diamond Sutra*'s diamond eyes, the *Diamond Sutra*'s right eyes, eyes which hold the right Dharma.

> *"World-Honored One, when virtuous men and virtuous women initiate the mind of anuttara-samyak sambodhi, how should their minds dwell? How should their minds be pacified?"*

This sutra is translated with such skill! Here we have, *"virtuous men and virtuous women,"* male and female clearly distinguished, but notice that both are "virtuous."

Then, it speaks of initiating the mind. To initiate is to start moving, to initiate what kind of mind? The mind of anuttara-samyak sambodhi, which is a Sanskrit term. Why was it not translated into Chinese? It's very difficult to translate. Well, actually, the scope of its meaning defies translation. If stretched, *anuttara* could be translated as meaning "the highest unexcelled," *sam* meaning "right or correct," *yak* meaning "equanimity" and *bodhi* meaning "awareness or awakened wisdom." The translation of the individual words all strung together would read: the highest, unexcelled, right equanimity and right awareness. This, however, is just a translation of the words, and does not reflect the entire meaning.

If its meaning were to be translated, then one could use the lingo of the Ch'an sect, "great awakening, great enlightenment," but still it falls short. The meaning also includes "Dharma door of the mind," "to behold the original nature of the mind," "to leap over the mundane and achieve the alambana of a Buddha." From the standpoint of one's deeds, it expresses the great mercy and compassion of the Bodhisattva's heart, the mind of *bodhicitta* wishing to enter the world and save all sentient beings. Theoretically, it means the great awakening and great enlightenment going beyond essence even, to the very heart of the original nature. The meanings are numerous, so it is best to just keep the original Sanskrit words. Let later generations worry about translating it.

Another way to define anuttara-samyak sambodhi is as merely the spirit of an ordinary person who wishes to practice Buddhism. Buddhism is different from other religions in that it professes that all sentient beings can become a Buddha rather than believing in an originator. Other religions believe that only "He" is perfect and we must wait for "Him" to help us. We must listen to "Him" and all other than "Him" are wrong. In Buddhist philosophy, every sentient being is a Buddha, absolutely equal. But, then why aren't sentient beings all Buddhas? Because they can't find their own mind—they're lost. If one awakens to enlightenment, never to be lost again, then one has become a Buddha oneself.

Without Power and Authority, Without a Supreme God

The Buddha is not actually the embodiment of power and authority, or a supreme God. The Buddha's power, authority and supremacy are all within each person's mind. This is why it is said that one who studies Buddhism does not have blind faith; rather, it is a clean, clear belief. Clear belief requires that it be initiated within one's self and by one's own discoveries, that one must awaken of one's self and achieve Buddhism of one's self. If one goes to the temple, kowtows, offers incense and hopes for the Buddha's protection, this is blind faith. To tell the truth, the Buddha doesn't really pay much attention to this small matter of yours. He will tell you the methods by which you can protect yourself. This idea is the same as in traditional Chinese culture. There's an old saying, "One must seek fortune for one's self." One must first help one's self and then heaven will help; one must first help one's self and then others will help. In other words, you must first help yourself and then the Buddha will help.

Some people do bad things, and then run to the Buddhas to ask forgiveness. If you think that by saying you're sorry, the Buddhas can pardon you, you're really fooling yourself. When I was in Tibet, I saw that even though it was a Buddhist country, there was still crime. However, the perpetrator would run to the temple and repent in front of the Buddha, saying he would never do it again. Then, after his money runs out, he goes and steals again. Again he goes to beg for forgiveness saying, "Buddha, I'm so sorry. The next time I won't do it again." Over and over the same story, his heart is never at peace. The Buddha has no sway with him at all. The only way is to "seek fortune for one's self." This is what Buddhism is all about.

Wanting to become a Buddha, wanting to find within one's own heart and mind that which is the Buddha nature is what's called initiating anuttara-samyak sambodhi. This, really, is the motivation for studying Buddhism. I always say to young students: You think that sitting in the lotus position is called practicing Buddhism and once you uncross your legs it's not practicing? This is called practicing one's legs, not practicing Buddhism. Meditation is but the practice of *dhyana,* which is one of the preparatory works of mind and body along the path. This must be clearly understood.

So where does the difficulty lie in truly practicing Buddhism? It's in being *"skillfully mindful."* This is the diamond eye. Subhuti said, Buddha, virtuous men and virtuous women (not the bad eggs, they don't practice Buddhism!), these good people who wish to clearly perceive their mind and essence and discover the origin of their existence and ultimate Tao, have a great difficulty. Their thoughts will not come to rest. They sit down to meditate and the thoughts just don't stop. If it's not one's husband, then it's the wife, the relatives, the parents, children, money... When one's not meditating, everything's fine and under control, but sit down and close the eyes and a myriad of thoughts fly.

Due to the pressures of society, the state of many people's minds can be described as, "the myriad of thoughts are listless." In other words, they're in a kind of depressed stupor. Many people come to me asking how they can help someone they know who is in that state. I say, "Tell that person to meditate." They say, "Ah! Of course, if he'd meditate and study Buddhism, he'd be all right." I say, "That's not what I mean. When he sits down to meditate, a whole slew of thoughts will arise!" His mind won't be in a listless, gray state. He'll start thinking and everything will come up. Almost everyone who meditates comes up against this problem. The mind's frustration cannot be cut off. This is the first problem one encounters on the spiritual path.

This Mind, How Should It Dwell?

Subhuti was fully at ease in discourse. On behalf of all the disciples, he asked, *"How should their minds dwell?"* How should the mind rest in the alambana of peace and, furthermore, virtue? One's mind is a crazy circus full of frustrations and delusions. How can it possibly be subdued? Whether it be in ancient times or modern, the East or the West, normally, when we speak of being ethical, learning the wisdom of the sages or practicing Buddhism, these all address this question: How can one tame the mind? This mind will just not abide in any one place. Even if one repeats the Buddha's name forever, still it can't be done. One thought is going, *Amitofo*, while at the same time another is pondering what to do tomorrow. "Amitofo, Old Wang still owes me ten bucks. Amitofo, he hasn't returned it yet. Amitofo, what to do? Amitofo..." The mind just won't abide. You pray to God, but he doesn't help because you are still you and the evil thoughts still arise. The Bodhisattvas are of no help, either. So how should the mind abide and how should one tame the mind? How can all the frustrations and wanderings be tamed? This is an enormous problem.

The *Diamond Sutra* from the beginning is like a camera or rather like a strong light which shows all of the dust. It's clear-cut and directly to the point, not in the least mysterious. No matter which sect you're in, which methods you use, the first problem you come up against is how the mind should abide and how it should be tamed. This is a very serious problem. When I was young, I was always deeply affected by these lines. Studying the *Diamond Sutra*, one sees that the sages of a thousand ages all sigh over this same point. The problem is just too difficult. A hero could conquer anything under the heavens, but cannot conquer his own mind. A hero could govern the whole earth, but have no way to govern his own mind. One's own thought world defies submission. Sainthood is so difficult to achieve; the Tao is difficult to attain! You, say, then learn a spiritual method, all kinds of spiritual methods, but even if you learned all the methods in the heavens, of what use would it be? The method remains the method and your frustration is still your frustration. Reciting mantras? Frustration is much more stubborn than mantra. The harder you mantra it, the harder it mantras you. This frustration is really that difficult to manage, that stubborn. The question of how the mind ought to abide and how it ought to be subdued was asked very well.

> *The Buddha spoke, "Excellent, excellent Subhuti, it is as you say. The Tathagata is skillfully mindful, perfectly instructing and entrusting the Bodhisattvas. Now listen well to what I say."*

The Buddha listened to the question Subhuti asked and then opened his eyes again. The question was asked well, right to the point. The sutras should be read as though they were stories—that way one can really understand what is happening in the situation and gain something from it. It's not disrespectful to look at sutras in this way. On the contrary, it is very respectful. If one cannot enter into the story, then the sutra is the sutra and you are you—it's fruitless.

Now we are kneeling there with Subhuti. Try to enter that alambana and have it be present for you. The Buddha says, Good, good Subhuti, you just said that the Tathagata is skillfully mindful, perfectly instructs and entrusts the Bodhisattvas, correct? Subhuti answers, Yes. The Buddha says, "*Now, listen well*"—you must be very attentive! *Well* is attentive and careful in this situation. "*...to what I say.*"— in other words, I wish to answer you. You've asked a most excellent question and I, of course, must give you an answer. All this while, Subhuti was still kneeling there.

> *"Virtuous men and virtuous women who initiate the mind of anuttara-samyak sambodhi should thus dwell and pacify their minds."*
> *"I assure you, World-Honored One, we joyfully await your answer."*

The Buddha said, When virtuous men and virtuous women decide to seek the supreme Tao, it's like THIS that their minds should dwell, like THIS that they should pacify their minds. After finishing this sentence, the World-Honored One then once again closed his eyes. Subhuti probably waited for ages and then raised his head to look. He said, *"I assure you, World-Honored One, we joyfully await your answer."* In other words, I'm on the edge of my seat listening, waiting to hear! Subhuti was just poised there, but the Buddha did not continue. Why? Because he had already answered, but Subhuti did not understand.

Well, everyone, is this story well written? Sutras are really good stories. Amongst those sitting here, we have some expert writers, but the ones who wrote this story were really the experts. The writing is so clear and insightful, isn't it?

Now let's return to take a look at what the Buddha was just saying. He was telling Subhuti to listen carefully. Listen very carefully, and I'll tell you. When you have the mind that seeks the

Tao, when all of your mind is just one thought that seeks the Tao, just like this should it rest. Just like this has the untamed mind been placated. That's all—just like that.

If I were the one speaking—of course I'm not the Buddha, but if I were to be speaking—I'd say it differently. If I were an actor playing Shakyamuni Buddha, at this point I wouldn't be so gentle and compassionate. There would be no slow speaking with the eyes half closed, no "Excellent, excellent Subhuti." I would say, staring directly at him the whole time, "Listen! Pay careful attention! The question you asked—the moment the thought of wishing to seek the Tao is initiated, THAT'S IT!"

A while later—I give Subhuti credit for having been under the Buddha's stare for so long—a befuddled Subhuti blurts out, Buddha! I'm here listening!—or rather, You haven't answered my question.

Has he answered him?

"Skillful mindfulness," the question you've asked is in fact the answer you seek. If you still need to seek a method to make your mind abide, to tame your mind, you're finished! That's a second thought. It's the mind wandering off. Seeking a Buddhist method in order to cultivate Buddhism is just the wandering mind. The moment you think, I want to be a good person, this moment of thought is a good person. In thinking, "How can I be a good person," one is then not a good person. Isn't it very clear? To put it in Buddhist terminology, this is Ch'an .

So I tell you, if you want to find peace and serenity, find Buddhism, then (first) sit in a meditation position or however you wish to sit. Now you wish to meditate, and at this moment everything is fine. Then, after you've settled in just right—"Shhh! Stop your racket!" At this moment, you've lost it because your own mind is making a racket. There is really nothing which is peaceful or not peaceful. That initial moment is just it.

The Buddha said that the question you asked, the moment you had the thought, the moment you asked, right there and then was the alambana of perfectly protecting the thought. "How should one dwell?" The Buddha said it should be like this: you just stop. In this way should the mind be pacified. This is what the Buddha said. If it were me, I'd say, "What are you babbling on about? You've already lost it!"

To Dwell Is to Repeat the Buddha's Name

We will now discuss how one should dwell and how one should pacify one's mind. The word *dwell* can mean to live someplace or it can simply mean "suspended someplace." The question is, how can one get one's frenzied monkey mind to stop? The Buddha says, "Like this, just stop."

Everyone knows that the greatest difficulty is to get one's contemplations, emotions and mental wanderings to stop. Actually, in every different religion in the world, the methods of cultivation are all directed toward developing a peaceful mind or what we call "abiding." The Buddhist cultivation methods boil down to a simple essence: samadhi and prajna. How can a person's thoughts be made to come to be one and just rest in that one spot?

The pureland sect uses a method of repeating the Buddha's name, "*NAMO AMITABHA*." The orthodox name of this method translates as "maintain the name, hold the Buddha in mind." In other words, it's as if the mind is held in one place. *NAMO* means to take refuge; *AMITABHA* is one Buddha's name meaning "infinite light." *NAMO AMITABHA* means to take refuge in this Buddha; so we call his name, holding this Buddha in mind.

There's a funny story that I'd like to tell all the young folks here. There was an old woman who from morning till night recited the name of Amitofo[1] in fervent belief. Her son couldn't stand it. One day when this old woman was reciting, her son called out, "Ma." The woman asked, "What is it?" Her son ignored her. "Amitofo, Amitofo..." she started up again. When she was in full swing, her son cried out, "Ma! Ma!" "What is it?" she asked. Again, no response. She was a little perturbed at this, but kept on reciting Amitofo, Amitofo. Then her son cried out, "Ma! Ma! Ma!" The old woman finally lost her patience and yelled, "Damn it! I'm reciting the Buddha's name, why do you keep calling me?" Her son finally answered, "Mama, look, I'm your son. I've called your name three

---

[1] Chinese practitioners say Amitofo, which translates to Amita Buddha, rather than Amitabha.

times and you fly off the handle. You call out Amitofo's name without stopping. Don't you think that you're driving him nuts?"

From all general appearances, this just seems like a funny story, but actually there is a lot of deep meaning in it. It's very meaningful, so don't just push it to the side as a joke. To recite Amitabha is to maintain the name, like calling "Ma." To "maintain the name" or "hold the Buddha in mind," has its meaning, but we won't discuss this now. However, the purpose of this method is to get to the point of single-minded concentration. Single-minded concentration is not easy to achieve! Ordinarily, when people recite Amitabha, they also go right on with their thinking and fantasizing as well. In the same way, when a candle is lit, there is black smoke coming up from the flame. Another way to look at it is like a rock pressing down weeds; they still manage to grow up along the sides. This situation cannot be considered single-minded concentration for the mind is still in full swing, a blur of action. If one gets to the point of forgetting one's self, one's body and any state, this can be called a bit like single-minded concentration, but still that would be stretching the term.

In the same way, to practice any kind of cultivation method— whether it be of the Ch'an sect, the esoteric sect, etc., even praying in other religions—is a method for developing single-pointed concentration. After one arrives at single-pointed concentration and holds the mind there, then this is called samadhi.

The Myriad Kinds of Samadhi

In one alambana of true samadhi, there is no element of time. We have all heard stories of old masters who can sit for seven, eight days, even a month. Well, we feel that a week or a month has passed, but they only feel it to be a fraction of a second. Everyone must be clear on one point—this is only one aspect of samadhi. It's not to say that all samadhi is like this. Take note of this!

Buddhism speaks of there being a multiplicity of samadhi. One particular kind, we could call it "action samadhi," is present in all different kinds of situations. While handling affairs of the world, even if one doesn't have a minute's rest, one's inner world still remains in a state of equilibrium, unrelated to and unaffected by the world outside. To have this presence of mind is difficult enough, let alone doing meditation and practicing Buddhism.

Some people have insomnia because their minds won't settle down. For some, the older they get, the more complicated their thought world becomes. This in turn affects their nerves and brain, making it even more difficult to settle down. Our brain is an organ as is our heart. Their movement and functioning are directly affected, and to a large extent controlled, by our thoughts, feelings and emotions—our state of mind. This is why people who study Buddhism or enter the spiritual path are essentially seeking a method by which to achieve peace of mind. I think that anyone looking for peace of mind wants to have the power of samadhi. Some people practice meditation for years, and even though they sit there seemingly quiet, their inner heart is chaotic. Sometimes they might feel very peaceful and comfortable, but this is merely a short-lived state of body and mind and is not true samadhi. There is practically no chance that they'll achieve true samadhi.

Buddhist sutras often use images of ocean water to describe people's minds. All of our different thoughts, feelings and emotions are like running water, ever moving and changing. There is a saying that the waters of the Yellow River come from everywhere under the heavens and flow to the ocean never to return. This is one particular image. In Buddhist scriptures, another image frequently used is of the fragrant elephant crossing a river. It stops the flow of the current as it crosses. One with great wisdom and great character can stop the flow of thoughts. They can stop the mad mind no matter how crazy or frustrating the situation may be, just like the fragrant elephant crossing the river.

To be able to cut right through this untamed mind in one fell swoop is to hold the Buddha in mind. It is the preliminary stage of the pureland method, true peace of mind, true stopping. Having reached this point of stopping, if one continues to persistently cultivate, his or her mind and body will undergo many changes. Only then can the state of samadhi be reached. There are many different levels and situations of samadhi. Both "stopping" and "samadhi" are very different and to achieve either is kung fu. Achieving this one can be said to have a stable base in the first steps of Buddhist cultivation.

At this point in the *Diamond Sutra*, *stopping* and *samadhi* have not yet been discussed, only the concept of *abiding* has. All three of these are different, very different. First let's discuss *stopping*. Stopping can be said to be from working with the mind, getting it to simply stop its thinking, knowing and feeling processes. It is applying force to have things come to an abrupt stop on one point, like driving a knife into a point. This is the alambana of stopping. Samadhi, on the other hand, can be likened to a spinning top with which children play. After moving about, it just stops spinning in one place. This is the simile to explain samadhi. This '*to dwell*,' well, it's very different than the other two. *To dwell* means to very peacefully stay in one place. These explanations look at the meaning of the three words in conjunction with Buddhism.

Whether or not one studies Buddhism, if a person wishes to at all times peacefully abide, it is extremely difficult. We have a phrase in Chinese which describes life's highest achievement of profound knowledge and morality, "to feel at ease under all circumstances". *To feel at ease* and *to abide* are the same thing in this context. People, however, can't get to the state of feeling at ease under all circumstances because they are not satisfied with themselves, not satisfied with reality, never satisfied—endlessly searching for a nebulous something. What are they searching for? People speak of many things from searching for a career to even saying that life is the search for the meaning of life. Philosophers say they are searching for truth, but for how much can truth be sold? There's no price on it. Truth is an empty name. How much is life worth? All of these are created by man. In the course of life, to get to the point where one can "feel at ease under all circumstances" is very difficult.

Many of my friends who are Buddhist practitioners say that it's not convenient being a lay practitioner, but then, they also have trouble living in a community. Some explain their trouble as not being able to sleep in an unfamiliar bed. They simply can't "feel at ease under all circumstances," they cannot "thus dwell." They can't even take changing beds, let alone anything worse. Do a bed or surroundings actually make that much of a difference or have that much of an influence? Actually, no, for it's the mind which isn't at peace and which doesn't have the capacity to deal with change. It's the mind not at ease which prevents one from simply abiding wherever one is. This is very ordinary logic.

The question that Subhuti asked about is the most difficult problem that a person who is starting to study Buddhism faces, the mind not being at peace. How can the mind be at peace? At this time, the Buddha answers him—just when you asked, your mind was at rest; just as you asked, there were no illusions or frustrations. There is an example which will help you to understand better. Someone is walking down the street and, seeing something very strange or horrible, just stands there stupefied. His mind has, for the moment, "abided." This experience of the mind coming to a stop from suddenly experiencing a shocking event, however, is not the abiding spoken of in Buddhism. It is a false abiding, unlike the abiding which comes from a mind at peace. Most people, though, can relate to the above experience and can therefore understand the logic of saying that the mind can "abide." When the Buddha answered Subhuti, he didn't frighten him shouting, "STOP!" He didn't use the logic of the above example; his explanation was a bit different.

Three-Step Melody

Let's talk about a funny saying which, on the surface, seems as if it's insulting to Buddhists, but actually has some interesting truth to it. Everyone has heard the saying "Study Buddhism one year, the Buddha is in front of your eyes; study Buddhism two years, the Buddha is in the temple hall; study Buddhism three years, the Buddha is in the Western Paradise!" A person who has just started studying Buddhism or any religion for that matter is usually very sincere and fervent. Therefore, it is said, "Study Buddhism one year, the Buddha is in front of your eyes." Often, though, the longer one studies, the further away is the Buddha.

Here is a story to explain this more clearly. One day a student said he ought to go home to visit his parents and show filial piety. At that moment, when he said that, it was true filial piety, just like seeing the Buddha before one's eyes. After he gets home, his father says, "Why did you wait so long before coming home?" Seeing his father's face and hearing his tone of voice, the son's thought of filial piety slips further away—the Buddha is in the temple hall. Dad then goes on to give him a sound lecturing, thus removing any last thoughts of filial piety—the Buddha is in the Western Paradise. Our student then just goes to his room to sleep. Buddhist thinking is the same as that of the ordinary mind.

How does one tame the frustrated wandering mind? The Buddha answered lightly, "Thus dwell and pacify the mind." Just like this, dwell; just like this, pacify the mind. Why did the Buddha answer him so seemingly offhandedly? We shouldn't take the *Diamond Sutra* to be a sutra, nor should we take the sutra's words to be somewhere over there in the temple or just scholastic writing. We should take the words into our hearts. If we really want to study it, we need to leave the religious framework behind and set all that aside. In the quest for the profound essence of life, one must come to know, be empowered by and truly experience what is "peace" and "abiding." The Buddha told Subhuti, When you were asking the question, your mind had no frustration. You should remain in this moment. This is the same as when they say in the Ch'an sect that the present moment is it. The moment between thoughts is in essence peaceful and serene. One need not go looking elsewhere. This moment of mind is it.

Whether we believe in Buddhism or in another religion, whether or not we are in a church or temple, if at this moment, we give rise to a feeling of remorse and repentance, there follows a moment of serenity. This moment is the alambana of a Buddha. There is no agitation; no second method is needed. If one thinks to create a method by which to tame the frustrated mind, it's this very same method which will create further agitation. It will not help one to peacefully abide.

The *Diamond Sutra's* contents are about the culmination of wisdom. The point at which true Buddhism will differ from other religions is in the cultivation of wisdom rather than skill. The culmination of wisdom, merit and virtue is prajna. What is spoken of as awakening, achieving the Tao or Great Enlightenment is, in essence, the awakening of prajna wisdom.

How to Abide and Abiding Nowhere

Now let's speak of Mahayana wisdom. *"Thus dwell and pacify the mind."* When the question of how to subdue the mind is asked, at that moment, the mind is calm and abiding—but only for a split second which you can't hold on to. It's too fast. If one could hold onto that moment of calm abiding, one would be home. The rest of the *Diamond Sutra* teaches us, who are in a state of busy confusion, how to calmly abide, how to abide nowhere, abiding in a serene state and not abiding. One who has made significant accomplishment in cultivation can go into a state of samadhi for many days or even months. We see this as being amazing and difficult. In the Mahayana perspective, the Hinayana arhat who can go into a state of samadhi for 84,000 eons is not actually in a state of samadhi because the mind is still engaged. What mind? The mind which abides nowhere. Abiding nowhere is still using the mind. This ability of abiding nowhere is slowly, cumulatively accomplished. Mahayana doesn't engage the mind because the mind originally does not abide.

Just what does this mean, "the mind originally does not abide"? For instance, I'm speaking right now. Having started at eight, I've now spoken twenty minutes. Every sentence I've spoken has come directly from my mind. After they've been spoken, they're gone like the passing clouds and flowing water. "Without abiding," if I were to abide or get fixated on the time I am supposed to speak, then I wouldn't be able to say anything because my mind would be abiding in my watch. If the listeners in the audience, having heard the first few sentences, started to criticize, thinking, The first part was good but this last part was just out to lunch..., nothing after that would go in because their minds would be abiding or, in other words, stuck.

In Mahayana Buddhism, how does one peacefully abide? Nowhere to abide is abiding. To speak in Ch'an terms: To abide is not to abide, and not abiding is abiding. Human existence lived at this alambana is what's called the Tathagata, or the mind like a bright mirror, the mind tidied up and very clean without any subjective point of view or bias. "*Que sera, sera!*" Situations arise, and the mirror reflects them. Today joy, anger, sadness and happiness come; we simply have joy, anger, sadness and happiness. What has passed does not remain. Whatever situations have passed do not remain. The famous Sung Dynasty poet Su Tung-p'o, who brought together his literary prowess and Ch'an studies in his poetry, wrote the following famous couplet: "*People are like migrating birds in autumn, sure to come; events are like spring dreams, gone without a trace."*

These are lines rarely seen from a poet, and only appear because he understood Ch'an theory. *"People are like migrating birds in autumn, sure to come."* Su Tung-p'o wants to go to a certain place in the countryside to drink wine. He was there last year, promised to come back this year and this is surely what will come to pass. *"Events are like spring dreams, gone without a trace."* All events which have gone past are like the dreams of springtime. In springtime, people tend to be more sleepy and dreamy, but upon waking, one finds that dreams neither stay nor leave tracks. Life is like a long dream; all things pass by like the Yellow River flowing off to the east, nothing returns. Old people tend to dwell on the past, thinking of the time they were doing this, that or the other thing. One just frustrates oneself because the hands of time cannot be turned back, like the spring dreams which leave no tracks.

If one can truly experience life as spring's traceless dream, one does not need to study the *Diamond Sutra*. For a mind like this, there is no taming for there is no need to tame it. The true nature of frustration is emptiness. What are called happiness, anger, sadness, joy, depression and bitter frustration, all disappear the moment we sit down to meditate. Everything prior to this moment is gone forever, never to return. One should abide like this and in this way tame one's mind. This is what's meant by the analogy of the spring dreams. First understand this point.

THE TRUE MAHAYANA SECT

The Buddha then said, "Subhuti, all the Bodhisattvas and Mahasattvas should quell their minds in this way: All kinds of sentient beings— whether egg born, womb born, moisture born or transformation born, having form or not having form, having thought or not having thought—through my reaching nirvana are saved. Yet when immeasurable, innumerable and unlimited numbers of beings have been liberated, verily, no beings have been liberated. And why is this Subhuti? If a Bodhisattva retains the notion of self a personality, a being and a life, he is not a true Bodhisattva."

All Sentient Beings

> *"The Buddha then said, "Subhuti, all the Bodhisattvas and Mahasattvas should quell their minds in this way."*

The Buddha told Subhuti that the moment one asks how to calm the mind, one's mind is calm. After a while, the Buddha saw that Subhuti still did not understand. Since the crucial pivotal moment, "the opportunity" as it's spoken of in Ch'an Buddhism, had already gone by, the next step was to speak and explain. He went on to say that all great Bodhisattvas should have some method by which they can tame their minds. Just what method ?

The next line starts, *"All kinds of sentient beings..."* We'll first explain what the term *sentient* means. The term *sentient being*, seen even earlier than the sutras in the writings of Chuang-tzu, refers not only to human beings; humans are just one kind of sentient being. Sentient beings include animals all the way down to bacteria. Every living being which has a spirit, feelings and consciousness falls within the parameters of a sentient being. Buddhism is different from other religions in that the Buddha wishes to teach all sentient beings to have love and compassion for all other sentient beings; to have compassion for and teach those who are good and, even more so, those who are bad; to help those in a heavenly situation and help those who need it the most, those trapped in hell. This is the spirit of the Buddha; this is what is called "saving all sentient beings."

"All" has no boundaries; it includes everything. Speaking of sentient beings, it makes me think of ten years ago. At that time, I was in Sichuan teaching Chinese philosophy at a university. One day in class, I mentioned the term *sentient being* and one student asked whether plants and rocks were included in the term *sentient being*. I explained that these were complimentary products of karma. They are extras that come with us and have a relationship with us. The student then said, "You can't tell me that Venus flytraps don't have consciousness!" I asked him what he studied and he answered agriculture. I said, it's strange you asked this, having studied agriculture. At the time, I liked to play intellectual games. You ought to know that Venus flytraps have a small sack of water which reacts to the heat of our hands. This makes it close up as if it were shy and afraid. It is a chemical reaction rather than an emotional one or an intellectual one. It was very funny that I had actually learned this only the night before talking with an agricultural student. Perhaps the Buddha had a hand in this serendipity played out by the Buddha knowing that the next day someone would ask this question!

T'an-tzu's Book of Transformation

"All kinds of sentient brings—whether egg born, womb born, moisture born, or transformation born, having form or not having form, having thought or not having though— through my reaching nirvana are saved."

The Buddha divided sentient beings into twelve categories, the first being those born by egg. This includes most kinds of birds, turtles, some reptiles, etc. Birth by womb indicates humans, horses and any kind of being which is born through a womb. Those born of moisture include fish, mosquitoes, fruit flies, etc. Those things born by transformation are cicadas, beetles, frogs, butterflies, etc. In ancient Chinese folklore, there was a kind of shark in the ocean which, after having lived several hundred years there, would then crawl out onto a beach, grow a horn, and become a deer, which would also be transformation.

There are writings about transformation in Chinese culture which include deep theoretical explanations that practically no one understands. In the Taoist treasury of writings, there is one book which is entirely on this subject. It is called *The Book of Transformation* and is written by the sage T'an-tzu (T'an Ch'iao was his original name, and T'an-tzu is an honorific title conferred by other scholars), who was a student of both Buddhism and Taoism. T'an-tzu's father was an official and the only university chancellor of the Sung Dynasty. He was a highly respected man who had only one son. T'an-tzu left home in his early teens to study Taoism and left behind a distraught father. Twenty years later, he appeared wearing the clothes of a Taoist, tattered shoes and a battered hat. He had a peculiar air, somewhat like the hippies of a few years back. T'an-tzu came back to convince his father to go with him and practice Taoism, saying that everything in this life has no meaning. T'an-tzu was then a very well-known, learned Taoist and had written *The Book of Transformation*. He thought that with this knowledge, he could control the transformations of life within this universe and thus gain immortality. Did he live on until now? Who knows, maybe he's enrolled in this class!

Later on, because people asked him how the Tao is cultivated, he wrote a poem. It's a bit like verses from the *Diamond Sutra*, very simple containing the alambana of Ch'an :

THE TRUE MAHAYANA SECT

A thread makes the Yangze River, an umbrella is the sky;
Cast the slippers away toward the ocean's eastern edge.
To this place, Peng Lai, there are not many roads
It's just in front of the walking stick held in T'an's hand.

He said the entire universe is ever so small. The Yangze and Yellow Rivers are but threads of a cloth, and the sky is like an umbrella. Slippers have no back to which to affix a heel and so they flap as one walks. The unwanted slippers are cast toward the ocean's eastern edge. Peng Lai represents the alambana of the Taoist Immortals. "To this place, Peng Lai, there are not many roads." In the next line, he says the *alambana* of the Immortals is not far away; it's just right here. Where? Just right here in my (T'an-tzu's) hand, the hand grasping a walking stick right here. This is the same logic as that behind what the Buddha said to Subhuti, *"It's like this that one should dwell, one should pacify one's mind."* Where is the Buddha? Here, not in the Western Paradise, the Buddha is right here.

While speaking of birth by womb, egg, moisture and transformation, I mentioned this very important book of Chinese theory on biological physics. I really love this book, but don't have the time or energy to study it in depth. If one is interested in true science or really understands Buddhist theory, perhaps he or she might wish to study this book and do research—see if in this world there are many things which have come of transformation.

His book was also very special in that in addition to explaining the theory of transformation, he also spoke of science as being philosophy and what is normally thought of as philosophy as actually being politics. He spoke of the realm of human life and how to teach others, how to change others. On the societal level, he believed that bad times or even a bad world could be turned around. The level of his theory and philosophy is very high. So when we speak of Chinese culture, the essence of Chinese culture, we need to at least have an inkling of it.

Form and Formless Beings

Aside from those born of wombs, eggs, humidity and transformation, there are also other kinds of life, two being the form and formless kinds. "Form" beings have a physical form which can be seen. The "formless" ones are unknown to us and cannot be seen, but they actually do exist. For example, ghosts, are they there or aren't they? Of course there definitely are ghosts, but they are actually not so horrible. To us, they are just a kind of "formless" life with a different energy level than our own.

We talk of ghosts, but it's not everyone who's seen one. If you go to Guizhou or the outlying areas of Yunnan, you will hear stories of living ghosts. They call these living ghosts *Shan-hsiao* (Mountain Hsiao). If we use Buddhist sutras to explain these, it's very easy. They fall into the category of "as if form; as if formless" because a Shan-hsiao will sometimes let you see it and sometimes not. It depends on its mood. If one goes into the woods and sees footprints with toes at the back and the heel in the front, one then knows that a Shan-hsiao has been in the area. If you cry out that there are mountain ghosts here, it will be your misfortune. They place a high importance on politeness. If you, however, say that "Mr. Shan-hsiao" is here, you won't have any trouble.

These Shan-hsiao are very interesting. I've said before, humans are the ones to fear, they being the most horrid of all beings. Everyone's afraid of ghosts, but it's really humans that are to be feared. Just how bad are humans? Around their New Year's time, Shan-hsiao will come to people's houses to borrow pots, bowls and chopsticks. Their appearance is very ugly, with short legs and backwards feet. Their language is unintelligible to humans, and so they must point to the things they need. The people living in the mountains all know about this and will prepare extra things. There are some mean people who will trick the Shan-hsiao. They will prepare paper pots and bowls. The happy Shan-hsiao take these back, and as soon as they're put on the fire, they burn up. Since they were borrowed in good faith, the Shan-hsiao feel they must somehow replace the things.

Within one *li* of their territory, they won't steal, but somehow, from some rich family far away, the replacements are procured. The Shan-hsiao return the real pots and bowls as replacements for the paper ones. Many poor people in the mountains play this trick on the ghosts. Is it the ghosts that are bad or the people that are bad? Those who know about the Shan-hsiao stories all have the same feeling—that the people are really the horrible ones. They even trick the ghosts!

"Thought and Thoughtless"

Another category of beings is called those '"having thought." These beings have thoughts and feelings as opposed to those beings in the category of the "thoughtless," which have none. Getting down into even finer categories, there are those beings without thoughts or consciousness, but who have feelings. Yet another large category of beings is that of heavenly beings. This category can be broken down into thirty large subcategories, which in turn can be broken down into sixty more and so on. Within each of their realms, there is also a hierarchy. An example of one of these heavenly realms is the realm of "not having thought." Those in this realm don't actually not have to think, but it is as if they are thoughtless. For example, when some people are meditating, it looks as if they don't know what's going on, but they actually do know. But, do they really know? They still don't really know!

In this world, there are many kinds of beings, but Buddhism generalizes them into twelve categories. Within all these categories, only humans are at the same time so bad and yet complete with everything one could ever want. We don't want to make the mistake of assuming that people are in the category of birth by womb only. We actually experience all twelve categories.

Conception begins with the union of a sperm and an egg. Within the category of birth by womb, there is also birth by egg. Inside the womb, we experience the category of birth by moisture. Then, by the power of the incoming vegetables, carrots, onions, beef, etc., we grow. Thus, we are also within the category of "birth by transformation." Humans are part of the form realm with physical bodies visible to the eye. Yet, if we come right down to the essence of our life force, we can also be said to be of the formless realm. As to "thoughtful," of course we have thoughts, but sometimes we'll go blank or have no thoughts. This experience and also that of the extremely dull-witted can be said to fall within the thoughtless realm. Many people who cultivate Tao have reached the state of "not having thought; not without thought." This state is not easy to accomplish but, mind you, it is not indicative of complete achievement. The point is, as humans, we fall within all twelve realms.

Speaking of "not having thought; not without thought," when I was in mainland China, I saw this twice. Once in Shaoxin in Zhejiang Province , there was a Taoist priest meditating in a small temple. It was said that he had been there for two hundred years. Each year at Chinese New Year, the townspeople would come to clip his fingernails which were still growing. He wasn't dead because if you felt him, his body was still a little warm. Some said he was in samadhi. Others who were Taoists said that he wasn't in samadhi, but rather his spirit couldn't come out. They said that his cultivation was finished, but his spirit was stuck inside the shell of his body.

The other case I saw involved a Buddhist. People said that his samadhi was very deep and he had incredible kung fu. He had been sitting there for seven or eight years, not dead, just not coming out of samadhi. Calling his name, for instance, evoked no response. So in essence, it was almost as if he were dead. He was all hunched up, and there was a protrusion on his back which had a pulse. Most people thought he was in samadhi, but people who really understood Buddhism or Taoism, however, knew his spirit was stuck. He had turned down a side path and traveled a deviant route of cultivation.

Some of you young people are afraid to meditate because you fear you'll become ensnared by demons. This type of condition I have just described could be called being ensnared by demons. So you see, it's not so easy. Most people aren't qualified to be ensnared by demons. You can relax, you are far away from that danger! Still, that monk's condition shouldn't necessarily be classified as being ensnared by demons. His life force is existent in what could be called a state of "not having thought; not thoughtless."

The human body and human existence are both microcosms. All the different states of existence are embodied within us, but we don't stop to recognize this. According to T'an-tzu's theory of transformation, humans can become Immortals, Buddhas, ghosts, gods...through transformation. This all depends on one's wisdom and power.

Red Fortune, Clear Fortune

" *All kinds of sentient beings"*, ("kinds" being the aforementioned twelve), *"...through my reaching nirvana are saved."*

One who is practicing Buddhism first needs to make a vow, to set an aspiration, "I vow to save all the sentient beings in the world," because sentient beings are in the midst of frustration and suffering. The rich and famous have rich and famous frustration; the poor alike have birth, aging, illness and death to suffer. Courtship has its frustrations, marriage has its own, and raising children yet more. All in all, this life is a chain of frustration and suffering. *Frustration* and *suffering* are two different terms that represent varying degrees of the same feeling, frustration being a lighter form of suffering. Those who are Mahayana Buddhists don't think of themselves first. Rather, they would complete their own cultivation in order to best help others and save others from suffering. They wish for others to enter a realm that does not know frustration and suffering, that is absolutely pure and blissful. What is this realm? It is called "perfect nirvana."

Nirvana is a transliteration which at times had been translated as "quiet extinction" or "complete stillness." Later on, this translation was thought to be too cold—only the quiet left after the extinction of everything, not even a little sound to be heard. Studying Buddhism changed to studying "quiet extinction." Isn't it strange? What then is the use of human life? Life is already full of enough suffering, and then to go study "quiet extinction." Why do that to yourself? Later on, others changed the translation to "complete serenity," perfect peace and serenity. Serenity is in itself a good thing, but some people don't know what serenity is. The state of peace and serenity is most comfortable.

I usually say there are two kinds of Buddhism, leaving the worldly for peace and serenity and entering the worldly to "tumble in the red dust." Why is the mundane world called the "red dust"? This term comes from the T'ang Dynasty period when the capital was in Xian, next to the Yellow River. The only vehicle then was the horse cart, which would kick up the red dirt native to the area. A layer of red dust hung in the air around the city; thus, the term red dust came to represent mundane life—"tumbling in the red dust." Now buses spew out black exhaust. Looking at Taipei from atop Kuan-yin Mountain, we see it is black rather than red, so it is a black-dust world now. We are all tumbling in the black dust.

Having wealth and high position is another meaning of life in the red dust, hence the familiar term, *red fortune* or *great fortune*. Peaceful, serene fortune is called "clear fortune." Great fortune is relatively easy to achieve and enjoy; clear fortune, however, is not. Without wisdom, one cannot enjoy clear fortune. In life's later years, when all affairs can be laid to rest and one can finally enjoy some peaceful fortune, many people, on the contrary, feel immensely frustrated and suffer greatly. Without having any business to attend to, some people feel as though they can't go on living. When the time came around for many of my older friends to enjoy the clear fortune of retirement, that clear fortune was the death of them. Fear of loneliness, boredom, and the feeling of having no reason to live, added together, killed them.

I usually advise young students that as part of their character development, they absolutely must learn to enjoy being alone. If one recognizes being alone as a great pleasure, they are almost at the point of a true understanding of human existence. Having experienced a higher state of existence, one can see red fortune as a vexation. In the sutras, it says that if you observe one to have developed the mind of intolerant detachment, or rather, aversion to red fortune, then this person has entered into the path.

It is most difficult to have the blessing of clear fortune. This is the fortune enjoyed in the heavenly realms. I'd like to tell everyone a little story. In the Ming Dynasty, there was a man who kept a traditional Chinese practice. There are probably some people in the countryside who still practice this now. Every night between midnight and one, they go outside, light incense and give reverence to the heavens. This is a traditional Chinese religious practice. They're all up there—the Buddha, the Immortals, the saints, Jesus, Kuan-kung, God...whether it be in the Western

Paradise, Eastern Paradise, Northern or Southern Heaven—and they're all covered in this practice.

This man in the Ming Dynasty had been doing this faithfully and sincerely for thirteen years. One evening, he moved the heart of a heavenly being who appeared in all his radiance before this mortal man. The man was not frightened. He knew this to be a celestial being. The Immortal said to him, "Every day you pay respect to the heavens very sincerely. For what do you wish? Speak quickly, I will leave soon." The man thought briefly and then said, "I do not want for anything. My only wish is for in this life to have enough to eat; clothes to wear; not to be poor; not to have too much money just enough to go and enjoy the mountains, ocean and some famous places; not to suffer from illness and to pass away without suffering." The Immortal heard this and said, "Oh my, so this is what you desire. This is the fortune of the gods and Immortals. If you had asked for fame and fortune, high position or great wealth, I could have given it to you but that which you ask for is the pure fortune of the heavens. I have no way to grant you this."

If throughout life, one never goes without food or proper clothing; once the money is used up more comes along but not too much, just enough; and on top of this one is able to go to all the wonderful places on this earth... Who has this fortune? Those with high positions are too busy to even have time to listen to the Diamond Sutra teachings. This clear fortune is the most difficult to attain. In this light, looking at the translation of nirvana as "quiet extinction," we see it includes the concept of clear fortune. However, most people are not so eager to obtain this. Actually, nirvana is an alambana. It's what was spoken of in the *Parinirvana Sutra* as "permanence, bliss, ego and purity." It also can be said to be like coming to a place without birth or death. "No arisal and no extinction; no filth, no purity; no increase nor decrease..." as it says in the *Heart Sutra*. Permanent happiness—this is a paradise world. That is the real ego, the true "I," not the physical form born of the womb, egg, moisture and transformation, the ever changing "I." The real "I" is the pureland, the realm of nirvana, the fountain of life, "permanence, bliss, ego and purity."

The Arhat's Nirvana

Arhats are divided into two kinds: those with incomplete nirvana (*sopadhisa-nirvana*, meaning, there are still subtle illusions remaining) and those with complete nirvana (*nirupadhisa-nirvana*, meaning, no illusion remaining). When arhats attain Tao, what they have attained is incomplete nirvana, where everything is empty. The great arhats can be in a state of samadhi for 84,000 eons. Not years, but eons! For the time it takes for the earth to be destroyed and created and destroyed many times over, these arhats can remain in a state of samadhi. It is very difficult for people nowadays to believe this kind of thing.

Let's go back to the time of the T'ang Dynasty, when the Venerable Hsuan-tsang went to "study abroad" in India. There is a legend about what happened along the way there. Accounts of it are recorded in both Hsuan-tsang's own writings and in the Annals of the Great Western T'ang Dynasty. The master was crossing Heaven's Mountain in Xinjiang, nearing the northern border of India at the back side of the Himalayas. In these snowy mountains, the weather was very cold, and the twenty or so people who had accompanied the master all died along the way. Only he saw the following sight. Amidst the ice and snow-covered mountain tops, protruded a bare peak. The falling snow didn't stay on it. Master Hsuan-tsang thought this was very curious, and so he climbed up to look at it closely. He discovered that the ground was covered with very long, thick hair, different from the kind of hair we have. He stared at it for ages, thinking. He supposed it was a being not of this millennium, or that perhaps it was a prehistoric man. He dug down and—lo and behold—it was a huge man!

Master Hsuan-tsang was standing on the shoulder of a giant man in deep meditation. He came up to about the man's ear, and so he shouted to awaken him. It was to no avail. Then, the master struck the meditation chime which monks carry in order to awaken people from samadhi if necessary. "Ding, ding, ding." He struck it by the giant's ear slowly three times; whereupon, the gentleman awoke from his samadhi.

As he opened his eyes, an avalanche of snow was created from the enormous crusts of snow covering his eyelids. He asked, "Who called me?" I'm not sure what language he spoke, but they must have been able to communicate. Hsuan-tsang called out, "It was me." The giant asked where the voice was coming from and the master said, "Here, on your shoulder." He turned to look. "Such a tiny person! Where are you from? You're so strange." Hsuan-tsang said, "I'm from the Great T'ang country to the East. I am a monk." The giant said, "Oh, you're a monk. So am I."

The master asked what his story was, and the man told him that he was a monk from the age of destruction during the period of the previous Buddha, Kasyapa. Since it was the age of destruction, all he could do was develop single-pointed concentration, enter samadhi, sit tight and wait for Shakyamuni Buddha to come; then, he could ask for instruction. The master informed him that Shakyamuni Buddha had long since come and gone. It was no longer the period of True Dharma; rather, it was the Semblance Age, in which there are still Buddhist teachings and images. The giant sighed, "Well, I'll just have to continue waiting for Maitreya Buddha to come then."

The master quickly yelled into his ear, "Dear Brother, just hang on a sec before you go into samadhi again, please. If you go into samadhi to wait for Maitreya, you're going to have to come out of samadhi again to find him. Who's going to wake you up at that time?" The giant said, "You've got a point there." The master then asked him if he was able to release his consciousness from this body.—This is not such an easy thing to do as we saw in the examples mentioned earlier of meditators stuck in their physical shells.—Hsuan-tsang had already planned to go to India, and so asked him to reincarnate in China so that later on the giant could become his disciple. The master directed, "If possible, go to Great T'ang, find the biggest palace, reincarnate as a prince there and wait for my return." No sooner said than done— his spirit immediately left.

Master Hsuan-tsang, after twenty years, returned as promised. He went to see the Emperor, T'ang T'ai-chung, who implored him three times to become his secretary general. T'ang T'ai-chung truly admired Hsuan-tsang. The master, however, wouldn't agree to take the position. He told T'ang T'ai-chung about the event that had happened en route to India and that he had come to find the prince born that day in the palace. However, there were none born to the emperor on that day. T'ang T'ai-chung asked if this kind of thing was really reliable and the master assured him that it was. The emperor then had all the surrounding palace buildings checked. It turned out that a son had been born to a great general, Wei Ch'ih-kung. The arhat mistook the general's palace for the emperor's. As it would be impossible for the master to simply entreat this great general to allow his son to become a monk, T'ang T'ai-chung took matters into his own hands. He called for Wei Ch'ih-kung and made the announcement that he wanted to become a monk, but his role of being emperor prevented him from doing so. He then appointed Wei Ch'ih-kung's son to go in his place.

Master Hsuan-tsang thought that since the arhat had achieved such a high state of samadhi, he would certainly recognize the master upon seeing him. However, arhats and

Bodhisattvas still will have "amnesia" going from one incarnation to the next—they forget. The young man felt an affinity with the master and chatted away happily with him. At last, the master said to him, "Come and be my disciple." Wei Ch'ih-kung's son, of course, balked. The emperor then commanded him to become a monk. He said he would agree to become a monk if three conditions were met. The first was that a carriage of maidens would accompany him and attend to his wishes. A vegetarian diet would be too much of a compromise, and so a carriage of meats and wines should also follow. Thirdly, he wished to learn more than just sutras, and so a carriage of books should follow as well. Thus begins the story of the master known as the "three-carriage monk," who in his next incarnation became the great Abhidharma master, the Venerable K'uei-chi.

Why do I mention this story? From this tale, we can have some understanding of how peaceful serenity, the state of single-pointed concentration on emptiness, leads to samadhi. Furthermore, even one's body will be totally forgotten, and it will withstand the rigors of changes of weather, even large physical changes of the earth. That arhat had great powers of concentration to be able to enter samadhi as he wished. However, this state of emptiness is not the state of dwelling. To dwell in a state of emptiness is a false dwelling. This arhat whom Hsuan-tsang awakened was in a state of dwelling in emptiness, or, in other words, "residual nirvana." What is residual? Habit energy. His habits were never changed and so, upon reincarnation, the attraction of fame, wealth, women, pleasures, etc. all remained. The *Vimalakirti-Nirdesa Sutra* calls this state "the knots of habit yet to be untied."

Some of my friends who study Taoism or Buddhism tell me that they are happy that I encourage them to come and meditate; however, there is something which they would find difficult to give up and they make the motion indicating mahjong. I tell them that there is no need to compromise completely. You can come sit in the Ch'an Hall and then go sit in the mahjong hall, whatever suits you. The reason I tell them this is because they have yet to untie this habit knot. Actually, there are many students here who experience "residual nirvana." Upon the sound of the wooden fish being struck, they sit excellently, abiding in an expanse of emptiness. As soon as they finish and put on their shoes, however, they're headed for a game of mahjong and a bottle of spirits. This is the great nirvana with remainders.

Buddha's Nirvana

Residual nirvana is the alambana of arhats; it's incomplete. Non-residual nirvana, *anupadhisesa*, is the alambana of Buddhas, final and complete. The Buddha says that when one studies Buddhism, the first thing one must have is the pure wish that all beings become Buddhas, that all can make the accomplishment that "I have," to enter complete nirvana and be saved. In Mahayana Buddhism, without the power of this great vow, one cannot succeed. If one feels one is frustrated and suffering greatly and wants to escape, this is not the great Mahayana vow. This is not the spirit of true Buddhism. Rather, it is narrow-minded escapism and doesn't even hold a candle to the state of an arhat. Having a practice of Buddhism or the power of the Buddhas doesn't help all sentient beings.

The Buddha said that to practice Buddhism, one needs that big a heart— a heart big enough to wish to teach every sentient being how to leave all suffering and frustration. Suffering and frustration are very difficult to escape, but the Buddha gives us the methods by which to do so. To actually escape, we must do the work for ourselves. The Buddha can only tell us how. We must then, ourselves, cultivate.

The Buddha has liberated immeasurable, innumerable and unlimited numbers of beings, and yet, in his own mind, there is not a single being he claims to have liberated. This magnanimous strength of the Buddha is what we who study Buddhism should aspire to. Suppose we did some great deed which helped thousands of people, we'd have the satisfaction of being able to say, "You see, I helped those thousands of people!" The Buddha doesn't have this alambana. If thousands of people helped by the Buddha were to achieve buddhahood, he would humbly pay respect to their achievement. He is extremely humble and reserved, truly wishing that all beings can escape suffering, yet not having even a shred of thought that he himself saved anyone. The Buddha is different from the pillars of other religions in that he is

129

not a powerful authoritarian. He is very plain and ordinary. He says your success is due to your efforts and has nothing to do with him.

"Why is this?" What is the reason? Here Buddha poses the question to add emphasis.

Four Notions and the Idea of "I"

"If a Bodhisattva retains notions of self, person, being and life, he is not a true Bodhisattva."

The Buddha said, Subhuti, if one is trying to practice the way of a Mahayana Bodhisattva and yet still holds in one's mind these issues of "you," "me," "him," "I'll rub your back if..." and so forth, this guy ought to be in the business of loyalties and favors instead. This is the way to get things done in worldly affairs. In Buddhism, if it's been given, it's been given. It's done with and forgotten. Just as the poem says, *"Events are like spring dreams, gone without a trace."* If one tries to forcibly forget, one is not a Bodhisattva on account of the effort. Charitable acts of course must be done, but with a heart as large as the earth and sky. The earth and sky give birth to all things and yet possess nothing. They are not selfish. This is why I always say, if I have Tao, the Tao common to all under the heavens and owned by none, and you, if you really have the "stuff" to take it, then take it! But if you don't have the stuff to do so, then don't blame me. I've said my piece. The Buddha also has this attitude.

The four notions spoken of in the *Diamond Sutra* are ideas that we hold. The notion of an ego is the idea of you and me. The notion of a personality and a being are, in modern language, the ideas of society and humanity. There are two kinds of notions of ego. The first is the idea of separate living physical beings—I am I, and you are you. The other kind is non-physical. This is especially true of those with scholarly achievement, or with high position, or elders. I myself tend to do this a lot. I'll say, "Oh, you young people, what do you know?" This is ego, grasping onto a feeling of "me," presuming on age to despise youth. To take advantage of one's seniority is a form of ego, but then again, so is presuming on youth to despise the elderly, femininity to despise men, masculinity to despise women, and so forth. These are all egocentric notions that congeal to form an idea of "I." It is a non-physical concept of the self.

A piece of one's own writing can be taken as a self. One finishes a piece of writing and that's it—it's finished. If someone else changes a part of it, it kills him. He can't stand it. Actually a piece of writing is just words. Or is it? If the editor wants to change it, if the publisher wants to arrange the words this way, let them. That's their job. It has nothing to do with us, yet still we can't stand it. These are all due to the notion of self which we hold in our minds. It is also called the notion-of-a-self phenomenon, *phenomenon* here meaning "the essence of" a self notion.

The notion of a being has the parameters of society and humanity. It has territories within it—you, me, him. The row of people in the front is the same as the row of people in the back until everyone sits down. The notions of self and personality come up right away, "Oh I can't stand those people in the row in front! They purposely came and sat in front of me, knowing I'm short, and blocked my vision." Following this, the notion of a being arises, "The atmosphere in here is really not so nice. I can't imagine what sort of person would come up with this sort of decor." Finally enters the notion of a life, "The air in here is really stuffy, probably full of contagious diseases. I can tell I've shortened my life by coming in here." No matter what the situation, all four notions come as one package.

These four notions all stem from the same root and from these four notions arise all klesa. Kumarajiva grouped them into four *categories*. Master Hsuan-tsang had seven categories, the last three of which Kumarajiva grouped into the fourth. The notion of a life is very serious; everyone wants to live a long life. When people see each other, they'll often ask, "So, how old are you now?" "Fifty-eight." "Oh, I'm sixty this year. You're two years younger! And you?" "I'm eighty-two. Quite a few years older than you two young people!" These are all notions of a life, the desire that "I" live a long, healthy life.

Of all the people who have come to learn meditation, even those who've come to learn Ch'an , nine and a half out of ten, and maybe even five pairs out of ten, have come because of the notion of a life. Now, this is a far cry from what is taught in the *Diamond Sutra*. Take note, to leave these four notions, to leave all notions is truly the alambana of a practicing Buddhist. In the original language of the sutra, the Buddha called them the four notions. In modern language, these four are the egocentric notions common to all humans. They are tough as nails and stubborn as oxen. If we can break these notions and get rid of them, our Buddhist studies are almost complete.

At this point, the Buddha has told Subhuti that one who wishes to study Buddhism must first open his or her heart. One must vow to help all sentient beings, and not just one's own self. Furthermore, one must actually make the effort to work for others and not advertise this effort as a great contribution to humankind. To advertise would be a sell-out. A true Buddhist would say, "I can't not work hard to help others," rather than, "I'll work hard and then make a contribution to you." You may wish to save all sentient beings, but do you have the stuff to do it? This is the reason one must work hard. The Buddha then said, After you have completed the hope of all Buddhists, you've saved all sentient beings, you don't feel as though you've saved a single one.

The Three Cycles of Emptiness

There is a Buddhist term called the *three cycles of emptiness,* which really describes this section. The word *cycle* here does not mean pedaling one's bike. It could be defined here as "part"— the three parts being the giver, the receiver and the act of giving. This section talks about the importance of charity. At this point the *Diamond Sutra* starts to talk about the six paramitas, the first of which is generosity. The first thing one must be able to act upon when practicing Buddhism is generosity. Now I will explain the meaning behind the term *three cycles of emptiness.*

There are three kinds of charity. The first kind is the giving of material goods, money, and things in general. The second type is the giving of dharma, which is on a more spiritual level. This includes passing on knowledge, opening another's wisdom, and is the spirit of a true educator. It is what's called internal, or inner, giving. The third kind of giving is that of giving fearlessness, such as saving others from suffering and catastrophes.

No matter what kind of giving one is doing, the giver should maintain the attitude that he or she is not giving. To entertain a hope that the other person will receive some benefit from your efforts is a religious attitude. One must work toward not having the notions of a person, a being and a life. You must forget who has received, as the one given to is empty. The act of giving is also empty. Upon seeing a pitiful creature, most people would feel bad for the poor thing. Feeling bad for it is just that, feeling bad for it. In performing a charitable act to help, it is finished. One then forgets the object of charity. "*Events are like spring dreams, gone without a trace.*" There are no giver, no receiver and no act of giving. This is the theory of Buddhist charity.

The Buddha came to this world and was the teacher of humans and *devas*, was the educator and the savior of all sentient beings. Upon finishing His life's work, He said simply: It's finished, goodbye. He called upon four of His disciples to remain on the earth without dying until Maitreya Buddha appears. The spirit of the Buddha is the charity of the three cycles of emptiness.

Happiness and Suffering, Both Do Not Dwell

The next part of the sutra talks about the meaning of giving. The title of this section is, "The Elusive Practice of Not Dwelling." Prince Chao-ming really chose this title very well. "Elusive practice" means Buddhist practice done without clinging to appearances. Thus, the next line of the sutra reads, *"Furthermore, Subhuti, a Bodhisattva ought to practice charity without dwelling."* Here the importance is placed upon the giving of dharma. Nothing is mentioned about the giving of material goods because Subhuti asked how those on the Mahayana path, the Bodhisattva path, could allay their frustrations and restless minds, how they could attain lasting peace. The Buddha first answered him by saying— Just like this. Subhuti didn't understand. So the Buddha went on to provide further explanation and theory. The Buddha further defined and explained the Mahayana path and its essential component—giving without attachment; in whatever one does, to not dwell.

"Ought to" is pointing to the method, telling you it ought to be done this way. Which way? Without dwelling. This is cultivation. At all times, not dwelling. In one's mind, giving away everything. In Ch'an , this is what is called "letting go." After doing a good deed, just let it go. The same goes for painful experiences—just let them go.

Some people say that they can let go of the good experiences, but not the bad ones. This sounds very noble, and when people hear it, they think, "Wow, he's a really great man!" He's really only half great. The good things can be let go, but misfortune cannot. In actuality, wonderful experiences and painful experiences are two parts of a whole, like the front and back of one's hand. So if one could truly let go of all the pleasant experiences, then when the painful ones came along, one could let go in just the same way. Painful experiences are a very good measuring stick. If when a person experiences frustration, pain or hard times, he cannot shrug it off, that person would be fooling himself to say that he could let go of pleasant experiences.

The Confucian *Analects* admonishes people not to get carried away by success. This is very hard to do. If one is rich, has a high position, is an elder or has status in the academic world, naturally he or she will assume an imposing manner, and there it is— carried away by success. So for one not to fall into this is difficult. I have discovered another side to the matter, which is that many people get carried away by failure. In their heyday of wealth and fame, they act so cultured and civilized. But, come the day they may no longer cavort as one wealthy and famous, this all goes out the window. They completely change their tune. It's as if they had suddenly become short and insignificant. In other words, they get carried away by failure.

To be carried away by either success or failure is both uncivil and deficient behavior. To look at it from another perspective, this is the mind dwelling. To have a dwelling place is to be tied down to something. This is not the condition of practicing Buddhism. In practicing the true Buddha Dharma, you are not called upon to worship false idols, nor are you asked to have blind faith. You are simply advised that you ought to practice charity without dwelling. This is liberation. This is the great liberation. All things come into being and come to pass in response to something else. When they are gone and finished, they leave no trace; just as when the bell has rung, we all exit down the stairs. The *Diamond Sutra* remains itself and you remain still yourself. Such is not dwelling.

Transforming the Twelve Types of Being

One student brought up a question about a lecture he'd heard me give many years ago. He said that at the time, in addition to what I've been explaining in these few lessons, I had talked about a deeper theory. Actually, this "deeper theory" is simply a Bodhisattva's vows and the actualizing of these vows to which he must aspire. He ought to save all the masses of beings under the heavens and still feel as if he'd not done a thing, as if it had never happened. Saving people, empowering people naturally should be done. If in one's mind there is still the notion of empowering others, saving the world, saving the human race, this is not the Bodhisattva's way. This is referring primarily to a Bodhisattva's outward behavior. His or her deep inner cultivation needs even more to follow this dictum.

We study Buddhism in order to reach the state of pure vinaya, samadhi and prajna. However, our cultivation and meditation are usually about grasping some notion or idea. For example, many people will study all sorts of methods like *vipassana*, concentration on the chakras or *ch'i-kung*—all for their health. This is grasping onto the notion of a life, and along with this come the other three notions. Therefore, in this case, success at cultivation will not be great. As for those friends who practice the pureland sect, if along with each recitation of the Buddha's name, lurking in the mind's shadows or in one's subconscious there are notions of ego, personality, being and life, then one will never reach ultimate success. It is up to each cultivator to look deeply into all the mind's nuances to discover for his or her own self these hidden notions.

As for all the different kinds of life forms that we spoke of in the last lesson, our human body contains all twelve kinds. Humans live for a few decades, maybe a hundred years, on this planet, but most of this time is not actually spent living for oneself. If we examine people carefully, we can see that they are living for their reputation, their physical appearance, for others to see or for their children. There was a student who told me that when he was in college, his parents put a lot of pressure on him to do well because he was an only child. He told his parents that if they didn't ease up, he wouldn't graduate for them. There is a lot of truth in this statement! Young people take the college boards for their parents, for society or for their future family.

Humans are actually very pitiful. Throughout our whole lives, only three-tenths of our three daily meals actually go toward sustaining our own life. The rest goes toward the moisture-born, egg-born and transformation-born organisms within our bodies. Our intestines, for example, are full of bacteria. All of the different types of life forms and phenomena that appear in the universe are all present within our bodies. So it is said that our bodies are microcosms of the universe. The left eye is the sun, the yang; the right eye is the moon, the yin. Our digestive track is the Yangze River. In *Journey to the West*, it is called the bottomless pit. Things go in one side and come out the other. It will never fill up. Our skeletons are like mountain crags and crooks. Every cell is a single organism, including each sperm and egg. All of this has a bearing on our practice of Buddhism.

Real cultivation working toward samadhi goes through the four dhyana. In the first level of dhyana, the thoughts quiet down. There are no scattered thoughts or daydreams. The second level is when the ch'i comes to rest. All the meridians have opened up. When one enters the third level of dhyana, the pulse will come to a stop. Even the heart beat becomes very slow, a slight pulsation every one or two hours. Only in the fourth dhyana does the mind become completely calm and there is no feeling of either mind or body. If we wish to attain this state of samadhi where the channels and meridians all stop, we must transform all twelve kinds of organisms within our bodies before this can be achieved. In the language of the Confucianist, this is called transforming our breath (body of ch'i). Therefore, if we wish to cultivate samadhi, we must transform the physical body, or else it will be impossible.

This student encouraged me to talk about this aspect, thinking that I was withholding information. Truthfully, when I explain the physical cultivation aspect, most people don't believe what is said, so most of the time I just gloss over it. This time, since I was requested to, I added it into the talk on the third section.

Stanzas on the Thirty-two Sections

Another person asked me to talk about the stanzas that I wrote on the *Diamond Sutra*'s thirty-two sections. Originally, I didn't want to talk about this. It is something from forty years ago. At the time, I was in the O'Mei Mountains doing a solitary retreat. It was very solitary; there was not even the shadow of a ghost let alone any humans! After the autumn, the snow would seal the mountains, and not even the monkeys could get up to where I was. If someone wanted to go down, it was easy. In the same way that Westerners ski, you'd get two slabs of wood, tie them to your feet with strips of tree bark and then, if you dared, slide down a thousand *li* of snow. As to getting back up, you best waited for the next spring.

One evening on retreat, I wasn't doing anything in particular and just picked up the *Diamond Sutra*. I have no idea why, but as soon as I put down words in my journal, I became elated and then became truly moved. It was as if something else were in control, moving my hands, as if it weren't me in my body. In the course of one night, I wrote thirty-two gathas corresponding to the thirty-two sections of the *Diamond Sutra*, capturing the meaning of each. After I came down from the mountains, word of this got around. However, when I arrived in Taiwan, my original copy was lost. I also couldn't remember them. It was my students who had saved them and passed them down. One of my habits is that I tend to forget my own works. This is a weakness, but it is also a strength. It means I can cultivate the Tao. What's passed is gone, like entering nirvana without a trace. You empty everything out. In addition to not remembering these things, I also don't like to introduce them. Teaching at the university, I am asked by many students what works I'd written. I was always muddled as to what works I have produced, and I also never have the impetus to promote them to people.

Now, since it's been requested, I will explain the gathas as we go. Please remember that they were done in less time than it takes to take the national exams—the meaning of the thirty-two sections, completely explaining the essence of Ch'an and Buddhism, all within one night. The first stanza on "The Reason for the Teaching" goes something like this:

Colored robes replaced the jeweled crown effortlessly.
Begging alms at a thousand doors, walking at ease.
A lifetime of toil ending in sorrow, for what?
A meditation cushion, a fresh wash, the path is clear.

"Colored robes replaced the jeweled crown effortlessly." Colored robes are the robes that a monk wears. In India at that time, monks wore dyed cloth, while merchants and common people wore white. This is why when we write to Buddhist clergy, we sign the letter "white-clothed so-and-so" to show we are laity. Monks wear dyed cloth, colored cloth; this is just to say that Shakyamuni Buddha became a monk. The king wears a crown of jewels. This part is saying that Shakyamuni, Prince Siddhartha, gave up claim to the crown to become a monk. What does it take to practice Buddhism? If a person can throw away the power and riches of a king, just let them go, this is what it takes, the way Shakyamuni Buddha cast aside his crown.

"Begging alms at a thousand doors, walking at ease." Next, Shakyamuni went begging alms. Someone of his background went to the homes of rich and poor alike, begging for food.

"A lifetime of toil ending in sorrow, for what?" Why do people work so hard? A lifetime of toil, a lifetime spent busy, but why? We arrive for no apparent reason with nothing in hand. We depart

just as arbitrarily, taking nothing and leaving a body for others to dispose of. For what is a lifetime of toil ending in sorrow?

"A meditation cushion, a clean wash, the path is clear." The path is this lifetime. It seems there is no better way to spend it—a meditation cushion, two legs folded, the myriad of thoughts empty—no better.

This is the stanza for the first section, the reason for the teaching. As for what I wrote, I can't say that I'm satisfied with it, but if you asked me now to rewrite all this, I could never do it in one night. Life is just that strange.

Gatha for Section Two

The second gatha is for the "Virtuous Manifestation Opens the Question" section. "Virtuous Manifestation" is Subhuti, Subhuti posed a question to which the Buddha answered, "Be skillfully mindful." The question asked was, how does one pacify this afflicted mind? How can one's mind come to abide? The Buddha told him, "Be skillfully mindful." This is the essence of the teaching. How to dwell, how to pacify? Just like this, come to rest. In this way, afflictions are pacified.

The myriad phenomena are all due to a thought ripple.
To protect the mind, why use a string of jewels?
In a cave, sitting at ease is doing enough.
Madness arises, why is there even a question!

"The myriad phenomena are all due to a thought ripple," All of the pain and affliction of human existence are one mind moment. There is no second moment. The billions and billions of different phenomena are simply the movement of a single mind moment. Like the great ocean, from the completely calm and still body suddenly arises a wave. The myriad afflictions follow. This is why I said the myriad afflictions are all due to a thought ripple.

"To protect the mind, why use a string of jewels?" Didn't the Buddha tell Subhuti to be skillfully mindful? To really and truly be skillfully mindful, why use the sutras? "A string of pearls" means the Buddhist sutras. If one is enlightened, even without reading the sutras his or her mind is calm and peaceful. So then to protect the mind, why use the sutras?

As to the third line, I need to first explain a background story. Subhuti was one of the Buddha's main disciples. In the sutras, it says that one day Subhuti went to a mountain cave to sit at ease. What does it mean "to sit at ease"? Everyone who wishes to learn meditation, take note! And the old students especially, take note. Not to rely on the body, not to rely on the mind, not to pay any attention to the body or mind and not to rely on this non-reliance. This is what's called "sitting at ease," or meditation. You'll notice that most of us sit there watching the breath, working on the legs or doing ch'i-kung, completely concentrating on the physical body. If not this, then one is fooling around with thoughts, trying to suppress them. This is like playing with a ball in the water, you push it under here and it pops up there. The thoughts are the same—push one down and another pops up elsewhere. This is all relying on the mind. If one wishes to enter samadhi, one must rely on neither mind nor body. However, this state of not relying is a state of emptiness, which is also not correct. Not relying and no non-reliance are what's called "sitting at ease."

So, one day, Subhuti went up a mountain to sit at ease. There was absolutely nothing. Then, suddenly, from a celestial goddess's hands rained down an offering of flowers. Subhuti had probably just at that moment opened his eyes. How else would he know there were flowers falling around him? He asked, "Who's offering flowers?" From the void came a voice, "It is I, a celestial goddess. The Venerable One is called Subhuti and is a great arhat with Tao. The Venerable One is expounding the Dharma, and so from emptiness, I produced offerings of flowers." Subhuti said, "I've not expounded any Dharma!" The heavenly goddess said, "Excellent! Excellent! The Venerable One, in not expounding, has expounded. We, in not listening, have listened. Thus, we honor you with these flowers."

"In a cave, sitting at ease is doing enough." Sitting in meditation, in samadhi, is already doing enough. The path is right here; bodhi is right here. Meditating or not meditating are both within bodhi. Just sitting there in meditation setting an example is busy enough.

"Madness arises, why is there even a question?" At this moment a question arises—Buddha! How should one dwell, pacify

the mind? Why do you still ask unnecessary questions? This is the way of Ch'an . If we all could understand, then we would instantly enter nirvana without a trace and achieve liberation.

Stanzas on the Third Section

The third section is called "The True Mahayana Sect." It's what we've just been talking about—those born of the womb, by egg, in moisture and through transformation entering complete nirvana and achieving salvation.

> *Four notions precipitate the four changes.*
> *Fu the Ancient is above all, there's not even one.*
> *Exceedingly pitiable, how many such guests along the cultivation path?*
> *Those bewitched by life and ego, as if they could conceal their ignorance.*

"Four notions precipitate the four changes." We all know that in Buddhism there are four notions—ego, personality, being and life. These correspond to the *I-Ching's* four basic changes—greater yang, greater yin, lesser yang and lesser yin. If you take the spatial dimensions, there are also four— north, south, east and west. Our entire lives are bound by phenomena. The four notions give rise to discrimination. The same goes for the *I-Ching's* four changes. As soon as a thought moves, in the outer world a change occurs.

"Fu the Ancient is above all, there's not even one." In Chinese culture, we say that the world started when Fu-hsi drew the eight hexagrams. One sweep opened heaven and earth. Before any movement of drawing occurred, there was no heaven or earth. The universe was empty. After Fu-hsi drew the hexagrams, heaven, earth and all were formed. "Fu the Ancient is above" is talking about the existential Tao. The myriad phenomena are originally empty. Since they are empty, one need not practice any methods to achieve emptiness. We are all quite pitiful. Everyone practicing Buddhism is after emptiness. Isn't this turning our backs on the obvious? Being empty to begin with, can emptiness then be achieved? If it is an achievement, it is not emptiness. That is why *"Fu the Ancient is above all, there's not even one."* There is absolutely nothing.

"Exceedingly pitiable, how many such guests along the cultivation path?" Exceedingly pitiable are just that. From ancient times until now, how many have there been like this on the path of cultivation? Their practice is for the notion of a life—live a few more years and there's more chance to achieve a higher level. They are simply being spun around by the four notions, and yet they think they're on the path of Tao.

"Those bewitched by life and ego, as if they could conceal their ignorance." Tumbling about in the four notions, in one's own ignorance and yet still believing that one is head and shoulders above the rest—No one else cuts the grade; they don't understand. Only "I" am clear on things, so I practice Buddhism. Why do you

practice Buddhism? "I'm empty." Where do you think you obtained this emptiness? This is foolishness! In attempting to pass oneself off as a high-level cultivator, one clearly shows one's ignorance.

SECTION 4

THE ELUSIVE PRACTICE OF NOT DWELLING

"Furthermore, Subhuti, a Bodhisattva ought to practice charity without dwelling. That is to say, a Bodhisattva should also practice charity without dwelling in form, sound, smell, taste, touch or even dharma. Subhuti, Bodhisattvas ought to practice charity, without dwelling in form.

Why is this? If Bodhisattvas practices charity without dwelling in form, the blessings will be inestimable and inconceivable.

"Subhuti, what do you think? Can you conceive of measuring the extent of space in the East?"

"Certainly not, World-Honored One."

"Subhuti, what do you think? Can the extent of space in the South, West and North, as well as the Zenith and Nadir be measured?"

"Certainly not, World-Honored One."

"Subhuti, for Bodhisattvas who practice charity without dwelling, the blessings are also immeasurable.

"Subhuti, a Bodhisattva's mind should thus dwell as taught".

First and Second Best

Prince Chao-ming entitled this section "The Elusive Practice of Not Dwelling." The practice referred to here is the practice of cultivation, the true practice of Buddhist cultivation. *"One should thus dwell."* How should one dwell? Without dwelling, not dwelling. And how does one not dwell? This sutra explains that.

Furthermore, Subhuti, a Bodhisattva ought to practice charity without dwelling. That is to say, a Bodhisattva should also practice charity without dwelling in form, sound, smell, taste, touch or dharma. Subhuti, a Bodhisattva should thus practice charity, without dwelling in form.

This is the charity we talked about the last time, and it is also internal cultivation. Generally speaking, charity is of two kinds— internal and external. Ch'an Buddhism popularized a saying—let it go! This is talking about charity, giving up everything. One of the hardest things in life is to throw away something and forget about it. If you really throw it away or give it away then you have let go. Letting go is internal charity. If one can truly do this, he or she can succeed in achieving the Path. Here the Buddha is telling Subhuti of the Dharma door of internal charity.

"Furthermore," in common terms means here, "second to this" or "second best." The highest way has already been shown. The Buddha didn't spell this out. What did the Buddha say, do you remember? Subhuti asked the questions. If one wants to practice Buddhism, how should one dwell? How should one pacify one's

mind, quell frustration and affliction? The Buddha simply answered, Just like that. Just like that pacify the mind. The Buddha didn't say anything more, didn't add anything. This is the original meaning.

The original meaning is very hard to understand. I always use the novel *Journey to the West* to illustrate this. You've all read this story about T'ang Seng's journey to obtain Buddhist sutras. T'ang Seng arrived in the Western Heaven and had an audience with Buddha. Buddha called in his main disciple, Mahakasyapa, and said to him, "They have come from the East, from Cina (the ancient Indian name for China). It was a long journey, but their merit is complete. Open up the storeroom of books and give them one from the highest level of Buddhist sutras to take back." So, Mahakasyapa led T'ang Seng and his three disciples to the library door; whereupon, he asked them for a gratuity. Sun Wu-k'ung was irate. "Everywhere you have to pay for things. Come to the Western Heaven and even here they want blood money!" He picked up his staff and was thinking of whacking Mahakasyapa. T'ang Seng reminded him not to be so brutish and that they didn't go through all that trouble to go back empty-handed. Then he said to Mahakasyapa, "We don't have any money," who said, "You have clothing." "Yes, my monk's robe." "Go pawn it."

T'ang Seng pawned his robe and handed over the gratuity, Sun Wu-k'ung cursing the entire while. Mahakasyapa found it very difficult to carry on. Everyone in the temple was looking at him, and he was quite embarrassed. Finally, they had the sutras in hand and were heading for the door. Sun Wu-k'ung said, "Master, I don't trust that old monk. Open them up and look." T'ang Shen said, "Oh, Sun Wu-k'ung, you're so suspicious! We're in the Western Heaven. There's nothing unreliable here." "I don't trust him, at the last minute asking for a gratuity! Open it up and look! Look!" T'ang Shen consented and opened the box. It was all full of blank paper, not a word.

Sun Wu-k'ung went berserk, screaming and yelling. The Buddha called in Mahakasyapa and the rest to know the meaning of the ruckus. Sun Wu-k'ung explained in vivid detail what had happened. Mahakasyapa piped up, "Venerable One, you told me to give them the highest level of sutra." " Ooh la la!," said the Buddha. "Sentient beings can't understand those. They don't understand sutras without words. You need to give them sutras with words. Grab the second best."

"*Furthermore*" is second best, the sutras with words. The true sutras don't have any words, originally empty, right! One ought to thus dwell, thus pacify the mind. This is the original meaning, blank white paper. Since the highest level was not understood, the only way was to go for second best.

Without Dwelling

The Buddha said to Subhuti, called him by name, Subhuti, I'll tell you how a true cultivator ought to practice. Bodhisattvas ought not to dwell in any dharma. "Ought" signals that a method will follow. One's mind ought not to dwell, anytime or anyplace. If your mind is always in a state of emptiness, this is already wrong because you are dwelling in emptiness. If your mind dwells in light, this is also incorrect. If you say that you are working on energy channels, circulating through the governing and the reproductive channels (*Tu-mai* and *Ren-mai*), you are then bound to your energy channels. It's also wrong. None of these is *"without dwelling."*

"Ought to practice charity without dwelling." What is cultivation? Every moment is empty; just let go. *"What is meant to come, will. When gone, naught remains."* Once a good deed has been done, it's done with, not held in mind. If even virtue is not held, then one, of course, will not engage in wrongdoing. All times, all places practice charity; anytime, anywhere do not dwell.

Supposing one day someone criticized and cursed you. You were so angry that you didn't sleep well for three days. You dwelled in your anger for three days. Another day, someone gave you "the eye," and that night you couldn't sleep because you were dwelling on that eye. Don't dwell on any situation; what's gone is gone. Look over here and then turn your head and look behind you. What you were just looking at is gone. Just like a dream, it's gone. We, however, can't actually not dwell. We're never able to really let go. "I haven't fed the dog! My husband isn't back yet..." Forget about all this; don't dwell on it. Practice charity; charity is letting go of everything.

Not Dwelling in Form

What is form? Form in Buddhism can be divided into form with appearance, form without appearance, microscopic and macroscopic. Form with appearance is talking about things of the physical world with color and shape. Everything in our world made of the four elements—earth, water, fire, and wind— including our physical bodies, is classified as form with appearance. Form without appearance has to do with the spirit of things. It is very difficult to describe. For example, there is energy. Energy—everyone knows the term but, unlike scientists, the common person doesn't have a clear idea of how it works. The essence of energy is empty, and because it is empty, it has infinite power. Perhaps even power so great that scientific equipment cannot measure the entire extent of it. One can only give a vague explanation, but cannot really express it. This is form without appearance.

Microscopic form is like atomic or rather sub-atomic particles. Only through the most advanced scientific equipment can one view these, and so they are called microscopic form. Macroscopic form is the forms so large they are difficult to conceive of, such as the milky way and other such formations within our universe.

These are all form phenomena. To put it simply, form is the four elements. Our physical bodies are the four elements. *"Bodhisattvas ought to practice charity not dwelling in any dharma."* This is telling us not to dwell on appearance or form when practicing charity, and also not to have the idea of a recipient, for example, giving money to a charitable cause or rescuing a person from some terrible situation. To tell people of giving such-and-such or helping so-and-so is not the spirit of Buddhism. In helping or rescuing, one ought not have the idea of a recipient. Rather, it is something one should just do and not dwell on. Don't think, "Oh, today I've done a meritorious deed!" Cultivating earthly or heavenly merits will bring only a small reward, unlike the blessings received by truly cultivating Buddhism. There is a big difference between merit and blessings. The *Diamond Sutra* speaks only of blessings and not of merit. What are the greatest blessings in life? Enlightenment, achieving the Tao and wisdom are the greatest blessings. The achievement of wisdom spoken of here is, of course, not just ordinary knowledge. This is the first point of not dwelling on form when practicing charity.

The second point is when meditating, most people are working on the body. Sitting there with eyes closed, legs crossed, and whether it be reciting the Buddha's name, reciting mantra, or vipassana, most people are dwelling in form while practicing charity. One can say they've let go, but in reality they've let go of nothing. If one's legs have aching numbness, there comes a point when one can't stand it any longer. Why does this happen? Because one dwells on the dharma of form. If one didn't dwell on this physical body, then the feelings, or rather the *skandha* of sensation, could also be emptied out. There would be no sensation of either legs or aching numbness. Thus, sentient beings cultivate while dwelling on form. Bodhisattvas practice charity without dwelling in form; they don't dwell on the physical body. Let everything go; even let the body go.

Not Dwelling in Sound, Smell or Taste

> "Practice charity without dwelling in sound, smell, taste, touch or even dharma."

Some students during a period when they've been practicing very well will hear the sound of mantra or the reciting of the Buddha's name. Some become fascinated by this phenomenon and later come to believe they've attained the Tao. In the end, however, these people have achieved only insanity and not Tao. They've slipped into the realm of the subconscious due to the fact that they didn't understand practicing charity by not dwelling on sound.

Many students have had the experience during meditation of smelling sandalwood incense. There is none burning, but one clearly smells it. From where does the fragrance come? It comes when we reach a state of inner equilibrium or samadhi, from the pure and calm clear light within our body. Actually, no one's body will give off any bad smells if one is truly healthy, not even one's sweat and breath. Of course, we will still have the basic human smell. In Journey to the West, the evil ghosts can detect even the slightest hint of human smell and will come to inhale it. If we go to a pigsty, all we smell is pig. In a kennel, there is an overwhelming dog smell. The same happens to the heavenly beings who come close to our realm. It wreaks of human smell, so they can't stand it. I've had this kind of experience. After living in the high mountains for three years, I came down the mountain. It was still about five or six *li* before I reached the city, but I was already gagging on the human smell. I'm also human but having gotten used to my human-free mountain top, the smell of people was acrid. It took quite some time to become accustomed to it. Those who study medicine know that the inside of the human body is not dirty. Why then do blood and other bodily fluids have a bad smell? It's only when they come in contact with the air or more specifically, air-borne bacteria, that they develop a smell. Some bacteria germs or cells die immediately upon contact, and we smell necrosis.

Now back to fragrant smells. If in meditation we are sitting very well, our body will give off fragrant smells internally. If we think that this is the fruit of our merit and that we can smell the Bodhisattva's fragrance, we have come to dwell in smell. This is wrong! One ought not to dwell in smell. Quickly let it go.

The Bodhisattva of the Internal Feeling of Subtle Joy

"Smell, taste, touch..." "Touch" is a very important aspect. Among our meditators here are some who've experienced a sitting so comfortable that they didn't ever want to get up. For most

beginners, the experience of the legs in meditation is only pain, aching and numbness. Once you've paid your dues, however, your legs will feel so comfortable that you won't want to get up. One who is in this state is called a " 'Bodhisattva' of the internal feeling of subtle joy." From within one's physical self arises a fantastic feeling of comfort and joy never before experienced in one's lifetime. The Bodhisattva's vows do not allow a Bodhisattva to enter into this kind of samadhi. Why is this? Who would want to leave this state to come and save all sentient beings? If you were experiencing that kind of bliss, would you want to come and stand here to give a lecture? It's only because you're feeling uncomfortable that you might as well come and stand here. A Bodhisattva's alambana is one of having an internal feeling of subtle joy, but not dwelling in this feeling. A Bodhisattva practices charity without dwelling in form.

"...dharma..." is the realm of thought consciousness which includes our views, our thoughts and our will. If your mind is in an alambana of cavern-like emptiness and quiet, then you've come to dwell in dharma. In addition to emptying out the physical body and sensations completely, one must also drop all thought consciousness. This is practicing Buddhism. It is also called practicing charity without dwelling in form, sound, smell, taste, touch, or dharma. The Buddha explained that this is the right way.

At this point, the Buddha again called out, "Subhuti." How dearly he speaks to them: Subhuti, I want you to know...! You see how loving and caring he is toward them, as if they were his children. He explains again and again.

Always Empty After the Geese Have Passed

"Subhuti, Bodhisattvas ought to practice charity without dwelling in form. Why is this? If Bodhisattvas practice charity, without dwelling in form, the blessings will be inestimable and inconceivable."

One who is a Mahayana Buddhist ought to practice charity, ought to cultivate in this manner. In which manner? Without dwelling in form, without even the slightest appearance remaining. If in one's mind there remains even the tiniest appearance, this is not the alambana of Buddhism. We can take an example from Chinese literature to illustrate our meaning. *"The wind comes to the surface of the bamboo; it is always empty after the geese have passed."* The wind blows through the bamboo and we hear a whoosh of rustling leaves. The gust of wind is gone. It doesn't stay on the leaves; it just passes. A Buddhist practitioner ought to have the same magnanimity. Birds fly through the sky without the slightest trace, *"...it's always empty after the geese have passed."* What has passed has passed. In cultivation, one needs this same breadth before it can be called practicing internal charity.

Su Tung-p'o wrote a famous poem which came out of his Buddhist practice:

Human existence anywhere can be likened to what?

One ought to describe it as a bird touching down.
On new-fallen snow, leaving by chance a track.
When the bird flies, does it plan to go east or west?

He posed the question; the course of one human existence can be likened to what? Like a bird on a snowy day, alighting on the snow for a moment, leaving a claw print, *"leaving by chance a track."* The snow continues falling after the bird flies off, covering over the print, no trace remains. After the bird has flown off, whether it be to the north, south, east or west, the bird is gone and no print remains.

Most people's goals in life are to raise a family, have a career, children, grandchildren, etc. The day one's eyes close, limbs go limp and one passes from this world—when the bird flies—does one plan to go east or west? At that point, there is no such thing. These are Su Tung-p'o's famous lines. Like the lines, *"The wind comes to the surface of the bamboo; it is always empty after the geese have passed,"* they have the same meaning as *"Bodhisattvas ought to practice charity, without dwelling in form."*

I've noticed that recently a lot of young people are really keen on practicing Buddhism or cultivating the Tao. It makes me worry. I always say to them: You are so young. Why do you want to practice this? I don't want to upset anyone by asking this, but there are two reasons why I do ask. The first is that most worldly pursuits can be accomplished with a little effort; while studying Buddhism, on the other hand, is by far the most difficult thing one could pursue. The second reason is that, "If one's life drawing of a tiger is unsuccessful, one can always change the subject to a dog." If your Buddhist pursuits are unsuccessful, what will you then turn to? What I hope that you young people will do is first learn how to be good people and take care of worldly affairs; then study Buddhism. However, if you insist on going down this path, then you must very seriously beware of dwelling in form. If you dwell in form, you will not succeed at any practice.

Merit and Blessing

"Why is this? If Bodhisattvas practice charity without dwelling in form, the blessings received will be inestimable and inconceivable."

Here suddenly pops up the word *blessing*. The Buddha says, supposing a person, a Mahayana Bodhisattva, achieves the state of not dwelling in form, the state of internal charity, this person will receive inestimable blessings. Blessings are not merit. Merit is accumulated through work and effort over time, which results in rewards. It's like when we work on a project—if you put effort into it every day, eventually you will get results.

Blessings are different, and we spoke of them before in terms of worldly, or red, fortune and transcendental, or clear, fortune. Clear fortune is much more difficult to enjoy even if the opportunity presents itself. Most people in their retirement have the opportunity to enjoy some, but most people are afraid of being alone, afraid of quiet. It's really a shame. This happens because people grasp onto appearances and hold tight to views of ego and being. One's children have grown and gone abroad. One sits alone staring at the television, the television staring back. If it's an old couple, they take turns crying. Two broken-hearted people comforting each other, "Oh, the children have abandoned us. We've done something wrong." Actually, this time of undisturbed quiet is the best time. It's just a matter of turning one's idea of it around.

Hence, this is all a matter of dwelling in form. It's grasping onto the ever changing phenomena of our world as real. When things change, one thinks it regrettable. One doesn't realize how comfortable this time of peace and quiet can be. A lot of my students say, "In my opinion, Teacher is the most pitiable." I say, You are right. I can't even get a moment's peace. Very pitiful, not even a minute of clear fortune. Most people who actually get a taste of this don't realize that this peace is true fortune. A peaceful safe life is the height of fortune.

Though, to ask what is the ultimate fortune, the answer of course is to become a Buddha, to transcend ordinary existence and enter sainthood. This is not the result of accumulating merit. It is also not blind faith. One must be able to throw away everything before one can achieve the blessing of wisdom. This is why the Buddha said to Subhuti, if you can practice charity without dwelling in form, the blessings received will be inestimable. This fortune is so big that your mind is unable to conceive of the size. It is unmeasurable. There is no unit by which it can be measured.

The Buddha was very serious about getting the meaning of this across, and so he said: *"Subhuti, what do you think? Can you conceive of measuring the extent of space in the East?" "Certainly not, World-Honored One."*

The Buddha asked Subhuti: What do you think? How big is the space in the easterly direction? Is there any way to measure it? Subhuti answered that there was not. Standing here facing east, there is no way of measuring the expanse of space stretching out in front of one. There is no way for humans to measure this size. The Buddha went on to ask: *"Subhuti, what do you think? Can the extent of space in the South, West, and North, as well as the Zenith and Nadir be measured?" "Certainly not, World-Honored One."*

South, West, and North together with the East make up the four primary directions. The four directions together with the space above and below is how big? Can you measure it? Subhuti answered: Certainly not, it's impossible. Remember, Buddhism came from India, from Indian culture. The *Diamond Sutra* was translated by Kumarajiva, who was from there also. He took the Indian way of writing or expressing things and adapted it for Chinese culture by condensing the language and yet still retaining the original meaning and flavor. It was extremely skillful. This became the literary style in Buddhism after the Northern and Southern Dynasty. If it was purely a Chinese style of writing, it would be condensed even further, such as, "Can the six directions of space be measured?" Just like that, very simple. Kumarajiva simplified the original Indian text to two sentences. The original would have read, "What do you think? Can the extent of space in the East be measured? It cannot, World-Honored One. What do you think? Can the extent of space in the South be measured? It cannot, World-Honored One..." and continued on in that manner through the six directions. The large 600-volume *Great Prajnaparamita Sutra* reads that way, so to actually read the whole thing, oh my Buddha! In the *Diamond Sutra*, Kumarajiva condensed this style, thus creating a new style of literature.

One young person here has just raised an important question. Why is the Easterly direction mentioned first? Why not the Westerly direction of Amitabha's sutra? Both the *Medicine Buddha's Sutra* and the *Diamond Sutra* put the East first. The "Enlightenment in this Body" practice of the esoteric school speaks of the North, while the practice of "The Great Clear Light" mentions only the South. Studying and practicing Buddhism has all these questions. Look into these rather than going round and round on the five skandhas, the eighteen realms, and the eighteen emptinesses. In the end, those all come down to, "form is emptiness, emptiness is form, form is not other than emptiness, and emptiness is not other than form."

The Buddha of the East and the Buddha of the West

The East is the direction of the birth of ch'i. If one seeks long life or offspring, one should recite "Homage to the (Namo) Medicine Buddha of the Eastern pureland." The Medicine Buddha's Buddha land is in the East. The West is the final resting place. The East is the cultivation of life, of multiplying endlessly. This is why in Eastern culture we multiply in endless succession! The sutras read by orthodox Chinese Buddhists actually contain a lot of hidden information. It's up to everyone to look deeply and to think. People who study Ch'an all want a *hua tou* or a *koan* to look into. The sutras are full of *hua tou*. If you think you already understand and say that it's simply because we Chinese always say the directions in the order of East, South, West and North. It's not actually so simple. Why the East first? Why then is it South, West, and North? Why are Zenith and Nadir mentioned last? These all raise further questions and tie into a lot of information having to do with the theory of cultivation.

If we want to practice Buddhism, to cultivate, we must first start with the arousal of the life force. The ch'i-mai must move and our physical body needs to go through various transformations before we can achieve the dhyana which can give rise to subtle bliss. These names, directions, are merely symbolic representations. The East represents the arising of the life force, just as the sun rises in the east. What then is the western direction of Amitabha's sutra? The sun sets behind the mountains of the West, *"The setting sun was infinitely pleasant; only, the dusk was too near!"* Go home and think for yourselves; think about the West. It's no accident that it is this way. In Buddhism, these things all have their meaning.

"Subhuti, for Bodhisattvas who practice charity without dwelling, the blessings are also immeasurable. Subhuti, a Bodhisattva's mind should thus dwell as taught."

The Buddha once again very seriously told Subhuti that one wishing to practice Buddhism must be able to practice charity without dwelling in any form whatsoever. Why should people practice charity, be compassionate? It's simply that which a person *ought* to do. The ancient Chinese wording expresses it well, *"to naturally act in accordance with one's principles."* One simply just ought to live one's life this way. One ought to be charitable, aid people, enable people, love others and be compassionate. One should practice in this way and with this mindset, without dwelling in form. All this is not for nothing. It is not empty, for the blessings received are as inconceivably large as is the extent of space.

Subhuti, you must take note! One who wishes to follow the Mahayana Bodhisattva's path ought to practice as I've taught, without dwelling. To put one's heart into one's practice without dwelling on it is real cultivation. If from morning till night, one's face is scrunched with worry, one is obviously wrongly dwelling in these worries. If a person spends his or her days aimless and scatterbrained, giving free reign to whim, this is also not right. Dwelling in an empty alambana is also erroneous. *"What is meant to come, will. When gone, naught remains."* This is the cultivation practice of Mahayana Buddhists.

The Fifth Ch'an Patriarch told the Sixth Patriarch to first read the *Diamond Sutra*. He wanted him to practice the Dharma door of not dwelling. This is the basic method for all of Mahayana Buddhism and is, at the same time, the ultimate method. Everyone must take note, people who teach the *Diamond Sutra* and prajna will often commit the very serious error of believing they are talking about emptiness. The *Diamond Sutra* does not have one sentence talking about emptiness. All it does is use the extent of space as a metaphor. So if a person believes that the *Diamond Sutra* is talking about emptiness, he is making a mistake. It is simply telling you not to dwell. "Not dwelling" is not emptiness. It is rather like the passing of clouds and the flow of water. If you watch the flow of water, it just goes by without stopping. It continually comes, never stopping. If you say that empty space is the main idea of Buddhism or prajna, this is a grave error. This is dwelling in the realm of form. The *Diamond Sutra* tells you not to dwell. It doesn't talk about being empty.

In the fourth section, the Buddha is telling us a method of cultivation which is the real practice of Buddhism, not dwelling. Not dwelling yet, not thinking one need not do anything and thereby slipping into the erroneous view of nonexistence. Bodhisattvas should practice as I've taught and just keep practicing in this way. The second point is that to achieve the state of not dwelling is also to achieve all blessings.

Everyone knows that to do business, you need to have three kinds of funds, or capital: first, start-up capital, and second, accounts receivable, and third, working capital. To practice Buddhism, you need only two kinds of capital. This kind of business is more affordable. Just what are the two kinds of capital needed? Sufficient amounts of wisdom and fortune. This is the reason that a traditional Chinese gift to give to friends is an inscribed plaque with the characters, "Cultivate both wisdom and fortune." To cultivate both wisdom and fortune is the way of the Buddhas. There are some people who have fortune—money, status, power—but don't have any wisdom. Others have achieved a high state of wisdom, but have not a penny to their name. They, too, are limited in what they can do. The alambana of a Buddha is one of complete wisdom and fortune. One who develops sufficient amounts of wisdom and fortune will become a Buddha. This is why when we recite the Buddhist services, we say, Take refuge in the Buddha, the Honored One with two legs. (In Chinese this character has a double meaning of legs or feet and of being sufficient or adequate.) What are the two legs or rather, which two are sufficient? Wisdom and fortune. In the *Diamond Sutra*, what does it say is the way to cultivate real fortune? By practicing charity without dwelling in anything.

King Ashoka's Sand

In the sutras, there is a story about the previous life of King Ashoka who lived and reigned in India five hundred years after the passing of the Buddha. Ashoka in his youth did not believe in

Buddhism. It was not until about middle age that he did, and yet during his lifetime, he erected thousands of stupas (pillars). He was the first famous patron of Buddhism in his country, and his influence spread from the borders of China to Macedonia, Epirus, Egypt and Cyrene. During the T'ang Dynasty, one of his stupas flew to China—I'm not sure how—and landed at a temple, renamed Ashoka Temple, in Ning-po in Zhejiang Province. This particular stupa, at the time it flew over, contained actual relics of the Buddha.

During his reign, Ashoka was very close friends with a highly respected monk called Upagupta, who was a great arhat. What was their karma to be friends? If you read the story of Ashoka, it speaks of the time when the Buddha was out begging for alms and met two small boys playing in the sand along the road. The two saw the Buddha coming along and were filled with respect. They were pretending that the sand was gold, and so one boy offered the "gold" to the Buddha, who accepted it in his bowl. The Buddha rubbed his head saying, "Wonderful, wonderful," and then the other boy also sincerely offered his "gold." The Buddha then said, "Due to this merit, five hundred years from now, one of you will be reborn as a great arhat and the other will be reborn as a king who will bring peace and order due to his enlightened governing." King Ashoka and the Venerable Upagupta were those two boys who offered sand to the Buddha.

Throughout his life Ashoka had one troublesome problem, skin disease. The offering to the Buddha had its great merit, but after all, it was sand, and so Ashoka's skin was incurably itchy his whole life. Throughout history, there have been many cases like this. For example, during the end of the Ch'ing Dynasty, there was a famous general, Tseng Kuo-fan, who pacified unrest and uprisings throughout the country. He had more popular support than the government and yet encouraged the people to remain loyal to the emperor. He also had a lifelong incurable skin disease. A myth started that he was actually the transformation of a huge python or of a dragon who would still shed his scales at night.

Ashoka was a legendary king. He loved to practice charity, build temples, help the poor, set up social programs, etc. and as a result, led his government to bankruptcy. As he was nearing the end of his life, from his bed he would direct the princes or ministers to allocate money for such and such. The ministers all put their heads together to resolve this crisis. With the cooperation of the princes, they would say to appease King Ashoka, "Yes, Your Majesty," but would not actually send any money. There wasn't money to send. After Ashoka figured this out, he was heartbroken, but lying there, he knew there was nothing he could do about it.

One day, he was eating a pear and called his sons and a general to his side. He asked them, "In the world today, who has got the most power?" They all answered, "Why of course, Sire, your power is the greatest." Ashoka said, "You do not have to deceive me. My power is great all right. At this moment, it only extends to half a pear. For if I told you now to give away money as charity, it could not be done. I cannot finish the other half of this pear. Take it to the temple and give it to Upagupta." After Ashoka had said this, they had no other recourse than to put the remaining half of the pear King Ashoka had eaten on a gold tray and take it to the temple. At the temple, Upagupta knew what was happening and called for the temple drum and bell to be sounded continuously. He had the entire sangha put on ceremonial robes and line up along both sides of the entrance road to the temple to receive Ashoka's last gift of charity.

Upagupta, upon receiving the half a pear, told the sangha that this was King Ashoka's last act of charity to send this, and since there was no way to divide it among so many people, it would be cooked in a huge pot of porridge so everyone would share his gift. Ashoka then passed away, and soon after, Upagupta also left this world.

This whole story is speaking of fortune and blessings. Ashoka, as the child, in that moment offered the sand in a pure act of giving, without dwelling. If you, however, try to do as he did and bring a handful of sand tomorrow to put before the Buddha, you may not even be so lucky as to get only a skin disease in the next life. The child didn't make a calculated plan to do this; it was a spontaneous act. The children were pretending to be selling gold and so offered the "gold" to the Buddha. If we did this as a planned action, it would be dwelling in form.

Suddhipanthaka's Broom

There is another story in the sutras about Suddhipanthaka. During the Buddha's time, he was one of the Buddha's monks. He was also unbelievably stupid. He couldn't remember anything people taught him. The Buddha finally just let him sweep the grounds repeating, "Dust away, dirt away." Suddhipanthaka would remember "dust away" and forget "dirt away," would remember "dirt away" and forget "dust away." After many years, he not only remembered both parts but also awoke to realize that the "dirt and dust" he was sweeping was actually that of the mind. Eventually, of the disciples, Suddhipanthaka was known for his great superpowers and Dharma discourses.

In the sutras, it also tells of Suddhipanthaka's karmic connection by which he became a monk with the Buddha. When he first came to join the sangha, many of the older brothers—Ananda, Sariputra...—were against it and wouldn't allow him in. Suddhipanthaka just stood outside the gate bawling. The Buddha heard and asked his disciples what was wrong. They told him, and the Buddha asked why they were so against this man becoming a monk. These disciples were arhats, and so they had some super powers. They said, "We checked and in the last 500 lives, he's had no connection whatsoever with the Buddha. He doesn't have the karma to be a monk." The Buddha then really gave it to them, "You guys only have arhat level knowledge. Your powers only allow you to see 500 lives. What about lives prior to that? Do you have any idea what happened five hundred and one lives ago? In that one, he was a dog who made a connection with me. I'll tell you the story of that connection."

This dog went to eat some excrement, as dogs will, and found his way to a mountainside outhouse. You've probably never seen this kind of outhouse before. In mainland China, they still have this kind in some places. It is a semi-enclosed platform that hangs out over a steep drop with a hole in the floor. Between the time that one expels and the time the expelled matter hits the ground, it picks up great speed. There is even a classic Chinese couplet about this: *"The stream of urine tumbles downward from the platform; the pit is deep and for the shit to hit, one must wait."* These are just some lines of sarcastic wit by some scholar of old.

So, the dog went to one of these places to feast. Way up above, someone shat, and it landed, "Smack!" right on the dog's tail. It gave the dog such a start that he took off running. After running a while, the dog saw the stupa of an arhat and stopped to take a pee. After peeing, the dog stood there wagging his tail and unwittingly flung the still warm excrement, "Whack!" onto the stupa. The Buddha said, "Because of this offering of feces, this man has a karmic connection with me. That stupa held the ashes of the life in which I achieved the state of a Pratyeka Buddha." You laugh, but really, think about it. That wasn't a human, it was a dog. Excrement is to a dog what Peking Duck is to us humans, just as fragrant. We think of it as filthy, but it's a dog's food. So this dog, with the utmost sincerity, flung that delicacy with his tail, thus making an offering of it. It was not only a sincere act, it was also completely without forethought. He was simply wagging his tail, not dwelling at all in form. Consequently, he gained immeasurable blessings, and due to this karma can become a monk.

After being ordained as a monk, Suddhipanthaka, knowing he was very dull witted, just quietly did the laborious work. The Buddha tried hard to teach him, but to no avail. The only thing left was to have him repeat to himself "dust away, dirt away" as he swept. Cultivation is just like sweeping—sweep away the scattered thoughts and practice charity without dwelling. Not dwelling is "dust away, dirt away." Whatever is in the mind just sweep it away. Keep practicing like this and at all times, in all places, empty the thoughts. Dwell in non-dwelling. This is real Buddhism. This is what is meant by "a *Bodhisattva's mind should thus dwell as taught.*"

This is the fourth section, "The Elusive Practice of Not Dwelling," and now we'll look at the gatha I wrote as a wrap-up. This gatha brings to light the theory of true cultivation practice, the elusive practice of Mahayana Buddhism.

Gatha of Section Four

Form holds the mind captive, ever moving dust captivates people.

In this floating existence, mind and body bustle about.

Glamorous opulence passes before one's eyes, the spring wind withers.
Coming and going, the two spheres revolve without dwelling.

"Form holds the mind captive, ever moving dust captivates people." This body of ours is the form which holds us captive. Our lives are really quite pitiful. We live as slaves of the physical body. When it's cold, clothe it; when it's hot, cool it; hungry, feed it; sick, medicate it... Day in and day out, we busy ourselves for this body. The outer world is the dust forever captivating us. We are in effect, servants of the outer world, the physical world, which is dust.

"In this floating existence, mind and body bustle about." In Chinese literature, human existence is sometimes called "floating existence." Like a bubble on top of the water, when it bursts "I" no longer exists. The water remains the water. Like duckweed, we float about without any roots. Every day we are very busy with our bodies, busy because of our ideas, busy fooling ourselves.

"Glamorous opulence passes before one's eyes, the spring wind withers." Fame and fortune, a house full of sons and grandchildren, five generations all together—it all seems so full of sound and fury, like the heralds of springtime, the flowers that bloom all over the fields. During the period from youth to middle age, it seems that since no expenses have been spared on one's upbringing, the possibilities for the future are limitless. One feels that "before heaven and earth, I alone am the Honored One," especially when one is looking down on the city from an executive penthouse. "I

am on the top." All of this glamorous opulence passes before one's eyes and, in the blink of an eye, a few decades have passed. It is no longer springtime; the flowers have all withered away. None of these things is actually "mine." What is left?

"Coming and going, the two spheres revolve without dwelling." The two spheres, the sun and the moon, eternally revolve. After we die, the sun and the moon will continue to revolve. The universe of infinite space will not, upon our death, cease to exist. Many older people lament about the youth of today saying that they are beyond redemption. I tell them that I once thought the same way but have finally made peace with this thought. Young people may seem a mess, but after you and I have passed away, the sun will still rise in the East. Their time, like glamour and spring, will pass. Time moves on its merry way, oblivious to all. The sun and moon revolve continuously. They don't dwell or stop for a moment. For if they did, the world would cease to exist. The sun and the moon also represent our minds and bodies, going through cyclic existence, around and around.

If we wish to understand how not to let our minds and thoughts dwell, we must not seek emptiness. For dwelling in the dhyana of emptiness is still dwelling. The *Diamond Sutra* does not talk of emptiness. If you still say it does, you have terribly misconstrued it. This is how I've summed up the fourth section. It's not to be relied upon, however. If you take it for the final word, then you are dwelling.

SECTION 5

PLAINLY, THE TRUTH IS PERCEIVED

"Subhuti, what do you think? Can the Tathagata be perceived by means of form or appearance?"

"No, World-Honored One, the Tathagata cannot be so perceived. Why is that? The form and appearance spoken of by the Tathagata is not true form and appearance."

The Buddha told Subhuti, "Everything with form and appearance is merely illusion. If all form and appearance are seen as illusion, the Tathagata will be perceived."

No Form and Emptiness

"Subhuti, what do you think? Can the Tathagata be perceived by means of form or appearance?"

"No World-Honored One, the Tathagata cannot be so perceived."

Now, everyone should note that in the sutra it was just telling us not to dwell on appearance or form, to practice charity without dwelling and that blessings would follow from this. The fortune or blessings one receives from the culmination of wisdom are infinite and immeasurable. Here it goes a step further in telling us the reality of seeing a Buddha. This is very serious. Everyone who is a Buddhist wants to see a Buddha. So, He asked Subhuti, calling him by name, *"Subhuti, what do you think?"* What's your idea, Subhuti, can people perceive the Buddha in a physical form?

In the sutras it says that the Buddha has thirty-two physical marks (*laksanas,* or physical marks of a chakravartin—"wheel king") which distinguish Him from ordinary mortals. These are described more fully in the eighty detailed physical characteristics. For example, He has thousand-spoked wheel signs on His feet, long slender fingers and toes that are finely webbed, a long broad tongue and so forth. These signs all arose from many lives of cultivating merit. If one makes offerings of flowers and incense to the Buddha, then in the next life, one will be more beautiful. If one offers clothes, in the next life one won't have to worry about going without and will have a healthy body. Also if one regularly offers medicine, one won't get sick in the next life. If in a previous life, a person refused to give medicine as charity, in this lifetime he will encounter many hardships and illnesses. These results just follow the laws of karma.

How then did the Buddha gain these thirty-two marks and eighty characteristics? They are the result of virtuous behavior. These are marks we could see when the Buddha was alive, in human form. Ananda, His cousin, had thirty of these marks as did the great translator, Kumarajiva. At this point, the Buddha was asking Subhuti if the Tathagata could be seen by means of these thirty-two marks. Subhuti answered, *"No, World-Honored One, the Tathagata cannot be so perceived."*

You might ask, if the Tathagata cannot be perceived by means of form or appearance, why then in the temples are there statues to which we prostrate? Buddhism is just like all other religions in that it is against worshiping idols. Then, is it that we shouldn't prostrate to the images of Buddhas and Bodhisattvas? The answer is simple: because of the Buddha, you prostrate to yourself. The Buddha's image causes respect to arise in you and you prostrate. The image is merely a representation of "I." When you prostrate, you are not bowing down to the Buddha, rather you are bowing down to yourself, and therefore you are saved. All religions boil down to the same essence: "I" don't save you. You save yourself due to your mind of true respect. In actuality, it doesn't even have to be an image of the Buddha to which you prostrate. It could be some wood or clay, but if in your mind it is the Buddha and reverent respect arises, then you have succeeded. This is what is meant by, "because of the Buddha, you prostrate to yourself." It is not bowing down to "me." You bow down to yourself. What part of yourself? Your mind, your respect.

Not only should an idol not be taken for the Buddha but also, while He was on this earth, if you took His physical body to be the teacher, you were grasping onto form. In the *Surangama Sutra*, it tells how Ananda made this mistake. The Buddha asked him why he had become a monk. He answered that he saw how beautiful the Buddha looked and how He gave off gentle, golden-hued light.

Ananda reckoned that this was not the result of ordinary karma. The Buddha then scolded him saying, Ananda, you are so foolish! You are not only attached to form but have become a monk due to attachment to physical beauty.   This same attachment drew Ananda into a potentially dangerous situation with Maugdalena. Thus, the Buddha said one cannot perceive the Tathagata by means of the physical form.

"*Why is that?   The* form *and appearance spoken of by the Tathagata is not true form and appearance.*"   What is the reason? The true body beyond birth and death is not this physical body. The physical body experiences birth and death.   Even if one lives to be a thousand years, in the end one must still die.   There was a famous monk called "Jewel-Fisted Ch'an Master" who lived a thousand years.   He practiced for about five hundred years in India but hadn't yet awakened to Great Enlightenment.   Knowing that Bodhidharma would bring Ch'an Buddhism to China, he went ahead to wait for him.   After seeing Bodhidharma, he had his Great Awakening and lived another five hundred years in China.   As a result, many places have temples named after him.

There are many examples of people who live extraordinarily long lives.   Mahakasyapa is an example of one still living on this earth.   Long life is merely a physical appearance.   It is not beyond birth and death.   A thousand years is still but a thousand years. That which is beyond birth and death is not the physical body, or the nirmanakaya.   It is the dharmakaya, which has no appearance. This is why the Buddha again emphasized the point:

*The Buddha told Subhuti, "Everything with form and
appearance is merely illusion. If all form and appearance are
seen as illusion, the Tathagata will be perceived."*

Kumarajiva in translating this part used very strong words,
"The Buddha told Subhuti." In this section, pay particular attention
to the words *"everything with form and appearance."* Whatever
may transpire because of one's cultivation work would not happen
without this effort.   People talk about different meditative
experiences, but when one is not meditating, these go away. Every
alambana is but an appearance, and every appearance is but an
illusion, not reality.

How then, does one perceive the real Buddha, the Tathagata?
Only when one has perceived the dharmakaya has one come "face
to face" with the real Buddha. If one perceives that all form is not
form, this is not emptiness. Most people explain this as achieving
emptiness. This is foolishly adding another meaning to the words.
The Buddha only said to perceive form as illusion. What then is
"not form"? He gave no definitive explanation. Please be careful!
Most people who study the *Diamond Sutra* will give their own
explanation of emptiness. Those are your own words and not the
Buddha's. The Buddha simply said to perceive that form is not
form is to perceive the Tathagata, the dharmakaya. The important
point is that the Buddha said "illusion" and not "empty." What is
this really saying? Simply, do not dwell.

Dharmakaya, Sambogakaya, Rupakaya— Substance, Appearance, Function

The most important lines in the fifth section of the *Diamond Sutra* are *"Everything with form and appearance is merely illusion. If all form and appearance are seen as illusion, the Tathagata will be perceived."* In the middle of the *Diamond Sutra*, there is a gatha which reads, *"One who looks for me in appearance; Or pursues me in sound, Follows paths leading astray, And cannot perceive the Tathagata."* And at the end of the sutra, there is another gatha which reads, *"All phenomena are like/ A dream, an illusion, a bubble and a shadow/ Like a dew drop and a flash of lightning/ Thus you should view them."* For the last thousand years, Buddhist and literary scholars as well have argued over which gatha contains the main point of the *Diamond Sutra*. These lines in the fifth section can also be taken as a gatha. I hope that when you are studying on your own, you will also take this question into consideration.

The Buddha said that we should not perceive the Tathagata in form. Everyone who has studied some Buddhism knows that when one becomes a Buddha, one also achieves the three bodies, or *kayas*. These are the dharmakaya (essence body), the sambhogakaya (reward body), and the nirmanakaya (transformation body). This is why in some temples you will see three of the same Buddha images on the same altar. They represent the three kayas. This became very popular in China, and by the T'ang Dynasty, the Taoist temples were also doing their own form of this. Taoists had the Three Clear Ones: the High Clear One, the Supreme Clear One and the Jade Clear One. This situation is representative of the world of religion in general. Whether they be "Western" or "Eastern," religions do influence each other quite deeply.

We've all heard the terms for the three kayas. What do these mean? The dharmakaya is clear and serene, the sambhogakaya has billions of appearances, shapes and sizes and the nirmanakaya is complete and perfect. Let's put Buddhism to one side and look from a philosophical perspective. The dharmakaya is the basic substance, that which all the phenomena in the universe have in common. In modern-day terms, one could loosely use the term "energy wave." The sambhogakaya is the outward appearance as it goes through various transformations which can perform many different functions, these functions being the nirmanakaya. From a philosophical perspective, the three bodies are substance, appearance and function. Everything in the universe has these three aspects. Take water, for example. It can be made into tea, ice-cubes, steam, and so forth, all with different appearance and functions, but no matter how it transforms, the basic substance is still water. We now have some idea of what the three kayas are, in theory at least.

In Buddhism, when we say a person has awakened to Supreme Enlightenment, achieved anuttara-samyak sambodhi, to what exactly has one awakened? It is exactly that basic substance of which all life in the universe is composed, the dharmakaya. In the *Heart Sutra*, it is called, *"neither beginning nor ending, pure nor impure, increasing nor decreasing."* In the opening verses preceding the *Diamond Sutra*, it is referred to in the line, *"How to achieve immortality, the indestructible vajrasattva?"* The familiar line, *"Not a thought arises, the entire body reveals itself"* also refers to the dharmakaya. The dharmakaya has no appearance.

As to the perfect reward body, the nirmanakaya, this is the result of one's cultivation work and is very difficult to achieve. I mentioned before the thirty-two marks of a Buddha and the eighty detailed physical characteristics. The body of anyone who has succeeded in cultivation, attained the Tao, has undergone a complete physical transformation. This physical body is the reward body. Why is it called the "reward body"? Actually, everyone's body is a "reward body." If throughout one's life one is very comfortable and fortunate, this is the reward of previous virtue. Others may experience a lot of pain and suffering and lead a very pitiful life. Their body is the result of non-virtuous actions in a previous life. Through cultivation work, we transform this karmic reward body.

In the Taoist school, they describe the process as getting rid of illness to lengthen one's life and achieving immortality. This is talking about transforming the reward body. Achieving the perfect reward body is gaining complete liberation, changing mortal bones into immortal bones and gaining every kind of superpower. This is extremely difficult to achieve. The perfect reward body is very difficult to cultivate. The Taoist cultivation, opening ch'i-mai, as well as Esoteric cultivation, opening the three channels and seven chakras, both start from the reward body. *Samatha* and *samapatti* (stopping and introspection), the pureland practice of reciting the Buddha's name and vipassana meditation are all examples of practices which mainly cultivate the dharmakaya. When one cultivates to the point where he or she has at will another body outside of this physical body, this is the sambhogakaya or transformation body functioning. This is a very basic overview of the three bodies.

The average person who practices Buddhist or Taoist cultivation works on the dharmakaya. The Esoteric school emphasizes the achievement of the three bodies because only when one achieves the three kayas has one successfully completed the Path. This is also called completion in one lifetime. "In one lifetime," means in this one lifetime to settle the question of life and death, to succeed at achieving the three bodies. In theory, this can be done, but in actuality, it is of the utmost difficulty. One must achieve perfection of vinaya, samadhi and wisdom as well as completely transform this physical body of four elements born of one's parents. Only this can be called completion in one lifetime.

Lotus Born

In Tibetan Esoteric Buddhism, in addition to worshiping Shakyamuni Buddha, they also worship Padmasambhava. It is said that Padmasambhava is the reincarnation of Shakyamuni Buddha, born eight years after the Buddha's passing. The Buddha was born of the womb and there were many things he could not teach as the founder of the orthodox teachings. Therefore, to found the esoteric teachings, he returned born of a lotus transformation. In southern India, there were a king and queen who were childless and in despair about their situation. While they were in the imperial gardens gazing at the lotuses one day, suddenly one lotus grew taller and larger. Out of the pod in the center burst forth a small boy of flesh and blood. Thus, he was called Padmasambhava, the Lotus Born.

As a prince, he was heir to the throne, but just as Gautama Shakyamuni did, he left the royal life at eighteen to follow the way of a monk. Unlike as in his last life however, he did not pass away into nirvana. Instead, he rode into the air on a white horse. Earlier on in Tibet, every year there would be huge celebrations commemorating this. People would perform fire pujas throughout the country. They would burn all kinds of things as offerings—clothing, grains, valuables. Some women would even cut their hair and burn it as an offering. The fires would be kept burning for seven days and seven nights. People encircled the fire, continuously chanting Padmasambhava's mantra. He would always appear on his horse, circle the fire once and then disappear again. Padmasambhava always looks as he did as a young man with two small wisps of mustache. This is to show that he had achieved the perfect reward body. In Taoism, this would be called immortality or *"The sun and moon rest together; heaven and earth have the same longevity."* Upon achievement of the perfect reward body, the sambhogakaya is also naturally achieved. In order to be the role model for Esoteric Buddhism, he had to have had completion in one lifetime for the teaching to be perfect.

Now that we understand this, we can see that the *Diamond Sutra* concentrates on perceiving the dharmakaya. What is perceiving the dharmakaya? It is enlightenment, seeing the Path. The *Diamond Sutra* is of the prajna teachings which mainly focus on True Form Prajna. This is the substance of the beginningless source of all life. The nirmanakaya and sambhogakaya are within the prajna alambana. This is why the Buddha said one cannot perceive the Tathagata through the physical form. The Tathagata is the origin of all life, the essential substance of all life. To have faith and reverence is no problem, but to become attached to a form is wrong. Not only in Buddhism is this wrong, but in any other religion as well.

Grasping onto Physical Appearance

In my experience, there are many people who grasp onto physical appearance. Those who grasp onto appearances tightly fall into one or another category of psychological illness. Sometimes it can be quite serious, even beyond treatment. This is something encountered not just in Buddhism. Any religious order or community will encounter these kinds of people. They are not open to receiving any teaching, because they are clutching to blind faith. In Buddhism, this is called grasping too tightly onto form. The full title of the *Diamond Sutra* is the *Diamond Severer Sutra,* which has the underlying meaning of the culmination of wisdom that does not grasp form and knows the Tathagata cannot be perceived through form.

Many people who do Zen or other kinds of practice will often ask, is this or that kind of experience good? Is this or that a good sign? You absolutely must remember that *"All phenomena are but illusions."* Today in meditation you reached a wonderful state, but without meditation, there is no wonderful state, so this is obviously not Tao. If by sitting in the lotus position the Tao is conferred upon one and then is taken back when one's legs uncross, this is the cultivation and attainment of one's legs and not the Tao. To borrow a line from Taoism, *"The Tao, it cannot for an instant leave; that which leaves is not the Tao."* It is also what the *Heart Sutra* calls *"no beginning or ending, not pure or impure, not increasing or decreasing..."* It's not as if by cultivation one can increase it, or that in slacking off it will decrease. The Tao cannot be perceived by appearance and thus, all phenomenal appearances are but illusions.

This being the case, what if a Buddha appeared right in front of your eyes? In light of the *Diamond Sutra*, how should this be taken? If you were really seeing a Buddha standing in front of you, you'd better go have your eyes checked or carefully examine your psychological state. Some people may hear sounds or have premonitions. Most people who have these happen to them love to play around with this stuff. Hey! Don't get sidetracked! All phenomenal appearances are but illusions. The highest bodhi is incredibly ordinary. The most wise and skillful actions are also the most simple. The same with people, the more wise and skillful they are, the more commonplace they appear. Lao-tzu said, *"The highest wisdom appears stupid."* The ultimate wisdom is plain and simple. This is true of philosophy and science as well.

People always feel that their life is special. That is just one's own feeling. It's not until one has experienced life at its most simple that one has tasted the height of it. I sometimes joke saying that human history, from a Western perspective, was shaped with two halved apples. The first was the apple that Adam and Eve ate which kicked off human history. The second apple was the one that Newton saw fall which then changed the course of human history. Throughout the ages, people in many lands had happily eaten apples without ever having discovered gravity. Then out of the blue, Newton sees an apple drop and realizes that the earth has gravity. An apple is a common thing. Every year apples drop to the ground. One person through this very common knowledge brought forth something extraordinary. Another example is steam. We've all seen boiling water and seen the steam, but someone saw in this common phenomenon the power to run an engine. Every common object and situation has this same potential. The extraordinary is within the ordinary.

In studying Buddhism, don't go chasing after the strange and mysterious. If you can live life at its simplest, then you will know the Buddha. In other words, you will perceive that all phenomena are illusions and not even the Buddha can be obtained. If at all times one does not grasp appearances, then one will perceive the Tathagata, the original nature of the dharmakaya. The fifth section is extremely important, especially to those people who work hard on their daily cultivation. Prince Chao-ming called this section "Like Theory, the Truth Is Perceived". The "theory" is the dharmakaya. The essence of Tao is a "theory," an understanding. The nirmanakaya and sambogakaya are one's ordinary affairs. Theory is in the philosophical realm while one's "affairs" are one's effort in cultivating the right way. This title, "Like Theory, the Truth Is Perceived" is pointing to the dharmakaya.

Gatha of Section Five

Repeatedly exhorting, there's no appearance or form.
Awoke clinging to dreams, dreaming wishing to be roused.
Hollow compassion continuously rains down tears of crying.
In a drunken stupor, the mind's doors have been bolted since antiquity.

"*Repeatedly exhorting, there's no appearance or form.*" The Buddha, with a lot of heart and serious words, repeats three times that to practice Buddhism one must not grasp onto appearances. To cultivate the Tao, one's thoughts must become the Tao, without form or appearance.

"Awoke clinging to dreams, dreaming wishing to be roused." This is human life. People throw around the phrase, "Life is but a dream," but are they clear and alert? No, neither clear nor alert, and so saying "life is but a dream" is but reverie. When people wake up from a dream state, sometimes they feel so foolish, "Oh, it was all just a dream." But are they actually awake? Their eyes are open, but they are in another dream. It's really funny when people have had a wonderful dream the night before and they revel in it throughout the day, not wanting to lose it. Human existence is really quite an elusive state. *"Awoke clinging to dreams,"* after waking, people cling to their dreams, and during some dreams, people wish to wake up as soon as possible. What then is a person to do? It is hard to know.

We have all read Li Shang-yin's poems and know this line, *"One could linger in sentimental reverie; at the time, however, it was already a haze."* This is also saying, *"Awoke clinging to dreams, dreaming wishing to be roused."* Another two lines often quoted are, *"At the time it was an ordinary affair; remembering it later, the fondness doubles."* In our lives, we all have things we remember with fondness, especially the romance of youth. At the time things occur, they seem rather mundane. Like this class tonight—we're all sitting here as usual, but if you meet each other thirty years from now, you'll say, "Oh! Remember those times in class? Boy, those were the days! Our classmate..." wishing you could relive the old days. They're gone!

Old people especially will do this, think of how good the old days in the country were. It wasn't as clean, the flies would get on the food, but thinking back it seems so wonderful. Shooing the flies, laughing and eating—ahh if only one could relive it. At the time, they were just flies, but remembering it later, the fondness doubles. People fool themselves very easily. And so I say, "*Awoke clinging to dreams, dreaming wishing to be roused.*"

"*Hollow compassion continuously rains down tears of crying.*" In relation to the stupor of sentient beings, in the *Lotus Sutra* there is a Bodhisattva called, "Always Crying." Each Bodhisattva's name has an inner meaning. This Bodhisattva feels that sentient beings are so stupid and pitiful that he can't help but cry for them. The Buddha time and time again exhorted us not to cling to appearance, but most people don't understand. Therefore, "*hollow compassion continuously rains down tears of crying.*" Despite the compassionate tears of Always Crying Bodhisattva, sentient beings still don't awaken to enlightenment. Why is this? "*In a drunken stupor, the mind's doors have been bolted since antiquity.*" The doors of wisdom within one's mind have been closed since the beginning of time. This is because you yourself have not opened them, and thus, they've always been locked tightly shut.

SECTION 6

TRUE BELIEF IS RARE TO FIND

Subhuti then said to the Buddha, "World-Honored One, will there be living beings who, after hearing these words and sentences, awaken to a true faith in them?"

The Buddha said, "Subhuti, do not speak that way. Even in the last 500 years after the passing of the Tathagata, there will be those practicing charity, performing good actions and observing the precepts who will hear these sentences and develop a true faith in them. You should know that such people will have planted roots of merit not simply before one, two, three, four, or five Buddhas, but under countless millions of Buddhas. Furthermore, if upon hearing these words clean, clear belief is instantly awakened, Subhuti, the Tathagata who knows and sees all assures that this person has attained immeasurable fortune."

"Subhuti, the Tathagata knows and sees that these people will acquire immeasurable blessings and merit. Why is this? Because this person also holds no notions of self person, being and life, of Dharma and non-Dharma. If such a person seized upon the idea of form, they would still be holding onto notions of self person, being and life If they clung to the idea of Dharma, they would still be holding onto notions of self person, being

and life. If they grasp the idea of non-Dharma, they would still be holding onto notions of self person, being and life. Therefore, do not grasp onto the concept of Dharma and non-Dharma."

This is why the Tathagata always says, "Ye Bhiksus, know that the teaching I expound is like a raft. Even the Dharma must be cast aside; how much more so non-Dharma"

Wen-hsi and Manjushri

> *Subhuti then said to the Buddha, "World-Honored One, will there be living beings who, after hearing these words and sentences, awaken to a true faith in them?"*

Now comes a new question. Let's take a more relaxed attitude toward the *Diamond Sutra*. Take it just as the record of a lesson taught in question/answer format, or as the script of a play. After all, the search for Truth need not be like doing academic research. It is more important to open up the doors of one's mind to gain some understanding. The Buddha had just told Subhuti that all appearances are but illusions. So if you wish to see the Buddha and one appears in your dreams or even standing on a cloud in front of your awakened eyes, you've fallen into the clutches of Mara if you take this to be real. This is not the Buddha. You can throw a stone at him or even whack him with the *Diamond Sutra*! Tell him, "Hey! You're the one who said it—All appearances are illusions, and if one perceives form as not form, one will perceive the Tathagata—so what are you coming around here for?" You have my word; you can really do this.

There is a story about a famous Ch'an master, Wen-hsi. He became a monk when he was very young, and at the age of thirty, started to practice Ch'an . After some time in spite of his diligence, he hadn't awakened, and so he decided to make a pilgrimage to Shanxi's Five Peaked Mountain (Wu T'ai Shan), the Bodhimandala of Manjushri. From Southern China, he walked, come rain or shine, making a prostration every three steps until he arrived there. It would probably have taken about half a year to get there. Manjushri has been the teacher of seven Buddhas and Shakyamuni Buddha, and countless other Bodhisattvas have been his students for many eons. He is the first in wisdom, and so many who seek wisdom or enlightenment will prostrate every three steps all the way to the Five Peaked Mountain. For some, it may even take three years to get there. Many hope that they will actually see Manjushri.

The story goes that when the monk, Wen-hsi, got to the Vajra Cave at the foot of the Five Peaked Mountain, he saw an old man with white hair and beard leading a cow. The old man cried out to him, "What incredible merit! Such an exhausting endeavor! Please come and join me for a cup of tea before continuing up." Wen-hsi followed him to a small shack and over the tea, the old man asked him from where he had prostrated. Wen-hsi said that he had come from the South in hopes of seeing Manjushri. The old man asked how Buddhism was in the South. Wen-hsi replied that it was only so-so and that's why he had come to the North, to find an enlightened teacher. Wen-hsi asked how Buddhism was in the North, and the old man said, "Dragons and snakes all mix together; men and saints live with each other." This describes quite accurately the whole world of human society. There are saints and demons, good and bad people, all in one package.

Wen-hsi asked the man how many monks there were on Five Peaked Mountain. The old man said, "In front three three, in back three three." In the thousand years since this was spoken, no one has been able to figure out what it means. Most people guess that it has to do with opening the Governing and Reproductive Vessels, the channels or mai through which the ch'i flows. Along the Governing Vessel in the back, there are three "gates," places where the ch'i will easily get blocked: the "Tailbone Gate," the "Spinal Straights" and the "Jade Pillow." Along the Reproductive Vessel in the front are the "Sealed Place," the "Guarded Point " and the "Spirit Door." This theory, though, is not necessarily correct. "In front three three, in back three three," has become a famous Ch'an *hua- tou.*

The old man then asked Wen-hsi about Buddhist theory, and Wen-hsi couldn't answer him. The old man called out, "Jun Ti, see the guest out!" and a young boy came in from the back of the hut. "Master, this way please." Wen-hsi followed him out. He turned back to apologize and thank the boy, but he and the rest had disappeared. Wen-hsi saw Manjushri riding a lion off into the air. Manjushri called out, "Don't apologize!"

Wen-hsi was devastated. He had prostrated hundreds of miles in hopes of seeing Manjushri and then not only met but also conversed with him for some time without even knowing it. The young boy was a transformation of Manjushri's lion. Wen-hsi wept in remorse and, in this fit of rage and regret, he suddenly had a Great Awakening. After his enlightenment, he went to a large monastery and worked in the kitchen as the rice maker. In the army, he would be called the "kitchen guard," but in the large monasteries, they were called the "Head of Rice." This was extremely difficult work because of the volume of rice that had to be cooked in order to feed over a thousand people each day. The metal vessel that was used was so big that you wouldn't see me if I stood inside it.[2] The stirring paddle, as you would imagine, was long and heavy. You have to be in good shape just to lift it. Put three years of cooking behind you and there's no need to go to the Shaolin Temple to practice martial arts!

Ch'an Master Wen-hsi just did what needed to be done to serve people. He made the rice that fed a thousand people every day. He did the difficult work that not many wanted to or could do. So you see, it's as we've said before. One who has great attainment actually seems quite ordinary. Master Wen-hsi made his pilgrimage to the Five Peaked Mountain, prostrating as many before him had. Then, he took on the most difficult menial labor to serve others. To do what others cannot do, to endure what others

[2] Translator's note: I have seen one and it's true!

cannot endure for the greater good so that others won't suffer is the way of a Bodhisattva.

One day, while Master Wen-hsi was cooking rice, Manjushri appeared above the vessel, riding on his lion. He kept circling around the rim. Once Wen-hsi caught sight of him, the same Manjushri that had appeared to him as an old man when he first arrived at Five Peaked Mountain, he took his rice paddle and swatted at him saying, "Manjushri is Manjushri. Wen-hsi is Wen-hsi. Why are you here? You are you, and I am I." Manjushri flew up into the air, laughed and said, "Even the root of the bitter melon is bitter, while the sweet melon is sweet through and through. I've been cultivating for three great eons, but not until today have I incurred the wrath of an old sage!"

Of course the root of a bitter melon would be bitter. Of course a sweet melon is sweet through and through. Three great eons of cultivation, even Shakyamuni Buddha was his student, but today Manjushri's luck ran out. This old monk ran him out of his kitchen. This is just to say that all phenomena are but illusions— again and again this lesson. This is also why the Ch'an masters would later on say, "If the Buddha comes, chop his head off; if the devil comes, chop his head off." This is the highest secret method of cultivation.

The Monk That Burned the Buddha

Once again, the most important lesson is not to grasp onto appearances. Once you grab, it can become a psychological illness. This is why I am telling you, warning you, not to do this. Phenomenal appearances cannot be obtained, nor are there really any phenomena to obtain.

There is a story about one of the later Ch'an masters named Tan-hsia who was the main disciple of Ma-tsu. He became abbot of a temple, and during one particularly cold winter, they ran out of firewood. Master Tan-hsia remembered that one of the Buddhas in the main hall was made out of wood. So he went and got it, chopped it up and started a fire. The managing monk of the temple passed through the main hall and saw that the wooden Buddha was missing. He was very upset and ran to tell the abbot. When he saw the fire going, he realized what was going on and was horrified. "You're a monk and you're burning a Buddha!" Tan-hsia tried to calm him, "Don't worry, we'll just borrow this one for now and replace it with an even better one later." But to no avail. "This is outrageous behavior and there will be karma to follow!" Tan-hsia, gazing at him, just listened.

The strangest thing happened then—the managing monk's beard and eyebrow hairs all fell out and one layer of his skin just peeled off, right then and there. It was Tan-hsia who burned the Buddha, but it was the managing monk who received the karma. This is one of the strange stories of the Ch'an masters, strange but with meaning. From it has come the *koan*, "Tan-hsia burned the wooden Buddha; the temple manager lost his beard and brows."

Real Buddhism is not found in any appearance. If you practice hard, whatever happens, don't dwell, don't grasp. Once you do it's a serious mistake. In response to this teaching in the sixth section, Subhuti voices his doubts asking, will there really be people later who when they hear this will believe it? Most people who believe in Buddhism are clinging to some appearances. Is it really possible to completely let go of *all* appearances? *The Buddha said, "Subhuti, do not speak that way."* Subhuti, don't hold onto this view.

Five Hundred Years Later

The Buddha said, "Subhuti, do not speak that way. Even in the last 500 years after the passing of the Tathagata, there will be those practicing charity, performing good actions and observing the precepts who will hear these sentences and develop a true faith in them. You should know that such people will have planted roots of merit not simply before one, two, three, four, or five Buddhas, but under countless millions of Buddhas. Such people, upon hearing these sentences, will instantly awaken a clean, clear belief."

This is very serious language! That's because it's referring to all things not having appearance and not grasping appearance, this being the Buddha. If one dwells on the forms of devils and saints, playing in this or that alambana day in and day out, then one has entered the state of grasping onto forms. This will not only bring upon you uncalled for troubles, but in doing this, you have already gone down a side path leading right into the realm of Mara—These are my words and not the Buddha's. This caused Subhuti to raise the question of whether later on people would really understand this and whether they could believe it. The Buddha told Subhuti not to think like that. He mentioned 500 years after his passing. Why this figure, 500 years? The time period during which the Buddha is alive is called the Right Dharma Age. This is the period when the Buddha is here in physical form giving teachings. Five hundred years after the Buddha's passing then starts the Semblance Age, in which there are sutras and Buddha images. Still to come is the Dharma Ending Age, during which the sutras, starting with the *Surangama Sutra*, and Buddha images disappear. The *Amitabha Sutra* will be the last sutra to disappear and Buddhism will be reduced to superstitious beliefs.

The Buddha for this reason said that 500 years after his passing, if a person really observes the precepts, practices charity and lives virtuously, his or her wisdom will open and he or she will believe these words.

Virtue, Merit and Wisdom

In order for real wisdom to open, one must observe the precepts, practice virtue and cultivate merits. For a person even to be born with a bit of intelligence, let alone wisdom, is the result of merit produced over many lives. Supreme wisdom is not something you get just by asking for it. You have to work for it. You must practice every virtue and cultivate all merits and blessings in order to attain this wisdom. One awakens to wisdom. If wisdom could be obtained by prayer or asking, one would still need to have observed the precepts and cultivated merit and blessings before one's request would be answered. How does one cultivate blessings? By quietly serving all beings one will receive blessings, fortune and wisdom. In this section, the Buddha specifically stated that 500 years after his passing, only those who observe the precepts and cultivate merit and blessings will be able to develop true faith.

In another 500 years, human culture will be completely different than it is now. I discuss this with the young students quite often because it is such an important question. People like to say that the world is improving or advancing, but I think this statement needs to be qualified. It depends on which area one is addressing. If it is material culture, this area is definitely advancing rapidly. However, from the perspective of human affairs, morality and spirituality, the essence of culture is in decline, moving backwards actually. From the perspective of any religious philosophy, this is true throughout the whole world. To say that society is advancing is speaking from the perspective of material culture only. Buddhism speaks from the perspective of human culture. People are becoming more and more intelligent and at the same time less and less wise. During the Dharma Ending Age, the situation will be that people's brains will be very well developed and their bodies will be very small and weak. Because of this, the average age for having children will go down to twelve. There will constantly be warring, plagues and catastrophes. Even the trees and vegetation will become deadly. This period has not yet started.

Five hundred years later, if one can live virtuously, keep the precepts and cultivate blessings, from within will arise a true and correct faith in the words of the *Diamond Sutra*, *"Everything with form and appearance is merely illusion. If all form and appearance are seen as illusion, the Tathagata will be perceived."* To see that everything is "not," for real wisdom to appear, is very difficult. Most religious people, for instance, get stuck in the outer ceremonies. They pray with a seeking mind for that which cannot be given. You'll see this especially at those big ceremonial temples. Buy some incense and bananas, and with bananas on the offering table and incense in hand, pray for the family to be safe, healthy, make lots of money...all these good things...then leave the incense, but take the bananas. For an investment of ten cents worth of incense, people seriously ask for all that in return. Think of this from a business point of view. Is it rational? If I were a Buddha or deity, I wouldn't pay attention to this kind of request. For ten cents, people think they can buy perfection. It doesn't happen that way. And those same people have the nerve to complain, "Oh, that deity is not very powerful."

Do you think it's easy being a deity or a Bodhisattva? It's like the old poem that describes the sky's difficulty in producing the weather:

> *April weather is not easy, said the sky.*
> *Silkworms need it warm, but wheat likes it cold,*
> *Travelers hope for sun, while farmers want the rain,*
> *And ladies who pick mulberry leaves wish for cloudy weather!*

So what is the poor old sky to do? It's not easy being the sky, and it's just as hard being an ordinary person. Being a Bodhisattva is even doubly difficult. Just imagine two families involved in a lawsuit, both with good reason. Each burns incense and makes offerings asking for help to win the case. What to do? See who has more food on the offering table and side with them? This is just religious ritual. If you take all this from the point of view of psychology, it looks even more ridiculous.

My reaction to people who dwell on religious ritual is like that of General Tseng Kuo-fan. He sat there listening to the second-in-command, Wang Shang-yi, go on and on, as some intellectuals tend to do, and just mumbled agreement from time to time. Tseng Kuo-fan was getting more and more annoyed. His hand was free, so he kept dipping his finger into some water on the table and tracing characters. Wang Shang-yi thought to himself, Ah! He is truly a great man. He doesn't waste time. He's even practicing calligraphy while we speak. Wang came over to look and saw that Tseng had been tracing the words *lost person* again and again. In my case, I would write one word, "nonsense." My mouth would still be saying, "Mmm, you could say that...no need to rush things...we'll talk again later." Perhaps three aeons from now we'll talk again because you really don't understand.

At this point, the Buddha is talking about a truth so simple that it is very difficult to believe. One needs incredible fortune, and not the worldly red fortune, to be able to develop a true faith. This faith is not blind but rather is a very rational faith that the words of the Buddha are true. The Buddha also wanted us to know that such a person has followed not one, two, three, four or five Buddhas but countless Buddhas and with them has planted roots of merit in order to give rise to such wisdom.

Clean, Clear Belief and Not Dwelling

> *"Furthermore, if upon hearing these words clean, clear belief is instantly awakened, Subhuti, the Tathagata who knows and sees all assures that this person has attained immeasurable fortune."*

205

This is talking about a person who hears what I've just said, *"Everything with form and appearance is merely illusion. If all form and appearance are seen as illusion, the Tathagata will be perceived."* and clean, clear belief instantly arises. You should note that here it is still talking about clean, clear belief. It is not the same as true faith. This belief is a clean, crisp, bright, intuitive belief arising out of a completely calm, clear mind free of any extraneous wandering thoughts. In other words, clean, clear belief arises out of the pureland of one's mind. This kind of person actually already has some enlightenment. This awakening of clean, clear belief is also the pure state of not dwelling and of *"not a thought arises, the entire body (of the dharmakaya) reveals itself."* The *Diamond Sutra* right from the beginning says do not dwell. Not dwelling is "not a thought arises, the whole body reveals itself" and this in turn is clean, clear belief. It arises not from mere intellectual understanding but from the deep understanding that comes from experience.

The Buddha said, Subhuti, if there is such a person, I will know and will see with my own eyes the moment that this person attains this supreme fortune and merit. To say this shows just how difficult it is to truly come to an understanding of His meaning, how difficult it is to achieve the alambana of wisdom.

> *"Why is this? Because this person also holds no notion of self, person, being and life, of Dharma and non-Dharma."*

That person in whom clean, clear belief instantly awakens knows that all forms, all appearances within any alambana are *not*. They are all not the form. So you may say, well then, "not form" is it. You are wrong. You're clinging to the appearance of "not form." *"Without dwelling, therein arises the mind."* So next you may say, there is not even no-form, right? Also wrong. You are abiding in "not even no-form." This is why the Buddha said, one who actually has this great wisdom, who has actually awakened, will gain immeasurable fortune. Why is this? This person has achieved the alambana of a Buddha within his or her lifetime. This person is a living Buddha. And why can it be said that this person has reached the alambana of a Buddha? Because this person has no notion of self, person, being and life, and thus has clean, clear belief. Completely letting go, one has no notions.

These four notions are extremely serious because every kind of pain, suffering, and frustration of human existence arises from these four. Whether one looks at these from the perspective of psychology or from common awareness, these four notions, or ideas, are quite apparent. The ego of most people is very strong. The egos of intellectuals are particularly strong. Suppose you ran into an intellectual on a bus and asked him to move over so that you could sit. He would first look you up and down, thinking to himself, "What a Neanderthal! Well, perhaps I should take pity," and then say, "Have a seat." This is the grand ego at work, giving the seat out of pity. It's the same when they see that someone doesn't understand them but rather than taking the time to explain, they just let the person nod in agreement. This is the notion of a self. So you see, intellectuals' egos are very hard to deal with, very stubborn. Of course I include myself in this category.

People, no matter where or when, are always functioning deep within the view of ego. If one can get rid of the notion of self, then one is almost there. Along with this, one would naturally not have the view of a person. All people would be equal in one's eyes. All are Buddhas. Every man and woman is one's father and mother, each child is one's own child. The same goes for the notion of being and life, not wishing for either a long or short life. Life and death are as Chuang-tzu describes them, part of a whole, like day and night. When night comes, just go to sleep. There is no awakening clinging to the dream, dreaming wishing to be roused. To let go of the four notions is just like this. "Form" when outside is phenomenal appearances; when inside is views and ideas, subjective views and ideas.

The next two are even more serious than the four views. First, "non-Dharma." Let go of all Buddha-dharma. All phenomenal appearances are but illusions; don't cling to any appearance. Let go of everything, even the Buddha. This is called having no notion of Dharma. However, if you fall into thinking that nothing exists, that there is no existence—the Buddha doesn't exist and non-existence doesn't exist—you have fallen into an "existence." What existence? A no-Dharma-existence. If I ask you if you think that everything is nonexistent, if you deny the existence of anything, and you say, "Right!" This "right" is "nonexistence of non-Dharma." In other words, the two extremes: there is no existence and there is existence.

There are those who study the *Diamond Sutra* and say that it is definitely talking about emptiness. Dead wrong. There is no form or appearance, but to say that all is empty is also incorrect because all phenomena arise from that very same "emptiness." In the *Surangama Sutra* it says, *"Beyond all form, all phenomena are found."* "Beyond all form" is the same as "no form or appearance." "All phenomena are found" is the same as "nor isn't there 'no form or appearance'." Beyond all form, all phenomena are found. One must even transcend going beyond all form. The *Diamond Sutra* isn't talking about emptiness. All it is saying is that when one sees the Path, when one perceives the dharmakaya, one realizes that all phenomena are but illusions. Following this, one's practice is to diligently, untiringly practice every virtue until each and every thought is virtuous. It cannot be empty.

All the Ch'an masters who have achieved Great Awakening to Supreme Enlightenment explain this as the basis, the foundation of all Buddhism. Their way of saying it is as follows, *"In reality this True Ground does not grasp a speck of dust. While practicing a thousand doors, not even one Dharma should be missed."* The first sentence, *"In reality this True Ground does not grasp a speck of dust,"* is speaking about the fundamental nature, the dharmakaya or Thusness. *"While practicing a thousand doors, not even one Dharma should be missed,"* is talking about actually walking the Path, cultivation practice. Functioning in the world cannot be empty. Each moment, each thought has existence. Not even the slightest evil is done and one gives selflessly for the benefit of sentient beings. While practicing a thousand doors, not even one dharma should be missed. Each and every thing has existence; it is not empty. We must be clear on this basic theory if we are to practice Buddhism.

In this paragraph, the three different ideas in the obverse and reverse are gone over again and again. *"If such a person seized upon the idea of form, they would still be holding onto the notion of self, person, being and life. If they clung to the idea of Dharma, they would still be holding onto the notion of self, person, being and life."* If one feels that one absolutely has to burn incense and make prostrations every day, this is grasping onto form. In my youth when I was a student, we were all against superstitious beliefs and traditions. If we went to a temple together, I really wanted to make prostrations but was too embarrassed. I was afraid the other students would ridicule me saying I was superstitious. So if there was no one in sight, I would quick, quick make a prostration and then stand up and act cool again. Once a monk saw me doing a prostration and, thinking it was wonderful that a student was being so reverent, hit the big gong as was their custom when people prostrated. I nearly hit the roof when that gong struck. Just the idea that the other students would then see me prostrating horrified me to that extent. I asked the monk why they did that and he said to me, "Prostrate with the gong, or the Buddhas won't believe; burn incense with some noise, or the

Buddhas won't receive." Hearing this one doesn't know whether to laugh or cry.

The temples from Hangzhou northward on up, all do this sort of thing. You go down, the gong sounds and all the change jumps out of your pockets. With all this attention, you feel you should at least give a little something. So perhaps there is some logic to this saying after all! But really, do you actually think the Buddhas are nodding off there and you need to make a little noise to wake them up? Most people's religious ideas are totally grasping onto form, grasping onto the ideas of ego, personality, being and life. Then there are those who say that they totally reject all forms and rituals, like some religions that say people shouldn't worship idols. However, are there any of these religions which do not have the custom of prostrating? No matter which way you turn, these notions of form and dharma are all there.

"If they grasp the idea of non-Dharma, they would still be holding onto the notion of self, person, being and life. Therefore, do not grasp onto the concept of Dharma and non-Dharma." To talk of emptiness is incorrect. This is not Buddhism. To grasp onto existence is also not Buddhism. "Not empty and not existent" as well as "both empty and existent" are not Buddhism. This is very, very difficult! True Buddhism is the severing diamond of prajna paramita. If one wishes to become enlightened, this is where it starts, at real wisdom.

Real and Not Real

To not grasp form and not to not grasp form is extremely difficult. Dealing with interpersonal relations is almost as difficult. I'd like to tell you two funny stories, both with a lot of truth in them. The first one is about Confucius. At that time, Confucius and a group of his students were staying at Chenjia and there was no food to eat. The students all protested to Confucius saying, "Teacher, why are you being so stubbornly ethical? Let's go and borrow some rice from the rich man across the way." Confucius felt badly about their situation and so said to them, "If you insist, then by all means, go and try." Tzu-lu was always the most impulsive and so he just naturally took up the task.

Tzu-lu knocks and the door is opened. The old man who answers it says, "Oh, you're from that bunch of unfortunate ones across the way, students of Confucius. Why did you wait this long before coming to borrow some rice! I'll have you know that my rice cannot be borrowed. Since you are a student of Confucius, you must be able to recognize Chinese characters. I'll write one and if you can recognize it, I'll give you the rice. If you don't recognize it, there's no rice for you even if you could pay money for it."

Tzu-lu thought, No sweat! Write as many as you like, I'm a student of Confucius. He came back with the character for *real* on a piece of paper. Tzu-lu scoffed, "You test me with this character, *real*? The old man slammed the door shut saying, "You don't recognize it! No rice!" Tzu-lu was left with a door slam to stave his hunger. He went back and told his teacher the story. Confucius asked what the word was and when he heard it, said, "Oh, no wonder he didn't give it to you. We've come to the point of not having any food. Is this any time to be so earnest?" (This is a play on words. In Chinese, the two characters which together mean "earnest", if taken separately mean, "recognize real.")

Upon hearing this, another student, Tzu-kung, who was much cleverer than Tzu-lu rushed out to try for himself. Tzu-kung made excuses for his fellow classmate saying that Tzu-lu was actually illiterate. The old man, impatient, once again held up the paper with the character *real*. Tzu-kung, knowing that Tzu-lu fell on his face with this same one, said cleverly, "That's false." The old man, now angry, just slammed the door. Tzu-kung ran back and reported to Confucius who scolded him saying, "Oh! Don't you know that sometimes you have to be earnest in life!" (Recognize real.)

It's very tricky handling human affairs. You have to get the right tension between being earnest and not being earnest just right, like fine-tuning an instrument. The same applies to not grasping onto the concept of Dharma or non-Dharma.

The second story is from the Ch'an sect. There were two brothers who were ordained disciples of a great enlightened master. The two monks themselves were also awakened practitioners. One day the two were walking along the road together. At that time, monks would all carry a walking staff with a small, flat, metal shovel on the end. Why did monks carry this? Because it was very useful. No matter where they wandered, they could survive by carrying this and some potatoes. Just dig a hole, plant the potato and before long, one has a constant food source of greens and potatoes. One doesn't have to depend on begging to survive. The second important use for this shovel was to compassionately bury any dead bodies one might find along the road.

The two monks, this particular day, happened upon the corpse of a man by the road. One of them, upon seeing this exclaimed, "Oh, what a pitiful sight!" He recited *Amitofo* and set about burying the corpse. The other one didn't even bother looking, went off and lay down somewhere. Another person, having seen this whole thing occur, went to ask the master about the matter. After recounting the event, he asked which one was right. The master said, "The one who buried him was compassionate; the one who didn't was liberated. People die and turn into dust whether or not they're buried. Lying on top, they turn to dust; lying underneath, they turn to dust. In the end, it's all the same. So, burying is compassionate; not burying is liberated."

Listening to these two stories, we can understand a little about living life, perspectives, and real Buddhism. In the *Diamond Sutra*, it tells us the exact method for true cultivation, "one should not dwell" and thus do not grasp a Dharma. If you seize upon a Buddha Dharma in order to cultivate, then you've grasped form. If you say, I don't grasp anything and so I am really practicing

Buddhism, you are even more wrong. Sometimes you need to be more earnest! So don't grasp onto a non-Dharma.

Where Is the Shore

> *This is why the Tathagata always says, "Ye Bhiksus, know that the teaching I expound is like a raft. Even the Dharma must be cast aside; how much more so non-Dharma."*

This paragraph is extremely important. The Buddha told his disciples directly: *"Ye Bhiksus,"* all of you who have been regularly receiving my teachings, all of the ordained monks, all one thousand two hundred and fifty of you, *"know that the Teaching I expound is like a raft."* My expounding, my teaching is like a rowboat, or one of those simple bamboo rafts that are used to ferry people across a river. When you reach the shore, you simply get off the raft. You don't drag the boat along with you, do you? Most people aren't stupid enough to do that. The Buddha said, my Dharma teachings are convenient methods. They are all rafts to take you across the river. Once you are on the other shore, you don't need the rafts. So like the rafts, *"the Dharma must be cast aside."* All of the "real," "true" Dharma in the end must be let go. *"How much more so the non-Dharma."* It goes without saying that all which is not Dharma must also be let go. If one cannot make a totally clean break with the "real" Dharma, one will never achieve the Tao. This goes even more so for non-Dharma. In this part, the Buddha spoke strongly with complete clarity.

In Chinese Buddhism, there is a saying one hears often, *"The sea of suffering is shoreless; turn around and the shore is there."* Where is the shore? You don't need to turn around! Right now is the shore. Each moment, let go. The shore is right here.

There is a Ch'an story about Master Pu-wen of Dragon Lake. Pu-wen was originally a prince during the T'ang Dynasty. He saw through this life and decided to become a monk. As a monk, he went to see the famous Ch'an Master Shih-shuang Ch'ing-chu to ask him about Dharma. Pu-wen said, "Master, please give me a simple method that will bring enlightenment." The master said, "I will," and Pu-wen immediately fell to his knees, "Quickly, tell me." Master Ch'ing-chu pointed to the mountain in front of the temple saying, "That is a 'strength giving mountain'."

"What is a strength giving mountain?" According to the feng-shui experts, if one has a "strength giving mountain" in the front, it is good feng-shui. The same goes for an office—if it has a good desk in the front, this is also a "strength giving mountain." His temple had a particularly good strength giving mountain. There are different subtleties to these, such as being shaped like a calligraphy brush rest. They are called "brush rest mountains" and the household across from it will have writers and scholars. Some are shaped like a box; "box mountains" will bring material fortune.

Master Ch'ing-chu continued to speak, "When that strength giving mountain nods its head, then I will tell you." Pu-wen upon hearing this immediately awakened. In other words, when the strength giving mountain nods, I will give you the Buddha's Dharma. What does this mean? The *koan* from this story goes, "Upon saying the head nods, the head has already nodded; since when has a strength giving mountain nodded its head?" It's said, turn around and the shore is there, but one needn't turn. The shore is here. By the time you turn around, the shore is already gone.

Some Ch'an masters say, *"If one laid down the butcher's knife, one would immediately become a Buddha."* Some students will say this to me, applying it to themselves. I say to them, "Sounds good but that's not you. You don't even dare to handle a paring knife; you're afraid it will cut your hand." When they say butcher's knife, they mean *butcher's knife*. A person who has what it takes to be a killer, a gang leader or an evil lord, such a person, the moment he makes a true decision to be virtuous and lays down the butcher's knife immediately becomes a Buddha. Your hand is not even holding a knife and you don't dare to do anything bad—what is there to lay down? From this we can understand the meaning of the line in the *Diamond Sutra* which says, *"Even the Dharma must be cast aside; how much more so non-Dharma."*

Many people will say that the *Diamond Sutra* is talking about emptiness and so, being empty, one can engage in any kind of evil action. This is wrong. The notion of virtuous actions must not be grasped; how much more so non-virtuous actions. These must even more so not be done.

Gatha of Section Six

The golden rooster crows like thunder in the early morning hours.
Startled out of a good dream, the dark is like the light.
Awakened, death and life are but dusk and dawn.
One truly understands, the myriad of phenomena are just a downy feather.

"*The golden rooster crows like thunder in the early morning hours.*" In this section, the Buddha is talking about life and death. Sentient beings are like somnambulists living in a dream state. In the early morning hours, the rooster's crowing wakes us. It's like the feeling when one becomes enlightened; it's as if one has awakened from a hazy dream and is very clear. Even though it's the wee hours of the morning and we're in the middle of a dream, a rooster's cry will still wake us. The teachings of the Buddhas and Bodhisattvas are like the cries of a rooster rousing us from slumber.

"*Startled out of a good dream, the dark is like the light.*" Don't think that you're already enlightened. If you think there is a state of enlightenment, you are just a silly fool. For those people who are enlightened, there is no state of enlightenment. Those who think there is are grasping onto the concept of Dharma, and so I say, "*Startled out of a good dream, the dark is like the light.*"

"*Awakened, death and life are but dusk and dawn.*" When one has truly awakened and really understands, what is life and death to such a one? Enlightened, death and life are like dusk and dawn. A life comes to be the same as the dawning of day, awakening us from sleep. And death? When night is upon us, it is time to sleep. Death and life are a single strand, nothing special. This way of thinking is part of Chinese culture and so we often hear, *"One goes out for life and comes back at death."* If one can awaken to life and death like dusk and dawn, then true faith will arise.

"One truly understands, the myriad of phenomena are just a downy feather." Chuang-tzu saw all the phenomena in the universe as such, *"Heaven and earth are but the tip of a finger and all phenomena, a horse."* All of heaven and earth are a fingertip; all the universal phenomena are also just the tip of a finger, just this very tiny bit. All phenomenal appearances are like a horse. A horse has a head, a tail, horse hairs and so forth. All of the things in the universe are as light and insignificant as goose down.

So now we know the theory behind this section and if we wish to understand it deeply, *"Even the Dharma must be cast aside; how much more so non-Dharma."* Everyone practicing Buddhism wishes to unlock the secret of life and death. How is one to do this? I will tell you in one sentence: Ultimately there is no life and death to understand. Only in this way can we understand life and death.

SECTION 7

NO GAINING, NO EXPOUNDING

"Subhuti, what do you think? Has the Tathagata attained anything by anuttara-samyak sambodhi? Does the Tathagata in fact expound a Dharma?"

Subhuti replied, "As I understand the teaching of the Buddha, there is no definitive Dharma called anuttara-samyak sambodhi, nor is there any definitive Dharma which the Tathagata can expound. Why is this? The Dharma which the Tathagata expounds is inconceivable and beyond words. It is neither Dharma nor not -Dharma. All of the saints and sages vary only in mastery of this."

What Is Gained? What Is Said?

"Subhuti, What do you think? Has the Tathagata attained anything by anuttara-samyak sambodhi? Does the Tathagata in fact expound a Dharma?" The Buddha asked Subhuti his opinion whether or not one who is enlightened has actually obtained anuttara-samyak sambodhi, Great Enlightenment, absolute equanimity and omniscient awareness. In becoming a Buddha, attaining the Tao, does one actually gain anything? That is question one. Question

two is whether or not in his regular teaching and discourse the Buddha has expounded a Dharma.

"Subhuti replied, ' As I understand the teaching of the Buddha, there is no definitive Dharma called anuttara-samyak sambodhi'." All of you who aspire to Buddhahood, please pay attention. Subhuti answered, Begging your pardon, if I might be so bold as to put forth my understanding, there is no definitive Dharma called annuttara-samyak sambodhi. To think that reciting the Buddha's name is the Buddha's Dharma is mistaken. To think that sitting in zazen, doing prostrations, reciting mantras and so forth are the Buddha's Dharma is mistaken. There is no definitive Dharma.

What does this mean, no definitive Dharma? The Buddha, like all great educators, does not rely on a set method. Rather, they see the opportune moments to teach something important and make use of them. They see where a person's capabilities lie and develop these. There are times you need to berate someone in order to teach, reward or praise a person or even embarrass him to teach something. Teaching is basically stimulating a person in some way so that his or her own innate wisdom will open. This is why there is no specific Dharma. Subhuti also said that as he understood it, there is no specific Dharma called anuttara-samyak sambodhi, Supreme Enlightenment. If there were a specific way to become a Buddha, a model to follow, this Buddhism would be cheating people. If one should develop a mind that does not dwell, where then could there be a prescribed Dharma?

"Nor is there any definitive Dharma which the Tathagata can expound." The Buddhist Canon, the Tripitaka, has twelve categories of sutras. The *Diamond Sutra* explains things one way; the *Sutra of Complete Enlightenment* another; the *Flower Adornment Sutra*, the *Surangama Sutra* and so forth, all have different ways of explaining things. If it's raining when you leave the house, you can say that it is the clouds of compassion and the Dharma rain. If the sun comes out, you can explain it as the sun of wisdom penetrating through emptiness. If it's not sunny or rainy, then it is the clouds of compassion forming a blanket of protection. Any way that one explains it is correct. This, in other words, can explain, *"Nor is there any definitive Dharma which the Tathagata can expound."* Where then is the Buddha Dharma to be found? Not necessarily in the sutras. Worldly affairs can be the Buddha Dharma. The *Diamond Sutra* is telling you that practicing Dharma, practicing Buddhism and everyday life are an inseparable whole. There is no such thing as a worldly versus spiritual dichotomy. When I was young, at times older people would ask me why I didn't become a monk and leave worldly affairs. I would clarify to them that indeed I had never entered worldly affairs. "Worldly" is just the outer appearance.

"Why is this? The Dharma which the Tathagata expounds is inconceivable and beyond words. It is neither Dharma nor not - Dharma." Pay attention here. You cannot cling to the Dharma spoken of by the Tathagata. If you take the Honored One's words and grasp onto them as being "right," then you have succeeded in

completely fooling yourself. *Inconceivable* and *beyond words*, even these words themselves are merely shadows. The real thing in no way can be expressed. Say for instance, you go out and try some new kind of food. Then, you come back and describe it to everyone—how delicious it tasted and all the details of its appearance and flavor. It sounds fantastic, but I haven't actually tasted it. It's just a reflection of the moon. It's not my experience of the delicious taste, right? It's the same with Buddhism. Any verbal expression of it is still just the reflection of the moon. The expression is not "it." Thus, the Tathagata says that the Dharma is inconceivable and beyond expression. It is not Dharma. There is no set Buddha's Dharma; and to have this idea is also wrong. It is not "not-Dharma." The Buddha doesn't profess nihilism. To think so is a misconception.

Varying Depths

"All of the saints and sages vary only in mastery of this." Buddhism is that magnanimous! This is the spirit of Buddhism. Many other religions will negate all but their own order; whereas, Buddhism affirms all religions, all saints and sages. In the *Avatamsaka Sutra* (*Flower Adornment Sutra*), even the side paths of the powerful spirit lords were affirmed to a tiny degree. If it encourages any kind of virtuous behavior, it is affirmed. Whether it be an Immortal, a saint, an arhat, a Bodhisattva, or whoever, the differences among them are due to their varying depths of

understanding of the Tao. The Tao of Jesus, the Tao of Buddha, the Tao of Mohammed, the Tao of Confucius, the Tao of Lao-tzu— which one is actually the Tao? Which Tao is bigger? Which is smaller? Actually, the truth is singular. In the sutras, there is a metaphor of blind people feeling an elephant. The one who grabs the ear describes the elephant as flat and round. Those who touch the tail, the leg, the underbelly, etc. all describe the elephant differently. This is just saying that people grasp onto their own subjective views and will therefore say: this is Tao, that isn't Tao.

Buddhists should not fall into this mistake because there is no definitive Dharma that can be espoused. Real and true Buddhism can accept all. All the saints and sages differ on account of their varying mastery of this point. There is only one truth, not two. If a person recognizes only a small fraction of this truth and thinks that only he is right and the rest are wrong, in actuality, he is the one who is wrong. To be at the alambana of a Buddha, the myriad of phenomena are affirmed, are denied and are created.

Worldly and Spiritual Are Equal

Today I'd like to talk about the main points of this chapter. Having attained Great Enlightenment, Great Awakening, there is no actual attaining of an "enlightenment." If there were, then one would have a concept of this state. To have a concept of the Tao in one's mind is already not the Tao. This is the first thing on which we must be clear. The next point is that there is no definitive Dharma the Buddha can expound. Buddhism in later centuries developed into many sects—orthodox, esoteric, Ch'an, and so forth, each with its own methods of practice. To grasp onto any of these and say, "This is real Buddhism" is wrong because there is no definitive Dharma the Tathagata can expound.

In the *Lotus Sutra* it says, *"All worldly dharmas are the Buddha Dharma."* One need not leave worldly affairs in order to practice Buddhism because all of these affairs are the Buddha Dharma. The *Lotus Sutra* also says, *"All the different industries and ways to make a living are not in any way contradictory to True Reality."* One need not leave worldly affairs, leave one's family, and go to a temple deep in the cold mountains to live in retreat in order to be practicing Buddhism. All of the different kinds of work, careers, ways to make a living are not contrary to True Form, nor to the essence of Tao. Indeed, they are one and the same. This is the main point of the *Lotus Sutra*. It espouses the One Vehicle Gate. The worldly and the transcendental are equal, and their ultimate achievement is the same. The paths leading to this ultimate achievement can be very different, and so the Buddha says there is no definitive Dharma that the Tathagata can espouse.

This leads into the Buddha's next statement, *"The Dharma which the Tathagata expounds is inconceivable and beyond words,"* which seems to repudiate his forty-nine years of teaching. In fact, this is actually a confirmation. All of the Dharma, the different reasonings and teachings the Buddha gave must not be clung to. If you grasp onto even one sentence, you're mistaken because it is inconceivable and beyond words. This discussion of the *Diamond Sutra* in which we are engaged is ignoring this basic premise! Just be aware of this in your minds. *"Neither Dharma nor not-Dharma"*; there is no fixed Dharma. If you believe there is an attainable Dharma, a conceivable Dharma, your belief is misconstrued. However, do not fall into thinking that all Dharma is empty or that there is no Dharma. Don't seize upon any notions. If you say, "I don't hold any views," you are grasping onto the idea that you don't hold any views. *"It is neither Dharma nor not-Dharma."*

The Difference Between Saints and Sages

"All of the saints and sages vary only in mastery of this." In Chinese culture, there is a distinction between a saint and a sage. Sages are those whose cultivation, knowledge, and virtue are of the highest level. Those who are still working toward this, but are not quite there yet, are the saints. This is the common cultural understanding. In Buddhism, there is an even clearer delineation of all the levels, which are called in popular terminology "the three saints and ten sages." There are three groups of ten stages which are the preliminary cultivation stages for becoming a Bodhisattva. The ten stages of abiding, ten stages of action and ten stages of dedicating together make up the so-called "three saints." The "ten sages" are the ten grounds (*bhumis*), or levels, of Bodhisattvas. Avalokiteshvara, Manjushri, Samantabhadra, Kshitigarbha and so

forth are all Mahasattvas, true sages according to this definition of the word.

All these levels and divisions were emphasized by later Buddhists. During the time of the Buddha, it wasn't taken so seriously. Here in the *Diamond Sutra*, the Buddha simply says, *"All saints and sages vary only in mastery of this."* A person who has been either a student or a teacher for a long time will know the following to be true: the teacher talks about one concept and one hundred people hear it all at the same time. Each of the one hundred people come away with a different perception, feeling and understanding of what was taught. In some cases, the teacher was very clearly saying that something was "white," but in two notebooks, the word "gray" was written, instead. All sorts of distortions occur. This is due to the fact that people's wisdom and understanding are all different. Different religions come about also due to the fact that there are different depths of wisdom.

Gatha of Section Seven

The traces of the bird with air for a nest are like water ripples;
By chance an exposition forms, like a brilliantly colored cloud.
That which is attained and lost, comes and goes, is not it;
When existence and non are altogether banished, the bedlam
comes to rest.

"The traces of the bird with air for a nest are like water ripples." In the sutras, there is a metaphor of a bird which nests in the air without ever touching a tree. This bird lays eggs, raises baby birds, lives and dies all in the air. In other words, this bird never dwells anywhere. It comes and goes without a trace, just as in Su Tung-p'o's poem, *"The air-nesting bird leaves no traces. On top of the water, a ripple passes and then is gone."* You can see the ripple, so you can't say that it's nothing, but a few seconds later, there's nothing left at all.

"By chance an exposition forms, like a brilliantly colored cloud." Once in a while, some literature or painting comes along which is just stunning. In Ch'an there is a saying, *"An insect burrowing in a piece of wood will sometimes form words."* There are some insects which burrow around in tree bark forming interweaving tracks. Sometimes it looks as if some spirit being has carved magical incantations all over the tree. It is just a natural occurrence. *"By chance an exposition forms, like a brilliantly colored cloud."* Sometimes a chance modification will yield spectacular results. This is just saying that the saints and sages, like the Buddha, expound the Dharma according to the opportunity. People asked questions of the Buddha and he answered. These are all by-chance expositions and do not remain. If we can understand this, then we can understand the wisdom teachings of Nagarjuna and of the *Diamond Sutra*.

"That which is attained and lost, comes and goes, is not it." If today in meditation we see light, see Bodhisattvas, or if we dream

many days in a row of Bodhisattvas who tell us things, we are so elated that we can hardly stop speaking about it. Other times, we may have horrifying nightmares. All of these kinds of things are but passing occurrences. Causal conditions are inherently empty. The conditions which come together causing something to happen weren't there originally.

"When existence and non are altogether banished, the bedlam comes to rest." Let go of everything and it's somewhat like the Buddha Dharma. Letting go of everything isn't a state of nonexistence or vacuous emptiness. It's simply not hanging on anymore.

The first to the seventh sections are all basically addressing the question: How should one cultivating the Bodhisattva path dwell? Or rather, how can one pacify the mind and bring it to a state of calmness and clarity? The mind is full of emotions, thoughts, frustrations, etc. How does one pacify these? The Buddha answered—just like that, dwell and pacify the mind — period. Seeing that Subhuti didn't understand, the Buddha then said—one ought not to dwell—telling us to protect the mind moment. At this point, the Buddha has not yet said, "not dwelling, the mind should arise." He has only said one ought not to dwell, do not dwell on anything. The Dharma also does not dwell anywhere; there is no specific Dharma of which to speak. To say that the Buddha's Dharma is prajna, is the *Diamond Sutra* or the *Amitabha Sutra* or a mantra is incorrect. This is all dwelling. Up to now, the Buddha has said only not to dwell because **IT** is inconceivable and beyond words. Furthermore, all the saints and sages differ in their depth of understanding of the essence of Tao. This is why we mustn't cling to any particular Dharma door. The least bit of clinging , the least bit of obstruction and one has completely misconstrued the teaching. This is not Buddhism. Up to this point, this big question has been addressed.

SECTION 8

BORN OF FOLLOWING THE DHARMA

"Subhuti, what do you think? If a person bestowed in charity an abundance of the seven treasures to fill the universal galaxies of worlds, would the merit and fortune obtained be great?"

Subhuti replied, "Very great, World-Honored One. Why? Because what the Tathagata refers to as merit and fortune is not real merit and fortune, the Tathagata calls it great."

"Subhuti, if, on the other hand, someone receives and retains even a single stanza of this discourse and expounds it to others, his merit and fortune would be much greater. The reason, Subhuti is that all Buddhas and their anuttara-samyak sambodhi arise from this teaching. Subhuti, the so-called Buddha Dharma is not Buddha Dharma."

No Fixed Fortune

"Subhuti, what do you think? If a person bestowed in charity an abundance of the seven treasures to fill the universal galaxies of worlds, would the merit and fortune obtained be great?

Subhuti replied, "Very great, World-Honored One. Why? Because what the Tathagata refers to as merit and fortune is not real merit and fortune, the Tathagata calls it great."

This question was asked by the Buddha of his own accord: Subhuti, what's your idea on this? Suppose someone filled the universe with the seven treasures—at that time there were seven precious substances, gold, silver, jewels, considered to be the greatest treasures—imagine enough of these precious materials to fill a universe, or in Buddhist terminology, a "three thousand great-thousand world." This is also the measurement for one Buddha land. One who has become a Buddha has the responsibility to teach all the beings in an area this large. If someone gave away in charity as much treasure as could fill a universe, would their merit be great? Subhuti replied, *"Very great, World-Honored One."* In other words, incredibly huge merit!

Most people's charity only goes as far as the food and incense they put on their own altar. They put this out and ask for fortune and blessings in return. Compare this with someone who gives away an entire universe full of treasures. How do you think their merit will differ? Of course this person will obtain much more, and why is this? *"Because what the Tathagata refers to as merit and fortune is not real merit and fortune, the Tathagata calls it great."* This is saying that we must be clear on the fact that this fortune for which we humans all wish has no actual self existence nor any fixed form. This holds true for any kind of worldly fortune.

Suppose the weather was very cold yesterday and you ran into a friend who wasn't wearing enough clothes to keep warm. You were wearing more than enough, and so you put your sweater around her. Yesterday, this friend had the good fortune to run into you. Now suppose it became very hot today and you ran into this same friend. If you performed this same act of "kindness," you put your sweater around her, she'd probably be annoyed enough to hit you. What is fortune in one time and place is punishment in another, and vice versa. This is because fortune in itself has no set form. Intrinsic within fortune is the fact that each instance is always unique. The good fortune that comes out of an opportunity may stay with you for some time, even several decades. At the end of those several decades when the fortune runs out, that's it— finished, gone, empty! This is because it never existed independently.

Not having independent existence is to say that it has no fixed form, nor does it exist forever. *"Because what the Tathagata referred to as merit and fortune is not real merit and fortune, the Tathagata calls it great."* There's actually a secret here which he has not disclosed—real merit is actually enlightenment, the ultimate accomplishment of great wisdom which liberates one completely from the mundane. This kind of attainment goes way beyond the parameters of any ordinary fortune. In saying that the fortune attained by the giving of all those seven treasures was so great, the Buddha was actually just teaching and encouraging people to be virtuous and charitable.

"If, on the other hand, someone receives and retains even a single stanza of this discourse and expounds it to others, his merit and fortune would be much greater." Once again, the Buddha is emphasizing the importance of wisdom and teaching others. Someone who gives away a whole Buddha land full of treasure does indeed gain a great deal of merit; but a person who has some understanding of the *Diamond Sutra* or even just four sentences of it and tries to pass this understanding on to others has much greater merit and more blessings than the former. The Buddha said: You ought to know that if you understand, print copies of, hand write or explain to others this sutra —and it doesn't even have to be the entire thing, even just four sentences will suffice— resulting in others' understanding and relief of suffering, your merit is much greater.

All Buddhas and the *Diamond Sutra*

"The reason, Subhuti, is that all Buddhas and anuttara-samyak sambodhi arise from this teaching." What is the reason for such great merit? All the Buddhas of the past, present and future come from this sutra. In this *kalpa* alone, 1000 Buddhas will appear. Shakyamuni Buddha is the fourth of these, and Maitreya will be the fifth. This kalpa is called "The Kalpa of Sages" because it is the kalpa during which the most saints and sages will appear. The time period spoken of here is not just an archeological or

anthropological time period such as the Paleolithic, Neolithic, and so forth. This division is on the scale of the lifespan of a universe.

The Buddha said all those who have achieved Buddhahood, who've had a great awakening, attained anuttara-samyak sambodhi, have done so by means of this sutra. Actually, it is by means of prajna, the coming forth of one's innate wisdom. The *Diamond Sutra* is a discourse by those whose wisdom has already come forth. True Buddhism is the appearance, the arousal of one's innate wisdom, and the *Diamond Sutra* is just a representation of this. From this perspective, each and every Buddha has issued from this sutra.

The Buddha's Dharma Is Not Buddha Dharma

"Subhuti, the so-called Buddha Dharma is not Buddha Dharma." If you look at this sutra, sometimes you're really not sure what is going on. First, there is an example of someone who achieves incredible fortune by an act of charity. As if this was not good enough, next, we have the Dharma in all its splendor, merits far surpassing those of a mere act of charity. Now, just when you think you've got things straight, the Buddha hits us with Buddha Dharma is not Buddha Dharma.

Just what is Buddha Dharma, enlightenment? There is no Buddha Dharma, nothing which can be held up as a Buddha Dharma. Mind you, this "nothing" is not a nihilist view nor a materialist one. If someone tells you that he or she is the living

Buddha, go right ahead and hit this person. This person is actually a wayward spirit and not a Buddha. Anyone who truly has great accomplishment is so humble and modest that he or she seems unbelievably ordinary, as though he or she has nothing at all. A Buddha doesn't think himself to be a Buddha, just as a sage doesn't think himself to be a sage. Likewise, the Buddha Dharma is not Dharma. There is no Dharma which the Buddha has attained. This is what makes the *Diamond Sutra* special. Great prajna sutras which talk about the highest wisdom leave no traces; everything expounded gets overturned. If one has taught a lot of students who've gone on to become very successful and one thinks one is indeed the teacher of the century, one has in fact become an antique and should be retired to make room for the new. One who is really great doesn't have the perception of himself or herself as god's gift to the world. He or she just does what he or she ought to do and moves on. If you have an idea of the Buddha Dharma in mind, you're grasping onto form. This is putting it nicely. To put it in stronger terms, you're grasping onto a wayward spirit.

Many people don't understand this manner of expression, especially Confucian scholars. For instance, the great Confucian scholar of the Ch'ing Dynasty Ku Ting-lin in his famous book *The Record of Daily Knowledge (Jih-chih-lu)* recommended that ordinary students should not read the Buddhist sutras. Ku said there was nothing of value to be gleaned from these. He likened the contents to pouring water back and forth between two buckets.

The Buddha Dharma is not the Buddha Dharma... Isn't this like pouring something back and forth? Nothing to it really.

The eighth section clarifies an important point in Buddhism: real merit and fortune are the accomplishment of great wisdom. The title, *"Born of Following the Dharma,"* means that following and according with the Buddha Dharma is the inception of each and every saint and sage. This section leads into a discussion of another big question in the next section. First, we will look at the gatha.

Gatha of Section Eight

Brilliant or rusted, divine or earthly, all are a grand game of chess.
Futile empyrean fortune leads one to ignorance.
Buddhism is nothing more than this whit after all.
Disentangle, unbind, release and escape, but who has?

"Brilliant or rusted, divine or earthly, all are a grand game of chess." In the world, the greatest fortune is that of being an emperor or king. I think that everyone has desired this at some moment in his life. If you study history and really take a look at their lives, you'll realize that these monarchs are actually most pitiable. The Emperor Kang-hsi of the Ch'ing Dynasty himself said, "My suffering is so extraordinary." So brilliant or rusted, divine or

earthly, mountains or rivers, in the light of history are like chess. You win a game, you lose a game and time goes on.

"Futile empyrean fortune leads one to ignorance." When Bodhidharma had his first audience with Emperor Liang Wu-ti, the emperor asked him: Master, I have built so many temples and given so much charity to the sangha, what kind of merit will I receive? Bodhidharma answered, "Naught but the small fortune of a heavenly being, as the cause has a leak." In saying this Bodhidharma was scolding the emperor: Where's your head? You've studied Buddhism for so long, do you still think what you've done is so great? The small fortune of a heavenly being only. After you die, you'll go up to the heavenly realms, but when this fortune has run out, you'll come back down. It's only limited fortune, not unlimited fortune without any leaks. Fortune without any leaks remains perfect forever. *"Futile empyrean fortune leads one to ignorance."* If one is born into royalty, power, money, fame and so forth as a result of prior merit, one's worldly fortune is enviable, but one's wisdom will decline.

There is a story in Ch'an Buddhism about Master Kuei-shan. Kuei-shan was the founder of the Kuei Yang Sect, one of the five major schools in China. Master Kuei-shan had been an emperor for three lives and as a result had lost virtually all of his power of wisdom. He decided not to continue on like this for fear that he would completely lose all enlightened wisdom. If one practices Buddhism and at the same time desires worldly fortune, one must be careful of the danger of actually getting what one wishes. Of course, it is not an absolute danger but it does exist. This is why I've said that futile empyrean fortune leads one to ignorance.

"Buddhism is nothing more than this whit after all." This is Ch'an talk. When Master Lin-chi had his awakening, he said, "Oh, so true Buddhism is nothing more than this whit after all." In modern terms, *whit* means "speck." Buddhism really isn't much more than this little speck.

"Disentangle, unbind, release and escape, but who has?" What is the purpose, the motive of Buddhism? To release and untangle oneself. We are completely enmeshed in our worldly sufferings and desires. If we wish to be liberated from the desire, frustration and misconceptions of the three realms, all that binds and entangles us, how is it to be done? How can we wash ourselves clean of this sticky glue and return to our original pure nature? This is where Buddhism ultimately leads one. All of the teachings in the twelve sections of the Tripitaka are simply to serve this purpose, to unbind us, to untangle us and to lead us to ultimate liberation. But who really understands? This is the essence of Buddhism.

SECTION 9

ONE FORM, NO FORM

"Subhuti, what do you think? Can a srotapanna have the thought, 'I have attained the realization of a srotapanna'?"
Subhuti replied, "No, World-Honored One. Why is this? The reason is that while srotapanna *means "entering the stream," actually one does not enter into form, sound, smell, taste, touch or dharma. Therefore, one is called a srotapanna."*
"Subhuti, what do you think? Can a sakridagamin have the thought 'I have obtained the realization fruit of a sakridagamin'?"
Subhuti replied, "No, World-Honored One. The reason being that while sakridagamin *means "only once more to come," actually one neither comes nor goes and therefore, one is called a sakridagamin."*
"Subhuti, what do you think? Can an anagamin have the thought, 'I have attained the realization of an anagamin'?"
Subhuti replied, "No, World-Honored One. The reason is that while anagamin *means "no returning," actually there is no such thing as no-returning. Therefore, one is called an anagamin."*
"Subhuti, what do you think? Can an arhat have the thought, 'I have the realization of an arhat'?"

Subhuti said, "No, World-Honored One. Why? Because there is no dharma called arhat. World-Honored One, if an arhat has the thought, 'I have attained the realization of an arhat', he would still be grasping onto notions of self, person, being, and life. World-Honored One, although the Buddha says that I have attained the samadhi of no dispute, am foremost amongst men and am the leading arhat who has left desire, I do not have the thought 'I have attained the realization of an arhat'. If I had the thought 'I have attained the realization of an arhat', the World-Honored One would not have said that Subhuti takes delight in calm and quiet abiding. The fact that Subhuti does not stir mentally is called the calm and quiet in which Subhuti delights."

We all know that Buddhism is divided into Mahayana and Hinayana, but strictly speaking, the Hinayana can also be divided into two parts. The three are called Mahayana, Hinayana, and Sravakayana—the large, medium and small vehicles. A practitioner of the initial Hinayana stage is called a Sravaka, or a hearer; whereas, the second stage is called solitary achiever, or Pratyekabuddha. Among the disciples, Ananda and Subhuti, for instance, were only sravakas. Those a step higher were solitary achievers, or Pratyekabuddhas. If a solitary achiever were born at a time when there was no Buddha, no culture, not even Buddhism, he could awaken of his own accord. It wouldn't be a great awakening, but the person would be a sage among ordinary mortals. This is the stage of a solitary achiever, or nirvana, and is within the Hinayana.

The main objective of the Hinayana is to save oneself, leave the mundane world and avoid having to return. There are form fruits of the Hinayana cultivation, not apples and oranges mind you. Those at the preliminary level are called a srotapanna, at the second level they are called sakridagamin, at the third level an anagamin and at the fourth level an arhat. Arhats are not necessarily ordained clergy. Both laity and clergy who achieve a certain level can become an arhat, but in fact during the Buddha's time, the larger percentage of arhats were monks or nuns.

How does one achieve these four stages? By breaking through the "entanglements of perspective" and the "entanglements of mental states." There are five entanglements of perspective which have to do with problems of one's ideas, ways of thinking and understanding. The five are the perspective of a body, perspective of parameters, ideology-grasping perspective, heterodox perspective and rule-grasping perspective. Many religious people, philosophers and academicians get caught in the entanglements of perspective. The perspective of the body is thinking that this body is actually ours to keep. The truth of the matter is that it is made of the four elements and we merely have "user's rights" for a few decades. The perspective of parameters is having borders or limitations. This includes any of our ideas, states, or alambanas. Even experiencing a state of emptiness is limited to the bounds of "an experience" and is considered entanglement within the perspective of parameters. If a person through his or her own experience and/or reasoning process comes up with his or her own philosophy or ideology about something, whether it be how to run a business, how to run the country or what the nature of Tao is, and will not listen to anyone else's ideas on the matter, this is entanglement in an ideology-grasping perspective.

Heterodox perspective and rule-grasping perspective for the most part have to do with religion. Heterodox perspective is grasping onto a wrong idea, one which does not correspond to reality, as being true, for example, the Doomsday cults. These people go to the top of a hill on such and such a day to meet their maker because they are convinced the earth is supposed to be destroyed on this day. As for rule grasping, you'll see many people who say things like, if they don't go to temple on the first and fifteenth of each lunar month, they've committed a sin. Some religions have strict rules about what one can and can't eat. This also falls into the entanglement of rule-grasping perspective.

Disentangling oneself from these five perspectives depends on being able to let go of and change one's view of things. It can happen instantaneously. The entanglements of mental states, however, are much more difficult. Of these, there are also five: greed, anger, ignorance, pride and doubt. Such is the character of man. These are what we bring into this life, our habit energies which take a lot of time and effort to break.

What is greed? The desire for fame, power, love, etc. of which we cannot let go. We all have desire for things of this world. I'll give you a story from the Ch'an sect to illustrate. There was a monk who had done a lifetime of meritorious deeds—building temples, expounding the Dharmas and the sutras, and so forth. However, he had neglected his own cultivation, his own meditation practice. He was getting quite old, and one day he saw two small spirits coming toward him. They were holding the notice from Yama and some handcuffs. The master said to them, "Let's make a deal, okay? I've been a monk my whole life and have performed many meritorious acts, but I haven't done any personal cultivation. If you give me seven days, I will succeed and you two will be the first ones I liberate. After that, I will liberate your boss, Yama."

The two thought it was a good risk, and so they consented to the deal. This monk, because of his great merit, sat down and the myriad of thoughts came immediately to rest. There was nothing worth dwelling on, and so, in three days, he had achieved the state of no ego, personality, being, or life, only light. When the spirits returned, they saw only light, no monk. "Damn! He cheated us!" They called out to him, "Great master, have some compassion. You should be true to your word! You said you'd save us. Don't let us go down and spend time in the hells on your behalf!"

The master had entered a deep samadhi and didn't hear them. The two turned to each other, desperate for a plan. In the light, there was a tiny speck of black shadow. When they noticed this, they were overjoyed. There's a way! This monk still has one iota which is not in accord with the Dharma, one bit of ignorance.

This monk had performed so many great works that the emperor had proclaimed him to be one of the nation's masters. For this status, he received a gift of a golden begging bowl and a gold-threaded monk's robe from the emperor personally. The master didn't care about any material things really, but he did like this bowl. He even cradled it while he was meditating. He had let go of everything completely—except this. The two spirits changed themselves into mice and started to chew on the bowl—crunch, crunch, crunch .... The monk's thoughts moved, the light disappeared, the master reappeared and in a flash the cuffs were on him. He was quite surprised but even more so couldn't believe that he hadn't achieved Tao. The little spirits ran the whole story by him. The monk smashed the bowl on the ground and said, "I'm going with you to see Yama." The two little spirits both awakened right then and there.

This story is just to illustrate the difficulty of getting rid of desire. Similarly, a friend once came to see me and chat. He said that he didn't want anything anymore and was now living in a small cabin in the hills, and oh, what a lovely cabin with refreshing breezes and a bright moon at night... I told him that he was quite extraordinary, almost a saint, but that he must beware of the mice, for being attached to a cabin is still attachment. Real cultivation is here at this place and not at opening the channels and chakras, or glowing in the dark. Those are not Tao. The Tao is at each moment of mind. To have all these different mental states at each moment is called entanglement in mental states. One's constant thinking, dwelling, musing, mulling over and mental espousing are huge knots which must be untied. Those who make up the intelligentsia all like to read books, and this is all the same attachment and desire. Don't fool yourself into thinking that this isn't a form of desire. Desire is at the root of our being, and its expressions are multifarious. Some people fool themselves, thinking they don't have desire—they're old enough, that they don't need fame or fortune. Do you believe this? If these were handed to them on a platter, of course they would take them!

Who has no anger? Who has no ignorance, pride and doubt? Anger, the mind of anger, thoughts of anger are things many people deny having. Hating people, killing people and having a terrible rage are all anger. Strict ideas of right and wrong are also anger. If you can't stand for things to get dirty, this is also a level of anger. Be careful not to brag that you don't get angry at all. A thought of anger is anger. You may practice repeating the Buddha's name or meditating, but no matter how well you do these, if you don't disentangle yourself from these mental states at all, don't kid yourself about practicing Buddhism. This is where the real Buddhist practice is done. It doesn't matter which sect you are—pureland, Ch'an , Esoteric, whatever—you still must break through these entanglements of mental states.

Ignorance, what's to say! Every one of us is ignorant and torpid. I have two good friends, a couple, whom I've known for about twenty-odd years, both of whom have been studying Buddhism with me. I was saying once to the wife that the time was ripe for them. The kids have all earned their degrees, are married and living abroad... Still, I said, when the grandchildren start coming, life will get very busy once again. She said, "No way! Absolutely not! We plan to completely devote ourselves to Buddhist practice." What happens? The grandchildren are born, they feel bored at home and so they bring the grandchildren to have some fun or go there to enjoy them. In effect, nothing has changed. This is, in fact, your average case because ignorance comes in many, many forms. Ignorance, greed and anger, commonly known as the three poisons, prevent us from attaining the Tao, prevent us from being able to rise above being an ordinary mortal.

As to pride or self-admiration, upon careful introspection, everyone will discover that the one person he or she admires most is himself or herself. Because of this, deep down inside people don't really trust anyone else. Even religious people have this doubt within them. As one bows down, there is a thought floating around saying, "I can only hope this will help." There is virtually no one who has absolute trust in another.

The five mental states—greed, anger, ignorance, pride and doubt—are the most basic, the roots of all mental entanglements which obscure the Tao. We practice Buddhism in order to gain liberation. If one can liberate oneself from even one of these, it is incredible, but it is only when we are liberated from all five that we have achieved the state of a first-level arhat. The four stages of a Hinayana arhat are quite important in Buddhism. Hinayana is the basis for Mahayana. If one has not achieved even the small vehicle, one shouldn't expect a big vehicle.

They're Called "Once Returners"

The first step of an arhat is the level called srotapanna, which means "the fruit of a stream winner." At this point, one has cut through the five entanglements of perspective, but is not yet liberated from the entanglements of mental states. The leftover mental habits are yet to be cut. One needs to return seven times to the human world before this can be accomplished. But if during these seven lives, one doesn't make an effort in their cultivation, they can still regress. Those who have achieved the fruit of a stream winner after each death will go up to one of the heavens to be reborn before returning to the human realm. They will live one life in the heavenly realm in which the life span is much longer than ours. After this, they are again reborn in the human realm and are now called "returners." Of course, upon return, you don't know if they'll be male or female, good-looking or not, rich or poor. One never knows. Not even a computer could assess all the variables. Each person has to settle his or her own accounts. Seven lives, life and then death, death and then life.

In society, there are many people at this stage, and amongst those sitting here as well, but they just don't realize it. They don't even realize if and when they've paid off all seven lives. If they know, they're not at the first level of a srotapanna anymore. They've leapt ahead to a higher level.

Is It All Right to Not Return?

At the second level, a sakridagamin, or "Once Returner," the root of entanglements of mental states has been pulled out a little. After death, those on the second level need to return once more to the world to completely clean up the loose ends and then they can go on to a more clean and pure place. Please note that this is only temporary. It's not a final resting place.

The third level, anagamin, is called the stage of "No Returner." They can achieve the fourth stage in the heavenly realm and directly enter nirvana. In the sutras, it says, *"When my life comes to an end, if the Buddhist ways have been established and all that must be done is finished, I need not endure another life."* If the Buddhist ways have been established, if one has worked diligently at their cultivation practice throughout one's life, it does not necessarily mean that one has attained Tao, but one has at least well established the clean and pure alambana of the heavenly beings. *"All that must be done is finished,"* when one has paid off the debts of sentiment, has worked off these karmic debts and has broken even, one won't need to endure another life. They don't need to return. Other sutras put it this way, *"Take a long bow to this world."* As you go, make a bow to this human world, "Goodbye, everyone! I won't be back!" This is what's called the fruit of a No Returner, the third level before the stage of arhat.

Many students who practice Buddhism say life is such suffering that they wish to achieve the fruit of the practice in this lifetime and not return. More easily said than done. One needs to achieve the third stage of an arhat before one can make a bow to the world. Furthermore, one needs to get to the fourth stage, arhatship, before one has really succeeded at cultivation in this realm. *Arhat* is a transliteration, the meaning of which is "forever without birth, suffering or obstacles." One's mind free of darkness is endless, pure, calm light. This is the fruit of the arhat stage. These four stages of an arhat cover the heavens of all three realms.

The Heavenly Beings of the Three Realms

A srotapanna and a sakridagamin go up to the heavens after death, not to the heaven of the Form Realm, but to those of the Desire Realm. In traditional Chinese culture, we talk about there being thirty-three heavens. This is actually only the number of those heavens in the Desire Realm's main center. This main center is located within our solar system. The Desire Realm is defined by the continuance of life through the union of man and woman. Not only human beings but all the various life forms in this realm come to be through a union of two different genders. Because there is love and desire, it is called the Desire Realm. The heavenly beings of the Desire Realm are of a higher level than humans. In old

Chinese tradition, people make offerings to the protector gods and different deities. These protector gods and deities are often Bodhisattvas of the Desire Realm heavens. A srotapanna and a sakridagamin both go to these heavens because they still have some desire. They have actually only managed to press/hold down their desire. It needs to be completely uprooted. I encourage the students who like to write novels to write stories about marriage in the different realms. In our world, a man and a woman marry. The woman conceives and gives birth to the child through the lower end. In the heavens of the Desire Realm, it's not the women, but the men who give birth, from their shoulder.

You can tell from their manner that certain people have come from the heavenly realm. The things that give them pleasure are different from those that give pleasure to the average person. Also there is nothing which they strongly desire. They enjoy planting flowers, hiking in the mountains, these kinds of things. As for worldly pursuits, they take only a mild interest. It is only because they still have a little bit of debt they must pay off that they return, but indeed they are very refined.

It is not until the third level, anagamin, that one will ascend to the Form Realm but only to the lowest heavenly level of the Form Realm. The highest heaven of the Form Realm is called Akanisthah heaven. In some sutras, it is called the "Cap of the Heavens." It is also said that if one dropped a fifty-kilo rock from this heaven it would take 120,000,000,000 years to reach this earth. The heavens of the Desire Realm are all still within this Milky Way.

Even above this is the level of the Formless Realm. This is only accessible to great arhats, whose level is much higher than regular arhats. Subhuti, Ananda and Mahakasyapa, for example, were great arhats. Even Shakyamuni Buddha could also be called a great arhat in a strict interpretation; however, His "great" is far beyond those arhats just mentioned. *This* stage of arhat is very, very difficult to achieve.

Our earliest ancestors didn't come into being due to a trick with an apple, nor did they evolve from bacteria. They were beings from the Abhasvarah (light and sound) heaven of the Form Realm who came down to this earth. They were probably doing deep-space exploration. Their bodies were made of light, and they didn't need to eat food. They could fly around of their own accord. Once they were on this earth, they tasted the earth's flavor, which I think was salt, not apples, and liked it. After eating more of it, they became heavy and couldn't fly away. This is the start of human life during this period on this planet. The pre-Ice Age beings are another story. The beings of the Abhasvarah heaven themselves had originally come from the Formless Realm. And those of the Formless Realm? The Buddha said this is not to be told because it will fall into theorizing on the origin of the first being. These questions comprise a huge topic which is all found within the sutras. There are plenty of such scientific and philosophical topics discussed in the sutras. Now we've finished the talk on matching the four stages of arhats with the three realms. Let's return to the topic of being a civilized human being. If one wants to be free of desire, anger, ignorance, pride and doubt and become clear, balanced, compassionate and loving toward all beings, then one must rid oneself of the entanglements of both perspectives and mental states.

Releasing the Knots and Breaking the Entanglements

Another classification of the entanglements of perspective and mental states is the eighty-eight knots of the Consciousness Only school. Beings of the Desire Realm have the most knots. These knots are like eighty-eight warts, all growing in a big gnarled bunch. If you can rid yourself of one or two, it is quite incredible. Your face will be full of luster. If you can undo four or five, even your hair will also become lustrous. True cultivation is undoing these knots, changing one's behavior all the way down to one's mental behavior. Doing this will allow one's wisdom to shine forth. To stop the mental states and perceptions which have misled one is the only way to become liberated. Whether one be Hinayana or Mahayana, there are five steps to follow: vinaya, samadhi, wisdom, liberation and liberation from perspectives.

Vinaya are the different vows which practitioners may take. Why do we need to follow the vinaya? To prevent these mental knots, or warts, from making a connection with the outside world. The outside isn't allowed in, and what's inside isn't allowed out. There is not the desire for these to go out. This takes a lot of strength and perseverance, so one must cultivate samadhi.

Meditation is but one method only to develop samadhi. One needs to cultivate samadhi in every moment, plant the mind firmly in virtue. Even if one accomplishes the four dhyanas, this is still just like laying a stone down to prevent the grass from growing. The grass will still grow out the sides. At this point, the eighty-eight knots have yet to move. Eventually, one's practice of vinaya and samadhi will result in one's wisdom opening; then the knots start to loosen. When these have opened completely, one is liberated from the entanglement of mental states.

One's perception is something different. The perception of wisdom, to perceive the nature of fundamental emptiness from which all phenomena arise is only one side. The other side is that of emptiness. The fundamental nature of all phenomenal arising is emptiness. Buddhists from different sects have opinions like, Madhyamika is the right way or some other thing is the right way. This is getting caught in the entanglement of ideology grasping, the subjective view that only such and such is correct.

One must liberate oneself from these entanglements as the real practice of Buddhism. We've spent a lot of time and effort on introducing these concepts and will finish this here. Now we will go back to the sutra and look at the actual text.

Beginning-Level Arhats

"Subhuti, what do you think? Can a srotapanna have the thought, 'I have attained the realization of a Srotapanna'?"

Subhuti replied, "No, World-Honored One."

The Buddha again asks Subhuti, what's your idea on this, can a Srotapanna have that thought? Can one who has attained the fruit of a beginning-level arhat have the idea in his or her mind that he or she has already attained the level of a srotapanna? It's like asking if one who is awakened to the Tao would go around trying to impress people saying he or she was an enlightened master. If someone were to go around saying these things, it'd be strange if no one committed that person to a mental hospital.

Think about the scenario of someone who is an intellectual walking around with a sign saying, "I'm an intellectual!" Utter madness! The Chinese have an old saying, *"True intellectuals are of a harmonious spirit."* If even an intellectual is of a harmonious spirit, how much more so would a beginning-level arhat be? And so, Subhuti's answer was "No, of course not."

"Why is this? The reason is that while srotapanna *means "entering the stream," actually one does not enter into form, sound, smell, taste, touch or dharma. Therefore, one is called a srotapanna."*

A srotapanna is one who enters the stream, but what stream? The stream of sages. One has made it onto the "sage team." Another way to look at it is that the Tao to which one has awakened is the flow of the Dharma nature. The Dharma nature is

255

not the narrow, ignorant, crude nature of man, rather it is the opposite side of this nature. This person has extracted himself or herself from the average person's lust, unrestrained emotions, love and desire, and entered into the calm purity of the Dharma. How is it that one can reach this state of beginning the arhat path? It's already been said. The basic principle is that in entering the stream, there is in fact, no entering. In other words, this person understands emptiness, no arising, the fundamental nature of arising being empty. In this fundamental emptiness, each moment is the alambana of emptiness.

This is the reason it says one does not enter form. One looks without seeing. People, images, mountains and rivers may look very beautiful, but it doesn't matter. Most people see something nice and get attached; the mind knots around it. A srotapanna can appreciate such, but doesn't get carried away by these things. The mind remains very mild and calm, not entering sound, smell, taste, touch or dharma. What kind of state is this? This is the state of not dwelling, truly not dwelling. In dealing with different people and situations, in working for the benefit of others, one does not dwell on anything. Nothing is kept in the heart. Even if one has performed thousands of virtuous deeds, what's gone is gone. To be like this at all times, whether or not one is meditating is the state of the srotapanna.

One of the younger students earlier on asked me if her situation was considered entering the stream. She said that she would often just "space out" and was still sort of aware of everything around her but not engaged with any of it. This is not quite the state of not entering form, sound, smell, taste, touch and dharma. Still, don't take this to be ordinary spacing out. There is something more to this than that. It is a phase she is going through as a result of her meditative work. If this is mistaken as the fruit of entering the stream, this is incorrect. Some people go through phases where food has no flavor. Is it that the person has lost all taste distinction? No, the person knows, but the experience of flavor is of a much lesser degree than usual. These phases are usually short-lived. It's like a blind cat finding a dead mouse—the cat just happens upon it. Not only are we this way, even for some arhats it is difficult not to enter form, sound, smell, taste, touch and dharma. In the *Vimalakirti-Nirdesa Sutra*, Kasyapa and some other Arhats show this to be so.

Kasyapa Dances and Pilindavatsa Has Pride

The Venerable Kasyapa was well-known for his high level of samadhi. Before he became a monk, Kasyapa was married, and he and his wife were partners in spiritual cultivation. Theirs was like a fake marriage as both were so totally committed to spiritual cultivation that they never consummated the marriage. After Kasyapa found the Buddha and became a monk, he went back for his wife and she became ordained as well. Even with all his discipline, while in meditation one day, he could hear celestial music and unconsciously (from a deep habit of loving and desiring the sound of music) started tapping and rocking in time with it. In essence, he was sitting there dancing.

Why did this happen? The *Vimalakirti-Nirdesa Sutra* calls it "remaining subtle habits not yet broken." In that sutra, celestial goddesses threw flowers down upon the arhats and Bodhisattvas who were visiting Vimalakirti at his home. The flowers stuck to the arhats and, no matter how they shook or brushed, wouldn't fall off. Not even one, however, stuck to any of the Bodhisattvas. Upasaka Vimalakirti explained that although the arhats have cut the eighty-eight knots, the remaining subtle habits have not yet been broken. It's the still remaining subtle roots of these habits which have not been broken. Even the arhats are like this, not to mention us ordinary folk.

There is another example from amongst the Buddha's disciples. Pilindavatsa was an arhat with great super powers. Still, he was always plagued with serious asthma throughout his life. In one sutra the story of Pilindavatsa crossing a river is told. This particular river was under the jurisdiction of a female dragon deity. Pilindavatsa wanted to get across, so he said a few mantras and called out to the river deity from the shore saying, "Daasi! Part these waters. I want to cross." Knowing she was no match for him, she could do nothing but part the waters to let him cross.

Afterward, this female dragon went and told the Buddha about this incident saying that not only did this "so-called" arhat with a big temper force her hand with his super powers, but on top of that, called her a derogatory name. The Buddha called

Pilindavatsa over and scolded him. "Using super powers to cross a river is against the vinaya. Next time hire a boat or swim. And, not only did you break this rule, but you were very rude to boot." Pilindavatsa exclaimed that he had been falsely accused. He turned to the deity for support, "Daasi, you tell him. Was I ever rude to you?" The deity said, "You see, you see, even in front of you, he's still referring to me as a slave girl!" The Buddha turned to her and explained, "Try to understand. This is not unusual for him. He's been a Brahman for 500 lives and is so used to using derogatory names that they are no longer derogatory to him. This habit has not yet been broken, and as a result, he has to live with terrible asthma. In his mind, he's not being derogatory." Pilindavatsa piped in, "I really didn't mean to hurt you, Daasi. Please don't feel so bad." It's like people who are used to being sarcastic. They will apologize if they've hurt your feelings, but with a little sarcasm still added.

One who has reached the level of a srotapanna is not free from being affected by the six senses and the six phenomena. One has entered the stream, but the stream of consciousness has not yet been emptied. It's like putting down a stone to stop the grass from growing. When the conditions are right, it will still grow out again. There are many examples of people, Su Tung-p'o for example, who were great cultivators in their last life but have completely forgotten everything upon their return.

From the Ming Dynasty, there is an historically recorded story about the famous Wang Yang-ming. He went to a temple in

Jiangxi and noticed a room which had been locked up for a long, long time by the looks of it. The monks told him that the room could not be opened. Wang Yang-ming was then suspicious that the monks of the temple were concealing something bad. He was a man of considerable power and authority and so ordered them to open the door immediately. Upon entering, all he found was the dried up corpse of an old monk sitting there. Around his neck was tied a cloth with words which read, "Fifty years before I was Wang Yang-ming; the one who opens the door is the same one who closed it before." Wang Yang-ming stood there in shock. He had no idea he had achieved such a high state. He never spoke of this event again during his life.

What does this all mean? This is all talking about the knots within us. As we said earlier, one who reaches the first stage of arhat still must return seven times. During these seven times, who knows what kind of lives one will lead! In Sichuan, there was an old couple that everyone knew about, just incredible. When I was young, I really envied them and would say that they must be part of some celestial family living here amongst us. They had a house up in the mountains, a happy couple with lots of kids. The two of them studied and practiced together from the *Lankavatara Sutra* . The wife had extrasensory perception of the eyes. I asked her if she knew what their karma was to be together. She said that in her last life she had been a lama who had accepted many offerings from a devotee. Instead of working hard on cultivation in that life, she developed the desire to eat and drink good things. So in this life, she became the wife of the then devotee to serve and take care of him in return. She could even tell me which temple, which lama, all the details. In this life, she worked hard on cultivation and really grasped the heart of it. She was able to see clearly this karma. In my opinion, these are all "returners" through whom we can understand the fruit of a srotapanna.

I've told lots of stories, but I don't want everyone to diverge into the stories. These so-called stories are not stories! Now, back to the sutra.

What Do Second- and Third-Level Arhats Do?

"Subhuti what do you think? Can a sakridagamin have the thought, 'I have obtained the realization fruit of a sakridagamin'?"

Subhuti replied, "No, World-Honored One. The reason being that while sakridagamin *means "only once more to come," actually one neither comes nor goes and therefore, one is called a sakridagamin."*

The Buddha asked Subhuti the same question concerning a sakridagamin. Second-level arhats have only to return once more to the human realm. In name, it is called returning one more time, but it's the same as not returning. Just what does this mean? There are many people who come to the threshold of life and death having paid off all their debts. Sometimes, they'll enter into a womb and just live briefly in the fetus stage. The woman experiences a miscarriage and the last return to human life is finished. This is really true even though it sounds as though there can be no evidence of this. Other times, they'll be born and will have a very good relationship with their parents, but do not live very long. The karma is finished. Parents should be happy for the child. She is a realized being. She owed you a little bit of love, and you owed her some tears. It's that simple, finished. This is the second stage of arhatship.

> *"Subhuti, what do you think? Can an anagamin have the thought 'I have attained the realization of an Anagamin'?"* *Subhuti replied," No, World-Honored One. The reason is that while an* anagamin *means "no returning," actually there is no such thing as no-returning. Therefore, one is called an anagamin."*

The third stage of arhat, anagamin, is a very high stage. It's not necessarily the case, however, that one does not return to the world. At this stage, one is beyond the question of life and death and has no fear of "coming." The only thing is that at this stage there is still the possibility that one may forget everything during the process of going through birth. Those above this stage will not have this happen.

In these recent years, I haven't gone running around the way I did in mainland China during my youth. At that time, I'd go looking for interesting things, and I heard many stories. For example, I met someone in Sichuan who was a famous writer and academician. He told me that he could remember three of his former lives. This is not something that he goes around bragging about, either. A lot of times the person knows their level but does not say anything, is even clear enough to come and go as s/he pleases, knows where s/he has come from. Yet, sometimes there is still the possibility of forgetting. Some are clear going into the womb, but forget while they are a fetus, and others don't forget until the moment of birth. Each case is different for it's all a matter of one's power of samadhi. The third stage of arhat is that of no returning, but actually there is no such thing as no-returning because one is more or less free within the cycle of coming and going.

Preliminary Ground of an Arhat

> "Subhuti, what do you think? Can an arhat have this thought, 'I have the realization of an arhat'?"
> Subhuti said, "No, World-Honored One. Why? Because there is no dharma called Arhat."

When we spoke of the level of anagamin, the stage of no-returning, we saw that in fact it's not the case that they do not return. The same goes for the level of the fourth stage, arhat. Great arhats can go into samadhi for 84,000 great aeons, a great aeon being the time that it takes for the earth to come into being, exist, be destroyed and then come into being once again. It's not easy for an arhat to come out of samadhi, but when he finally does, then what? Return here to cultivate the Mahayana prajna wisdom so that he can be truly liberated, become a Buddha.

Hinayana is the preparatory ground for Mahayana. One must first accomplish the stage of sravaka before the stage of Mahayana can be completed. There is no cut-and-dried method, path, or Dharma which is the stage of arhat nor any Dharma of emptiness. If you have a state of emptiness, you are stuck in an incorrect perspective. If you say that you have no perspective, then this is the entanglement of ideology grasping. It's still an incorrect perspective. True emptiness has no state which can be experienced. A lot of students here are sitting quite well during their meditation and feel that they have experienced a "state of emptiness." You must absolutely not grasp onto a "state of emptiness." It's actually only an area just a little bit bigger than your body. If not emptiness, it's just a hole, a tiny state due to an incorrect perspective. Why do our experiences of emptiness have boundaries, why do they fall into incorrect perspectives? It's because our power of mind and wisdom is still finite and thus gives rise to limited understanding based on one's perspective. The *Diamond Prajna Paramita Sutra* has no limits, no boundaries; it is infinite. In the next part, Subhuti summarizes:

"World-Honored One, if an arhat has the thought, "I have attained the realization of an Arhat', he would still be grasping onto notions of self person, being and life."

According to Subhuti, one who has reached the stage of arhat has not even a wisp of a thought that he or she is of a certain level of realization. If this thought is present, then the myriad of thoughts are also present, for this one though is connected to all the other thoughts. In the *Avatamsaka Sutra*, it talks about Indra's net (*Indra-jala*) where our ideas, thoughts, feelings and emotions are part of an enormous net, and when one part of the net moves, the rest of it will move as well. The karmic force of our cultivation, the force of our mind in one thought movement will affect all the rest of our thoughts. To say that it is phenomena, it is phenomena. To say that it is empty, it is empty. This is the gist of it.

If a great arhat feels that she has the realization and is in the state of being an arhat, then she is grasping onto the four notions of self person, being, and life. Such a person is just an ordinary trickster. If a person had ten thousand dollars, would he walk down the street telling people this? Think about it; it is just ordinary logic. Need we even speak of the case of one who is an awakened being?

Next, Subhuti gives his own report.

Number One in the World

"World-Honored One, although the Buddha says that I have attained the samadhi of no dispute, am foremost amongst men and am the leading arhat who has left desire..."

The Buddha said that Subhuti had already attained the samadhi of no dispute. If you insult him, criticize him or even yell at him, it doesn't phase Subhuti in the least. It's not that he doesn't hear you. On the contrary, it's just that his mind remains calm and even. He doesn't get happy and excited nor does he get sad and upset. Right and wrong are two sides of the same coin. All is without dispute.

The next line is very important. The Buddha said that Subhuti was "foremost amongst men." He's still a human amongst humans but his knowledge, civility and morality are of the highest level. Therefore, the Buddha said he was foremost amongst men. Thirdly, it was said that Subhuti was the "leading Arhat who last left desire". At that time, the Buddha elevated Subhuti to just having risen above the level of the Desire Realm. He had not yet liberated himself from the three realms. In the book *Journey to the West*, Subhuti was portrayed as one who had very high attainment. That was just a novel. In the *Diamond Sutra*, he is only at the level of an arhat who has left desire, is without desire only. The desire referred to is the larger meaning of *desire,* not just that which is limited to male-female love. It includes all kinds of desire, even the desire for meditation, purity, calmness and the cultivation of Tao. Subhuti had emptied himself of all desire and so was called the leading arhat who has left desire.

"I do not have the thought, 'I have attained the realization of an arhat'. If I had the thought, 'I have attained the realization of an Arhat..."

Subhuti said, even though the Buddha has given me such a rating, I, myself have absolutely no such idea in my head. I do not think that I am the foremost amongst men, and even more so I do not think that I have attained the realization of an arhat.

"World Honored One would not have said that Subhuti takes delight in calm and quiet abiding (Aranyak - literally, one who lives in a forest hermitage*). The fact that Subhuti does not stir mentally is called the calm and quiet in which Subhuti delights."*

So, what is being said? Suppose the Buddha gave me such a rating —having the realization of an arhat who has left desire, being foremost amongst men and fellow monks—I myself would have not even the least little idea or feeling of such. If I had even the slightest notion of this floating around in my mind, He would not say that I enjoy abiding in calm and quiet. This calm and quiet is the deep peace and calm within a person, usually someone who likes to live in the mountains. Just naturally there is a temple created. Where is this temple found? In one's own heart and mind. It's just like the lines of the poem mentioned earlier:

Vulture peak is at the seat of one's own heart.
Each and all have the stupa of Rajagriha.
It's just a matter of getting to the bottom
Of Vulture Peak stupa to observe.

There is a temple within our minds and hearts, a calm peaceful place. Where outside can one find peace and calm if it is not in one's mind and heart? This section explains the four stages of an arhat's realization. What is the main focus of the *Diamond Sutra*? Not dwelling. If one has ideas in one's mind of obtaining different realizations, this is dwelling. It is wrong.

Gatha of Section Nine

The four steps of realization are all mental constructions.
Another moment of mind, still no peace.
A toddler's tears stop as a yellow leaf wafts to the ground.
Empty-fisted pretending, this one's bigger and this one's smaller.

"*The four steps of realization are all mental constructions.*" There are four stages, or fruits, in the development of an arhat. There are ten grounds, or bhumis, along the path of a Mahayana Bodhisattva. Upon what are these distinctions based? Actually, it is all a question of one's perspective, the range and depth of one's perspective. The moment of mind is also of great importance. So, to answer the question, they are all based upon mental constructions.

"Another moment of mind, still no peace." If this moment of mind is calm and peaceful, the myriad phenomena are empty. However, in a lifetime of practicing Buddhism, for one to remain this way in each present moment is the most difficult thing. Due to our states of desire, anger, ignorance, pride and doubt, as well as the tendency to seize upon these, the present moment is not unusually peaceful. In the face of this, most of our Buddhist practice has been in vain.

"A toddler's tears stop as a yellow leaf wafts to the ground." There is a story that goes with this from the *Avatamsaka Sutra*. In the *Diamond Sutra* the teaching is that one shouldn't grasp any Buddha Dharma; if one grasps a Dharma as the Buddha Dharma, one is not a true practitioner. In the *Avatamsaka Sutra*, it is explained in another manner. The Buddha said that his Dharma was like pretending a yellow leaf is a gold treasure to stop a toddler from crying. If a toddler is crying how can you make him stop? Grab something nearby, like a yellow leaf and coax him into laughing, "Look, look what I've got! Gold treasure! Wow!" Use whatever is available, a leaf, a feather, whatever, to trick the child out of crying and you've succeeded. The Buddha said that the Dharma he taught was the same thing, pointing to a leaf and calling it gold treasure to stop a toddler from crying. All of the

Dharma and the methods are like this. Once the mind comes to rest, the leaf is not needed.

The old Ch'an masters used to say, "The Buddha taught all kinds of Dharma to appease each state of mind. I haven't these states. Why use all that Dharma?" That is the level of a Buddha. Zen, Vipassana, reciting the Buddha's name, reciting mantras, skeleton visualization... It doesn't matter if you visualize white bones or pink ones. If the white doesn't work, try the pink. The Buddha taught all kinds of dharma to appease each state of mind. I have naught these states, why use all that Dharma. This is really what the *Diamond Sutra* is saying. The Buddha has told you very clearly, and yet you still go seeking more methods. You travel to other countries because that's where it's really at. Of course it is! This is because you have all states of mind. You need to find all kinds of Dharma.

"Empty-fisted pretending, this one's bigger and this one's smaller." The Buddha said that the Dharma he taught was like using one's empty fist to coax a child out of crying. One pretends to have something in one's hand and trades it for the imaginary thing in the child's hand. The hands are empty, but this can appease a child. One can say this one's big and this one's small; this one is Hinayana and this one is Mahayana. We're all children in essence. We want superpowers, E.S.P., prajna wisdom, great enlightenment but there's really nothing to all this.

There are two stories which the Fifth Patriarch, Hung-Jen, used to tell in order to explain the rationale behind Buddhist cultivation. The first story is about a thief. I'm sure that many of you have heard this before, but I'm going to tell it again. There was a man who was a master thief. His son had come of age and wished to learn his father's skill. The father didn't want him to learn this, but his son was so persistent that he finally agreed to take him along one night. They went to the house of someone who was very well-off and very quietly snuck into one of the rooms. There was a large closet which was locked. The father got the lock open, and then told the son to climb in and get the things. As soon as the son stepped in, the father closed the door and snapped the lock back on. The father jumped out the window and cried out loudly, "Thief, thief!!" And then ran off.

The family and servants woke up and lit candles to look around. Finding no evidence of a thief, they were going back to bed. Inside the closet, the son was scared that they would either open it and find him or that he would die locked in the closet. Thinking quickly, he started to make noises like rats. The servant heard this and said, "Mistress, there's no thief, but rats got into the closet!" The mistress gave her the key and the servant unlocked the door. The thief's son jumped out of the closet, blew out the servant's candle and ran away.

Upon returning home, he found his father asleep. He yelled to wake his father and asked why he had done such a thing to his own son. The father said, "You're out, aren't you? Congratulations! You're now a thief. There's no special method for becoming a thief. All a thief needs to do is get out and he's succeeded." This is the first story told by the Fifth Patriarch to his disciples to help them understand that there is no set method by which one becomes a Buddha.   The next story talks about there being Hinayana, Mahayana and the *Diamond Sutra*.

There was a convict who was sentenced to life imprisonment. After being inside for a while, he wished to escape, and so he discussed the matter with some of the other prisoners.   Among these was a thief who, after their talk, started to dig a hole.   Each day he'd dig a little until one day he did succeed in escaping.   The other convict, however, felt this was not the way to go.   He made friends with the guards.   Eventually, they shared food with him, joked around together and confided in him.   No one was worried that he would try to escape.   During a big holiday, the man's family brought him lots of good meats and wines, which he of course shared with the guards.   He cheered them until they were dead drunk and fell asleep.   Then the man took the keys from one of the guards, unlocked his cell, exchanged his clothes for a guard's and walked out in uniform, saluting the guards at the front door.

The Fifth Patriarch explained that the Hinayana was like the thief who expended all that energy digging a tunnel to escape gloriously.   Once out, he was still a fugitive in convict's clothing. He was then perhaps even more pitiful than when he was in jail. Practicing Mahayana is like the other man sentenced to life in prison.   This world is the prison, and one must become friends with the other convicts, the guard and Yama in order to successfully escape.   This is what practicing Buddhism is all about, escaping from the prison of the three realms. Be it with the aid of mantra, prostrations, visualizations, whatever method works for you—if you can get yourself out, you've succeeded. There is no set method called the Buddha's Dharma.

SECTION 10

MAJESTIC BUDDHA PURELANDS

The Buddha then said to Subhuti, " What do you think? When the Tathagata in the remote past was with Dipankara Buddha, did he gain anything from the Dharma?"

"No, World-Honored One. When the Tathagata was with Dipankara Buddha, He did not gain anything whatsoever."

"What do you think, Subhuti? Do Bodhisattvas establish majestic Buddha lands?"

"No, World-Honored One, they do not. Why is this? Majestic Buddha lands are not majestic but are called majestic."

"This is why, Subhuti, Bodhisattvas and Mahasattvas should develop a clear, pure mind which does not dwell in form, sound, smell, taste, touch or dharma. They should develop a mind which does not dwell anywhere.

"Subhuti, suppose a man has a body as large as Mount Sumeru. What do you think? Would not his body be considered great?

Subhuti replied, "Very great, World-Honored One. Why is this? That which the Buddha says is not a body is called a great body."

Returning to an Empty Mind, One Passes

Before I start commenting on the text, I would like to say something about "establishing majestic Buddha purelands." This is actually the pureland of prajna wisdom. The pureland of the Buddha does not just refer to the Western Paradise of Amitabha. "Establishing majestic Buddha purelands" is "not a thought arises, the whole body reveals itself." In other words, the pure mind, the empty mind is the true pureland.

This reminds me of a couplet written by Ch'an Master Tan-hsia of the T'ang Dynasty. Master Tan-hsia and his contemporary Lu Ch'un-yang both went to take the civil examinations, but on the way there, Tan-hsia took another route. Along this route, he met somebody who asked him why someone with his ambition and talent was going to take the civil examination. Tan-hsia replied that he might as well try. The person kept asking him, "And then what?" until Tan-hsia's answer as to his future possibilities was as high as one could go in terms of worldly achievement. This person asked yet again, "And then what?" Finally, the question hit Tan-hsia. The person then said to him, "Go to Jiangxi and take Ma-tsu's test. You might become a Buddha. It's better than power and fame." Thus, Tan-hsia went to go find Ch'an Master Ma-tsu. This story is told in Tan-hsia's *koans*.

In Tan-hsia's Ch'an hall there hung a couplet which read, *"This is the hall of the Buddha examination; returning to an empty mind, one passes"*. Our Ch'an hall is also an exam hall; it is the hall of Buddha examinations. An empty mind is a pureland. If one can remain empty in the moment, one passes; returning to an empty mind, one passes. Ultimately, practicing Buddhism is simply to remain empty in the moment. This is the real, true pureland. This is why in the sutras it says, *"The pure mind is the pureland."* The pureland is everywhere; the Western Paradise is everywhere as long as the mind is pure. Thus, Prince Chao-ming titled this section "Majestic Buddha purelands."

"The Buddha then said to Subhuti; What do you think? When the Tathagata in the remote past was with Dipankara Buddha, did he gain anything from the Dharma?"

At this time, the Buddha is talking about His own experience: At the time I was with Dipankara Buddha, did I obtain any Dharma? The time He is talking about is not the previous life, but rather many, many lives ago. Dipankara Buddha was the first teacher to predict Shakyamuni's coming enlightenment. Dipankara Buddha is a very ancient Buddha from the time before this earth even came into being. At the time of this prediction, did Shakyamuni obtain anything?

> *"No, World-Honored One. When the Tathagata was with Dipankara Buddha, He did not gain anything whatsoever."*

Subhuti said, "Negative! According to my understanding, when you were with Dipankara Buddha, the alambana in which you were was one of truly understanding no gain and emptiness.

Emptiness so empty that there wasn't any gain or no-gain nor even a state of emptiness." Subhuti answered up to here. The Buddha didn't say anything more about this; instead, he asked Subhuti another question.

Where Are the Majestic Buddha Lands?

> *"What do you think, Subhuti? Do Bodhisattvas establish majestic Buddha lands?"*
> *" No, World-Honored One, they do not."*

The Buddha said, "Let me ask you. Do you think that Bodhisattvas actually have another world, a heaven, a beautiful majestic land out there?" I think someone should compile a book comparing the descriptions of heaven in different cultures and religions. Usually, they are very much a reflection of the culture in the style of clothing, the architecture and so forth. What does heaven or a Buddha pureland actually look like, though? One can describe it any way one wishes because none of us has been there. The picture that we have in our mind is different for each person. People who like gold imagine it full of gold; those who like natural beauty imagine spectacular nature scenes, snow-peaked mountains with Buddhas. Oh! How lovely! It's all a matter of one's preferences.

In the *Surangama Sutra* it says, *"In accord with each one's mind and karma, understanding has different sizes and appearance varies. So could there then be a fixed direction?"* Actually, the parameters of knowledge, philosophy and religion are all a function of the limitations of one's own mind. Your heaven, your Buddha land has its own size in accord with your understanding and mind's capacity. *"Appearance varies"*—within a group of people who practice Buddhism and meditation together, a few might see Buddhas. Each one sees a slightly different version. One has a higher nose; the other a flatter one. Why does this happen? Each person has a different karmic state or filter within his or her mind's eye. *"So could there then be a fixed direction?"* There is no fixed direction, no fixed location of mind. It is completely just a product of our consciousness.

The Buddha asks, "Do Bodhisattvas establish majestic Buddha lands?" Subhuti denies the existence of majestic Buddha worlds.

"Why is this? Majestic Buddha lands are not majestic but are called majestic."

The *Diamond Sutra* often uses this type of argument. The so-called "majestic Buddha lands" is just a descriptive phrase. *"Not majestic"* means it's not the kind of majesty that we usually imagine. For instance, most people would think of a place which is really pristine. Close your eyes for a moment and whatever you think of, even if it is a big empty space, is but that which we can imagine. An imagined state is already not majestic. Absolute purity and emptiness are not that which we have the capacity to imagine. Real majesty is beyond imagination. So, in this process of reasoning, there is the obverse, the reverse and then a combining, or middle ground. That which we experience, describe or imagine as emptiness is already not empty. Without experiencing the actual majesty of the Buddha lands, there is no way possible for the ordinary mind to conceive of it. This is the meaning behind Subhuti's answer.

Cigarette Lighter

"This is why, Subhuti, Bodhisattvas and Mahasattvas should develop a clear, pure mind which does not dwell in form, sound, smell, taste, touch or dharma. They should develop a mind which does not dwell anywhere."

Take special notice! Here again the Buddha is teaching us how to practice, the method of cultivation. This is a second-rate method. First-rate has no words, and so no one understands. Second-rate methods have words: one should not dwell. What exactly is not dwelling? One should at all times give rise to a clear, pure mind. If, for instance, a student comes up and says, "Teacher, the past two days of practice have been really good. My mind has been so pure and clear." All of you have been listening to the *Diamond Sutra* teachings and know the score. Having this experience of a pure and clean mind still has the parameters of understanding, very limited parameters.

Now the Buddha explains what this clear, pure mind is: not dwelling in form, sound, smell, taste, touch or dharma—a mind which does not dwell. The Sixth Patriarch, Hui-neng, upon hearing the line, *"Develop a mind which does not dwell"*, had his great awakening. Our mind originally has no dwelling place; it's simply that we don't recognize this. Not dwelling is of course emptiness. To have an alambana of emptiness is not right because this is still a form of dwelling. It is developing a mind dwelling in emptiness. A truly clear, pure mind has no state of "light." There is no particular state, no dwelling in form, sound, smell, taste, touch or dharma. The Buddha said that real cultivation was not dwelling. Developing a mind that at all times, in all places, does not dwell. Just that simple! *"What is meant to come, will. When gone, naught remains."* These two familiar lines can be used to sort of describe the state of a mind free of phenomena. The mind is like a bright mirror—whatever comes is reflected in it. Nothing remains after its use. Many years ago, a friend of mine shared with me his latest understanding from his Buddhist practice. At the time, cigarette lighters had just come out. If someone asked him what the Buddha was, he would pull out the lighter, snap it on and then off. "When you use it, it's there. When you don't, it's not."

Blinded by the Teacher

"Subhuti, suppose a man had a body as large as Mount Sumeru. What do you think? Would not his body be considered great?"

Subhuti replied," Very great, World-Honored One. Why is this? That which the Buddha says is not a body is called a great body."

"Suppose a man had a body as large as Mount Sumeru." This Mount Sumeru is referring to the dharmakaya, to the achievement of developing a mind which does not dwell, which is the preliminary stage of experiencing the dharmakaya. The dharmakaya is neither beginning nor ending, pure nor impure, increasing nor decreasing. The dharmakaya is called the great body, the body without borders. The Buddha said that we need to achieve a mind which does not dwell anywhere. This dharmakaya is the majestic pureland of the Buddha. Describing this body as the size of Mount Sumeru, the size of the Himalayas with a stomach as big as the Kunlun Mountains is just a descriptive comparison. Actually, it is infinitely large without beginning or end.

Subhuti wraps up with the Buddha's words that it is not a body and thus is called a great body. If one can break the false perception of body, the first of the eighty-eight knots which bind us, if we can totally empty this out, then we will catch an

281

experience of that which is beyond birth and death, the dharmakaya.

The dharmakaya body beyond birth and death is described by Confucianists as, "Buddhism can only be experienced." You must have the experience for yourself ,and then you'll know that the Dharma is indescribable. Whatever words one uses to talk about it are not it. The first step in awakening to the Tao talked about in Ch'an is the experience of the empty nature of the dharmakaya. It is only then that one can be liberated from the perception of one's physical form. It is only then that it can be said that one is practicing Ch'an.

These two days the quiz question has been, what is Ch'an ? The answers given are all just a little off. Ch'an is the heart of Buddhism. In the *Lankavatara Sutra* and the *Diamond Sutra*, the Buddha spoke very clearly, but nobody notices. People throw around the term "practicing Zen," but their basic understanding is not clear. If one's basic understanding is off, all the rest will be off as well and one will go down the wrong path of practice. One should not practice blindly, nor play around irresponsibly. There is an old Ch'an saying, *"Originally, my eyes were clear, but I was blinded by the teacher."* This is a saying by an enlightened master. An earlier teacher had misguided him, but he realized later on that he himself had actually been clear on things. It was as though his teacher had blinded him. Those crazy teachers, like me, will often lead the students astray. So everyone must be careful!

Gatha of Section Ten

Letting go of "me," there is no body but the great body.
If you dwell in the pureland you remain in the dust.
Dipankara bid the establishment of a majestic Buddha land.
Where can be found antelopes hanging by their horns in trees?

"*Letting go of "me," there is no body but the great body.*"
Outside of me "there is no body" is taken from one of Lao-tzu's
phrases, "*past the body, that behind the body is formed.*" In
practicing Buddhism and cultivating the Tao, we must first get rid
of our perceptions of our bodies. "*Letting go of "me," there is no
body,*" is the achievement of breaking the perception of body. The
first step is taken and has a little experience of the dharmakaya,
which is the great body.

"*If you dwell in the pureland, you remain in the dust.*" If in
your mind, there is a pureland and you believe it to be the state of
Buddhahood, this clean purity you experience is still "red dust." It
is still an obstacle.

"*Dipankara bid the establishment of a majestic Buddha land.*"
The Buddha told us that when he was with Dipankara Buddha,
Dipankara verified his awakening and said that after returning
many times to continue his cultivation, he would eventually
become a Buddha called Shakyamuni and establish Buddhism in
this world. This awakening is the majestic Buddha land, and so
Dipankara bid the establishment of a majestic Buddha land. It

283

could also be called the pureland, the pure mind, the mind seal... There is no actual state. If there were, or rather if he dwelled in a pureland, he would remain in the dust.

Just like the Ch'an masters of old used to say, *"Where can be found antelopes hanging by their horns in trees?"* It is said that at night when clever antelopes want to go to sleep, they leap up and grab onto a tree branch with their horns. They sleep peacefully hanging from the tree while below hunters search for them to no avail. Thus, we should develop a mind which does not dwell anywhere. Our minds are originally like the hanging antelopes. In the two hours, the one hundred and twenty minutes of time that we devote to the *Diamond Sutra*, all that you hear is but antelopes hanging in trees.

The present moment is the pureland.

SECTION 11

THE FORTUNE OF EASE SURPASSES

"Subhuti, if there were as many Ganges Rivers as there are grains of sand in the Ganges, would all of their grains of sand be many?"

"Very many, World-Honored One! Even the Ganges Rivers would be innumerable, how much more so their grains of sand.

"Subhuti, I tell you truly. If a good man or woman bestowed in charity the seven treasures sufficient to fill a number of galaxies, as many as the number of grains of sand in all these rivers, do you think his or her merit would be great?"

Subhuti replied, "Exceedingly great, World-Honored One."

The Buddha then said to Subhuti, "If a good man or woman receives and retains even one stanza of this sutra and teaches it to others, his or her merit would be even greater."

Today we're up to the eleventh section, "The Fortune of Ease Surpasses." Although this title was a later addition to the sutra, still it really captures the main point. "The Fortune of Ease" is a kind of clear fortune. "Fortune of ease surpasses" is saying that clean, clear fortune far surpasses any of the mundane fortune of wealth, power, fame etc. In the last section, it talked about the great body, that which is the essence of life which is behind this physical body. It is our original body, the dharmakaya, which is beyond birth and death. Everyone wishes to find this origin of existence, that which is beyond birth and death, but in order to do this, one needs incredible fortune or merit. The merit one needs is that which comes effortlessly. Therefore, this question is discussed in this section. The *Diamond Sutra* is an account of a conversation, a dialogue between the Buddha and Subhuti.

> *"Subhuti, if there were as many Ganges Rivers as there are grains of sand in the Ganges, would all of their grains of sand be many?"*
>
> *"Very many, World-Honored One. Even the Ganges Rivers would be innumerable, how much more so their grains of sand."*

The Ganges is one of the major rivers in India, like the Yellow River in China. The Buddha put forth a word problem. The first part was about the number of grains of sand in the Ganges, these being uncountable. The second part of this equation is then to have as many big rivers as there are sand grains in the Ganges. Now comes the gist of the question: would the number of grains of sand in all these rivers be great? What do you think? Subhuti said, "World-Honored One, of course the number is great! Even the Ganges Rivers would be innumerable, how much more so their grains of sand!

In this world alone, each country has its own great rivers. India has the Ganges, China has the Yellow River, America the Mississippi and so forth. There are so many rivers just on this planet alone. The question put forth by the Buddha has two ideas behind it. The first is the idea of universal size. In this universe of three thousand great-thousand worlds, how many rivers might there be? The Buddha has no way to tell us because our minds lack the capacity to conceive of such things. Science is just starting to be able to verify things the Buddha taught. The second idea behind it was to give us a feeling for what is infinite. Even the Ganges Rivers would be innumerable, how much more so their grains of sand.

> *"Subhuti, I tell you truly. If a good man or woman bestowed in charity the seven treasures sufficient to fill a number of galaxies as many as the number of grains of sand in all these rivers, do you think his or her merit would be great?"*

This builds on the previous question. The Buddha first states that the following things he will say are not fabricated but are absolutely truthful. The Buddha then prefaces his statement with this question: Suppose there is a man or a woman in this world who has as much of the seven treasures as would fill as many galaxies as the number of grains of sand in all these rivers. And suppose this man or woman gives away all that in charity, helping every living being in existence. Would such a generous person gain great merit by doing so? Would they gain great fortune?

"Subhuti replied, "Exceedingly great, World-Honored One."

Of course, a person having done such a wonderful deed would gain incredible huge fortune.

Receiving and Retaining One Stanza

"The Buddha then said to Subhuti, "If a good man or woman receives and retains even one stanza of this sutra and teaches it to others, his or her merit would be even greater."

This is a pretty serious statement! It is talking about someone who receives and retains, one who completely understands the teaching of the *Diamond Sutra*. "To receive" means that from one's own experience, one understands the meaning of the *Diamond Sutra*. Not a mere intellectual understanding but rather one's whole being understands and goes through a physical and mental transformation because of this understanding. Still, unless one can retain this state, it doesn't make the grade. There are people who recite the *Diamond Sutra* by memory every day, still just glossing over these two words. They could also be called receiving and retaining but only at a very ordinary level because once they are finished reciting, they don't give it a second thought.

Deeply understanding the teaching is like eating vegetables. Once our body has absorbed the nutrients, it has no need for the cellulose. The Buddha himself said in the sutra that the Dharma was like a raft used to cross a river. Once across, you don't need the raft any longer. So if one deeply understands the teaching within, it doesn't matter whether or not one recites the sutra.

Furthermore, it need not even be the entire sutra that one receives and retains. All that's needed is a four-line stanza from the sutra. If one can truly receive and retain even just a stanza and then teach and explain this to others, one's merit and fortune will surpass that of the person who gave away all of that treasure. This is quite incredible! One who teaches the *Diamond Sutra* has merit and fortune so big that it can't even be contained within this universe. It's not the earthly red fortune but rather clean, clear, pure, effortless fortune.

Concerning the four-line stanza, we had mentioned earlier that this has been a question of debate for thousands of years among those who study the *Diamond Sutra*. Within the sutra there are many groups of four lines which could be taken as a stanza. I will throw something out for you young people to consider, but what I suggest may not be right. You must use your own prajna wisdom to verify things. The Buddha himself said that his words don't count. They are like a medical prescription for an illness. If you still hold tightly onto this prescription once you are cured, this has now become a mental illness.

In Ch'an Buddhism, you often will see or hear this, *"avoid the four positions and cut off hundreds of unfounded illusions"* This is the way to research Buddhism. Throw everything away. Everything is wrong. There are four sentences, or concepts, which are within the *Diamond Sutra* and not within the *Diamond Sutra*, these being: emptiness, existence, both empty and existent and neither empty nor existent. All worldly things are of a dialectic nature: obverse and converse; both obverse and converse, and neither obverse nor converse. So to "avoid the four positions and cut off hundreds of unfounded illusions" is to really receive and retain the essential meaning of the *Diamond Sutra*. This is also the central meaning of the four-sentences stanza.

This section is talking about the fortune of ease, which is also the fruit of Buddhist practice. In Chinese we call it "ease"; in Sanskrit, it is called nirvana. They mean the same thing, the unsurpassable achievement. From this we can see that all of us sitting here meditating and doing our practice are actually at the other end of the stick. Everyone is working hard to make sure that meditative achievements don't fade, scared that the wondrous mental states will leave and grasping on tightly to any passing feeling of calm and peace. Some people sit in meditation with their eyes open, staring at the ground. When I was young, I would go up and ask if they were looking for something. They would answer, "No," and I'd say, "Well, why do you keep staring at the floor like that?" Most people are in a state of un-ease. If a person can retain a state of ease, this is the alambana of one who has achieved the Tao.

Sufficient Amounts

How is it that one can actually achieve the Tao? First one must reach a state in which one's behavior is virtuous through and through. When one's fortune and merit are complete, one will naturally reach the state of Tao. This has important parts to it—a sufficient amount of wisdom and a sufficient amount of fortune and merit. Reading and studying the sutras, such as the *Diamond Sutra*, are ways of building up wisdom. Not engaging in even the slightest evil and working for the benefit of all beings are building up fortune and merit. If either is lacking, one will not reach the highest achievement.

There is a great difficulty in that our world is one of imperfect existence. There is not one being who experiences a perfect life. If they did, they've actually died and gone somewhere else! The Buddha calls this world Sahaloka, meaning enduring the imperfection. Tseng Kuo-fan deeply understood this, and in his library hung some calligraphy which read, "Seeking imperfection is admirable". If one is too fulfilled, if life is too perfect, it can be kind of frightening. We need a glitch now and then. Because this world is imperfect, some people will have great affluence but no wisdom, and some people with great wisdom will have no worldly means. One may have money but no free time; one is blessed in one area while another is lacking. If you wish to have it all, you must become a Buddha, but a Buddha has no desire for this worldly fortune. He has the fortune of ease!

Gatha of Section Eleven

> *Ten thousand bushels of pearls to challenge a rich man's house.*
> *Over the rivers and mountains, three is no sovereign as high as the moon*
> *The three thousand world Sahaloka is an ocean of tears.*
> *Past the eyelashes of the King of Emptiness, all is pure.*

"Ten thousand bushels of pearls to challenge a rich man's house." This first line uses a story from Chinese history from the Wei-Chin Dynasty of the Northern and Southern Epoch. There was an extremely wealthy man named Shih Ch'ung who managed to so impress the beautiful Lu Ju with his gifts that she became his wife. Another man, who was a wealthy official, wanted Lu Ju for himself. He challenged Shih Ch'ung to compare their wealth, which was such that they could use pecks and bushels to measure their riches and jewels. Shi Chong was not about to give up Lu Ju. This other man later rose to higher office and was able to have Shih Ch'ung executed on false charges. He decreed that Lu Ju was now his wife

but she loved Shi Chong so much that she committed suicide rather than give herself to the official.

"Over the rivers and mountains, there is no sovereign as high as the moon." Looking back through history, all the emperors and kings with their incredible wealth have one by one passed away. In this world of mountains and rivers, who can stand as supreme ruler? One generation after another leaves this world, but for thousands of years the moon has been there. Today it is here; tomorrow it will still be here. It was here during the T'ang Dynasty as well as the Han, and it could care less about what's shaking the world. Thus, the wealth and power of the emperors are but a passing spring dream.

"The three thousand world Sahaloka is an ocean of tears." People in this world still pay homage to wealth and power. They strive for it from the time they come into this world until they leave it, and even at the moment of death won't let go. The Sahaloka world's affairs are full of tears, full of pain, suffering and ignorance. Always Crying Bodhisattva continually weeps for the pitiful sentient beings. The Sahaloka is an ocean of tears.

"Past the eyelashes of the King of Emptiness, all is pure." The King of Emptiness is Shakyamuni Buddha. One who is a Buddha is also called the King of Emptiness. Raising his eyelids, the King of Emptiness sees all as empty. When he closes them, ten thousand years of history pass by in that moment. All the splendor and fortune are but dust blowing past. If one wishes to have such attainment as the Buddha, one needs fortune and merit beyond

the greatest worldly fortune. Only then can one understand the meaning of the *Diamond Sutra*, only with the culmination of wisdom can one become a Buddha.

Now as far as we can understand, the fortune and merit spoken of in this section are the real fortune and merit, they being wisdom. Great wisdom is the greatest fortune one can have, but the fortune of wisdom is not worth a penny. The Buddha always says that sentient beings are all upside down. The most important things in life, like wisdom, are viewed as insignificant. Take rice and other grains, for example. If it weren't for these, people couldn't live. They are in open fields everywhere, part of the roadside scenery. Money, on the other hand, in and of itself is a useless thing. However, it gets bundled, then banded, then stacked, then metal-boxed, then locked in a safe and finally a guard with a gun is stationed outside to protect it from thieves. The rice is just out there in the fields. No one gives this a second thought. Sentient beings are all upside down, and we could go into many more examples of this. Wisdom is like the rice in the fields—no one notices or pays attention to it. Secondly, the most common things, the most ordinary teachings hold the highest wisdom. The Dharma of which the *Diamond Sutra* speaks is in life's most ordinary things, the central teaching being on prajna wisdom, and the Buddha encourages us to experience it for ourselves. Experience which kind of prajna wisdom? The true form of prajna, the essence of wisdom and the Tao—this is the most important wisdom and is also the fortune of ease.

SECTION 12

THE PLACE WHERE ONE PUTS THE DIAMOND SUTRA

"Furthermore, Subhuti, you should know that wheresoever this teaching or even one of its stanzas is kept, that place will be held in reverence by all beings including gods, devas and asuras as if it were the Buddha's sacred temple or stupa."

"How much more so if someone is able to receive, retain, read and write the entire discourse throughout. Subhuti, be assured that such a person will achieve the highest and most precious Dharma. Wheresoever this teaching is kept, the Buddha and his respected disciples will be there also."

"Furthermore, Subhuti, you should know that wheresoever this teaching or even one of its stanzas is kept, that place will be held in reverence by all beings including gods, devas and asuras as if it were the Buddha's sacred temple or stupa."

The Buddha is giving a directive, and we need to pay special attention. He said, Subhuti, I once again wish to impress upon you just how powerful is even a stanza from the *Diamond Sutra*. You ought to understand that wherever you might place a copy of this sutra or even one of its stanzas, that place is considered Buddha's

295

stupa or temple. Whether it be celestial beings from any realm, spirits, Immortals, asuras, etc., all must bow down and prostrate to show reverence. He said this sutra or even one of its stanzas represents a Buddha's stupa or temple—this is pretty serious! Even so, ten years ago I had occasion to buy some fried dough and some sesame bread which were wrapped in pages of the *Diamond Sutra*! At that moment, the *Diamond Sutra* wasn't a stupa or a temple; rather, it was a fried-dough wrapper.

> *"How much more so if someone is able to receive, retain, read and write the entire discourse throughout. Subhuti, be assured that such a person will achieve the highest and most precious Dharma. Wheresoever this teaching is kept, the Buddha and his respected disciples will be there also."*

This sutra or even a stanza of it put wherever is equivalent to the Buddha's being there. Boy, this *is* serious! Of course, the devas, immortals, spirits, etc. must prostrate. This is not even speaking of the case where one is studying the sutra, understands it, puts it into practice, keeps it always in mind or maintains the alambana of a Buddha. Even if one recites the sutra or just a section of it each day, the merit gained is just enormous, and the power of this is incredible. If one has copies of the sutra printed, there is merit as well. In the old days, people would hand write sutras, and some monks have even written out sutras with their own blood. This is done for the purpose of showing reverence more than for making a copy for people to use. Especially since the blood will turn a light coffee color on white paper, which itself yellows, it's not very clear for reading.

When I was young, I took refuge with a great master named Pu-ch'in. He wrote out the entire *Avatamsaka Sutra*, eighty volumes mind you, in his own blood, which took him three years to complete. The *Avatamsaka Sutra* is eighty volumes, mind you! The *Diamond Sutra* is only one volume, so you can understand the magnitude of this undertaking. Master Pu-ch'in also had only eight fingers because two were burned as offerings. To do this, you wrap your finger in cloth, then soak it in oil and light it. You then hold up your hand in an offering position without moving or making a peep while it burns, your face shouldn't even turn red. Later on, the master let me in on the secret of writing with blood. If you just squeeze it out into the ink tray and dip the calligraphy brush in it to write, it congeals too fast to write very much. You must add "Bletilla striata" (*Bai Ji*), a kind of Chinese medicine, to the blood as well as a little bit of ink in order for it to be used more efficiently. In the old days, everything was done by hand, and so there was great merit in writing out a sutra. Nowadays, we can make use of the printing presses.

Where Is the *Diamond Sutra* Found?

The Buddha told Subhuti that people who can exalt in the *Diamond Sutra*, study it and make it available to others have already sealed their success. They are foremost in this world and have achieved the most precious Dharma. They themselves are rare and precious amongst men. In Sichuan and Hubei provinces, there is a local term for the occasion of a rare visit from a faraway friend, "precious guest." and that is how we understand this term.

We were just saying that having a copy of the *Diamond Sutra* in your home is almost the same as having the Buddha there, and not only the Buddha but also his disciples—Subhuti, Sariputra, Mahakasyapa, Mahamaudgalyayana and so forth. Quite incredible, but then in the next breath, I told you about how people had used pages of the *Diamond Sutra* to wrap fried dough and sesame bread. Another incident I haven't told you yet happened when I managed to get the book *The Record of Pointing to the Moon* first printed. A Mr. Hsiao and some other friends helped in the endeavor, but it wasn't selling very well and we owed a lot of money. So one of them went to the Butcher's Association and sold the last 30 copies to them. Upon hearing this, I just knew what they would do with it and asked him to get back as many copies as possible. He got a few copies back, but the other twenty-something were used to wrap meat. Anything can happen; even the Buddhist sutras can be used to wrap pork chops! This is a modern *koan*!

Think how many copies of the *Diamond Sutra* are around now. Many households in Taiwan have one—so just think, all these stupas, temples and Buddhas. You all must take note, however, you absolutely must not let the *words* of the sutra fool you! Does this sutra (this ink and paper) actually have that much power? I'll tell you a story. There was a scholar in China a long time ago who said that the *I-Ching* (*Book of Changes*) could repel ghosts. Because of this, a young scholar of more recent time took a copy with him when he went to live out in the woods while he studied. He put the copy under his pillow at night because he was deathly afraid of ghosts. One night, he heard a ghost wailing and took his *I-Ching* in his hand and waved it about. The more he waved it, the louder the wailing became. He spent the entire night waving the *I-Ching* in complete terror. Finally, in the morning, when it became light, finding himself still alive, the scholar ran to the window to see what was out there. It was a line of rope caught in a tree which made a noise when the wind blew it around.

The *I-Ching* couldn't even subdue a rope let alone a ghost! Don't you think the same would be true of the *Diamond Sutra*? Of course it would. How then is this to be explained. You can't depend on the sutra there on your shelf. The sutra must become "yours." You must take it into the heart of your mind because this is the place where the stupa and the temple are. The Buddha never said "wherever a *printed copy* of this teaching is kept," nor was a particular place named.

We need to be reminded again of these verses which contain a real reason, *"Buddha is in the very heart of one's own mind. No need to go rashly seeking. Vulture Peak is at the seat of one's own heart. Each and all have the stupa of Rajagriha, It's just a matter of getting to the bottom of Vulture Peak Stupa to observe."* The Buddha is at Vulture Peak in Rajagriha. There really is no reason for you to go rushing to India, however. Vulture Peak is at the heart of your own mind; this is why in the *Diamond Sutra* it says you should receive and retain this teaching. This is where the Buddha is found. This mind is the Buddha. When one awakens to the great wisdom of the *Diamond Prajna Paramita Sutra*, the Buddha is therein found. This is the stupa and temple of the Buddha to which the devas, asuras and so forth will bow down and pay reverence.

Gatha of Section Twelve

> *The teacher of devas and men has words like needles and stones.*
> *With respect we realize there is nothing to doubt.*
> *Tears of deep gratitude well, but to prostrate is not enough.*
> *Drop all affairs and let your eyebrows hang down.*

The summary of this section really has nothing to it. It is merely a show of reverence and gratitude. To speak of the true Buddha Dharma, this section is the Buddha Dharma. If you wish to become enlightened, this is the important section. The basic message is simple: handle all your interpersonal relations and your daily affairs of business with respect and honor. One must first be able to honor and respect oneself before one can do so for others. In honoring and respecting others, one's self-respect and self-honor will also grow. If one's mind embodies honor and respect, one experiences the alambana of a Buddha.

This section calls us to true faith. Whether one's religious faith is Buddhist, Hindu, Christian, or any other, if one sees a stupa or temple and just very innocently makes some motion of respect without any words or thoughts, this moment is the alambana of a Buddha. With whatever thoughts come after this moment, the alambana is lost.

"The teacher of devas and men has words like needles and stones." This is what I call the celestial-and-human single-needle lifesaving treatment. Chinese medicine of old followed a code of treatment which went: press before piercing, pierce before moxibustion and moxibustion before using internal medicine. The practices of acupressure, scraping and cupping popular today all use pressure to heal. In ancient times, different stone implements were used for pressure healing, but this later developed into various practices. For a more serious problem, the doctor would pierce the skin with acupuncture needles. The third level is using moxibustion treatment. Finally, in the case of more serious or chronic illness, herbal internal medicines would be administered. It's only in recent times that Chinese medical doctors have made separate practices of these. Traditionally, Chinese doctors knew all these arts.

The Buddha is revered as the teacher of men and devas. His words are the healing needles and stones which can cure us of all our dis-ease. Any one sentence of his can awaken, enlighten and liberate us; it's just that we don't believe.

"With respect, we realize there is nothing to doubt." With true respect and faith in the Buddha's teachings, we can become enlightened. Then one realizes that the Buddha has not said anything false. There is no doubt about any of His teaching, and profound respect, reverence and gratitude will arise. *"Tears of deep gratitude well, but to prostrate is not enough."* This deep, profound gratitude will sometimes move you to tears, but at this moment to prostrate is not enough. You couldn't do enough prostrations. There is only one way to express your feelings. Let go of everything and rest at ease. *"Drop all affairs and let your eyebrows hang down."* The Bodhisattva's eyebrows droop downwards, making them look very compassionate. If you have true belief in the Buddha's words, completely drop everything and rest in the alambana of the Buddha. This is the best way to show gratitude.

SECTION 13

RECEIVE AND RETAIN IN ACCORD WITH THE DHARMA

At that time, Subhuti addressed the Buddha saying, "World-Honored One, by what name should this teaching be known and how should we receive and retain it?"

The Buddha replied, " This teaching should be known as the Diamond Prajna Paramita by which name you should receive and retain it. For this reason, Subhuti, what the Buddha calls prajna paramita is not prajna paramita but is called prajna paramita.

"What do you think, Subhuti? Has the Tathagata ever expounded a Dharma?

Subhuti replied, "World-Honored One, the Tathagata has never expounded any Dharma."

"Subhuti, what do you think? Are there many atoms of dust in the great universe of galaxies?"

Subhuti replied, "Many indeed, World-Honored One!"

"Subhuti, when the Tathagata speaks of the 'atoms of dust', they are not atoms of dust but merely called atoms of dust. Similarly, the great galaxies are not but called great galaxies.

"Subhuti, what do you think? Can the Tathagata be perceived by means of the thirty-two marks of excellence?"

"No, World-Honored One. The Tathagata cannot be perceived by the thirty-two marks of excellence. Why is this? The reason is that which the Tathagata calls the thirty-two marks are not marks but are called the thirty-two marks."

"Subhuti, if on the one hand a good man or woman for the sake of charity has sacrificed as many lives as there are grains of sand in the Ganges, and on the other hand someone has been studying and observing even one stanza of this teaching and expounding it to others, the merit of the latter will be far greater."

Now begins the *Diamond Sutra*'s discourse on the practice of cultivation. Everyone mustn't forget what was previously taught. Section one through section ten constitutes one division in which the Buddha tells us the first method of cultivation, *"one should not dwell,"* the method of not dwelling on anything. If one has actually achieved this, then one already understands prajna paramita. Before telling the next method of practice in Section 13, in Sections 11 and 12 the Buddha tells us how very important this teaching is and how one ought to respect it. Having wrapped that up, the Buddha now goes on to give us another cultivation practice.

At that time, Subhuti addressed the Buddha saying, "World-Honored One, by what name should this teaching be known, and how should we receive and retain it?"

The names of the Buddhist sutras were discussed and decided on the spot. Here Subhuti asks, for the purpose of record keeping, what the record of this teaching should be called and how those who've read it should act upon what's been taught. In other words, how should one practice it? *The Buddha replied, "This teaching should be known as the Diamond Prajna Paramita by which name you should receive and retain it."* You can call today's discourse on this sutra by the name of Diamond Prajna Paramita. Also, it is by this name you should receive and retain it. *"For this reason, Subhuti, what the Buddha calls prajna paramita is not prajna paramita but is called prajna paramita."* This familiar pattern of logic used throughout the *Diamond Sutra* is exactly what the Confucianists used to rail against. They said it was the same things poured back and forth, prajna paramita isn't prajna paramita is exactly prajna paramita, with no logical reason. The Buddha himself said the *Diamond Sutra* is truly the Supreme Dharma door of wisdom. Why is this? Subhuti, you should know that there is no specific Dharma called the Buddhist Dharma. If you say you must do prostrations or else; if you say you must eat meat as in some Tibetan traditions or else; if you say you must be vegetarian as in the Chinese orthodox school or else; if you say you must do this or that, this is having a specific dharma. It is not Buddha Dharma. Those are just methods of teaching something specific to the time and place and are not the ultimate. The Buddha here is saying loudly and clearly, do not grasp a dharma as the Buddha Dharma. Doing so is slandering the Buddha because there is no specific Buddha Dharma.

This is also saying that it is not necessarily only this format which is called Buddhism. Any other format can also be "Buddhism." Later, when you young people go out to teach others Buddhism, if you can get the meaning across, even without saying a line of Buddhism or the name Buddha, this is the Buddha dharma! Why do you need to add the word *Buddha*? That is just like a coat or a jacket which you can take off. Very early on we said that Buddhism goes beyond religion, philosophy, or any outer trappings.

The achievement of wisdom is not prajna paramita. The culmination of wisdom has no alambana of wisdom, that is real wisdom. It's as Lao-tzu said, "Great wisdom looks foolish." One who is truly wise, is actually the most ordinary. Those with the greatest capability are very common and practical. The opposite is also true that the common people are the greatest heroes. Students will always ask, then where can this great enlightened wisdom be found? I tell them, right where you are. Ordinary teachers have a "Tao" to pass on to you. "Be Careful!" This sentence is "Tao." Can you be full of care? "Mind you," this is "Tao." Can you "mind"? Don't look at things of the world as being only for the common denominator, they are diamond prajna paramita. If you can really understand one sentence, these then are the words of a sage. Who can be "full of care"? Who can "mind"? If you can, this is Tao, prajna paramita which is not prajna paramita.

Huang Shan-ku and Hui-t'ang

There is another level of meaning within *"prajna paramita is not prajna paramita but is called prajna paramita"* which needs to be brought to light. The Buddha talks about the culmination of great wisdom, prajna paramita, the wisdom which brings one to the other shore, and so everyone who studies Buddhism seeks wisdom. Prajna paramita is not prajna paramita; to achieve the Buddha's wisdom, do not seek it from without! It is not found outside of the ordinary worldly things. Worldly dharmas are Buddha dharmas; any knowledge or events which happen are all Buddha dharma. This point must be understood. You absolutely must not fool yourself into thinking that prajna paramita is a special wisdom which bursts forth upon awakening. Many people have this incorrect concept. The Buddha said clearly that prajna paramita is not prajna paramita but is called prajna paramita.

All worldly knowledge, wisdom, reflections; all worldly goings on; all places and times are fraught with the possibility of awakening you. This is why the Ch'an masters have the saying, *"Crisp green, green bamboo are all the dharmakaya. Lush, lush yellow flowers are nothing but prajna."*

Where is prajna? It's everywhere. The Chinese Ch'an sect takes the *Diamond Sutra* as its major teaching and many have awakened because of it. This, though, is not to say that they awaken during or due to reading it. People could become enlightened any time, any place. For example, one might look at the road and see the stream of cars or the hordes of people and this is prajna, one sees, understands and awakens. It is also *"crisp green, green bamboo are all the dharmakaya"*. The dharmakaya beyond birth and death is found everywhere. *"Lush, lush yellow flowers,"* is just an descriptive phrase. One could be talking about cabbage; it also is *"nothing but prajna."* It means that one could be enlightened while gazing at a flower, or become a Buddha while feeling a cool breeze.

In the Sung Dynasty, there was a poet named Huang Shan-ku whose work was on a par with Su Tung-p'o's. Huang Shan-ku was a student of the Ch'an master Hui-t'ang. Although he was very well-read and well-versed in the *Diamond Sutra*, still after three years of diligent practice, he hadn't even a shadow of awakening. He went to beg the master for a more convenient method which would bring better results, just like all the students today who wish to be given a secret method. Hui-t'ang then asked him, "Have you studied the Analects before?" To ask this question of someone of this day and age is quite acceptable but to have asked someone like Huang Shan-ku, this was an insult. Anyone with any scholarly training at that time would have memorized the Analects as a young child. Huang Shan-ku was peeved but answered, "Of course." The master quoted to him a line from the Analects, "Those of you here, have I concealed anything from you?" Those of you here refer to the core of students. Confucius said: I haven't concealed any teachings or kept any secrets. I've given you everything.

Huang Shan-ku's face turned red and then green and he told the master that he *really* didn't understand the point. The master shook out the long sleeves of his robe and left in displeasure. Huang Shan-ku's spirits were completely crushed and the only thing he could do was follow. The master silently strode up into the mountain, not looking back knowing full well Huang Shan-ku would follow. Huang Shan-ku followed along like an admonished school boy. It was autumn and the cassia flower was in bloom everywhere. The whole forest was exquisitely fragrant. The master suddenly stopped, turned and asked, "Do you smell the flowers of the Cassia trees?" Huang Shan-ku also stopped and turned his attention to his nose. "I smell them." The master then said, "Those of you here, have I concealed anything from you?" and Huang Shan-ku finally awakened. The so-called prajna paramita is not prajna paramita but is called prajna paramita. This is a very famous Ch'an story.

Huang Shan-ku and Huang-lung Ssu-hsin Wu-hsin

After his awakening, Huang Shan-ku became quite unbearable. He had a high office, high academic standing, highly acclaimed poetry and prose, nothing mediocre about him *and* he understood the Tao, understood the Buddha. He was rare and peerless among men, as was the size of his pride and ego. He felt no one other than Master Hui-t'ang was worthy of associating with. Eventually, the master passed away. Before he left this world, he passed his position on to a young monk called Huang-lung Ssu-hsin Wu-hsin, who received his dharma. The master said to him, "Your dharma brother, layman Huang Shan-ku, has had an awakening, but he's only half way there. He has not yet had a great awakening. No one can seem to get anywhere with him. I'm leaving. If you have a way to really reach him, then teach him well."

Huang-lung immediately sent word to Huang Shan-ku that the master had passed into nirvana and they would cremate the body. The master had passed away in the meditation position and was seated on the pyre in the same way. The young monk stood in front of the pyre holding the flame. Before lighting it, he was to say some words of Dharma. Just at this time, Huang Shan-ku finally arrived. He saw his master on the pyre and this—in his eyes—very young monk. Even though he was young, Huang-lung had achieved Great Awakening and Enlightenment. He was of a very high level and his grasp of the Dharma was as solid as a mountain. He took the flame he was holding and pointing it at Huang Shan-ku said, "In a moment from now, I will light the pyre. The master's body will be burned. After his body has turned to ashes, where will you and the master meet? Speak!" Huang Shan-ku couldn't answer. "Ha, you call yourself enlightened!" This was a serious question. Eventually, he too would die, and where would he meet his master?

I'm sure many of you sitting here would say, in the Western Paradise, but Huang Shan-ku wouldn't give such an answer. Forget about this. Let me ask all of you sitting here. Tonight, you will go to sleep and so will I. Where will we meet?

This time Huang Shan-ku's face turned gray. He left without saying anything. Returning home, he encountered great misfortune. Due to political unrest, the emperor removed him from his office and sent him to the hinterlands past Guizhou to man some picayune rural office. To go from a position of such prestige to this, most people couldn't stand it. Because one who was demoted was officially guilty of a crime, he had to walk to this new post like a common criminal, escorted by two guards. The guards treated him well because you never know about the emperor's favor and he might be promoted again.

We were talking earlier of the fortune of ease, well, Huang Shan-ku took the opportunity of this misfortune to practice as they made their way along the road. He would even sit and meditate when they stopped. One day, the weather was quite hot and by noontime it had become unbearable. Huang Shan-ku suggested they stop and rest for a while. Getting ready to lie down, he knocked the headrest down off the bed. In those days, they used a wooden block for a pillow so it made a loud "clap" as it hit the ground. It startled him, and at that moment, he really had an awakening. He had no desire to sleep anymore and quickly wrote a letter to Ch'an master Huang-lung Ssu-hsin Wu-hsin. Then, he had someone carry it immediately back to Lu Mountain to deliver it. The letter read: *Completely ordinary! My writings, my Tao, under the heavens there is not one who doesn't flatter me except you, Venerable One.* Finally, Huang Shan-ku sees fit to address his dharma brother in a way worthy of such a monk. He said, you were the only one who didn't praise me and I thank you for it.

Prajna paramita is not prajna paramita. Through this story we can understand another level of this. All worldly dharmas are Buddha Dharma. If you don't get bound by Buddhism when studying Buddhism, this is really practicing Buddhism. If you have this Buddhist air about you and your words are all Buddhist language as well as your thoughts, you're already a goner.

That is prajna paramita. We've gone through important explanations first and the rest you will slowly understand.

Molecules, External Form Atoms and Internal Form Atoms

"What do you think Subhuti? Has the Tathagata ever expounded a Dharma?"
Subhuti replied, "World-Honored One, the Tathagata has never expounded any Dharma."

Let me ask you once again, has the Buddha really ever expounded any Dharma? Subhuti answered right off the bat: World-Honored One, according to my understanding, you've never expounded or passed on a Dharma. Look at that—the two of them lying to each other! Shakyamuni Buddha became enlightened at age 31. At age 32, he started teaching and taught for 49 years. Now, in this conversation, they say, on the contrary, that he did not ever expound anything.

> *"Subhuti, what do you think? Are there many atoms of dust in the great universe of galaxies?"*
> *Subhuti replied, "Many indeed, World-Honored One."*

This sentence does not seem to follow the train of thought of the previous statement. Subhuti just finished saying that the Buddha never expounded a Dharma and the Buddha follows on its heels asking, "What do you think, in the great universe of galaxies, the material universe, would all of the molecules taken together add up to a lot?" Subhuti answers, "A lot, World-Honored One."

> *"Subhuti, when the Tathagata speaks of the 'atoms of dust', they are not atoms of dust but merely called atoms of dust. Similarly, the great galaxies are not but called great galaxies."*

What kind of talk is this? The Buddha said the atoms are not the atoms, and the dust is not dust but for the time being, we'll call it dust. The Buddha then said the great universe is not the great universe, but we'll call it the great universe for now. Just what is going on? No wonder the Confucianists say the *Diamond Sutra* should not be read. Prajna paramita is not prajna paramita but is called prajna paramita. The galaxies are not the galaxies. Did you expound? No, I didn't. What is going on?

"Atoms of dust" is a Buddhist term (*suksma* in Sanskrit), another name for which is "outer form atoms" (of the five *gunas* dealing with the visible, the audible, the aromatic, that having taste, and the tactile). The "outer form atoms" are what science now calls electrons, protons and neutrons. There are also "inner form atoms" (of the 6 gunas associated with mind) which are very intense. If practitioners recite the Buddha's name or mantra, or practice visualization or whatever until they reach the point of the source of the mind and body, they can mentally generate another being outside of themselves. This mentally created being can be seen by others and can function as any other person. This is the power of the "inner form atoms" being released. In this world, there are very few who really understand this kind of theory, but it is absolutely factual. To be able to actually achieve this is "causal arising is inherently empty, inherent emptiness causally arises."

Now we will further divide these atoms or outer form atoms. They can be broken down into seven parts: form or color, sound, smell, taste, touch, dharma (mental component) and emptiness. So during the past 2000 years, Buddhism has been very difficult to expound, especially these parts. Most masters in the past didn't talk about these things. Now, because of the advances of science, the language can be stretched and Buddhism can be spoken of in scientific terms to a certain point. Don't forget though, this was all spoken of by the Buddha over two thousand years ago.

If you take an atom and split it, it's empty, but in the process of splitting, it gives off light, noise, heat, force, etc. It can even kill people. The power of the atomic bomb, of the atoms splitting, for instance, is in the power of emptiness, which can alter people at a cellular level. The damage won't necessarily kill the person, but it is irreparable. The atoms themselves, made of appearance, sound, smell, taste, touch, dharma and space return to their original emptiness.

Another way of looking at this is that if you add one atom after another and keep adding, eventually these will form the great universe of galaxies. If you blow this up, blow apart all the atoms, there will be nothing but empty space left. This is because, to begin with, it was originally empty. There is no truly existent physical world nor are there atoms. Their original nature is empty. When the emptiness of the physical world, and the emptiness of prajna paramita wisdom, the mind substance, come together, this is the original source of the mind and body (mental and physical realms). It's only true emptiness when these come together. This is the emptiness of the Buddha realm, enlightenment. At that point, one's enlightenment or great awakening is on an experiential rather than a theoretical level. That experience, though, is inexpressible, absolutely inexpressible. You could go on for days but not even begin to be able to express it, which is why the Buddha said that he never expounded the Dharma. Subhuti affirmed this as well because it is absolutely inexpressible. To say something is already not it. Everything in the universe will return to emptiness so you cannot say: empty or existent, both empty and existent or neither empty nor existent.

The words of the *Diamond Sutra* read very smoothly. It's easy to understand at an intellectual level; however, deep understanding at an experiential level is not so easy. It is at this level one can be said to truly be practicing Buddhism. This said, the Buddha moves on to yet another question.

"Subhuti, what do you think? Can the Tathagata be perceived by means of the thirty-two marks of excellence?"
No, World-Honored One. The Tathagata cannot be perceived by the thirty-two marks of excellence. Why is this? The reason is that..."

Practicing Buddhism we do not grasp onto any form. This is the same as other religions saying, do not worship idols. What then is an idol? In the sutras it describes how incredible the Buddha is. Anyone who becomes a Buddha will have these thirty-two marks of excellence, thirty-two marks which differentiate a Buddha from ordinary mortals. There are also eighty wonderful qualities which come from and further describe the thirty-two marks. This is a very big question. It is a *hua tou*.

If we look at a picture of a Buddha, we will see that in between the eyebrows, there is something like a pearl. The top of the head has an extra lump. From the pearl, this lump grows a white hair, not just growing any which way, mind you, *"The fine white hair, the length of five Mt. Sumerus, curls neatly.*" All the Buddha's hairs curl to the right. If you pulled this one out, it would go something like five times the length of the Himalayas. *"His eyes are so clear and bright as the four seas."* The irises of his eyes are blue, the whites are crystal clear. The color is even more clear blue than the seas we are used to seeing. We mentioned this one before—if for three great aeons, one has not said even one false word, when one sticks out one's tongue, it will cover all the galaxies in the great universe. Image that! You can forget about hanging the clothes out to dry when that tongue goes out, it'll block the sun, the whole sky even! The Buddha's skin is smooth; each cell is perfect and gives off light.

People have asked of the Ch'an sect before saying: You people say that someone who has had a great awakening is a Buddha, so why don't we see the thirty-two marks on them? What we see is the same old hands, no long hair growing out, the teeth have fallen out and they don't grow back, the hair is white and doesn't become black, nothing changes! You say it's enlightenment but this enlightenment is unreliable.

Thinking about this later one, I realized that we all have thirty-two marks of perfection. Each has their own special marks which makes them individual. I am not you and you don't have my "marks." If you suddenly looked like me, then you wouldn't be you. Looking around, each being has their own thirty-two special marks and eighty wonderful qualities. To grasp onto this idea of thirty-two marks is still just the level of religious belief, is grasping onto form. This is why the Buddha asked Subhuti, can the Tathagata be perceived by this idea of the thirty-two marks and eighty qualities? Subhuti said no, it's not possible; you cannot see the Tathagata through the thirty-two marks.

If you see a glowing Buddha during your meditation, or in your dream last night and He told you things, you were dreaming. You absolutely must remember that you cannot perceive the Tathagata through the thirty-two marks. Are the things we see in our dreams real or false? The things we see in our dreams are real. They come from our alaya-vijnana, the eighth consciousness. They are one and the same as you, and are also real. Still you mustn't grasp them. Why is this?

"That which the Tathagata calls the thirty-two marks are not marks but are called the thirty-two marks."

I can tell you for sure that the Buddha said each person who becomes a Buddha and has achieved the culmination of all merits will have the thirty-two marks of perfection. These are not marks found in the dharmakaya. The dharmakaya has no appearance, no marks. You could say there are thirty-two marks and you could also say there are sixty-four. If you understand the meaning of the *Diamond Sutra*, then you will also understand the *I-Ching* (*The Book of Changes*). There are sixty-four hexagrams, which are sixty-four marks; the meaning is the same. In all there are 8 X 8 = 64 changes in the I-Ching. Actually, not even one hexagram needs to be thrown because a hexagram doesn't dwell; it is changing—they are all faces of change. Speaking of this, I've remembered the story of a Ch'an master. If you can understand it, you young people with wisdom might even become enlightened.

Master Chia-shan

There was a great master of the Ch'an sect called Ch'uan Tzu-cheng affectionately known by his nickname, the boat monk. He and two Dharma brothers, all of whom were enlightened, came down from their retreat in the mountains. One was going to Hunan to spread the Dharma and the other to Jiangxi. They asked the boat monk where he was going. He said to them: Brothers, I can see that the two of you will have great fortune throughout this life. You will be great masters, teachers of many. My fortune this life is one of hard work and suffering. I will just lead an ordinary life and try to create some virtue. I'd like to ask a favor of you, though. In the future, if there is someone of the highest caliber, please send them to me so that I can pass down the flame, so to speak. The master passed on his learning to me. If I don't pass it on, I will have let down not only the saints and sages of our lineage but also our master. If I can pass my Dharma on to just one person, I will be completely satisfied.

The boat monk went to a very small place in Jiangsu called Huating. There he had a small boat in which he would ferry people across the river all day long. If people gave money, he would accept a little, if not then that was all right as well.

Later on in time, one of his Dharma brothers, Brother Tao Wu heard of another monk called brother Chia-shan, who was a very learned practitioner famous for his Dharma talks. Many people would go to listen and his name was quite well-known. Brother Tao Wu, thinking of his Dharma brother Ch'uan Tzu-cheng still ferrying people across the river decided to go hear brother Chia-shan give a Dharma talk. He wore ragged clothes and appeared very quiet and unobtrusive.

Brother Tao Wu went in through the back door and sat in the back corner of the Dharma Hall to listen. Someone asked the question, "What is the dharmakaya?" Brother Chia-shan answered, "The dharmakaya has no form." Another question, "What are the Dharma eyes?" He answered, "The Dharma eyes have no blind spot." Both were very good answers. The dharmakaya has no form. This is completely in accord with the *Diamond Sutra* which says the thirty-two marks are not marks. The dharmakaya has no blind spots, for the mind is like a bright mirror, nothing unreflected, nothing not known. The answers were completely in accord with Buddhist theory.

Still, from the back corner came a snickering laugh from Brother Tao Wu, a very cold sounding laugh. Chia-shan stopped dead and came down from his seat. Throwing the end of his robe onto his shoulder, he went straight to Brother Tao Wu to show his respects. He asked, "Elder Brother, where did I go wrong in my answers?" Tao Wu said to him, "There was nothing wrong. It's just such a shame you haven't received a master's inheritance." In other words, he was saying that the theory is right, but there is no experience to back it and you ought not be speaking blindly. Chia-shan asked which great master of today would be suitable. Tao Wu said, "There are two great masters, but you have such great fame, I'm afraid you won't succeed. The only possible way is if you can let go of all of this, then I will point the way to the right one." Tao Wu really could make things happen. Imagine having someone like this for a Dharma brother.

Chia-shan actually did it—he gave up his fame and position and got ready to take to the road with just a small pack. Chia-shan could leave all this for the Tao. This just goes to prove that his enlightenment wasn't without reason. Tao Wu told him that the one he sought, *"had not a roof tile above and not a spot to hammer a stake below."* No roof, no ground, where in the world was one to seek such a person? Was he floating in the air? Actually, he was referring to one who lived on a boat. Tao Wu told him to go to Huating and about thirty *li* away on the river he would find a monk. Chia-shan went and eventually found him. What happened to him on his journey you can read about in *The Record of Pointing to the Moon.*

Chia-shan Meets the Boat Monk

The boat monk took one look at Chia-shan and knew that he had the destiny to become a great master. He also knew that it was one of his Dharma brothers who had sent him there. Chia-shan didn't mention a thing about Tao Wu nor did he introduce himself. Rather, the two then started to test each other. The boat monk asked, "At which temple does the Venerable Master reside?" The two were very well-read and so were used to expressing themselves in a very formal and elegant manner. Chia-shan answered, "There is no temple of residence; to reside isn't it." My! These are the words of someone who's enlightened. It seems as though he is saying, not dwelling—therein arises the mind. To have a dwelling place isn't it. He just answered without having to stop and think. In Ch'an , this is called shooting from the hip. If you have to stop and think, you are dwelling and that isn't it.

The two continued on in rapid fire like this for some time, until finally, as a last resort, the boat monk took the oar and whacked Chia-shan so hard he fell into the water. Chia-shan couldn't swim and went under. In a flurry of movement, he surfaced and the boat monk said, "Speak! Speak!" Chia-shan opened his mouth, preparing to give some quip when the oar came down on him again. Surfacing again, "Speak! Speak!" Although gagging with water, he still had his wits about him and could shoot from the hip, but again that oar! Of course, he would have had a mouth full of intellectual theory, "there is no temple of residence," in addition to water. Having gone under for a third time, his mind was laundered clean of all theoretical learning and answers. When Chia-shan came up again, he quickly shouted, "I understand, I understand!" No more oars—he was enlightened. The boat monk said, "The Buddha Dharma is as such. You may leave."

Of course, he first got back into the boat. Chia-shan took the oars for his master for some while until the master said it was time for him to leave. Chia-shan kept looking back at his teacher as he walked away. We all think that he was just feeling sentimental and having a hard time saying goodbye completely, but his teacher saw this and said, "Brother, do you think I haven't taught you everything?" He flipped his boat and went under in order to seal his disciple's faith.

While in the boat earlier, the boat monk had told Chia-shan he should not go back to be a Dharma master and live in a busy place. First go to the mountains; find a remote hermitage where nights are cold and food and access are scarce. There, verify your understanding through cultivation until it is completely refined. Then return to spread the Dharma. Chia-shan followed the master's advice and years later again taught Dharma. An Elder Brother asked him, "What is the dharmakaya?" He said, "The dharmakaya has no form!" "What are Dharma eyes?" "The Dharma eyes have no blind spot!"

Still the same answers, but before enlightenment, they were answers from intellectual knowledge, now they came from personal verification. Previously the answers were correct but were "mouth Ch'an." In other words, mind and body had no experience of what was being said. So, with regard to the question of form or appearance, to grasp form is to think that there is an outer physical form of a Buddha. Whether it be in meditation, in a dream or in a state of samadhi that a Buddha appears to you, grasping this form as the Buddha is not in accord with Buddha Dharma. The thirty-two marks are not marks is what this means.

Vast Merit

At this time, there is a point I would like to clarify. In the world, the thing which is most supreme is not material, rather it is of the mind. The "mind" is that which is found at the source of the mental and physical realms and not the "mind" which is the mental realm opposed to the physical realm. This "mind" cannot be seen for it has no marks or signs not does it grasp any. True Buddhism is breaking apart any superstitions. It is clean and clear belief which doesn't grasp onto any appearance. The Dharmakaya without any marks is enlightenment. These are the two points which were brought up previously. The Buddha now tells Subhuti.

"Subhuti, if on the one hand a good man or woman for the sake of charity has sacrificed as many lives as there are grains of sand in the Ganges and on the other hand, someone has been studying and observing even one stanza of this

teaching and expounding it to others, the merit of the latter will be far greater."

Imagine if in this world there was a person who gave as many lives as there are grains of sand in the Ganges in the name of charity to help others. This merit is much greater than that of giving away a whole universe full of treasure. In the end, the two things that people can't bear to part with are their acquisitions and their life. While one is alive, one's many possessions are the things one can't stand to lose. So for people to give money away in charity is quite admirable. If one tumbles into a freezing cold river and is about to die, the only thing that person wants is for someone to rescue him. That person will give you anything at that point, just "save my life!" At that point, one doesn't want to lose one's life and so money and possessions lose their importance.

The last time the Buddha took as a comparison the merit of giving away as much treasure as would fill a universe. In this section, the stakes are *much* higher. It is the merit of sacrificing as many lives as there are grains of sand in the Ganges for charity. Is the merit of this great? Of course it is great. Still, it doesn't even hold a candle to the merit of understanding a gatha of the *Diamond Sutra*. To receive, retain, practice and even more so, save oneself and save others, enlighten oneself and enlighten others; expounding this Dharma to others has inconceivable merit and fortune. This merit and fortune is that of ease and that of clean, clear belief.

Gatha of Section Thirteen

The great universe of atoms is a tiny water bubble.
Let go of the precipice and the outflow will spread the flame widely.
Yellow flowers and crisp bamboo, all very commonplace things,
Derived from prajna, the shore is everywhere to be touched.

"The great universe of atoms is a tiny water bubble." The first line comes from the *Surangama Sutra*. In it, the Buddha says that within our original nature the great universe of galaxies is like a small bubble floating on water. Our original nature is *that* stupendous. If all of space and the galaxies are but a small bubble, our world in relation to that is just a tiny, tiny bubble within that bubble, not to even mention the microscopic bubbles of our existence on that bubble. All just bubbles. The whole universe is just an atom. In the eyes of the Buddha, these bubble bodies arise for a moment and then, "pop!" are gone. How does one become a Buddha then? Let go of this body and awaken to the original nature, the true nature of emptiness. How does one do this?

"Let go of the precipice and the outflow will spread the flame widely." A Ch'an master of old said how one can awaken. Go to the top of the Himalayas and do a swan dive! *"At the precipice, dare to let go. Having gone completely beyond, one is reborn and can no longer be fooled."*

This is saying that one who has gone through something oneself cannot be cheated about it. People talk very easily about the subject of life and death but have those who talk about death actually died and returned? Having gone through, you can't be cheated. Many people talk about emptiness but can they actually empty everything out? Can they let go at the edge of the precipice?

The Buddha gave these words of direction. He passed on the real secret to everyone but it is up to you to do it or not. *"Spread the flame"* comes from the words of Chuang-tzu. *"Before the fire is extinguished, pass it on to new wood."* The Ch'an sect is the transmission of the mind seal. The flame, or light, is passed on from teacher to student. The firewood is used up but the flame doesn't die.

"Yellow flowers and crisp bamboo, all very commonplace things." This is from the Ch'an master of old who was asked what is prajna? Where can it be found? "Crisp green, green bamboo is all the Dharmakaya. Lush, lush yellow flowers are nothing but prajna." Look at the tree outside the window, "crisp green, green bamboo." This is the Dharmakaya! The beautiful flowers in bloom, "lush, lush yellow flowers" are prajna. Do you understand? Prajna is not something inanimate—bamboo is the Dharma body; prajna paramita is flowers. If you understand this, you understand the *Diamond Sutra*. You understand Buddha Dharma. The very ordinary things are Tao.

"Derived from prajna, the shore is everywhere to be touched." Prajna paramita is everywhere! You come in contact with it, but

you don't realize it. At all times, in all places it is revealing itself. So, when your stomach hurts, "Oh, what pain!" It's prajna here! If you really have to go but can't find a toilet, when you finally do— ahh!—prajna! Prajna is everywhere. You are at the shore. The original nature of the Buddha and sentient beings is the same.

SECTION 14

SERENITY BEYOND FORM AND APPEARANCE

At that time, after listening to this teaching, Subhuti realized its profound meaning and was moved to tears. He said to the Buddha, "Most rare, most extraordinary World-Honored One! The Buddha has expounded such a very profound teaching. Since I have acquired the wisdom eye, I have never heard such a teaching. World-Honored One, if someone listens to this teaching with a pure and faithful mind, this person will surely realize reality. One should know that such a person has achieved the most precious merit. World-Honored One, this true form is not true form and so the Tathagata calls it true form.

"World-Honored One, after listening to this teaching, I have no difficulty in believing, understanding, receiving and retaining it, but in the ages to come, in the last 500-year period, if there be a person who happens to listen to this Teaching, believes, understands, receives and retains it, this person will be most rare. The reason is that this person will no longer hold on to notions of self, person, being, and life. Why is this? The notion of an ego is not real. The notions of self, person, being, and life are not real. The reason is that those having gone beyond all notions are called Buddhas."

The Buddhas said, "Just so, Subhuti, just so! If there be a person who, listening to this teaching, is neither awed nor frightened nor filled with dread, you must know that such a person is rare. The reason is, Subhuti, as the Tathagata says, the first paramita is no first paramita, but is simply called the first paramita.

"Subhuti, the Tathagata speaks of the perfection of patient endurance which is no perfection of patient endurance, but is merely called the perfection of patient endurance. Why so? Subhuti, in a past life my body was mutilated by the Raja of Kalinga, but I was at that time free from the notions of self, person, being, and life. While in the past when my limbs were cut away piece by piece, if I still held notions of self, person, being, and life, I would have been stirred by feelings of anger and hatred. Subhuti, I remember five hundred lives, I was an ascetic practicing patient endurance and held no concept of self, person, being, and life Therefore, Subhuti, Bodhisattvas should go beyond all conceptions of form and appearance in order to develop the Supreme Enlightenment mind. Their minds must not dwell in form, sound, smell, taste, touch, nor dharma. Their minds should not dwell anywhere. In the mind that dwells, one should not dwell. This is the reason the Buddha says that Bodhisattvas' minds should not rest in form when practicing charity. Subhuti, a Bodhisattva in order to help all sentient beings ought to practice charity in this way. The Tathagata

says that all form is not form and the so-called sentient beings are not sentient beings.

"Subhuti, the Tathagata's words point to the true and correspond to reality. They are as Such, and are neither deceitful nor heterodox. Subhuti, the Dharma which the Tathagata attained is neither real nor illusory.

"Subhuti, if a Bodhisattva practices charity with a mind dwelling in Dharma, he is like a man entering the darkness who cannot see anything; but if a Bodhisattva practices charity with a mind not dwelling in Dharma, he is like a man with open eyes in the daylight who can see things clearly.

"Subhuti, if there be virtuous men and women in the future ages able to receive, retain, recite and write this sutra, the Tathagata with His Buddha wisdom knows and clearly sees that such a person will receive unlimited merit beyond measure."

Today we will look at Section 14, and I would once again like to call everyone's attention to the overall picture. The *Diamond Sutra* is talking about the cultivation of prajna, not all the expressions of prajna but of the pure form, or body, of prajna, the body of Tao and the way in which we perceive this. In the very first part, it talks about practicing the *sila,* or discipline, of prajna, "being skillfully mindful." From the very first inklings of bodhicitta to the time one becomes a Buddha, it's all a matter of "keeping well the moment of mind." Keeping well the moment of what mind?

The mind which doesn't dwell. A mind not dwelling is samadhi. The prajna of the *Diamond Sutra* is itself wisdom. This is looking at the *Diamond Sutra* in terms of sila, samadhi and prajna wisdom.

If we look at it in terms of the six paramitas, the *Diamond Sutra* first explains "not dwelling" by saying one must lead all sentient beings to enter nirvana and be liberated. This is charity, giving or dana. Through this mind of giving, one completes the merits of wisdom, develops the mind of bodhicitta, the mind of anuttara-samyak sambodhi and achieves the Great Awakening and Enlightenment of a Buddha. After developing the mind of giving, one must develop discipline, or sila. What discipline? The great sila of a Bodhisattva, perfectly protect the mind of no ego, no personality, no being, no life. This is the paramita of discipline, or sila. On the path to the culmination of prajna wisdom, this is one of the basic stages. These are the bases on which one can practice Buddhism, cultivate and become a Buddha. This is the main point of Section 13.

Now we will start Section 14, in which the Buddha explains the paramita of patient endurance, or *ksanti*, and how it leads to prajna.

At that time, after listening to this teaching, Subhuti realized its profound meaning and was moved to tears. He said to the Buddha, "Most rare, most extraordinary World-Honored One! The Buddha has expounded such a teaching. Since I have acquired the wisdom eye, I have never heard such a teaching.

World-Honored One, if someone listens to this teaching with a pure and faithful mind, this person will surely realize reality. One should know that such a person has achieved the most precious merit."

This section can be broken down into three parts, the first of which is a dialogue between the Buddha and Subhuti. *"At that time,"* after Subhuti has heard the Buddha expound this sutra, this teaching on the Dharma door of prajna, he is deeply moved, *"...realized its profound meaning."* I hope everyone will pay special attention to these words. It's very easy to read right over them without even noticing. *"Realized its profound meaning"* is to arrive at a very deep understanding. It's what we commonly refer to as an awakening. In later years, the Ch'an sect talked about two different levels of this. The first is called "awakening" ("releasing and awakening" is the exact translation) and the second is what's referred to as a "Great Awakening" ("verifying and awakening"). An awakening is when one's wisdom perspective has shifted and is on track or rather on the Path. It is not just an ordinary intellectual grasping of the concepts but one feels a great sense of liberation in this shift. This is the feeling of releasing and awakening which is one alambana of awakening. This is why he says, *"...realized its profound meaning",* a feeling of deep release and awakening. Now the question is, awakening to what? To the profound meaning of this teaching. With this awakening, one has clear direction, one sees clearly the path and is sure of where it leads. It is absolutely not a mere empty intellectual understanding of the words.

After Subhuti had this deep awakening to the profound Path, he cried. Why did he cry? His feeling of joy was so overwhelming that he was moved to tears. If people work very hard to accomplish something or attain something, when at long last the moment comes that it is theirs, they will cry. The tears they cry are tears of sheer joy; they are also tears of compassion. When the clean, clear body of the self-nature is about to reveal itself, the one who practices Buddhism or cultivates the Tao will cry tears of compassionate joy (*mudita*). This is a natural occurrence. The other possibility is that the person is just a kook. When one's clean, clear self-nature, one's original face just naturally reveals itself, one experiences an unsurpassed feeling of joy and bliss (*mudita* and *karuna*). If you ask them why they cry, they will say they do not feel bad, but they just can't help themselves. It is a kind of heavenly dew or ambrosia. It's a feeling of having found something one has lost and has been searching for for a long time. It's that kind of joy, bliss, relief and congruence.

Subhuti was in tears as he said, "*Most rare, most extraordinary, World-Honored One.*" These are sincere words of praise. "*The Buddha has expounded such a very profound teaching.*" He said that this teaching that day was deeply profound, this teaching on the achievement of liberating prajna wisdom. "*Since I have acquired the wisdom eye.*" Of the Buddha's disciples, Subhuti was known as the foremost in discourse on emptiness. He was born with the eye of wisdom and thus his accomplishment in the area of prajna wisdom was the greatest. Subhuti said that since he had acquired the wisdom eye, he had *"never heard such a teaching."* He had never heard such an ultimately profound teaching before.

Pure and Faithful Mind

At this point, Subhuti once again calls out in praise of his Teacher, *"World- Honored One, if someone listens to this teaching..."* He says that if someone, someone outside of those who are here today, hears this teaching of the *Diamond Prajna Paramita Sutra* —the teaching on how to liberate yourself through wisdom, the Dharma door through which one becomes a Buddha—*"with a pure and faithful mind, this person will surely realize reality."* These words are the heart of the main point of this section. Do not forget these words. After the Buddha's passing, anyone who wishes to become a Buddha must follow this path, must enter this Dharma door. If one has not achieved this level, one is very far from becoming a Buddha. One is still at the stage of studying and hasn't even seen the shadow of the real thing. To achieve that level is to have entered the door of wisdom and laid the foundation for becoming a Buddha.

    "Pure and faithful mind" has two levels of meaning. One is the level of faith, a true faith which is not blind faith. Why? Because it arises from realizing the profound meaning. One who has this

level of understanding is practicing Buddhism. If one doesn't completely understand but has enough faith to pay respect and bow down, this is called the level of blind faith. In strict interpretation, one must have reached the level of realizing the profound meaning. First have this understanding of the theory, and then work at cultivation. This is what's called practicing Buddhism, having entered the path to one's own enlightenment.

In what does one develop faith? Faith in the mind, faith that each and every sentient being is a Buddha, that one's very mind is the Buddha. Each sentient being has a mind and thus is a Buddha. It's just that we have lost our true self and cannot perceive our true mind or original nature. It is covered over and so we are sentient beings. Actually not even a sheet of paper could fit between sentient beings and Buddha. Once one perceives one's original nature, one *knows* that the mind is absolutely clean and pure. All of the sutras; sila, samadhi and wisdom; stopping and introspecting; reciting the Buddha's name; reciting mantra or any other method are a means to get to the clean, pure mind. There are, in fact, different levels of this realization of one's self-nature and thus the different bhumis, or grounds, of Bodhisattvas.

Speaking of faith in the mind, we all say that we have it, but these minds of ours are full of afflictions. A mind of affliction is the mind of ordinary beings. The clean pure mind has no frustration, no wandering thoughts. To perceive in an instant one's original nature is to have clean, clear belief. To perceive the nature of mind is true form prajna; it is Tao. If you wish to perceive the nature of mind, you must have clean, clear belief in order for true form prajna to arise. Subhuti is speaking from his own experience to speak as he did. He spoke in order that people in the future who hear the Buddha's teaching may develop clean, clear belief, true form prajna.

Rare Merit

"One should know that such a person has achieved the most precious merit."

Supposing someone studying this sutra has achieved this stage. That person, then, has also achieved the most precious merit. Who is the person with the most precious merit? Earlier on in the sutra we've seen it mentioned. Subhuti lauded the Buddha as *"Most rare, most extraordinary World-Honored One."* So, in other words, this Buddhist practitioner can become a Buddha because he or she has already the most precious merit. We must be clear on this before we go on to discuss the next part dealing with true form prajna.

At the beginning of our lectures, we spoke first about the five kinds of prajna, the most difficult of these being true form prajna. This is the same thing as perceiving the body of Tao. True form prajna is Bodhi, nirvana, original nature, suchness and so forth. There are many names applied to this "thing." If you're not sure how big it is or whether it's larger or smaller than say a pineapple, you are grasping onto form and are still quite lost.

Subhuti once again calls out the Buddha's name and continues to report his understanding and explanation. *"World-Honored One, this true form is not form and so the Tathagata calls it true form."* This thing called true form, reality, is without form and so is formless. Remember earlier in the sutra there was a line which read, *"If all form and appearance are seen as illusion, the Tathagata will be perceived."* All appearances of form should not be grasped, no ego, no personality, no being, no life, nor form of Buddha nor is there not the form of Buddha. Nothing is to be grasped. Even "not grasping" is not to be grasped.

What then is true form? It is formless. To break it down—no ego, no personality, etc. In a nutshell "seeing all form and appearance as illusion is to perceive the Tathagata". Subhuti's understanding is that the so-called true form is that all is without form and appearance, to achieve an understanding of no form or appearance. The Buddha in order to give a name called it the true form of the Tathagata.

"World-Honored One, after listening to this teaching, I have no difficulty in believing, understanding, receiving and retaining it." Subhuti is still moved to speak and so he continues saying that, being there and hearing for himself the Buddha's teachings, he can definitely believe what was said, understand it, experience it for himself, retain this alambana and cultivate it. "Believing, understanding, receiving and retaining" are four cultivation stages.

These four correspond to four stages named by later generations: learning, theory, practice and fruits of achievement. "Believing" is having developed a true faith in the teachings. "Understanding" is awakening to the deep meaning. "Receiving and retaining" are the different stages of achievement from one's cultivation after having awakened. This part is also called verifying. These four words shouldn't be overlooked. Subhuti said that for us who were able to receive teachings directly from the Buddha, believing, understanding, receiving and retaining were not difficult nor unusual. But of course, the Buddha was personally instructing them.

Who Are the Precious Ones Five Hundred Years Later?

"But in the ages to come, in the last 500-year period, if there be a person who happens to hear this teaching, believes, understands, receives and retains it, this person will be most rare."

Why five hundred years later? Why not a thousand or three hundred? This is the Buddha's own timetable. The period that he was on the earth is called the Right Dharma Age. After his nirvana, his disciples were still there. This period of the Right Dharma Age lasted five hundred years and then the Semblance Age began. The disciples had all passed into nirvana and from then on there were only the sutras, the images and so forth to rely on. It is said that the Semblance Age also lasted only five hundred years or some say one thousand, and then we entered the Dharma Ending Age, the tail end. The Dharma Ending Age doesn't mean that Buddhism just disappears, but rather that the correct Buddha Dharma, methods of practice etc. are being lost. This is being talked about in the teachings on vinaya and mentioned in other places by the Buddha.

Still it is not necessarily exactly like this. For example, in many sutras, the *Avatamsaka Sutra,* for example, the Buddha himself admitted that there is never a time without Buddha Dharma because the Buddha Dharma is absolute reality which never changes. It is beyond beginning and ending, increasing and decreasing, so everyone can relax.

Subhuti said that supposing someone of the Semblance or the Dharma Ending Age reads or studies this sutra and can achieve this same state that the Buddha's disciples achieved: believing, understanding, receiving and retaining. This person is most rare and precious. "Most precious" is a special term which appears in the *Diamond Sutra* meaning one who has gone beyond the mundane and entered the realm of the sages. One who is "most precious" is almost a Buddha.

> *"The reason is that this person will no longer hold onto ideas of self, person, being, and life"*

During the time on the earth when neither the Buddha nor his disciples are present, one who has achieved this most precious merit has of course, no ego, no personality, no being, and no life notions. This person has gone beyond these notions and does not cling to any form or appearance.

"Why is this? The notion of an ego is not real. The notions of self person, being and life are not real. The reason is that those having gone beyond all notions are called Buddhas."

You must pay close attention to these sentences. Any Buddha exam would have this on it. The notion of an ego is originally a false notion. Continuing on, the notions of self, person, being, and life are all false notions. In Buddhism, we break down the notion of self. Most people feel they have a self, they have a body. This body is a composite of the four elements which make up bones, muscles and so forth which in turn make up the body. The day after we are born we've already aged a day. A month later one is completely different from the day of one's birth, and ten years later, even different still. If all of us sitting here today come back ten years from now, we would all be completely different right down to the bones. This physical body is not the self and to think so is a false notion. This body of ours is a tool, like a light bulb, and we just use it for a while. It is not the self and such a notion of self is a false notion which shouldn't be grasped. Don't take the false to be the real.

The body is definitely not the self. So then, what about mental consciousness? Are the thoughts the self? They're also not the self.   Every minute, every second, thoughts, ideas and awareness are changing. Old people especially forget what exactly happened ten years ago, even ten minutes ago.   They say something and then they forget what they've just said. So, the thinking mind of ideas is not the self. This self is made up of all non-self components. Where then are you, me, him...to be found? They are all non-self, all without form or appearance. All form and appearance are but the coming together of causes and conditions. It is a false combination coming together of illusionary appearance, not the face of reality. Still one cannot say that the illusions do not exist. They are merely serendipitous existences. This is why it is said that the notion of an ego is not real. The same thing is also applied to the notions of self, person, being, and life . The *Diamond Sutra*, at the same time, helps us see clearly that we mustn't let this illusionary human life, this fleeting appearance of a material world cheat us out of our wisdom, cheat us out of the emotions of our true nature.

Is there something wrong with the idea of the emotions of our true nature? Yes, there is. How could our true nature have emotions? Our true nature doesn't not have emotions. Emotions are not emotions but are merely called emotions. Emotions are also illusionary appearances, but if the Buddha had no emotions, He wouldn't have great compassion. The mind of compassion is emotion, but the Buddha's emotions are not blind or ignorant. All appearances are not real. The true mind of compassion has no tracks or traces. This is the basic principle.

How to See the Buddha

The next part is quite important because everyone who studies Buddhism wishes to see the Buddha, *"Those having gone beyond all appearances and notions are called Buddhas."* Going beyond all appearances and notions is the Buddha, the real Buddha. So then, you say, we don't need to pay respect to the big Buddha statue in the hall. You still must pay respect for beyond the false is the real. Appearance is illusion and by paying respects to this illusion, within your mind will arise true respect. This is the clean clear mind of faith which can give rise to true form, the alambana which is beyond all appearances. So if one pays respect to the Buddha without grasping appearance, one need not prostrate, one need not even bring one's hands together. Just in that moment one has paid respect and prostrated to all the Buddhas of the three times and the ten directions.

There is a public record in the Ch'an sect which tells the story of a little boy who had to pee. He ran around and around the Buddha hall looking for the toilet but in the end just peed in front of the Buddha statues. A monk came by at that time and said, "Child have you no manners whatsoever? How could you just urinate in front of the Buddha!" The child retorted, "The three times and the ten directions all have Buddhas, in what direction should I pee?"

All of the directions have Buddhas; Buddhas are everywhere to be found. In the middle is Vairocana Buddha. If in the middle of one's mind arises respect, all the Buddhas are there in front. How is it that they are all in front? Beyond all form and appearance is the Buddha. We must be clear on this principle.

Up to now Subhuti has been speaking. He gave a speech for the Buddha who was the audience. Subhuti told him of his understanding so that he could get verification from Buddha, which He indeed did give.

A Rare Person

The Buddha said, "Just so, Subhuti, just so! If there be a person who listening to this teaching, is neither awed nor frightened nor filled with dread, you must know that such a person is rare."

The Buddha said to him, Yes, yes, that's right. It's just like you said. In the times to come, if a person hears the meaning of the *Diamond Sutra* and is not scared, this person is most rare. Fright is to be startled, to be surprised and frightened. For example, if you are walking down a dark street and see a shadow move, you may take fright. Terror is a feeling of intense fear which lasts much longer than fright. Dread is the state of fear which, out of the three, lasts the longest. So all of us sitting here are most rare. We're listening to the *Diamond Sutra* with no fear or dread, and it's not that you don't understand; everyone here understands.

Are there actually people who have fright, terror or dread over these teachings? Among practicing cultivators one will see this. In their practice, many people are seeking the alambana of emptiness but when this alambana actually appears, they take fright or are terrified. People say they are scared out of their wits and sweat bullets because they've "disappeared." I say to them, Aren't we seeking to be selfless? How can you be frightened? Wisdom needs strength behind it. If the power of one's wisdom and one's merit is insufficient, one will experience fright, terror or dread. So the Buddha said that in the future, if one can achieve the Dharma door of the *Diamond Sutra* without fright, terror or dread, this person is most exceptional. When the Buddha calls someone rare, this is most serious. This rare is almost to the extent of being nearly impossible, going beyond the ordinary into the realm of the saints and sages.

"The reason is, Subhuti, as the Tathagata says, the first paramita is no first paramita but is simply called the first paramita."

What makes the *Diamond Sutra* special is that it allows us to understand not dwelling, no form and no vow. This is the mind seal of the Mahayana. This mind should at all times not dwell, at all times not grasp onto form, and at all times have no vow. You will say, But mustn't we give rise to the great vows? Why then do you say to have no vow? Great compassion is of course the power of the great vow. Once compassion passes, it doesn't dwell. No one told you to sit around crying all day long. Once something has passed, don't dwell on it. This is why it is said that having a vow is not having a vow.

The first paramita is the achievement of great wisdom, Great Awakening, Enlightenment and Buddhahood, as well as being true form prajna. True form prajna originally doesn't dwell, has no form and no vow. Please don't get the wrong idea. If you can't bring yourself to make any vows do not think that this is the case of originally there is no vow. You have deviated from the Buddha's meaning by doing this. "No vow" means that after you use your great compassion, it is again empty, it doesn't dwell. Therefore, the first paramita is not the first paramita but is called the first paramita. The first paramita is also prajna wisdom and within prajna wisdom, true form prajna is perceiving the body of Tao. In Ch'an, it is called perceiving the mind and one's original nature.

What Is Ksanti?

> "Subhuti, the Tathagata speaks of the perfection of patience (Paramita of Ksanti) which is no perfection of patience but is merely called the perfection of patience."

A big question arises here. From the beginning until now, Subhuti and the Buddha have been talking about the cultivation of wisdom, which is the last of the six paramitas, called prajna. We mentioned before the six paramitas: charity (dana), discipline (sila), patience (ksanti), zeal (virya), meditation (dyana) and wisdom (prajna). These are all steps to practicing Buddhism.

First one must practice charity. This is not merely taking money out of your pocket, but rather it is changing your habit energy. You have to change, drop, transform these habits, and in the process, your life will transform. To let go is also to give. To completely let go of everything is charity, internal charity. When one truly practices charity, one's mind becomes clean and pure. This is the state of discipline. If one's mind isn't clean and pure but keeps the rules of discipline, this is the stage of Hinayana. It is a state of contrived discipline. Once your mind is at the stage of clean purity in each moment, you need not have rules of discipline because this mind is already disciplined. To discipline all bad or evil behavior, to have a mind which is in every moment pure and clean and to not think of good or evil is called the supreme level of virtue. This is keeping the sila, or discipline. Keeping this is not difficult to do; patient endurance is very difficult.

You might think that your mind is very clean and pure and that you have excellent discipline, but you haven't been dealt a blow. If you face a serious blow in life, you could care less about maintaining calm, pure discipline. Every fault in your character comes out; you hit the roof, blow your top or whatever. This is why patience is at the heart of the six paramitas. It is absolutely the most difficult. It is for this reason that Mahayana Bodhisattvas must enter the non-arising Dharma of patience before they have actually achieved the stage of bodhisattvahood.

Non-arising, this is the original state of the clean, pure mind where not a thought arises. One doesn't get to the place where "not a thought arises" by holding down thoughts, and it is not that in this place one doesn't think or know. Rather, there are no extraneous wandering thoughts. Clean clear belief is non-arising. To simply be in this place of the non-arising is not enough; one also needs to cut off the myriad happenings in order for it to be considered the Dharma of patience. In Chinese literary terms, this is called drawing the sword of wisdom and cutting the fine threads of sentiment. Sometimes we can't pull out this sword, or we only pull it out half way, or pull it out and then are too frightened to use it. There is also the case where the sword won't cut as it has been dull for some time. Nevertheless, the Dharma of patience is the heart of the six paramitas.

The full translation of the name of this paramita is "Patient Endurance Under Insult." Not just insult but in the face of disgrace, dishonor, abuse, etc. as well. Normally, we would understand this in the sense of being told off, insulted, attacked or some other form of unwanted tribulation, but in Buddhism, this definition is expanded to encompass any unwanted experience. The process of aging or illness is also a form of "insult" which brings with it much unwanted suffering. This is not only true of the human world. If we look at the animal world, this is also the case. Take ants, for example, if you study them closely you will see that young ants will keep more physical distance from the older ants than they will with each other. This is a kind of insult. It's these kinds of things which are very hard to bear and test our patience.

This imperfect Sahaloka is indeed very hard to endure. There is never anything which is perfect, and so we must just "grin and bear it." It is for this very same reason that beings on this earth have the greatest opportunity to become a Buddha. In the heavenly realms, there is no suffering, nothing to disturb the mind, and no one thinks of cultivating the Tao. With all that fortune, it's not necessary! Those who are in the hells are suffering so badly there is no room for thoughts of cultivation. They don't have time to think about meditation. It's only in the Sahaloka that we have suffering as well as happiness, evil as well as good. It's all half-half, and so we are inspired to be liberated and to cultivate wisdom. This is the path toward Buddhahood.

Patient endurance under insult isn't only talking about misfortune but about patience within any imperfect situation. Take for example one's career. A person may be making lots of money but if you ask if he is satisfied and content, he will probably say no. If you ask if things are bearable, he will most likely say, "Of course, I have no choice but to cope." The people of this world have an innate ability to cope, to endure.

The Buddha and Subhuti have conversed up to this point. If one isn't mindful as they read this sutra, one will think it very strange that suddenly the perfection of patient endurance appears. This is why I brought it to your attention . Here ends the discussion of the six paramitas within this sutra. Why, though, was the subject of the perfection of patient endurance brought up at this point?

Model of Patience

In our efforts to cultivate and become a Buddha, the practice of patient endurance is most difficult. Just take meditation, for example. Why is it that you don't have samadhi? Your legs ache and you can't stand it anymore—this is only a small test of endurance! Of course, to just grit your teeth and endure can be done, but still the whole mind is intensely aware of some part of the body whether it be the legs or anything else. The four elements are originally empty, but at this moment they are anything but empty. So of the six ferries, also called the six paramitas, this is the one you can't get on. And if you can't get on this one, the rest is empty talk. Reciting the *Diamond Sutra* in time with the wooden fish, "no ego, no personality, no being, and no life," it sounds very nice but—Ahchoo! Ahchoo! Oh, no! I've caught a cold, better get some medicine, see a doctor.... Up come the views of a being, a life, and you've missed the ferry again.

To place the theory of patient endurance in the middle of the *Diamond Sutra* is *very* significant. So pay special attention. The Buddha also told us of his own experiences as a model to follow. He also said that one with real enlightenment, real wisdom, knows that the paramita of patience is actually not patience. If one has the thought and feeling of patiently enduring, it is not a paramita. One is not at the other shore and thus has not yet succeeded.

"Why so? Subhuti, in a past life my body was mutilated by the Raja of Kalinga, but I was at the time free from the notion of self, person, being, and life."

The Buddha held himself up as an example to Subhuti. He spoke of an experience from a past life during the time the Raja of Kalinga reigned in India. Accounts of him are only found within the sutras, however. This raja was infamously cruel and heartless. During the time of his reign, Shakyamuni was a holy man who had attained quite a high level. In fact, he was already a Bodhisattva at that point, a Pratyeka Buddha who had awakened on his own during a period when there was no Buddha on this earth. The raja had some argument with this holy man and decided to kill him. The raja asked of him, "Being a holy man, will you hate me for killing you?" The holy man Shakyamuni said, "My mind and heart are absolutely calm and clear. You can tear me from limb to limb and if I have no thoughts of hatred, my body will become whole again." The Raja of Kalinga then cut him apart one limb at a time. The holy man made no sound nor had even the slightest feeling of hatred in his heart; rather, he was filled with compassion. The raja, having finished, then called out for his proof. It was as he had said. He didn't stir from his Bodhisattva mind of compassion and his body immediately became whole again, and his life was restored.

This is a much more impressive resurrection story than that of Jesus! The Buddha explained that while his body was being mutilated by the Raja of Kalinga, he had no thoughts of self, person, being, and life. This was his own personal story which he shared as an example. Of course, this isn't saying that we need to get someone to hack us apart as a test. Forget about severing your limbs, even having you keep silent or meditate without moving is practically unendurable. This all has to do with patient endurance, samadhi and wisdom. It is because your wisdom isn't strong enough, you haven't had a great awakening and so you don't have this endurance.

Bodhidharma and Socrates

Just then when we were speaking of patient endurance, we mentioned that not only did this endurance include all the kinds of suffering in this world but also, this endurance had no idea of endurance. There is no thought in the mind of patiently enduring. This mind is naturally calm and clear in order that it be called the paramita of patient endurance which ferries one to the other shore. The Buddha said he had no notions of self, person, being, and life. First of all, he did not feel that this life was his. Pay careful attention to these words. This body is yours to use on a temporary basis and not as a permanent possession because this body is not the self. This theory needs to not only be understood clearly but also needs to be known at its deepest level in order for there to be clean, clear belief, in order to perceive true reality, true form. This is real kung fu.

From where does this kung fu come? It comes from the perspective of prajna. If one's wisdom is not penetrating enough, one cannot have a Great Awakening and enlightenment. Great Awakening and enlightenment is an alambana of wisdom and is not an alambana of kung fu which can be attained through practice. If you think the opposite, your head is still in a fog. Wisdom is a state of clarity.

"When my limbs were cut away piece by piece, if I still held the concepts of self, person, being, and life, I would have been stirred by feelings of anger and hatred."

At this point, we need to first understand that the Buddha is not just talking about an illusory idea. This is real cultivation work. No notion of an ego or a being is the wisdom which liberates. For example, the great western philosopher Socrates was plotted against and told to drink poison. All his friends urged him not to drink it. He knew very well it was poison but still drank it and went out with a laugh.

The famous Ch'an master Bodhidharma nearing the end of his period of teaching met with some monks who wished to do away with him. Five times they tried to poison him but without success. The sixth time he took the poison and said to his disciples, "My time with you has come to an end. I will leave now." His disciples urged him not to leave them, but he told them that he had already drunk the poison. A famous esoteric master of the Sung Dynasty called Lama Mona was also poisoned. All of these masters knew that their work here was finished and they must repay a debt with their life. Debts must be paid off and when one's time is up, the time is up. Jesus is another example, his hanging on the cross. They were all liberated due to their wisdom.

In the *Avatamsaka Sutra* it says, *"Unobstructed theory, unobstructed action—with unobstructed theory and action, each and everything is unobstructed."* When one's understanding of the theory is penetrating enough, there are no obstructions. Only reading and studying is not enough. One needs to actually cultivate the principles in order for them to be of any use. People don't really understand the ramifications of the teachings of the Buddhist Canon, the Tripitaka. Without this understanding, we still have notions of self, person, being, and life. When the Buddha was being mutilated in his past life, he only had thoughts of compassion; no hatred arose. Due to his penetrating understanding of the theory, his wisdom, he rested in the paramita of patience without any feeling of pain.

The Practice of Patient Endurance

Speaking of the kung fu that comes of practice, one Ch'an master, having attained the transmission of the bowl and robe from Bodhidharma in the end still had to pay a karmic debt from many,

many lives before. There was the debt of a life which remained to be paid off. The basic teaching of Buddhism is the law of karma and cyclic existence in the six realms. Before he was killed, he wrote the following verses:

"The four elements have no self,
The five skandhas are originally empty.
My head is about to be chopped for naught
The same as beheading the wind"

He fearlessly stretched out his head, "Here, chop!" In a similar story, one of the earlier Indian Ch'an masters had his head chopped off. When it was cut, there was no blood. White milky liquid gushed out, spouting a meter high. This goes to prove that through his cultivation practice he had transformed his physical body. This white blood can be further transformed into emptiness and at this stage, one cannot be killed. At the stage where one has the milky white blood, even before the body is transformed into emptiness, one does not feel pain while being killed or sustaining physical injury. That is not the paramita of patience. In the alambana of patient endurance, there is pain felt, incredible pain, but one can let go of the pain and transform it into compassion. This is the paramita of patient endurance. To experience no pain is a stage of kung fu and is not the merit of the perfection of patience. Even though it is very difficult to attain this level of kung fu through one's practice, still it is not unusual. To experience the feeling of extreme pain without any anesthesia and yet not be in pain is consummate wisdom. If, on the spot, you let go of the skandhas of sensation and conception, you are liberated. Practicing Buddhism is also learning how to liberate oneself. This needs to be understood.

There is a form to the patient endurance of a Bodhisattva. Pain and suffering is still pain and suffering; frustration and anguish are still frustration and anguish. If one can transform the idea of pain, suffering, frustration and anguish into emptiness, this is virtuous behavior. It deals with the nature of mind beyond the ordinary mind and is a Bodhisattva's merit. We as practicing Buddhists must all be attentive. If you meet with someone's bad attitude or harsh language and immediately start giving it back or hating this person, all of your so-called kung fu or cultivation of Tao is out the window. To hear the *Diamond Sutra* speak of patient endurance and then avoid interaction with the world is also cheating oneself. This is not patient endurance. You must interact with the world and endure what others cannot endure, do what others cannot do in order that it be considered the spirit of patient endurance of a Mahayana Bodhisattva. For example, why did the Buddha allow someone to cleave apart his body? In order to give proof that the Buddha Dharma is as such. We all must be clear on this.

"Subhuti, I remember five hundred lives ago I was an ascetic practicing patient endurance and held no concept of self, person, being, and life."

The Buddha goes on to tell Subhuti that He was remembering back to five hundred lives ago when He was specifically practicing patient endurance. In that particular lifetime, He only worked on improving his kung fu of patient endurance and definitely had no notions of self, person, being, and life. He mentioned this and then emphasized the point of how one should practice Buddhism.

"Therefore, Subhuti, Bodhisattvas should go beyond all conceptions of form and appearance in order to develop the Supreme Enlightenment mind."

This is the essence of practicing Buddhism, not being fooled or enchanted by phenomenal appearances. There's a temple, a house, a shirt, a place...these are all phenomenal appearances. Don't be fooled by a temple, a house, money, fame and so forth. Earlier it was said, beyond all form is what's called the Buddha. Bodhisattvas walk the path of Mahayana, seeking the mind of Supreme Enlightenment beyond all form.

The Mind Not Dwelling

"Their minds must not dwell in form, sound, smell, taste, touch nor dharma. Their minds should not dwell anywhere. In the mind that dwells, one should not dwell."

People who study and practice Buddhist cultivation should pay special attention here. Most people who practice are tumbling about within the six sense objects: form, sound, smell, taste, touch, dharma, and the sixth sense, consciousness. "One should develop a mind that does not dwell in form." All of our alambanas, all phenomenal appearances are not existent. They are the post-natal illusions of our minds, bodies, and energies. "One should develop a mind that does not dwell in sound." Of all the sense consciousnesses, the ear most easily gives rise to inner phenomena. In other words, as a result of the ear stimulating the ocean of ch'i.

So, if you hear Buddhas, Bodhisattvas, Jesus, the Saints, God or someone else whispering in your ear, and you start listening to them, you have a serious problem and not even Shakyamuni Buddha can help you. If you look at the vinaya teachings, many pertain to this because during the Buddha's time on earth, many people lost their way down this path. The Buddha could do nothing but let them go.

These words saying one should develop a mind which does not dwell in form, sound, smell, taste, touch or dharma, are spoken very seriously. If you want to practice Buddhism, you must forsake all phenomena and develop a mind that does not dwell. You must constantly check yourself, keep watch over your mind and do not let it dwell. If you find yourself dwelling on something or stuck in some habit pattern, you are not free. Early on in China this was called "mo" which is the character for grinding or milling, implying that you were in a state of affliction or torment. Later the character was changed by Emperor Liang Wu-ti to "mo" meaning demon or evil (a different character with the same pronunciation), implying that you were in the clutches of evil and so would give rise to a stronger determination to free yourself. I can't stress enough the importance of forsaking, going beyond all phenomena and developing a mind which does not dwell.

Those students who practice quiet meditation and awareness of the mind should pay careful attention to the next line, *"In the mind that dwells, one should not dwell."* If in your practice, your mind has a "scenario" of clean purity, you are dwelling in a state of clean purity and this is already not clean and pure. It's only just a smidgen of what real clean purity is. The same goes for an experience of emptiness, such a state is only as large as a water tank and probably even smaller. These are scenarios within your conscious, thinking mind. They are not real emptiness. It is the mind grasping onto form, to the idea of emptiness. *"In the mind that dwells, one should not dwell."* This is pointing to an incorrect understanding of emptiness, an incorrect method of dwelling on the mind. With the dwelling mind, one can practice concentrating the mind on a single point and one will become more calm and quiet. However, if you take an experience of emptiness the size of a water tank or an experience of purity to be the Tao, you haven't fooled the Tao. The Tao has fooled you. *"In the mind that dwells, one should not dwell"* is the best method of awareness of observing the mind.

How to Practice Charity

"This is the reason the Buddha says that Bodhisattvas' minds should not rest in form when practicing charity." Why is it that the Buddha was talking about patient endurance and then suddenly jumps to charity? Earlier on I mentioned that the *Diamond Sutra* covered charity, discipline and then patient endurance, in that order. The sutra was written at a time when everyone wasn't so scientifically minded and organized. The writing at that time was more like clouds moving and water flowing. It seems to not have order or sequence but this also has its beauty. *"A Bodhisattva should practice charity with a mind not dwelling"* is saying don't grasp onto appearances. Grasping to the appearance of charity is simply material giving. In other words, one is still controlled and turned around by the physical world and surroundings. You have to let go of all this, let go of the myriad happenings and *this* is practicing charity with a mind not dwelling.

"Subhuti, a Bodhisattva in order to help all sentient beings ought to practice charity in this way. The Tathagata says that all form is not form and the so-called sentient beings are not sentient beings."

For a third time, the Buddha repeats to Subhuti that the spirit of a Mahayana Bodhisattva is to empower all sentient beings through every aspect of their conduct. In each moment, any situation and every place to sacrifice one's self for the benefit of others. This is how charity should be practiced. Let go of each and all and work for the betterment of other people's physical and mental well-being. Why is it, though, that we can't let go? We don't dare to, we don't *really* want to let go or give away because we grasp onto form and appearance.

"The Tathagata says that all form is not form." Which form stays as is without changing? Don't grasp onto form because form is not form. The form which we grasp most tightly is our life. Everyone wishes to live a bit longer and this wish is especially strong in people who are middle-aged or older. The process of life cannot stand still. It never did stop for a moment, and you never can or could grasp hold of it. Ordinary people, ordinary beings all know this principle very, very clearly, especially Buddhists, but still in their minds they hope against hope and fool themselves into thinking that it doesn't apply to them, that they are in control. Everyone feels that they are special. In some cases, those who aren't Buddhist or know of these theories are a little better off. I

am always reminded of my teacher's words, "The five skandhas are so obviously illusory; yet, here, there and everywhere happens ignorance." People who profess to practice Buddhism know very well that the five skandhas are empty, but in every instance one is ignorantly enchanted and like a somnambulant. This is the inability to practice or actualize what one knows. Cultivation *practice* is putting the theory into practice in each and every aspect of one's conduct.

"And the so-called sentient beings are not sentient beings." To go a step farther, whether it be no ego, no personality, no being, no life. These are not excuses to not practice cultivation. Many young people use this excuse to avoid cultivation, but you must first liberate yourself before you can liberate others. How can you help others if you can't even help yourself? I often laugh at myself. At first, I wished to help sentient beings but in the end, they helped me. I haven't even practiced well myself, so who have I actually helped? Worry about not becoming a Buddha rather than not having anyone to save. There are more and more people on the earth, plenty of things need to be done, but if you rush into things without a stable base, who are you really going to save?

The Buddha himself even said that sentient beings don't need you to save them. Each will save himself or herself. Some Bodhisattvas will help sentient beings and not say a word of Dharma. On the contrary, they will add to the suffering of another until that person hits rock bottom and strongly seeks a way out. Teaching someone to meditate is not necessarily the way to help them, but it takes wisdom to know the difference. A lot of young people spend every moment thinking about Buddhism and wishing to become a Buddha. Why do you want to become a Buddha? To save people? People save themselves. They don't need you to save them. *"The so-called sentient beings are not sentient beings."* If you understand Buddhism, you will know that all sentient beings are Buddhas. Why do you want to save Buddhas? In the end, it's one's own self nature that saves one. This is why after awakening, the Sixth Patriarch said to his master, *"When ignorant, the master saves; after awakening, one saves oneself."* One's original nature saves one. In Buddhist ceremonies, you will come across this line, *"Original nature is the vow which liberates sentient beings; original nature is the vow which severs all affliction..."* One saves oneself through one's original nature.

How Does a Buddha Speak?

"Subhuti, the Tathagatha's words point to the true and correspond to reality. They are as Such and are neither deceitful nor heterodox." In total, there are five kinds of speech or words. The Buddha's Dharma corresponds to reality; it is not false talk. It is very true and sincere, stated like it is. It is easy to understand what is meant by true and corresponding to reality, but what is meant by *"as Such"*? It cannot be expressed, there are no words for it. With mouth closed and no words, the sound is like thunder. This is speaking "as Such." Suchness is the same as the true form of prajna.

The absolutely clean and pure original nature is so clean and pure it cannot be expressed in words. This is speaking *as Such*. The Tathagata speaks *as Such*.

The entire *Diamond Sutra* is spoken "*as Such*." After all was said, after 49 years of teaching, not a word was spoken. This is speaking "*as Such*." It can't be said; it's inexpressible.

Not "deceitful" is not lying. "Nor heterodox" is saying that the Buddha has never contradicted himself. If you take the entire Buddhist canon, both the Mahayana and the Hinayana teachings, there are many seemingly contradictory statements. Still, if you look deeply, you will see that the Buddha has only been pointing to *one* thing. For 49 years He's been talking about one thing which is not clearly expressible, and so the Buddha said that He hasn't said anything. He's afraid we won't believe Him and so is asking, "Have I ever not been honest?" He wants us to have clean, clear belief and to give us absolute faith in true Buddhism. What is true Buddhism?

Neither Real nor Illusory

"Subhuti, the Dharma which the Tathagata attained is neither real nor illusory."

Real Buddhism is as stated. Here the Buddha is speaking clearly, with absolute certainty about the Buddha Dharma. It there something to be attained? If you buy a radish or a pumpkin, you take something home with you, but after attaining Tao, you go home empty handed. Not "real," there is nothing to show; "nor illusory," but it is not fraudulent. If you say it's empty, that's wrong. Having a notion of emptiness is wrong, as is a notion of existence. It is a theoretical essence, neither real nor illusory. This is the main point of the *Diamond Sutra*. Right here is the whole sutra in a nutshell. Practicing charity, discipline, patient endurance all the way to consummate wisdom, all of Buddhist cultivation is not dwelling, not grasping to form, no grasping, letting go of everything.

Is simply letting go right? It's also not right! That is why Ma-tsu told his disciples, "If you can't let it go, then pick it up." "Pick it up," this is the mind dwelling but the dwelling mind is not the dwelling mind. Some can't pick it up. There are many who practice Buddhism but can't pick it up, nor let it go. One student came to see me and told me that now she couldn't pick it up or let it go. Well isn't this the state of enlightenment? Shouldn't I be prostrating? Actually, this was a state of "not picking it up nor letting it go." It was a state of emotional depression. If one can understand "not picking it up nor letting it go," one understands "neither real nor illusory." It is the state where if you need it, you pick it up and use it; when you no longer need it, you put it down. It's that simple. Real Buddhism is "neither real nor illusory." This was a very serious statement by the Buddha. He first emphasized: In my life, I have never been deceitful. I have always been sincere and so you must have faith in what I'm going to say. The Buddha

Dharma is neither real nor illusory. If you understand—it's yours. If you don't understand, it's still mine. It's just that simple, and if you can understand, then of course it's yours. The Buddha is not deceitful, and the Buddha Dharma is neither real nor illusory.

> *"Subhuti, if a Bodhisattva practices charity with a mind dwelling in Dharma, he is like a man entering the darkness who cannot see anything; but if a Bodhisattva practices charity with a mind not dwelling in Dharma, he is like a man with open eyes in the daylight who can see things clearly."*

Here the Buddha goes on to tell Subhuti that if one who is practicing the path of a Bodhisattva, holds on to the idea that there is a Dharma to be attained, a Dharma to be practiced or any idea of a Buddha Dharma, he or she has misconstrued the meaning. A small example of this is some practitioners who say they've given up everything. You ask them then, what they are doing and they say they are going off to practice Buddhism. I beg your pardon, but you haven't given up everything. Isn't "practicing Buddhism" one of the items included in "everything"? Could it be that it has a place outside of "everything"? This is just to say that this so-called practicing Buddhism has a form to it. This Bodhisattva's mind is dwelling in Dharma, and will never perceive the Tao. It's like a person in a dark room with his eyes closed. He will never find his way out. There are some people who prefer the dark. They feel more comfortable without light. The dark can also be fascinating.

If one wishes to perceive the nature of mind, perceive the Tao and then "practice charity with a mind not dwelling in Dharma." This is real liberation, really letting go of everything and not dwelling. This person will definitely be able to perceive the Tao. This is called having the wisdom eye. If one has normal eyes, on a sunny day they of course can see everything clearly, as it appears.

Unlimited Merit Beyond Measure

> "Subhuti, if there be virtuous men and women in the future ages able to receive, retain, read and write this sutra, the Tathagata with his Buddha wisdom knows and clearly sees that such a person will receive unlimited merit beyond measure."

Amitofo! We need to show a bit of gratitude. You are really just too good to us. The Buddha told Subhuti that in the ages to come, whether it be a virtuous man or a virtuous woman—that is to say, one whose merit and wisdom are replete—can understand the deep meaning of the teaching on prajna in this sutra and cultivate in accord with it, reading and reciting it, this person is like the Buddha. This is quite serious! World-Honored One, we really don't deserve such an honor.

Why is the Buddha speaking so graciously yet so seriously? There is a reason for which we can use the words from the *Surangama Sutra* to explain, *"When mind can transform the physical world, it is the same as the Tathagata."* These are the Buddha's words. Later on, Bodhidharma said, *"At the pivotal moment one turns back, this is the same as original nature."* This is all to say that if one can truly understand the essence of the *Diamond Sutra* and cultivate in accord with it, this is the same as the conduct of a Buddha. It's not saying you *are* the Buddha, but rather, the same as. With the Buddha's wisdom, He completely understands that a person like that, one who has a penetrating understanding of the *Diamond Sutra*, will achieve unlimited merits beyond measure.

This section can be summed up by saying that only with the consummation of great wisdom is one's conduct able to function or arise from the mind ground. The functioning of one's conduct within wisdom is the patient endurance of aiding all sentient beings from within the sea of suffering. Such a person has unlimited, immeasurable merit.

Gatha of Section Fourteen

"The Udumbara flower, is it real or illusory?
Atoms and sand grains, the current self is not the earlier self.
Smiling, He points to the place where the white lotus blooms.
Within the mire, the fragrant nourishes the wondrous pearl."

"The Udumbara flower, is it real or illusory?" The Udumbara flower spoken of in the sutras is the epiphyllum, or orchid cactus.

You rarely see this cactus in China, but in Taiwan it is common. The flower is very beautiful and fragrant, but its existence is rare and fleeting. As the flower wilts, it gives off its most enticing fragrance. If we look at human history from the perspective of the universe, it is but the flowering of the Udumbara. If we look at our own lives, we live for some decades but looking back, it's as ephemeral as the epiphyllum. It's neither real nor illusory, true nor false, empty nor existent. One should experience it from this perspective. Are there people who practice Buddhist cultivation and actually succeed? Absolutely! But don't grasp onto appearances, it's neither real nor illusory. When the epiphyllum opens, it exists. So fragrant, so beautiful and then, it's gone, empty again.

But is empty non-existent? No, it's not non-existent. Atom upon atom, grain of sand upon grain of sand—this is a Buddhist description of the physical world. A grain of sand represents the earth and atoms are all things. *"Atoms and sand grains, the current self is not the earlier self."* The self of this time and space in the physical universe is not the self earlier in life, is not the self of the previous life nor of the life to come. This is the false self. *"The current self is not the earlier self."* It is not the original face of life which is the origin of all life. It's only when one can let go of and go beyond this self that one finds "permanence, bliss, self and purity" of the real self. The world of today is not the same as the world of tomorrow.

The Buddha uses the lotus to express this. *"Smiling, He points to the place where the white lotus blooms."* Look, the lotus is in bloom. You say there is no lotus but it will open again. You say, but it opened already yesterday.... it will open again tomorrow. In the sutras it always talks about the lotus, such as being reborn in a lotus in the Western Paradise. The Buddha sits upon a white lotus with eight petals, just like our heart front and back. Where are the lotuses to be found? Not in nice clean places. The more stinky and rotten the mud is, the more healthy and beautiful the lotuses.

"Within the mire, the fragrant nourishes the wondrous pearl." The essence of Mahayana is to enter the world, cultivate the Tao from within the sewage. This is the way to succeed in cultivation. Lotuses won't grow on clean mountain tops, they can only grow in murky water. Born out of the dirtiest place, the lotus itself is not in the least dirty. It is fragrant and every part can be used—seeds, pods, root, leaves, flower, stem—all have a use. The center is hollow, empty and so it represents Buddhism. To really practice the Tao and to succeed is not possible on top of a pristine mountain. You must succeed from within the dirtiest muck. As the most beautiful lotus comes from the mud, if we wish to become a Buddha, we can only do so from within the world where there is suffering, strife and dirt. Cultivate and protect your wisdom. Wisdom is like a wondrous pearl.

SECTION 15

THE MERIT OF THIS SUTRA

"Subhuti, if on one hand a virtuous man or woman, in the morning, sacrifices as many lives of theirs as there are grains of sand in the Ganges, and sacrifices as many again at midday and as many again in the evening, and continues doing so throughout numberless aeons. If on the other hand a person after listening to this teaching believes without contention, the latter's merit will surpass the former's. How much more so if this sutra is read, written, received, retained, recited and expounded to others.

"Subhuti, to sum up, this teaching has inconceivable, inestimable and unlimited merit. The Tathagata has expounded it for the benefit of those awakened to the Mahayana and Supreme Paths. If they are able to retain, observe, read and write, recite and expound it to others, the Tathagata knows and sees that their merit is beyond measurement or calculation, is unlimited and inconceivable. They bear the responsibility for transmitting the Tathagata's anutara-samyaksambodhi. Why? Because, Subhuti, those who are satisfied with lesser doctrines are attached to the idea of self, person, being, and life. They are unable to hear, retain, read and recite this sutra and explain it to others.

"Subhuti, wherever this sutra may be found, all realms of devas, men and asuras should offer worship, for you know that such a place is a stupa and should properly be venerated by all with ceremonial obeisance, circumambulation and with offerings of flowers and incense."

The Most Difficult Charity

> *"Subhuti, if on one hand a good man or woman, in the morning, sacrifice as many lives of theirs as there are grains of sand in the Ganges, and sacrifice as many again at midday and as many again in the evening, and continues doing so throughout numberless aeons,"*

Giving of one's body is the most difficult of all charity. For example, giving blood, donating a retina or other organs and so forth are all examples of giving one's body. As an aside, giving birth and raising children can also be regarded as a kind of charity of the body, but this giving is done very happily of free will for the most part. The older some children get, the more disrespectful they become; yet, still the parents love and care for them. Strictly speaking, this is not charity because of the love parents have for their children. Is this saying that if someone loves another and serves him faithfully, this is not charity? It is the act or conduct of giving. It is still done with a mind of ignorance—desire, hatred, ignorance, pride and doubt. *"Falling petals are not without*

sentiment; they become the spring mud protecting the new flowers."
Real charity and giving is when you give up what you don't really
wish to give. It is a personal sacrifice. For example, only if I give
my arm—no one else's will do—will you be cured, and I am willing
to do this for you. To do what others can't or won't do, to endure
what others can't or won't endure is charity. To practice charity
with one's own body is very difficult.

Why is giving of the physical body mentioned here? People
of this world have two things of which they don't wish to let go;
the first is money and the second is one's life. In Sichuan they say,
"Money, wealth and riches are life's breeches." Money is hard to
give away, but under the threat of losing one's life one will let it go
in an instant. The second most difficult thing to give away is the
self. If you had to give up your leg or even half of your body to
save your life, you would say without hesitation, "Chop away."
Here the Buddha is saying that this person gives away his body, his
life—not just one but as many lives as there are grains of sand in
the Ganges—in charity. What does this mean? It means that this
person sacrifices his body and life, immediately is reborn and then
sacrifices himself again. Again and again and again, sacrificing his
life for the betterment of humanity and of all beings. This person
engages in the Bodhisattva's conduct rebirth after rebirth. To
continuously give one's life in sacrifice throughout numberless
aeons, will the merit not be great?

The Old Man's Life Jacket

Many people ask me if I am a Buddhist, I say that I don't call myself anything. I am not qualified to be a Buddhist because I don't dare to sacrifice my life. There are many people in this world who don't call themselves Buddhists but their behavior is that of a Bodhisattva. Twenty-three years ago, in Keelung, there was a boat which met with a typhoon. The boat was sinking and one of the crew gave a life jacket to a friend of his, an old man with emphysema. He saw a woman with a baby and took his life jacket and tied it around them. The crewman saw him without the life jacket and found him another one. Still, the old man didn't jump into the water. He saw a young man and gave the life jacket to him saying, "You're young and can still do many things with your life. I'm old and sick and useless." In the end, he sacrificed his own life in saving others. This is a Bodhisattva. In times of trouble and emergency, they don't consider themselves first.

I don't say that I am a Buddhist because I don't offer my life. If someone takes up more of my time than I had planned for, I get annoyed. In my mind, I'm thinking, "What's your problem, can't you see I'm too tired?" This is because I don't give of myself in charity. If someone asks me to go somewhere out of my way, I'll complain that I'm too old to go running around on his or her behalf. This is not being willing to give of one's life. To really practice Buddhism and give of one's body and life is very difficult.

The word "charity" shouldn't be thrown around lightly. Giving ten dollars here, one hundred dollars there, is this charity? If you think about it beforehand, if this one hundred dollars gone won't cause me any pain because I still have eight thousand dollars on me, then it doesn't count as charity. It's only when one makes a personal sacrifice that it can really be called charity, and this is why it is so difficult to do. Some people give money and look for their name to be written down and credited. Charity is letting go, and this is why it is so difficult.

In this part of the sutra, it doesn't talk about giving away money but of giving away lives, countless lives over countless aeons. This merit is enormous. Still, the Buddha went on to say...

The Fortune of Belief Without Contention

"If on the other hand, a person after listening to this teaching believes without contention, the latter's merit will surpass the former's. How much more so if this sutra is read, written, received, retained, recited and expounded to others."

The Buddha said that supposing there was someone who sacrificed their life time and time again, over countless aeons without even a thought of gaining something in return, this person would have great merit. However, if another person studies the *Diamond Sutra* and believes without contention—this is the crucial point, to absolutely believe without contention in the self-liberating, self-nature prajna wisdom of the *Diamond Sutra*, to believe in one's own mind and self nature—this person's merit and fortune will surpass the other person's. Just believing won't do it; you must believe *without contention* and without acting contrary to it.

Believing without contention is very difficult. Many people study Buddhism and understand it quite deeply but their behavior and conduct are contradictory and in contention with what they understand. For example, there are some people who can really sound convincing, telling you to let go or take a different perspective, but can they themselves let go or take another perspective? If you insult them or poke fun at them, they can't take it. This is in contradiction with one's belief. Belief without contention is not merely intellectual acceptance but is absolute faith. When one's conduct concords with their belief, this is from where fortune and merit arise. This fortune and merit supersedes that of sacrificing lives. This is not to mention the case where one provides means to make the Dharma of the *Diamond Sutra* widely available. In earlier times, before the printing press, this was accomplished by transcribing the sutra by hand. One who keeps the sutra, recites it, cultivates it and explains it to others will have greater fortune and merit than the other person.

To Whom Is the Tathagata Speaking

"Subhuti, to sum up, this Teaching has inconceivable, inestimable and unlimited merit. The Tathagata has expounded it for the benefit of those awakened to the Mahayana and the Supreme Paths. If they are able to receive, retain, observe, read and write, recite and expound it to others, the Tathagata knows and sees that their merit is beyond measure or calculation, is unlimited and inconceivable."

The *Diamond Sutra* itself has inconceivable (impossible to understand), inestimable and unlimited (impossible to measure by length, by strength or by anything) merits. Notice the next line! We all read and study it but can we get even one of its merits? We can't get them because *"the Tathagata has expounded it for the benefit of those awakened to the Mahayana and the Supreme Paths."* The inner meaning of this sutra is for those who've awakened the mind of bodhicitta, the mind of a Bodhisattva, for those on the Supreme Path and not those of ordinary wisdom. The Buddha also said that for those who are able to receive and retain, retain and observe, read and recite it, one doesn't need to be of the highest wisdom. *"The Tathagata knows and sees,"* He absolutely knows for sure and sees very clearly that those who can recite it or study it and make this Teaching more widely available to others will receive merit beyond measure or calculation, unlimited and inconceivable. This person will, in the near future, attain immeasurable merits. Why is this? *"They bear the responsibility for transmitting the Tathagata's anuttara-samyak sambodhi"*

Thus the Buddha said that this kind of person is like a Buddha. He or she has a feeling of responsibility and takes upon his or her shoulders the transmission of the Buddha Dharma. Such a person has such great wisdom, such great fortune. If you can give rise to such magnanimity and shoulder the responsibility, then you have this merit and this wisdom. What responsibility exactly does one bear? anuttara-samyak sambodhi, Supreme Enlightenment, Great Awakening; if you take responsibility for the transmission of this, naturally you one day will have a Great Awakening.

Are You Satisfied with Lesser Doctrines?

"Why? Because, Subhuti, those who are satisfied with lesser doctrines are attached to the idea of self, person, being, and life. They are unable to hear, retain, read and recite this sutra and explain it to others."

In the *Lankavatara Sutra* it divides beings into five categories of spiritual roots. There are those who have the roots of Hinayana. They naturally take pleasure in the doctrine of the Hinayana and if you encourage them to practice in accord with the Mahayana or the Supreme Path, they cannot accept it. It is beyond them to be able to accept it. Just as in school, there are students of different capabilities, and some will only be able to achieve the most rudimentary levels of learning. Buddhism is the same, but it doesn't have to do with one's capability. It has to do with the root of one's intention. Those who aspire to the Hinayana path are captivated by the effects of kung fu associated with meditation—seeing lights, hearing sounds, ch'i moving, legs feeling hot, rosy cheeks etc.

People who seek and take pleasure in these things are stuck in the view of self, person, being, and life. They're doing this for themselves. "Being," they hope to become someone extraordinary. "Personality," they hope to be healthy until a ripe old age and "life," if this wasn't enough, they hope to achieve immortality. As to the Mahayana Path, perceiving one's original nature and becoming a Buddha, "If a man hears about the right way in the morning, he can die in the evening without regret." Still, they absolutely cannot comprehend. This is why the Buddha says that those who take pleasure in lesser doctrines have no way to really hear and comprehend the real meaning of this sutra; nor will they read and recite it or make it widely available.

"Subhuti, wherever this sutra may be found, all realms of devas, men and asuras should offer worship, for you know that such a place is a stupa and should be properly venerated by all with ceremonial obeisance, circumambulation and with offerings of flowers and incense."

From the beginning, the Buddha has been telling us how very, very important this sutra is. Here again, he is telling Subhuti that anywhere and everywhere this sutra is found, whether they be devas, asuras, spirits or demon kings, all must pay respect to this sutra. Wherever this sutra is found, that place is a Buddha stupa and should naturally be venerated, prostrated to and made a place of offerings.

If I might be so bold as to make a slightly disrespectful joke, the Buddha is quite good at advertising and promotion! This sutra seems to be almost entirely promotional—the Dharma door of prajna is so important, so incredible... If you read this sutra, you may start to get the feeling that it's all marketing and no product! Is there something or not? This is the unique feature of the *Diamond Sutra* and of expounding the Dharma. The first important point is having absolute faith that if a person does not dwell in a single form or appearance, if one can let go of everything, then one is there. Still everyone in their deepest heart isn't really convinced and so they can't do it. They may say they can let go, but when real situations occur they get stuck in their perspective and can't let go. I have a little saying which talks about this, about human existence, *"I can see my folly but I can't be jolly; I have the dreams but not the means."* This is lack of conviction, contention with one's belief.

The second important point is taking responsibility for transmitting the Buddha Dharma, the Tathagatha's Right Dharma

Eye. One must be the heir to the ancient sages and carry on the heritage so as to pave the way for future generations. One must stand on the earth and reach for the heavens. From within this world's turbulent affairs, one must strive for the betterment of mankind and to pass the torch of wisdom. To do this, one needs unlimited patient endurance and self sacrifice.

In light of these two main points, one can see that the Buddha is not just doing a sales job. Read the section again, keeping these points in mind and you will understand what he is saying.

Gatha of Section Fifteen

A galloping horse, the whip is loosed and the stars are shaken.
Breathe one word and hundreds respond to the thunderous cry.
Rivers and mountains, no worries, in the old fisherman's pot is a catch.
What can compare with the ease of wearing a patched robe?

A galloping horse, the whip is loosed and the stars are shaken. This is using worldly dharma as a simile. We think of heroes, such as Han Kao-tsu, T'ang T'ai-chung, Chu Yuan-chang and so forth as all riding on horses. *"The whip is loosed"* is from the story of Ch'in-wang Fu-chien. He was leading the troops to battle, his men numbered in the tens of thousands. When face to face with the enemy commander, he boldly challenged him saying, "If all of my men threw their whips into the river, it would stop the flow of the water. Surrender now!" In the face of such confidence, the earth quakes and even the stars shake.

Breathe one word and hundreds respond to the thunderous cry." A person who has the enormous fortune to hold the power of an emperor needs only to breathe a word and all of those beneath him affirm it. It's like thunder from the heavens. In our world, an emperor or king has the greatest fortune and so everyone wishes to be the king but this is not real fortune. Where can real fortune be found?

"Rivers and mountains, no worries, in the old fisherman's pot is a catch." Dynasties come and dynasties go, but the rivers remain the rivers, and mountains still stand. There's nothing worth worrying over. The old fisherman represents people who wish to be someone great. They finally have a catch and not being sure what it is, just put it in their pot. It's all so meaningless.

"What can compare with the ease of wearing a patched robe." To practice Dharma is fortune without comparison. Some years ago in China, one would still see the monks wearing patched robes. Nowadays you'll hardly ever see any. Monks, usually those who lived in huts in the mountains would wear clothing made of scrap cloth that had been washed and then sewn together. Sometimes you could hardly see the cloth for all the thread that was used. Of all the manifestations of fortune in this world, clear fortune is the most difficult to obtain and enjoy. How does one get this kind of fortune? By initiating the great mind of the Mahayana, by daring

to want to become a Tathagata, one will have this most true form of fortune.

SECTION 16

CLEARING OBSTACLES

"Furthermore, Subhuti, it may be that some virtuous men or women are despised by others for receiving, retaining, reading and reciting this sutra. This karma is due to their evil conduct in a past life, for which they are to experience this evil state. However, because they are despised by others in the present life for receiving, retaining, reading and reciting this sutra, whatever evil karma they had produced in the past will be eradicated and they will attain anuttara-samyak sambodhi.

"Subhuti, I recall countless aeons ago, before I was with Dipankara Buddha, I made offerings to and respectfully served 8,400,000 multimillions of Buddhas without missing one. Nevertheless, if in the last period of the Buddha kalpa, a person were able to receive, retain, read and recite this sutra, his merit would be such that the merit I received from making offerings would not constitute a hundredth or even a millionth of it. Indeed it would be beyond calculation, beyond analogy.

"Subhuti, in the last period of the Buddha kalpa, if a virtuous man or woman is able to receive, retain, read and write this teaching, my full statement of the resulting merits may create derangement, doubt, and disbelief in the minds of some listeners. Subhuti, you must know that the significance of

this teaching is beyond conceivability, as is the fruit of the reward."

Lessening the Strength of Cause and Effect

> *"Furthermore, Subhuti, it may be that some virtuous men or women are despised by others for receiving, retaining, reading and reciting this sutra. This karma is due to their evil conduct in a past life, for which they are to experience this evil state. However, because they are despised by others in the present life for receiving, retaining, reading and reciting this sutra, whatever evil karma they had produced in the past will be eradicated and they will attain anutara-samyak sambodhi."*

This opening brings up quite a big topic. Suppose a person has spent his whole life as a very earnest, dedicated Buddhist, and has studied the *Diamond Sutra* but yet this person's whole life is a series of bad luck. There are others whose careers and businesses are going very well. They have money and a name for themselves and then get the idea to start practicing Buddhism. I warn them against it, saying that Buddhism is not for play and that tough times lie ahead on this road. They say that the Buddhas will protect their assets, but I tell them the Buddha doesn't care about such things. Buddhism is the way of emptiness, of letting go. Of course, there are those who get rich after starting to practice

Buddhism, but most meet with many difficulties. Not only is Buddhism this way; other spiritual paths have this same phenomenon as well. People say that they've been so good their whole life but have received only hardships in return. The bad guys are strong and healthy, have money and means—it's as if the laws of cause and effect are completely upside-down. This is really quite a big question.

We must first be clear on the fact that the law of karma and cyclical existence in the three realms is the most basic of Buddhist teachings. There is not only just this one life but rather life is a continuum. The Buddha discussed the above question in relation to this in other teachings. Students asked the Buddha why there were so many virtuous people in this world who suffer so much. The Buddha said that it was karma from a previous life which had not yet been cleared up and the rewards from the virtuous conduct in this life would manifest throughout future lives.

It is not easy for people to believe in the wheel of karma because they feel they cannot see it. Actually it is very easy to see and I will tell you the method. Why are you all looking at me with such big eyes? I'm not going to be transmitting some secret method to you! All you need to do is to look at your own life. People middle-aged and older especially can see that their experiences as a youth are what has shaped the person of the middle years and what one does in one's middle years will result in the kind of later life one has. You could for instance divide the time periods by 20 and under, 21 to 40 and 40 and up. You could also look at the cycle on a smaller scale such as yesterday, today and tomorrow representing the past life, present life and future life.

A lot of students ask me what they were in their past life. I don't have E.S.P.! Still, you can see for yourself, *"If you wish to know your past existence, the present one can unlock all the secrets."* In this life what you are, what habits you have will shape your future life. *"If you wish to see your future existence, closely examine this one."* The most difficult part of Buddhism is understanding karma and the cycle of existence. Life is a never ending continuum but it is constantly transforming itself.

Traditional Chinese culture also talks about karma but, in the *I-Ching* for instance, it does not talk about the concept of the three realms. Confucius, Lao-tzu, Mencius and Chuang-tzu all spoke of karma but not so directly. Here in the *Diamond Sutra*, it is pointed out specifically in the situation where a person recites this sutra and because of this is the object of another person's ridicule or hatred which could even be as bad as ostracization from society or persecution. The Buddha explains that this is karma which would have manifested as rebirth in the lower realm in a life to come but *"this karma is due to their evil conduct in a past life, for which they are to experience this evil state. Because they are despised by others in the present life for receiving, retaining, reading and reciting this sutra, whatever evil karma they had produced in the past will be eradicated and they will attain anutara-samyak sambodhi."* In other words, this serves as atonement for past mistakes. One is now a good person with virtuous conduct and so, this karmic debt from a past life is lightened or burned up. Instead, one will receive another fruit. This fruit is incredibly difficult to come by, anuttara-samyak sambodhi, Great Enlightenment.

To this, the only thing we can say is that we don't deserve this honor. Worldly fortune alone is so very very hard to attain, let alone becoming a Buddha. Ch'an has recently gained popularity again and everyone talks about sudden enlightenment. Many people sit in meditation waiting for their enlightenment to come. One student came up to me and asked why she hadn't experienced an awakening yet, saying that she had been meditating for a month already. I said be patient and keep sitting, eventually...just be patient! Here the *Diamond Sutra* is telling you what to do. Do you understand what it's saying? You need to clear up your past karma before any awakening will happen. This is why Ch'an Master Yung-chia said, *"One may understand that karma is originally empty but still must repay the debts long overdue."* Our life in this world operates by karma, cause and effect, and so there is no use railing against heaven and men. Everything with which we meet has a definite cause and each cause has a result. This part of the *Diamond Sutra* must not be taken lightly. It is telling us how we cultivate in order to get results. One must really work hard to decrease one's karmic obstacles. Only in this way will one's wisdom be able to shine through. If you haven't put any effort into getting past your personal obstacles, wisdom will not arise and no awakening or enlightenment will come.

"Subhuti, I recall countless aeons ago, before I was with Dipankara Buddha, I made offerings to and respectfully served 8,400,000 multimillions of Budddhas without missing one."

Shakyamuni Buddha, here is telling of His own background. He remembered back throughout countless aeons during which He was with countless Buddhas and teachers. The first time Shakyamuni Buddha had an awakening was when He was a student of Dipankara Buddha. At that time Shakyamuni vowed to practice Buddhism and between then and this life He had 8,400,000 multimillions of teachers and guides. He studied with and made offerings to each of them. What does it mean to make offerings? As he would have honored and respected his parents, he would have done the same for his teachers. This includes gifts such as clothes, food, lodging and medicine. The Buddha made such offerings to each of them as a disciple, as well as doing for them work that needed to be done. He let no opportunities pass by Him and always learned something from the experience. This is the kind of attitude He had during His period of learning—hard work, dedication and humility.

"Nevertheless, if in the last period of the Buddha kalpa, a person were able to receive, retain, read and recite this sutra, his merit would be such that the merit I received from making offerings would not constitute a hundredth or even a millionth of it. Indeed, it would be beyond calculation, beyond analogy."

Buddha was saying, actually no one taught Him the theory of the *Diamond Sutra* and so now He was saying this for the benefit of those to come. If a person can get a handle on the essential point of this sutra, *"receive, retain, read and recite"* it, their merit will be greater than that gained from having made offerings to thousands of Buddha. Neither an abacus nor a computer could calculate the comparison. The fact that we are now engaged in this study of the *Diamond Sutra* will bring to us more merits than Shakyamuni Buddha had accrued. This is the Buddha's way of giving us encouragement.

Inconceivable Fortune

> *"Subhuti, in the last period of the Buddha kalpa, if a virtuous man or woman is able to receive, retain, read and recite this teaching, my full statement of the resulting merits may create derangement, doubt, and disbelief in the minds of some listeners. Subhuti, you must know that the significance of this teaching is beyond conceivability, as is the fruit of the reward."*

The Buddha was telling Subhuti that during later ages, if someone was to receive, retain, read and recite this sutra, that person's merit would be so huge that He dare not try to explain it. He is afraid the person who hears such an explanation will be so stupefied he or she will go off the deep end, or that this person will doubt the Buddha Dharma thinking that the Buddha is exaggerating because it couldn't be possible. Therefore, the Buddha didn't dare try to explain, and yet did he offer absolutely no information? On the contrary, he did offer one conciliatory sentence saying that the meaning of the *Diamond Sutra* was inconceivable. Don't be fooled by your mere intellectual understanding of the words for there is layer upon layer of meaning here. This meaning or these principles are not within the realm of your ordinary consciousness and so there is no way for the thinking mind to access them. The merit and fortune which arise from this sutra are likewise inconceivable.

Gatha of Section Sixteen

> "Karmic consciousness flows in an uninterrupted tumult.
> All astir, there is no shore to which one can turn back.
> We are all just lonely sojourners floating about the sea of suffering;
> But understand no mind, and in the moment rest."

"*Karmic consciousness flows in an uninterrupted tumult*" In Buddhist studies, it is often said that the continuation of life is the result of karma and consciousness. First, we need to define these terms. Karma is not sin. It is the power which comes through habits which include habits of virtue, habits of non-virtue and neutral habits. We are constantly creating karma. We make many small movements. For example, some people stroke their ear lobe, others scratch their head, without being aware that they are doing so. This is a manifestation of habit energy.

How is it that we are unaware of our actions? What is unawareness? In modern psychology, action done without awareness comes from the subconscious. In Buddhism, it is the work of the back side of the sixth consciousness, called the shadow consciousness. One's "sixth sense," instinct and inspiration all are within this consciousness. Beyond this is a realm of karmic consciousness, an example being that when we are moving about, we have a feeling of being an individual entity. In Buddhist psychology, this is within the realm of our seventh and eighth consciousness, the klistamano(adana)-vijnana and the alaya-vijnana. In western psychological terms, these are very difficult to define.

The length of one's life, the condition of one's body, the kinds of illness one will develop and even the state of one's environment is the functioning of one's karmic consciousness. To engage in a full-scale explanation of karmic consciousness is quite difficult, but at least you have some inkling of this concept. We sitting here are living beings by the mere fact of our bodies functioning. Every cell exists, is alive due to the functioning of karmic consciousness. In the previous section, the Buddha spoke of the giving of one's body. The difficulty in this giving actually lies in the giving up of karmic consciousness.

Why is it that when one sits down to meditate, the mind will not settle down? Because blood is still coursing through the veins, the physical sensations are still present—the karmic consciousness will not quiet down. Karmic consciousness is active and will not be still. If you can really grasp hold of the power of wisdom and use the power of the mind to cut through the karmic consciousness and completely drop this body and these feelings, you may have a Great Awakening. Well, if not a Great Awakening at least a small one will occur. To actually sacrifice as many lives as grains of sand in the Ganges is no easy feat because no matter what, you cannot give up the feeling of having a body. The more one meditates, the more discomforts will come up. The closet of old debts stored in our karmic consciousness opens up. Some people who meditate will experience all their old physical ailments again. These debts have to move through and clear up before one can be liberated, before there can be an awakening. Within one's lifetime—yesterday, today and tomorrow; last year, this year and next year; youth, middle age and old age—the manifestation of karmic consciousness is unbroken.

We always hear in Buddhism, "Turn back and the shore is there". *"All astir, there is no shore to which one can turn back."* The sea of suffering is endlessly stirring. Turning back there's the shore. Everyone can say this line, but have you ever thought about it deeply? Just exactly where is this shore? You cannot turn back, and so you do not know. We all engage in some kind of practice such as meditation, but no matter what, our two eyes can only look forward. Whether or not they are closed, our eyes cannot look backward. The statement "turn back and the shore is there" already tells us where the shore is and what the shore is. It is the wide open sublime emptiness. What is it like when one is at the other shore? Don't forget the sentence in the *Diamond Sutra* which says, *"This Dharma is neither real nor illusory."* If you say it is devoid and empty, it is wrong. If you say it exists, you are wrong. It is at this point of not real and not illusory, at this alambana, that you are on the shore. If you don't know that turning back in itself is the shore, your *"karmic consciousness flows in a continuous tumult; all astir, there is no shore to which to turn back."*

"We are all just lonely sojourners floating about the sea of suffering." We all have a kind of feeling, myself included, that we are just floating, tossed about in the ever-stirring sea of suffering. How can we really become liberated, really attain the Tao? *"But understand no mind and in the moment rest."* No mind in the moment, "no mind" is not no thoughts. To think of them as "thoughts" and press them down is not what this means. There is a poem from the T'ang Dynasty which reads, *"Before one reaches the ground of no mind, the hundred thousand efforts flow away."* Until one gets to the point of "no mind," whatever sort of cultivation efforts one makes are just water under the bridge. If you can remember that the sutra said to develop a mind that does not dwell and the Dharma is neither real nor illusory, then at least you have found an inkling, "an eyelash" of real cultivation. I hope you will all pay special attention to this section. The last line of the

text sums it up. *"This sutra is inconceivable as are its merits."* Just how inconceivable? Through them, you become a Buddha. This is the path to Buddhahood.

SECTION 17

NO SELF IN THE END

At that time, Subhuti addressed the Buddha thus, "World-Honored One, when virtuous men and virtuous women initiate the mind of anuttara-samyak sambodhi, how should their minds dwell? How should their minds be pacified?"

The Buddha said to Subhuti, "Virtuous men or women who seek anuttara-samyak sambodhi must develop a mind to liberate all sentient beings. Yet, when all sentient beings have been liberated, verily, not a single being has been liberated. Why is this? Subhuti, if a Bodhisattva still has any notions of self, person, being, and life, she is not a Bodhisattva. This is because, Subhuti, in actuality there is no dharma called attaining anuttara-samyak sambodhi.

"Subhuti what do you think? When the Tathagata was with Dipankara Buddha, did He have any Dharma by means of which he attained anutara-samyak sambodhi?"

"No, World-Honored One. If I understand the Buddha's meaning, when He was with Dipankara Buddha, there was no such Dharma with which He gained anutara-samyak sambodhi."

The Buddha said, "Just so, just so, Subhuti! Subhuti, I tell you truly, there is no Dharma by which the Tathagata attained anuttara-samyak sambodhi. Subhuti, if there was a Dharma by which the Tathagata attained anuttara-samyak sambodhi, Dipankara Buddha would not have predicted, 'In the future, you will be a Buddha called Shakyamuni'. But since there is no Dharma by which one can attain anutara-samyak sambodhi, Dipankara Buddha predicted that in the future I would become a Buddha called Shakyamuni. Why is this? The Tathagatas and all dharmas are as Such. If someone says the Tathagata attained anuttara-samyak sambodhi, Subhuti, I tell you truly, there is no Dharma as 'the Buddha attained Supreme Enlightenment'. Subhuti, the Tathagata's Supreme Enlightenment is neither real nor illusory. This is why the Tathagata says that all dharma is Buddha Dharma. Subhuti, all dharma is not dharma but is merely called dharma.

"Subhuti, suppose there was a person with an enormous body".

Subhuti said, "World-Honored One, this enormous body of which the Tathagata speaks is not an enormous body but is merely called so."

"Subhuti, this is the same concerning Bodhisattvas. Although a Bodhisattva says, 'I have liberated countless sentient beings', he is not a Bodhisattva. Subhuti, in reality there is no dharma called Bodhisattva, and this is why the Buddha says that all dharma has no self, no person, no being and no life. Subhuti, if a Bodhisattva says, 'I make the Buddha lands majestic', this person is not a Bodhisattva. Why is this?

The majestic Buddha lands spoken of by the Buddha are not majestic but are merely called majestic. Subhuti, if a Bodhisattva deeply understands the Dharma of no self and no dharma, the Tathagata calls him a true Bodhisattva."

We have now come to the seventeenth section. Prince Chao-ming put a lot of effort into studying the sutra and making these divisions and titles. In total there are thirty-two sections and we've just completed the sixteenth, exactly at the halfway mark. The remaining sixteen sections form the remaining half. This division of sections has an order to it which should not be overlooked. It's not like books today where whatever one feels like writing and however one wishes to number things will suffice. Here careful study was done and the principles and philosophy of numerology from the *I-Ching* were applied. So now we will look at section seventeen which is a kind of a new beginning.

What Kind of Commitment to Make?

At that time, Subhuti asked the Buddha, "World-Honored One, when virtuous men and virtuous women initiate the mind of anutara-samyaksambodhi, how should their minds dwell? How should their minds be pacified?"

You see, we've come back to the starting point! The same old question again. This Subhuti is just like us, rehashing things again and again. Subhuti at the beginning asked this very same question and Buddha has been speaking since then in response to it. Then Subhuti asks again in the same way. We would say, "I still don't understand." If a person has just set his or her mind on the Mahayana Path, on becoming a Buddha, on perceiving his or her original nature, *"how should their minds dwell?"* The mind won't settle down, but how and on what should it dwell? *"And be pacified?"* We feel so much frustration and dissatisfaction. How can this be pacified? The same exact questions, it seems almost nonsensical. If this were a script for a play rather than a sutra, it would be a farcical play.

> *"The Buddha said to Subhuti, "Virtuous men and virtuous women who seek anuttara-samyak sambodhi, must develop a mind to liberate all sentient beings. Yet, when all the sentient beings have been liberated, verily, not a single being has been liberated. Why is this? Subhuti, if a Bodhisattva still has any notions of self, person, being, and life, she is not a Bodhisattva."*

The question is the same but the answer is not. This answer has some meat to it. At the beginning of the *Diamond Sutra* the Buddha answered this question by saying, *"Be skillfully mindful,"* *"one should thus dwell."* Here the answer is quite different. He said those who are ready to practice Buddhism and wish to achieve Great Enlightenment or anuttara-samyak sambodhi, *"must develop a mind..."* What mind is being referred to here? The mind of total commitment. Commitment to what? *"Liberating all beings."* I wish to save every living being in the midst of suffering and frustration and help them achieve liberation.

What is the meaning of liberation and salvation? It means to leave behind all suffering and enter into joy, enter into nirvana. The alambana of nirvana is leaving behind all suffering and entering into joy. *Liberation* is the pacifying of, the leaving behind of all suffering and entering into a state of clean, purity and peace. It is turning around and finding the shore. If one wants to practice Buddhism, the first motivating force must be this. This commitment must arise.

"When all sentient beings have been liberated, verily not a being has been liberated." If you have saved all sentient beings, it's finished—over and done with. If you have an idea in your mind that it was I who saved so many beings, you are quite mistaken. Yesterday a student told me that her mother gave birth to sixteen children altogether. I told her that her mother was a very great woman. She raised sixteen children and yet she left without a one. It's as if she hadn't given birth to anyone at all.

We all leave the world the same way in which we arrived—alone and empty-handed. No one is happy about arriving and so an infant cries upon taking its first breath. Upon leaving, there is often not enough time to cry for oneself and so others cry on your behalf. Something else which is very interesting is that an infant has a grasping instinct from the start. Their little fists tightly clamp and will grasp at whatever they feel. The entire span of our lives is spent trying to find something on to which we can hold. No matter what it is, at death all must be given up. This is the alambana of ordinary life, career, children...whatever but, in the end, we can take nothing.

The Buddha said that within our lifetime, we can understand what it means to make the commitment to save all beings and actualize this. If we hold onto nothing in our minds and just act out of knowing what one ought to do, this is the Bodhisattva Path, the mind of bodhicitta. If, on the other hand, you do a small favor for someone and then make a mental note of it expecting praise and honor in return, you not only cannot be said to be practicing Buddhism but also lack basic human integrity. To be a Buddhist you must make the commitment. If you wish to be on the Bodhisattva path but still have feelings of pride and think that you are doing something great, you are grasping onto notions of self, person, being, and life. This kind of person should stop kidding himself because the Buddha says, "He is not a Bodhisattva." They don't make the grade. Only one without notions of self, person, being, and life, one who has let go of everything under the heavens, one in whose mind nothing dwells, can be called a Bodhisattva.

Did Dipankara Buddha Attain Anything?

"This is because Subhuti, in actuality there is no dharma called attaining anuttara-samyak sambodhi."

The Buddha is saying to them—you spend every day wishing to awaken to the Tao, to perceive your original nature, to achieve Great Enlightenment. Well, I'm telling you there is not a dharma. There is no such thing which can be called Tao. Great Enlightenment is the great awakening to not a thing. There is no such Tao to attain. If you think there is a Dharma to practice, you are mistaken. You have fallen into the four views and are not a Bodhisattva. This is why the Sixth Patriarch, Hui-neng spoke the following gatha upon his awakening:

Enlightenment originally has no tree,
And the clear mirror has no stand.
Fundamentally there is not a single thing.
Where then can dust gather?

This is saying the same thing; there is not a dharma called attaining anuttara-samyak sambodhi.

"Subhuti, what do you think, when the Tathagata was with Dipankara Buddha, did He have a Dharma with which he attained anuttara-samyak sambodhi?
No, World-Honored One."

The Buddha asked Subhuti to really think about the question of whether or not he had attained anything during the time spent with Dipankara. Just how big or how small is this anuttara-samyak sambodhi? And what exactly is it? Did I really come away with something? Subhuti answered, *"No, World-Honored One."* It was a very decisive answer. As I understand it, when you awakened to the Tao, you attained nothing.

> *"If I understand the Buddha's meaning, when He was with Dipankara Buddha, there was no such Dharma with which He gained anuttara-samyak sambodhi."*

Subhuti said, having studied with you for so long, if I'm not mistaken, I understand you to be saying that when you were with Dipankara Buddha you gained nothing whatsoever. There is nothing which could be called anuttara-samyak sambodhi or Supreme Enlightenment or Great Awakening. Subhuti spoke quite clearly but at the same time was implying that since he had not reached that level, he was still just putting forth his reasoned understanding.

> *The Buddha said, "Just so, just so."*

The Buddha said, It's just like this, just like this. If we really wish to practice Ch'an Buddhism and to know what "just like this" is, these words are a *hua tou* which will give you the answer if you can truly penetrate them. Look deeply into the words *"just so"* every day. During the Ming Dynasty, there was a famous dancer whose name was Liu Just So (Liu Ju-shih). Her family name was Liu and she took the words "just so" from the *Diamond Sutra* as her first and middle name. The Buddha gave us this *hua tou* as a way to Great Enlightenment.

> *"Subhuti, I tell you truly, there is no Dharma by which the Tathagata attained anuttara-samyak sambodhi."*

Subhuti, it is no lie when I tell you that there is no fixed thing which can be called the Buddha Dharma. There is no physical body, no sensations, the five skandhas are empty. There's no light and not even the most subtle form. Not a single thing can be grasped—this is anuttara-samyak sambodhi, Great Enlightenment.

> *"Subhuti, if there was a Dharma by which the Tathagata attained anuttara-samyak sambodhi, Dipankara Buddha would not have predicted, 'In the future you will be a Buddha called Shakyamuni'."*

The Buddha said that if I felt there was something to be attained at the highest level of Buddhism, if I felt I had attained something upon awakening, my teacher Dipankara Buddha, would not have said that in a certain lifetime to come I would have a Great Awakening and Great Enlightenment. Prediction of enlightenment is something found in Buddhism. When students are going to have an awakening, Buddhas since antiquity, would rub the top of the student's head and give them some words of prediction telling them at which time, which place they would become a Buddha.

Why Did Dipankara Buddha Give Verification?

"But since there is no Dharma by which one can attain anuttara-samyak sambodhi, Dipankara Buddha predicted that in the future I would become a Buddha called Shakyamuni."

At the time He awakened, He truly did not feel as if he had gained anything, and so Dipankara at that time verified that he would become a Buddha called Shakyamuni in the Sahaloka. We always hear it said, *"Do not seek with a mind wishing to attain, the fruit of nothing to attain."* Still we all seek the fruit of "nothing to attain" with a mind wishing to attain. The very foundation is wrong. At that time, Buddha reached the alambana of "nothing to attain," and so Dipankara Buddha verified him. Finished. Now a question arises.

"Why is this? The Tathagatas and all dharmas are as Such."

This is the key point! Pay careful attention please! We who practice Buddhism will make prostrations to the Buddha. The Buddha is also called the Tathagata, (in Chinese, *ru lai*) which means "as if to come." *Tatha* means "as if" and *gata* means "to come". "As if to come"—there is really no arriving and yet to say there is absolutely no coming is also wrong. We can use the example of television. If we turn on the television, are the T.V. celebrities right in front of you? They are actually not there, but it's as if they're there. When you make a phone call, does the other person come and speak into your ear? Not actually, but it's as if they have.

Where is the Tathagata? Where is the Buddha? The Buddha is right here. You need not search elsewhere. The Buddha is right in the heart of your mind. Both inside and outside of your mind, the Buddha is always there. It's just a matter of your finding this for yourself and then you have perceived the Buddha, perceived the Tathagata. How then is the sentence, *"All of the Tathagatas and all dharmas are as Such,"* to be explained? This is the most important sentence. If you practice Buddhism, you must pay special attention. Most Buddhists have a religious air about them. Where is the Buddha? In the temple? In the Buddha Hall? In the Western Paradise? To think so is wrong.

"All dharmas are as Such." All worldly dharma is the Buddha's dharma; there is not a speck of dharma which is not the Buddha's Dharma. As it says in the Doctrine of the Mean, *"The folly of a husband and wife can impart great knowledge."* This is also the Tathagata; all things lead to this. In any moment, any one atom, any clean and pure place as well as any filthy place the Buddha can be found. This is the Tathagata and this is why it says, *"All dharmas are as Such."* Please pay special attention to this point.

"If someone says the Tathagata attained anuttara-samyak sambodhi, Subhuti, I tell you truly, there is no Dharma as the Buddha attained anuttara-samyak sambodhi."

The Buddha said that some people might say that the Buddha sat under the Bodhi tree for seven days and seven nights and then attained something called anuttara-samyak sambodhi. Subhuti, I'm telling you the day the Buddha became enlightened, he did not attain a single thing and so this is called Great Awakening and Enlightenment.

"Subhuti, the Tathagata's Supreme Enlightenment is neither real nor illusory."

You might say, if there is absolutely nothing to gain, then why practice Buddhism? Well, we originally gain nothing anyway! Everyone says that in Buddhism we are trying to get emptiness, but if you used your noggin and thought about the idea of "trying to get emptiness" a little, it would dawn on you that you don't have to try to get it! The self is originally empty. Why seek emptiness, right? If Buddhism was about existence, then there'd be something to get with a little flavor to it at least. But seeking emptiness deep in the mountains or in a temple, you will only find mountains and temples, not emptiness. Why seek when they are originally empty? Don't forget that the Buddha said, it's not emptiness and it's not existence. *"It is neither real nor illusory."*

"Not real" is emptiness and "not illusory" is existence. In many sutras, this is described *as "not empty nor existent, both empty and existent."* The *Diamond Sutra* simply uses these other words to express this same meaning.

All Is the Buddha Dharma

All dharma is the Buddha Dharma. There are some people who become very narrow-minded after they start studying Buddhism. They won't pay respect to any other "Devil's" path. When I sometimes go to the countryside and see one of those small, crude temples dedicated to the local protector god, I will put my hands together and respectfully bow. Other people will say, "But you're a Buddhist, why should you do that?" I tell them that I don't buy into that kind of attitude. If one is very virtuous in this lifetime, he himself may become a local protector god after death. I might not necessarily have been so virtuous and so perhaps after death I might come under the jurisdiction of the local protector god. It is better to establish a good relationship beforehand. If you think that by becoming a Buddhist you're one up on all the others, think again.

A real Buddhist is respectful to all others in any situation. This is the Buddhist spirit. The Buddha never taught us to look down on others. All he said was not to lose yourself in your studies. In the *Diamond Sutra*, the Buddha said, *"All saints and sages differ on this point,"* and now He says, *"All dharma is the*

Buddha Dharma." These are the Buddha's words, not mine. If one has religious parameters, one cannot practice Buddhism. When I go to a Christian Church, I am very respectful. Jesus was a virtuous man who taught others to be virtuous as well. His teaching influenced the people of Europe and then America, encouraging them to do good. Jesus was a magnanimous man. To practice Buddhism, we need this kind of magnanimity. To learn Buddhism, you must first learn how to be a good person, learn how to smile. You must become a bodhisattva with enormous capacity of acceptance, become the Buddha with an enormous "stomach" which can hold everything. In other words, everything is alright with you; all dharma is the Buddha Dharma. With this magnanimity you can face anyone with a feeling of compassion and a smile on your face. This is Buddhism.

"Subhuti, all dharma is not dharma but is merely called dharma."

Once again the contradictory language. What is all dharma? All dharma is empty! We were just speaking of paying respect and bowing; after this has been done, it is empty. *"All dharma is not dharma"* is a matter of your point of view. If you think there is something, there is something, but if you think it's empty, it's empty. *"All dharma is not dharma but is merely called dharma."*

The Bodhisattva with Nothing

"Subhuti suppose there was a person with an enormous body." As soon as He started asking, Subhuti knew exactly what He meant. A body so big, so huge—I understand, it's a metaphor. There is no one as big as this that I've ever seen. The Buddha heard his answer and followed up by saying, *"Subhuti, if a Bodhisattva says. 'I have liberated countless sentient beings', he is not a Bodhisattva."* You are right Subhuti. What's more, if someone spent all their time reciting sutras, *"Thus I have heard,"* on your behalf and they want your everlasting gratitude for it, this person is not a Bodhisattva. Don't pay any attention to this nonsense. Real Bodhisattva conduct is to save others, to help others, but not to have a feeling in one's mind of having saved or helped anyone. If this feeling remains, this is breaking the sila, the sila of charity, of giving. A Bodhisattva's conduct is to save all the beings under the heavens and not have any feelings of pride or self-satisfaction.

"Subhuti, in reality, there is no dharma called Bodhisattva, and this is why the Buddha says that all dharma has no self, no person, no being and no life."

Great Bodhisattvas are the same as Buddhas in that they haven't a thing. If you say they have the Dharma Treasure, that is just a worldly idea that goes along with power and might. How is it then that one is called a Bodhisattva? It is due to the fact that one is absolutely empty, completely wide open, grasping nothing, dwelling on nothing that one is called a Bodhisattva. Real Bodhisattvas have no notions of self, person, being and life. *"Subhuti, if a Bodhisattva says, 'I make majestic the Buddha lands', this person is not a Bodhisattva."* The Buddha said to Subhuti, suppose someone said, "If I become Buddha, I will make my Buddha land into the grandest place ever seen. It will make Amitabha's Western Paradise seem like merely a four-star hotel. In the sutras, it describes the place as having floors of glass and trees made from jewels. This is nothing compared to what science and technology today can create. If I were a Buddha, I would make a Buddha land that would give Amitabha a run for his money!

Is this the mind of a Bodhisattva? It most certainly is not. This paragraph is implicitly telling us that everyone who becomes a Buddha will have his or her own Buddha land, but this so-called majestic Buddha land is not actually a physical world but the majesty of the mind. The merits of virtuous conduct being complete, the mind is pure and clean and this is what is majestic. If, though, you have something which is called a majestic mind, this is not the mind of a bodhisattva.

"Why is this? The majestic Buddha lands spoken of by the Buddha are not majestic but are merely called majestic."

That which the Buddha calls majestic Buddha lands is nothing more than a metaphor. If you look at today's modern

411

world, science and technology have had so many advances that everything around us is very refined. However, if one day you ever get the opportunity to stand on the edge of space, to experience real emptiness, then you will know what beauty and majesty are. This kind of majesty is ungraspable. There's not a thing you can get from it or take away with you. That is why the Buddha says the majestic Buddha lands are not majestic but are merely called majestic.

Egoless Bodhisattva

> "Subhuti, if a Bodhisattva deeply understands the Dharma of no self, and no dharma, the Tathagata calls him a true Bodhisattva."

This is the first step of practicing Buddhism, and it is also the end result. You must first deeply understand "no self." What is "no self"? You must rid yourself of the idea of a body. Most people when they meditate cannot achieve the state of dhyana or samadhi because they hold onto the notion of a body and the feelings of a body. This is not to mention those who play around with ch'i-mai trying to open the Governing and Reproductive Vessels, make small and large cosmic rotations, cultivate the Tan-t'ien, etc.—you are just playing games with illusory feelings. It is all within the realm of the notion of a body. When Pai Chu-i studied Buddhism, he wrote two lines: *"Warm and full, cold and hungry, when is there*

enough Tao? The long and short of this body is illusory emptiness."
Whether we feel comfortable or not, whether we can eat our fill
are not worth discussing. For no matter how long we live, in the
end this body again becomes dust, nothing to show for it. So the
first step in Buddhism is to forget the idea of a body.

Forgetting the body is not "no self," it is only no notion of a
body. You must be able to completely let go of the body and mind,
inside and out in order to achieve "no self" and subsequently
achieve samadhi. Achieving this state is not the final achievement
of Buddhists. It is the level of human selflessness, which is one
level of Hinayana achievement. The self is gone but the dharma is
still there. Once you have achieved no self and no dharma, this is
anuttara-samyak sambodhi, also called the state of self and
dharma both empty of self. In the end, emptiness is also empty.
There is no emptiness existing.

In this section the old question is repeated but a new answer
is given. Subhuti asked the same question again, and Shakyamuni
Buddha gave him a new answer with five important points to
which everyone should pay attention.

Gatha of Section Seventeen

A wad of emptiness is a particle; a particle is not real.
Splitting the particle you get emptiness; emptiness is also dust.
Deceptive images hold the mystic jewel and yet the tracks are
silent.

Thus, lingering color and form do fool each and all.

"A wad of emptiness is a particle; a particle is not real." A while ago we mentioned the story of a Taoist named T'an Ch'iao who wrote *The Book of Transformation.* In the book it says, *"A granule is a wad of emptiness; when you see the granule you don't see the emptiness."* If you take an open space and enclose it with a house, you no longer see the space. Rather, you see a house. In the same way, a wad of emptiness is a particle or granule, when you see the granule, you no longer see the emptiness. *"Split the granule and you have emptiness; when you see emptiness, you don't see the granule."* If you take a physical particle and break it apart, it will return to emptiness. When there is emptiness, you no longer see the particle. This is just to say that you must rid yourself of the notion of a body. We are sitting here, physically present because we haven't worked hard enough. Our wisdom isn't strong enough, and so we cannot enter samadhi. We are stumped by this particle, this large physical particle. This is the logic behind using this Taoist idea. *"A wad of emptiness is a particle; a particle isn't real."* Physical, material forms are not real.

"Splitting the particle you get emptiness; emptiness is also dust." If you can knock out physical form, is the resultant emptiness what you want? Holding onto a state of emptiness, is still yet another obstacle, karmic dust, if you will.

"Deceptive images hold the mystic jewel and yet the tracks are silent." This line has its origins in the ideas of Chuang-tzu. The

basic physical material of the universe is fundamentally a projection, like a holograph. On top of this, the second level of projection is the physical world and within this is the projection of a self, mind and body. It's like a movie—you can't say it's real and yet you can't say that it's not. Looking deeply into this you will find the jewel, subtle and ungraspable. Deceptive images and mystic jewels, if you say they exist you're wrong, and if you say they don't exist, you're also wrong. If you really go to find an answer, no matter how hard you search, the tracks never lead to anything. Turning back, one finds one's original nature and true mind.

Thus, lingering color and form do fool each and all. Don't think that Chuang-tzu is saying that the world is false. Within the false is found the real. All is but illusion; illusion is also real. The Buddha said that the Dharma is neither real nor illusory.

SECTION 18

ONE SUBSTANCE, SAME PERCEPTION

"Subhuti, what do you think? Does the Tathagata have physical eyes?"

"Yes, World-Honored One, the Tathagata has physical eyes."

"Subhuti, what do you think? Does the Tathagata have deva eyes?"

"Yes, World-Honored One, the Tathagata has deva eyes."

"Subhuti, what do you think? Does the Tathagata have wisdom eyes?"

"Yes, World-Honored One, the Tathagata has wisdom eyes."

"Subhuti, what do you think? Does the Tathagata have Dharma eyes?"

"Yes, World-Honored One, the Tathagata has Dharma eyes."

"Subhuti, what do you think? Does the Tathagata have Buddha eyes?"

"Yes, World-Honored One, the Tathagata has Buddha eyes."

"Subhuti, what do you think, does the Buddha say that the sand in the Ganges River is sand?"

"World-Honored One, the Tathagata says it is sand."

"Subhuti, what do you think? If there were as many Ganges Rivers as there are grains of sand in the Ganges, and if there were as many Buddha realms as there are grains of sand in all these Ganges Rivers, would those Buddha lands be many?"

"Very many, World-Honored One!"

The Buddha said, "The living beings in the multitude of lands have many different kinds of minds which are all known to the Tathagata. Why is this? That which the Tathagata calls the mind is not really the mind but is merely called the such. Being as such, Subhuti, the past mind is ungraspable, the present mind is ungraspable and the future mind is ungraspable."

Eyes Are the Mind's

"Subhuti, what do you think? Does the Tathagata have physical eyes?"

"Yes, World-Honored One, the Tathagata has physical eyes."

"Subhuti, what do you think? Does the Tathagata have deva eyes?"

"Yes, World-Honored One, the Tathagata has deva eyes".

"Subhuti, what do you think? Does the Tathagata have wisdom eyes?"

" Yes, World-Honored One, the Tathagata has wisdom eyes."

"Subhuti, what do you think? Does the Tathagata have Dharma eyes?"

" Yes, World-Honored One, the Tathagata has Dharma eyes."

" Subhuti, what do you think? Does the Tathagata have Buddha eyes?"

"Yes, World-Honored One, the Tathagata has Buddha eyes."

In Buddhism, what is spoken of here is called the Five Kinds of Eyes. The Buddha himself raised the questions to Subhuti asking, "In your opinion, does the Buddha have physical eyes, deva eyes, wisdom eyes, Dharma eyes and Buddha eyes?" These are "self-initiated" questions. In the Tripitaka, the Buddhist canon, there are twelve divisions and one of these is "self-initiated". "Self-initiated" teachings are not prompted by others' questions but rather the questions are proposed by the Buddha himself. Here in these questions, the Buddha refers to the "I" rather than the "Buddha". The Tathagata represents the true essence of the dharmakaya, the nature of the mind which is the same in Buddhas, bodhisattvas and sentient beings and is the origin of all existence. The Buddha says that this has five kinds of functions and so there are five kinds of eyes.

The first kind are physical eyes, the same kind of eyes we have. They are the eyes born of our parents. Through these eyes we see our world, and due to this seeing, our feelings and understandings arise. These eyes are connected to our hearts and minds. In fact, in many sutras the words *mind* and *eyes* are interchangeable. In speaking of the mind, the eyes are often first mentioned. They are the door to the mind. In the *Yin Fu Sutra* of the Taoist canon it says, *"Eyes are a mechanism of the mind,"* the entrance to the mind. This is why many of the ancients speak of the relationship between the mind and the eyes. Mencius, for example, when explaining how to observe others stresses the importance of observing the eyes.

Everyone has a pair of eyes but what and how each person sees is different. For example, if we look at this wall, we can all see that it is white, but what that means to each person is completely different. There are those people who are near-sighted, far-sighted, those who have stigmatisms, those who are color blind, those who are near-sighted in one eye only and so forth.

Each and every person's eyes are different, as are their hearts, minds and faces. There are no two people on this earth whose faces are exactly alike, nor are there any whose thoughts are all alike. People don't look at things in the same way, and so you shouldn't think that everyone sees just about the same colors white, yellow, red.... There can be enormous differences. There are different karmic forces at work in each person which affect our mental and physical health. Some people prefer hot weather; some prefer cold. This is because of the different states of their bodies caused by karmic forces. All illness arises due to karma. Virtuous conduct leads to fortunate karma, and non-virtuous conduct leads to unfortunate karma. Karma is created by the mind. This is an undisputable principle of the Consciousness Only school.

Here, the Buddha puts the question to Subhuti of whether or not a person who has become a Buddha has physical eyes. Of course they do. They have physical eyes with which to see the physical world.

What Are Deva Eyes?

The second kind of eyes are deva eyes. People rarely have these kinds of eyes. Deva eyes have powers beyond the ordinary physical eyes. For example, there are those who can see ghosts, or devas, celestial beings. Those with deva eyes can even see other worlds within our desire realm. Strictly speaking, being able to see worlds outside of this Milky Way, outside of this realm, constitutes having deva eyes. Some people will close their eyes in meditation and see spots of light or shadows. They think that their deva eyes have opened—heaven's no!

In Buddhist artwork, there is an extra eye in the middle of the Buddha's forehead which represents both the deva and the wisdom eye. There have been a few humans as well as some animals who have three or sometimes four eyes. There are cultivation methods for both opening the deva eye and for opening "ten eyes". The "ten eyes" are the pairs in front, in back, and on the top of the head, at the heart, and at the throat. These eyes of course are not like our physical eyes but rather they function like a movie camera, a lens through which images are seen.

There are two ways people get deva eyes. The first comes as the fruit of many lives of cultivation and meditation work. Such a person is born with this natural ability because of the merit of his virtue. The second kind is the result of hard work in one lifetime, cultivating discipline, samadhi and wisdom. Such people do not grow another set of eyes, but rather they naturally develop the function of being able to see worlds and things that ordinary people cannot. There is another situation in which people who do a lot of meditation work will open up the energy channels (ch'i-mai) in the back of their head where the optic nerves end. When the energy stimulates the nerve, the person will at first have many optic illusions and hallucinations. This is not the opening of the deva eye. Don't fool yourself! The eyes of a person who has this ability will be bright and clear as if electrically lit. They will see everything as if it were transparent. There are no physical obstacles to what they can see with their penetrating vision.

During the Spring and Autumn Warring States Period, there was a famous doctor named Pien-ch'ueh. The story goes that he met a celestial being who gave him a gift of penetrating vision. With this vision, Pien-ch'ueh was better than an x-ray machine in that he could clearly see all of the organs functioning and his diagnosis was infallible. There are other recorded examples of historical figures, especially from the T'ang Dynasty onward, who have similar abilities. For example, there were those who were born with natural ability in geomancy; others could see into the ground and would find water or other things for people. These sorts of penetrating vision do not constitute a deva eye. They are only at the level of extrasensory perception. To achieve the true deva eye, one needs to cultivate samadhi as it says in the *Avatamsaka Sutra* and then these physical eyes of ours can have the ability to see everything in the ten directions.

Physical eyes can only see a limited amount of physical phenomena while Deva Eyes can see worlds that these eyes cannot. Deva eyes arise from samadhi and from the power of one's samadhi. When one's life force is strong enough, it can go beyond all the obstacles of the physical world. It needs the full power of one's ching, ch'i, shen and samadhi in order to function.

Wisdom, Dharma and Buddha Eyes

The next ones are wisdom eyes. Wisdom eyes are not beyond the physical eyes. They must also function through the eyes in the body given to us by our parents. Wisdom eyes come from cultivating discipline, samadhi and wisdom. Wisdom arises from samadhi and so is unlike worldly wisdom. As one's wisdom builds up, it gains strength, and when the strength is enough, the wisdom eyes will form. How does wisdom gain strength? People with ordinary intelligence can have an understanding of something, like, smoking and deep fried foods are bad for your health, but still can't change their habits. In this case, there is no power to their wisdom understanding because nothing changes. They still smoke and eat fried foods. We can all see very clearly our bad tempers, greed, laziness and so forth and yet, can't change them for all the Buddhist theory in the world. This is because our wisdom has no power behind it. When faced with actual situations, our meek wisdom can't help us. We can't actualize our wisdom, and therefore, we can't achieve the Tao.

Real wisdom eyes need to have sufficient power of wisdom behind them in order to function. What are dharma eyes? Wisdom eyes can perceive the emptiness of our original nature. The body of emptiness, the dharmakaya, is the dharma eye. The dharma eye sees all sentient beings as equal, not empty and not existent. To dwell in one-sided emptiness is the fruit of the Hinayana. One must be able to perceive the subtle existence arising from within emptiness. In worldly terms it is existence "arising from the nature of emptiness," but in the wisdom alambana of an enlightened being, it is true emptiness that gives rise to subtle existence. This is the principle behind dharma eyes which perceive everything in equanimity.

The fifth kind are Buddha eyes. Buddha eyes not only perceive everything in equanimity but also with only compassion and love. Compassion has two different facets to it. This first is the facet of benevolence, which represents the male side of our love. The second is the facet of sympathy, which represents the female side of our love. This love is not ordinary love but rather the highest manifestation of love. Great compassion is of the highest virtue, is unconditional and is with complete equanimity. In the Buddha's eyes, all sentient beings are deserving of pity, and so he must give, must help, must save them all. This is the great compassion of the Buddha eyes.

When you really practice Buddhism and make accomplishments in your cultivation, you will naturally develop these five kinds of eyes. Someone who achieves sudden enlightenment in that moment will achieve all these five functions. If you think that you have achieved Great Enlightenment but do not have these five functions, your enlightenment is fictional. The five kinds of eyes naturally appear with the consummation of discipline, samadhi, wisdom. Every person has the innate potential to develop these eyes. It's just a matter of putting the time and effort into cultivation.

Now the question is, why does the Buddha suddenly bring up the question of five kinds of eyes at this point in the sutra? Furthermore, he brings up the question and then just leaves it to Subhuti's response. Without saying anything more on the subject, he goes on to ask another question. There is no conclusion or follow-up. It's as if Shakyamuni Buddha suddenly becomes an eye doctor who gives his patient an eye examination and then says nothing. The patient didn't even make an appointment for the exam. What is the reason for all this?

These represent one's perspective and perception. Understanding the mind and perceiving one's original nature will naturally result in the functioning of the five kinds of eyes. This is the true perspective and perception, understanding the mind and perceiving one's original nature. Here in this section of the sutra the Buddha did not reveal the deeper meaning. If we wish to research the sutra, we must not overlook this part too easily. There is something more to be learned here.

Countless Galaxies of the Universe

"Subhuti, what do you think, does the Buddha say that the sand in the Ganges River is sand?"
"World-Honored One, the Tathagata says it is sand."

The Buddha now brings up the second question. The eye examination is finished and now starts the sand examination. Subhuti, does the Buddha see the sand in the Ganges as sand? If it were one of the Zen practitioners of today, they would say that in the Buddha's eyes it is not sand, or else they would say that the Buddha sees it as flowers or whatever. People have all sorts of crazy ideas and no straight answers. Subhuti was very earnest in his response—of course the Buddha sees sand. Do you think the Buddha's eyes see something different than ours? Sand is just sand, very ordinary. If someone is crying, the Buddha is not going to say they are laughing. An individual who says such is not a Buddha, rather, that person is a nutcase! When the Buddha sees someone crying, he says they are crying. It is absolutely ordinary. If you say the Buddha sees the world as empty, I ask you, who told you? The Buddha sees the sand in the Ganges as sand, cement as cement, and a wall as a wall, the same as we do. You must pay special attention here. Many Buddhists make the mistake of putting the Buddha up on a very high pedestal which has nothing to do with reality. When you put someone up on a pedestal, the result is that your perspective and thinking becomes warped. The *Diamond Sutra*'s full name is the *Severer Diamond Prajna Paramita Sutra,* which reflects this idea because it cuts through all false ideas. Real Buddhism has very, very ordinary principles.

The Buddha asked Subhuti if he thought the Buddha saw the sand of the Ganges as sand. Subhuti answered, Of course. The Buddha has eyes like ours and he sees sand as sand. If the Buddha were here with us in this room and you asked him whether he minded the heat, should we turn on the air-conditioning, unless we were seeing one of his transformation bodies, his physical body still feels heat and cold the same as ours. Of course he'd feel uncomfortable in such heat. It's these places in the sutra to which we need to pay attention. All of the sages of this world were humans. The Buddha was also a human being who succeeded in his cultivation.

This reminds me of a poem. As far as I can remember, this poem was written a hundred or two hundred years ago by someone from mainland China who went to Taiwan to search for a certain sage who lived on a mountain in Illan. He wrote the poem on the peak of this mountain. *"Thirty-three heavens, heaven upon heaven; the saints are found amongst white clouds; Of human flesh were saints originally made; just worry that your human heart is not resolute enough."* How did we get on to this poem? This is just to say that a Buddha is made of an ordinary person, very, very ordinary. When the Buddha sees the sand in the Ganges, he sees very clearly grains of sand, and now comes the third question.

"Subhuti, what do you think? If there were as many Ganges Rivers as there are grains of sand in the Ganges, and if there were as many Buddha realms as there are grains of sand in all these Ganges Rivers, would those Buddha lands be many?" "Very many, World-Honored One!" The Buddha asked Subhuti's opinion. Are there many grains of sand in the Ganges River? Each of these grains of sand represents a world. The total sum of grains of sand in all these Ganges Rivers is beyond computation. The Buddha used this method to help us understand the concept of an infinite number of worlds. Subhuti affirmed that this was certainly an incredibly large amount. Here, the Buddha also lets us know that there is an infinite number of Buddha lands. From his perspective as the founder of Buddhism in this age in this Sahaloka, he is one and the same as all the other countless Buddhas in the ten directions. Not only are the sentient beings all equal in his eyes but also are the saints and sages. He sees all in equanimity, absolutely ordinary. It's not only I that have become a Buddha. I'm nothing special. It's not as though if you don't listen to me you can't become a Buddha. That is not Buddhism. All sentient beings and all Buddhas are equal. Each Buddha is in charge of teaching in a world. There are an infinite number of worlds as well as an infinite number of Buddhas. "Are there many Buddha worlds?" "Very many, World-Honored One."

427

Infinite Number of Minds

The next question arises. The Buddha with his physical, deva, dharma, wisdom and Buddha eyes can see the multitude galaxies of worlds throughout space. Science can now verify that there are countless galaxies in the universe but still hasn't verified whether or not there is life on the moon. It's very easy for people of this day and age to understand these concepts about the universe. The Buddha taught all of this knowledge 2,000 years ago. What instruments did he use? How did he know there were so many worlds and beings in this universe? Simply by the Tathagata's five kinds of eyes, the strength of his wisdom, and his inconceivable power, and yet the Buddha is still completely ordinary. He sees sand as sand, and water as water. If he got hit in the back of the head, he might not see things as they ordinarily appear, but he ordinarily sees things as they are.

"The Buddha said, 'The living beings in the multitude of lands have many different kinds of minds which are all known to the Tathagata'." In this part, the Buddha seems to give a conclusion, but you must think for yourself whether or not this is the conclusion. Ch'an Buddhism encourages people to read this sutra in particular because it has so many of these *hua tous*. A *hua tou* seems very easy to understand when looking at it on the surface, but we actually don't understand at all. These give us a big test. We glance at it briefly as if we know the score but we know nothing really.

A lot of young people nowadays have this kind of attitude. They say they've read something but if you say, "Oh really, how about that part where it talks about...," they don't remember. It's the same in most social interactions—people gloss over the important issues in life and therefore make a lot of big mistakes. There really are no simple affairs in life. Each affair is a *hua tou* in and of itself. Whatever issue you can think of can be used. We could talk about it without ever reaching a consensus. The Buddha brought up all these different questions without giving any conclusions. He wants you to look into them for yourself. Actually the answers are all there! They just can't be understood by the thinking mind. It's only through samadhi and wisdom that the understanding comes. Buddhism isn't empty talk, but you must verify it yourself.

The Buddha asks how many kinds of minds there are among the myriad of beings in the multitude of lands. This is an imposing question. Even with the advance of psychology and computer technology, it would be next to impossible to figure out the answer. Yet, the Buddha says that he knows clearly all the different kinds of minds of all these beings. "The Tathagata clearly knows..." The Buddha gives an answer to this query, but it seems to have no connection to the questions before it, nor is there an overall conclusion and we are once again left hanging. This is, in fact, extremely skillful. For two thousand years, many Buddhist scholars either gloss over it or give an incorrect explanation. Let's take a look now at what the Buddha himself says as an explanation.

Your Mind

"Why is this? That which the Tathagata calls the mind is not really the mind but is merely called such."

As the Buddha sees it, all of these minds of the sentient beings are *"not really the mind."* The Buddha here is wagging his finger at us. These "minds" of sentient beings are not actually any "thing." There is no mind. Where is there a mind? The mind is lost; it is not really the mind. There is fundamentally no mind. Since there is no mind, the Buddha was probably expecting that the next question would be—then, what is there? So, he quickly added, that is why it is called the mind. All of the minds of sentient beings are known by him. The Buddha just kept on going saying that these minds are not minds. Subhuti couldn't get a question in edgewise. The minds of sentient beings are not only the minds of humans. Dogs, horses, ants and so forth are also sentient beings with minds that are not minds but are called minds.

From the beginning the *Diamond Sutra* has been saying that all sentient beings grasp onto the idea of a "self," the idea that "I" exists. We are completely entrenched within this self identity. We also have this idea that we have a mind. We take all these random thoughts, ideas, discriminations, frustrations and so forth, all these insubstantial and illusory phenomena as being an existent form. All beings make this fundamental mistake. All of these ever changing thoughts, feelings, ideas and so forth are merely phenomena of and within the real mind. All sentient beings, however, seize upon this kaleidoscope of images as being the mind itself. In the evening services at the temples, they recite the following verses: *"This day has passed and one's life is shorter yet; like a fish in water which is draining away, what happiness can there be?"* At the end of today, this life of ours is just a bit shorter. After today has gone by, it can never return. Youth has passed and one cannot stop from aging. It's so sad.

Actually, we are all fooled by these appearances. There is always tomorrow. Why get hung up on yesterday? There is never a shortage of tomorrows. Space is not divided into yesterday, today and tomorrow, past, present and future; nor does it come to an end. It is forever just space. Yesterday, today and tomorrow are just the changing of phenomenal appearance. The dawn's light covers up the darkness but, is the darkness really covered over by the light? The darkness then covers over the light of the day. Darkness then light, light then darkness; within these rotational changes, nothing increases and nothing diminishes. All functioning is illusionary and unreal. The body of space itself neither increases nor diminishes. Don't be fooled by the illusory and the unreal. The Buddha understands this but sentient beings don't. The Buddha says it is but merely called mind. Sentient beings take this feeling of the illusory as real and grasp onto the functioning calling it mind.

The mind, forever ungraspable. *"Being as such, Subhuti, the past mind is ungraspable, the present mind is ungraspable, and the future mind is ungraspable.*" The Buddha himself brought up the question concerning the mind, from the eyes to the mind. The summation of this discussion was that there is no mind. Sentient beings' "minds" are the constant transformation of phenomenal appearance; the same as the physical world, never stopping, forever ungraspable, forever onward flowing. The past, present and future mind are ungraspable. As soon as you say the word *future*, it has already become the present which then immediately becomes the past. It is ungraspable. All feelings and understandings are the same way. Sentient beings do not really comprehend this and in the midst of the "three minds," past, present and future, desperately seek something onto which they can hold. People want something upon which they can absolutely rely.

All of you students of Buddhism sitting here must also pay special attention. You meditate wishing to bring your mind to rest. This is making a fundamental mistake. As soon as you sit down and cross your legs, the mind wishing to quiet down is gone. It's gone with your aching legs. How could it possibly be held? If you say that you felt so clear and calm during your meditation, this feeling leaves after you get up from sitting. Didn't the Buddha say that the past is ungraspable, the present is ungraspable, and the future is ungraspable! Who told you to seize upon clear and calm? Clear and calm are ungraspable! Frustration is ungraspable, ungraspable is also ungraspable. How is it that we can get a grasp on anything? Within the ungraspable, this is just the way it is. It's that simple. Does the Buddha say the grains of sand in the Ganges River are grains of sand? Of course! Grains of sand are just grains of sand.

Most people who explain the *Diamond Sutra* say that prajna is emptiness and therefore ungraspable. This is a depressing perspective. It is ungraspable and so it is not empty. It is continuously coming. This is why the Buddha says that all this of the world are existent dharma. The "existent dharma" are not real. The fundamental fabric of existent dharma is non-existent while its functioning is existent. We are in the existent seeking the non-existent. With our back to the Way we rush onward. This is why all cultivation practice is useless. You don't stop existence and then have a realization of the Tao. Existence is within non-existence. It's only when you can observe the Tao beyond existence, within existence that you can be said to have perceived the Tao.

Existent dharma is endlessly re-becoming, transforming without cessation and without limitation. All things which are born and die never actually desist. If you think that by stopping the functioning mind, the mind of birth and death, beginning and ending, you will attain the Tao, this is an incorrect perception. It is not the right Buddha Dharma. This is why it is said, the nature of phenomenal arising is emptiness; from the nature of emptiness arises all phenomena. This is the middle way. It is the heart of the heart of the *Diamond Sutra* and is also the heart of the heart of enlightenment. If one is not clear on this point, then one dwells within an incorrect, skewed perspective, the perspective of a nihilistic, vacuous emptiness held in materialistic philosophy. If this were the case, why bother with Buddhism?

The Buddha clearly said that the past mind is ungraspable. He did not say there is no past mind. Right? The word "ungraspable" functions as a roadblock to deter people from going down the wrong path. Ungraspable signifies that there is no possibility. Many people explain these lines in terms of "capability." It is not a question of one's capacity. This is off the mark and following this direction will lead you farther and farther away. It's a mammoth mistake. The Buddha said that the past, present and future mind are ungraspable. Don't seek the mind of supreme Tao, anuttara-samyak sambodhi, within the realm of phenomenal appearances because they are constantly changing. Very skilled masters will always utilize the method of slicing through the three time mind in order that the student get an incipient understanding of emptiness. When the ungraspable past mind moment is gone and the moment of mind to come has yet to arise, the present moment is it. And just what is this present moment? It is not empty! Nor is it existent! You first need to see clearly for yourself what this mind is and then seek the Tao.

Section eighteen is all pointing to one thing. What is that thing? The "perceiving" of "perceiving the Tao," "perceiving one's mind," "perceiving original nature"; all that which is ungraspable, is not empty and yet is not existent. It is between existence and non-emptiness. It is bright clarity. When you have existence, there is existence; when you have emptiness, there is emptiness, very ordinary. If you are feeling sad and depressed, there is sadness and depression. When that passes, it is gone, empty. "Empty" simply means that the phenomenon is ungraspable. It doesn't mean there is no such occurrence. You're sad and when that passes, you are happy. Happiness and joy also cannot be held. They will also pass. They are also empty. "Empty" isn't non-existent. It is a convenient method of expression, a name. Don't think of emptiness as being the final goal of the Buddha Dharma. This is falling into nihilism. It is not even the emptiness which is the fruit of the Hinayana path. This idea is completely off the path of Buddhism. This is why it is so important to clear away the entanglements of perspective and the entanglements of mental states. Without doing this, it is impossible to achieve the fruit of enlightenment. It is that specific.

There are so many Buddhist commentaries out now which I feel are extremely dangerous. Something like that is even worse than deadly poison. It is a poison which affects one's understanding and perspective. I hope that all of you will use your wisdom and your discretion when you come in contact with teachings. Don't fall into incorrect perspectives which could sidetrack you.

Gatha of Section Eighteen

Shapes, sizes, colors and tones, perceptible variations are manifold;
Hand and eye are clearly different but the Tao perceives as one.
The universe is a floating bubble, while mind arises and ceases;
For, whom can you pacify, when space has naught to hold?

"*Shapes, sizes, colors, and tones, perceptible variations are manifold.*" Of the shapes, sizes, colors and tones of the physical world, there are myriad variations. If you look at people for example, they come in such diversity: big ones, little ones, black ones, white ones and everything in between. The world of phenomenal appearances is not one of uniformity. "*Hand and eye are clearly different but the Tao perceives as one.*" All are seen through the Buddha eyes, the wisdom eyes and the dharma eyes with complete equanimity. To what are the hand and eye referring? You've all seen the image of Avalokiteshvara with a thousand hands and a thousand eyes, one thousand arms and hands, each with an eye in the center of the palm. If a person with this many eyes and hands walked in off the street, half of you would cover your heads in fright! Actually, this is just a representation of the function of wisdom. There is nothing which isn't in view. The hands employ many methods of teaching, helping, protecting and saving. However, for all these thousands upon thousands of hands and eyes, there is only one hand and one eye. The hand is used for holding and the eye is used for seeing.

"The universe is a floating bubble, while the mind arises and ceases." Each universe, each world system is just like a small bubble, merely a function of one's original nature and great mind. Each thought, sensation, emotion and so forth is just a bubble within our original nature. Creation and destruction are an endless cycle, the nature of mind arises and ceases.

"For, whom can you pacify when space has naught to hold?" All dharma exists when it is functioning and is empty when not. Because there is no dwelling, therein arises the mind. Fundamentally, nothing abides. The second Ch'an Patriarch of China sought out Bodhidharma and asked the master how to pacify his mind. Bodhidharma told him to bring his mind hither and he would pacify it. Shen-kuang said, I have looked and indeed cannot find my mind. Bodhidharma said then, I have pacified your mind. In reality, Bodhidharma didn't pacify the mind of the second patriarch; the past mind is ungraspable, the present mind is ungraspable and the future mind is ungraspable. What is there to pacify? That is why I said, *"For whom can you pacify when space has naught to hold?"* Where does one go to pacify a mind? The mind needs no pacifying. Everywhere are worlds of lotus flowers and the mind is peaceful. Within the ordinary one finds the pureland and the mind is peaceful of its own accord. This is

because space is everywhere and space neither grasps nor dwells. This is the main point of this section.

SECTION 19

FORTUNE IS UNGRASPABLE

"Subhuti, what do you think? If a person filled the universe of worlds with the seven treasures and gave away all in his practice of charity, would he not thereby gain great merit?"

"Yes, World-Honored One, because of this one would attain great merit and fortune."

"Subhuti, if the fortune and merit were real, the Tathagata would not say the fortune and merit attained was great. He says so because there is no merit."

Here again, the Buddha poses a question, quite an interesting question. The *Diamond Sutra* just keeps recycling these couple of questions again and again. The Buddha has just finished talking about the highest wisdom and now we suddenly switch to another peak, the height of fortune. In Buddhism, there is a phrase which is, "fortune and wisdom both majestic." If an ordinary person wishes to become a Buddha, he or she must have majestic wisdom as well as majestic fortune. It takes true and correct merit and fortune to attain true and correct wisdom.

A lot of times, we may feel that we are really not very smart, we forget what we've read or we're not quick to understand. This is because our merit and fortune are lacking. Everyone comes into this world in the same manner; why is my brain power so deficient? Do you really think that when you came into this incarnation, you somehow picked a moldy brain out of the brain closet? Everyone's brain has the same capacity, but the problem is that one has not enough merit and fortune. The health of one's heart and one's brain depends on one's cultivation efforts.

The Buddha told Subhuti to suppose that someone gave away gold, silver, jewels and so forth, the seven most precious things in the world, enough to fill the universe. These precious things are actually completely worthless in that you can't eat them, clothe yourself with them or use them. All they're good for is to sit there looking pretty. Human beings are all upside down; the really useful things aren't even given a second glance in the face of these glittering trinkets. People will toil and risk their lives for these things. Completely upside down! Still, this being the case, if someone gave in charity a universe full of these precious things, would their merit be great? *"Yes, World-Honored One, because of this, they would attain great merit and fortune."* Subhuti's answer confirms it—yes, Buddha, if someone were to actually do this, the fortune he'd receive in the future would be incredibly great!

"Subhuti, if the fortune and merit were real, the Tathagata would not say the fortune and merit attained was great. He says so because there is no merit."

The Buddha is saying you must recognize that in worldly terms great fortune consists of having lots of money, long life, many fine children...the best of everything. There's a story about a man who lived a very simple and virtuous life. Upon passing from this world, he went to see Yama, who checked his life's record. Everything he did was good, not remarkable, but there was not a bad mark against him. Yama checked in the book of guidelines for karma and told him that he would once again become a human, but this time with great fortune. Since his case was so unusual, there were no specific guidelines as to what kind of fortune he should enjoy. Yama asked the man if he had any specific requests. The man thought a while and then said, "A thousand acres of good fields with water aplenty, no need to work for money and four beautiful wives; my father would be the Secretary of State under the Emperor. I, the son, would be made a prince and need only lean back and kick up my feet."

Yama told him to take a seat, and then came and stood next to him. Yama leaned toward him and said, if it were that such fortune could be had, I would go and leave you in my place!

There are certain kinds of daydreams about the perfect life which are shared by most people. Many famous poems and couplets of old were written expressing these. We spend our lives daydreaming that such fortune will suddenly drop from the heavens into our hands, but each time, wake to find we are still the same old self. The past, present and future minds are ungraspable, and so all of this is useless. Human existence is just chasing after an idea. It is so obvious that this idea cannot really be obtained, but still we strive. This is especially the case with one's life span. We're obviously all going to die and yet, people still hope to become an Immortal. Worldly fortune and merit do run out. We can only be in the limelight for a fleeting moment. It's like a flashlight—you can't expect the batteries in it to last you the rest of your life. The same goes for fortune and merit. This is why the Buddha says worldly fortune is like a twinkle of light in the sky. By the time you snap your fingers, it's gone, and *"there is no fortune and merit."*

The Fortune No One Appreciates

What is real fortune? The ease of purity and clarity. Being pure, clear and at ease. One's mind holds no frustration, no sadness, no gain, no loss, no pride, nor malice; there is no obverse and reverse, right and wrong, front and back, no polar opposites. This mind is always in a very peaceful state. This is the fortune of the highest realm, immaculate fortune. Every person has immaculate fortune. We've all experienced moments of joyful relaxation, but if all you had were free time to relax at home, the last thing you would feel would be relaxed! You would feel lonely, forgotten, worthless... No one has called me or written to me; no one comes to see me... I'm so depressed! This person cannot enjoy immaculate fortune. In practicing Buddhism, you must first get clear of this. The Buddha knows the minds of all sentient beings. Everyone takes the unreal to be the real. When real peace and purity come, people don't know how to enjoy this kind of fortune. So it's only when people experience the real nature of emptiness, the clean, pure ease of the self nature, that wisdom is consummated. This is true fortune. Is true fortune that difficult to find? It's incredibly easy but when this kind of fortune lands on your doorstep, you do not want it and go looking for some frustration instead.

How is it that we've been led here to this place? The Buddha told us that the mind of three times is ungraspable but to reach this alambana is extremely difficult. If you wish to reach this state of awareness, you need real merit and fortune. Another manifestation of this contradiction is that if one not only has free time but also a healthy body in which to cultivate, most people then can't resist the urge to throw these away, use them up at idle pursuits which only end in sadness and regret. Sentient beings are all upside down!

Gatha of Section Nineteen

> *Story upon story, the stupa reaches halfway to heaven;*
> *Drop by drop, could meritorious works possibly occur effortlessly?*
> *Fell the bamboo post, then turn back to look;*
> *Sumptuous opulence disperses into air and dreams are like mist.*

"Story upon story, the stupa reaches halfway to heaven." There is a saying in Chinese popular culture "saving one person's life is like building a seven-story stupa." This was actually something said by the Buddha. One has done a really good deed in saving the life of another. This act is equivalent to having built a stupa or temple by yourself. Both of these are acts of great merit.

"Drop by drop, could meritorious work possibly occur effortlessly?" Merit is produced slowly, little by little. Everyone does good deeds and after a while they start to build up. It's as if one is single-handedly building a temple. One can only do so much work in one day, but slowly it gets built. However, *"The Northern Chi Dynasty left four hundred and eighty temples; how many buildings and towers have faded away in the rain?"* There is not one left.

"Fell the bamboo post, then turn back to look;" Emperor Liang Wu-ti built hundreds of temples in his lifetime as did Empress Dowager Wu Tse-t'ien. Of these, practically none are left. One day Kasyapa suddenly said to Ananda, "How can one perceive the Tao?" Take down the temple banner post and then you can perceive the Tao. This is pointing to the fact that we have our own post with a banner of self-praise. "I am great." If we can get rid of this, then fortune can flow in and we will be able to perceive emptiness. *"Sumptuous opulence disperses into air and dreams are like mist."* Worldly fortune, even that of an emperor is all just the sumptuous opulence dispersing into air like mist or a dream. After a cloud or a mist disperses, is there even a hint of it left?

Everything is like a dream. Even dreams don't really exist; they vanish like the mist. This is why the Buddha said, "There is no such thing as fortune." What is it to gain truly great fortune? It is to realize emptiness, to awaken and become a Buddha. This is the real fortune and success.

Don't forget that if you really wish to awaken and become a Buddha, you mustn't do even the least little evil and you must work tirelessly for the benefit of others in order to nurture your wisdom. Wisdom doesn't come from books. You can't rely on those to give you wisdom. You also can't squeeze it out of your two legs no matter how hard you grit your teeth against the pain of sitting. The cultivation of this kind of discipline and dhyana will result in the one type of merit with form. The formless merit and fortune of ease is everywhere to be found, but your wisdom can't reach it and so you can't cultivate it. Even though practicing Buddhism is this true wisdom, one must still accumulate all of the merits of virtue for it to come forth. Do not forget this! Don't fool yourself into thinking that because Buddhism is the study of wisdom that you throw all your virtuous conduct out the window. One with true wisdom naturally conducts him or herself virtuously. Wisdom and virtue are inseparable.

SECTION 20

BEYOND COLOR, BEYOND FORM

"Subhuti, what do you think? Can the Buddha be perceived by means of his perfect nirmanakaya?"

"No, World-Honored One, the Tathagata cannot be so perceived. The reason is that the Buddha says a perfectly formed nirmanakaya is not a perfectly formed nirmanakaya but is merely called a perfectly formed nirmanakaya."

"Subhuti, what do you think? Can the Tathagata be perceived through any of the characteristics of his perfect nirmanakaya?"

" No, World-Honored One, the Tathagata cannot be so perceived. Why is this? Because the Tathagata says the so-called characteristics of his perfect nirmanakaya are not really so but are merely called the characteristics of his perfect nirmanakaya.

The Looks of a Great Man

"Subhuti, what do you think? Can the Buddha be perceived by means of his perfect nirmanakaya?"

"No World-Honored One, the Tathagata cannot be so perceived. The reason is that the Buddha says a perfectly

formed nirmanakaya is not a perfectly formed nirmanakaya but is merely called a perfectly formed nirmanakaya."

In the first half of the *Diamond Sutra*, Subhuti was doing the asking and Buddha was doing the answering. In the second half, the Buddha was asking the questions checking to make sure Subhuti really understood. The whole thing started right after the meal when Buddha was about to sit and have a relaxing meditation. Completely ignoring this fact, Subhuti kept on plying him with questions. The Buddha, having had his deep compassion aroused, decided to fully discuss the topic. He put aside all intentions of meditating and answered the question in a step by step, layer by layer process.

The thirty-two physical characteristics are not the Tathagata for, *"If all form and appearance are seen as illusion, the Tathagata will be perceived."* The Buddha was being very motherly in his response, making sure that Subhuti really understood what he was saying to him. Subhuti, what is your understanding, can the Buddha be perceived by means of his perfect nirmanakaya? Notice that the question was asked about the Buddha's perfect nirmanakaya and not the Tathagata's. In some places, the Buddha will say "Buddha" and in others, he will say, "Tathagata." You must be aware of and think about these nuances or else you are wasting your time just glossing over the sutra.

The word *Buddha* here is referring to the reward body of the Buddha, his actual physical body. The Buddha's reward body was actually quite beautiful! Even though he practiced ascetic living, virtually starving himself for twelve years, nonetheless, his body regained its fine shape. The Buddha was also considered to be a very handsome man. Having the thirty-two marks of physical excellence and eighty complimenting characteristics, is it any wonder his looks were so highly acclaimed? As it was told in the *Surangama Sutra*, Ananda became a monk because he so admired his cousin's physical appearance. Of course, the Buddha ran him through the ringer about the fact that his motivation for becoming a monk was physical attraction, which by the way, also got him into other kinds of trouble!

The perfect nirmanakaya is what is called in Chinese vernacular, "the bearing of a great man." There is something which sets this person apart from the average man. A Buddha has not only the thirty-two distinguishing physical marks but also there are eighty complimentary characteristics. When a person becomes a Buddha, he or she will automatically have the bearing of a great man. In many places in the sutras it talks about the importance of such looks. In some places in the sutras, it even says that a female needs to first reincarnate as or transform into a male in order to complete the path to Buddhahood. In the Mahayana sutras, however, the Buddha has to eat his words on this point. The female water deity and Queen Srimala, both of whom had married and given birth to children and, in spite of this, had achieved Buddhahood in this lifetime, openly challenged the Buddha on this point. The Buddha had to say "It is so, it is so! My apologies to you women. You are right, there is no such distinction." Females can also become Buddhas where they stand. There is no need to become a male first. To think that way is to get stuck in the Hinayana perspective. Here in the *Diamond Sutra* the Buddha also refutes the idea that females cannot become enlightened. Can the Buddha be perceived by means of his perfect nirmanakaya? Thirty-two marks, the perfect face, is that what is called a Buddha? Subhuti says, "No, World-Honored One, the Tathagata cannot be perceived by his perfect nirmanakaya."

All of you keep hoping to see a Buddha. If you are meditating and you see a Buddha, that is actually a demon and not the Buddha. The Buddha takes his meals and then sits there meditating. He doesn't feel like going to see you. Your paying him a visit would be the more likely situation. Still, you absolutely must not grasp onto form. Don't look for Buddha in the ideas of form. It is clearly stated, " *The reason is that the perfectly formed nirmanakaya is not the perfectly formed nirmanakaya but is merely called the perfectly formed nirmanakaya."* In this statement the Buddha is revealing one of the secrets of the Buddha Dharma. A person who has realized the Tao has the bearing of a great man within their own special appearance. This is what is called the "perfectly formed nirmanakaya."

"Nirmanakaya" means the physical body made of the four elements—earth, water, fire, and wind. Often I have said the same thing but the heart of the matter is that it "is not the perfectly formed nirmanakaya." Do not grasp onto form; all things with form are not, and thus it is called "the perfectly formed nirmanakaya."

Living Bodhisattvas of the World

The reason for saying this is that one who has great attainment naturally has the bearing of one of Tao. This "bearing" is not one's physical features. When I was young, my friends and I would seek out different cultivators. Among them were a few monks and masters who had reached great achievement and everyone called them living Bodhisattvas or living arhats. One, by ordinary standards, was incredibly ugly. His eyes were like protruding grapes, magnified to look even larger by his thick glasses. His nose reminded me of a bulb of garlic. The corners of his mouth almost reached his ears and a smile revealed small, thin teeth like kernels of white corn. To top it off, he walked with a lopsided gait. If taken separately, each feature was unsightly but all together his appearance was extremely appealing, even dignified. The longer one looked, the more appealing he appeared. Because he hadn't washed his clothes for probably more that ten years, there were lice all over him and he would walk along unconsciously scratching here and itching there. If one of his disciples would flick a lice off of him, he would quickly pick it up and put it back telling the disciple that we mustn't take lives.

There was another monk who for many decades had not bathed, nor even washed his face. A mosquito net in the same condition surrounded his bed like a tent. He would be sleeping or meditating inside the netting but you couldn't see him in there because the holes were all clogged up with dust. The day came that I was to leave and I went to say my farewells. He was meditating inside his tent and told me to come in and join him on the bed as he had some things he wished to say to me. I, with my compulsive cleanliness, was terrified. The thought of what it must smell like inside those tent walls made me quite reluctant to move. Out of deference to this teacher, however, I ducked my head into the netting. Much to my surprise, it had the fragrance of spring flowers, but unlike any I had smelled before. I didn't want to leave his tent because it was so pleasant. I learned immediately how different a man of Tao was from ordinary people.

Another example of such a person was a Tibetan lama who was considered to be a living Buddha. He really liked Chinese tea. Usually, the tea which is sold to the outlying areas of China is not of the best quality. Tibetans like to add yak butter to their tea. Those who are used to the taste really enjoy it, but if you're not used to it, you may just not be able to swallow your first mouthful. This Lama had only one bowl. All his eating and drinking were done with that one bowl and having no other, it was the bowl for guests as well. This bowl had never been washed. I can't even begin to describe how dirty it was. We enjoyed going to visit the lama because we heard he had extrasensory powers. If he felt an affinity with you or had respect for you, he would offer you a drink of tea from his bowl. Some people declined because they were put off by the condition of the bowl while the reticence of others was due to respect and he knew exactly which was which. Those with true respect, he would persuade to take a sip and it was said that by doing this a lot of bad karma was dissolved. Those who were squeamish would get an earful. Lama would say that his mouth was made of flesh like all humans and ask directly why the person wouldn't drink from his bowl.

To carefully observe such people, one sees how incredibly dignified and majestic they are. It's not the nose or the eyes, but just that there is a certain bearing which speaks to you of the Tao. This is why the Buddha says one should not look for Him or the Tao in the perfectly formed nirmanakaya, they are not there. The presence of someone will most certainly change when they awaken to the Tao. They will have the bearing of a man of Tao, but it is *"not the perfectly formed nirmanakaya"*. Do not grasp onto form. The body of flesh and blood experience creation and destruction. *"It is merely called a perfectly formed nirmanakaya."* Take note that the nirmanakaya is the physical body.

> *"Subhuti, what do you think? Can the Tathagata be perceived through any of the characteristics of his perfect nirmanakaya?"*
> *"No, World-Honored One, the Tathagata cannot be so perceived."*

The first question discussed whether or not the perfect nirmanakaya really existed. The physical body is what is called the perfect nirmanakaya. Now the Buddha brings up the second question of whether he could be seen in any form. If the Buddha were standing in front of you, could the image seen through your eyes be held onto as the Buddha? Subhuti, of course, answers no, as has been discussed previously in this sutra. You shouldn't fall into the religious trappings of worshipping an idol because you cannot perceive the Tathagata by means of the thirty-two characteristics. And why is this? *"Because the Tathagata says the so-called characteristics of his perfect nirmanakaya are not really so but are merely called the characteristics of his perfect nirmanakaya."*

The real Buddha is only perceived when the dharmakaya is perceived. The dharmakaya can be perceived, but not attained. All is without form or appearance as the dharmakaya has no form or appearance nor any alambana. If you have an alambana or state of being then you are dwelling in something. If one dwells in anything, one cannot perceive one's mind and original nature. To perceive the empty nature of all phenomena is to perceive one's original Buddha nature.

Gatha of Section Twenty

Form appears yet again but is not real.
All depend on the mind's form as the arising cause.

> *Able to endure, all guests of this world are either foolish or*
> *mad.*
> *They keep searching around the old withered stump of tree.*

"Form appears yet again but is not real" This form is just a happenstance occurrence and has no true existence. It is not real. From where then does the physical world and phenomenal appearance come?

"All depend on the mind's form as the arising cause" Formed by consciousness, mind and phenomena are of the same origin. They are products of the power of the mind. *"Able to endure, all guests of this world are either foolish or mad."* Buddhism starts out by telling you not to grasp form or appearance, not to grasp anything in this physical world. Those of this world are really quite pitiful. Most have no wisdom and therefore, *"They keep searching around the old withered stump of tree."* Around and around the old tree stump, searching again and again. Sitting in meditation, not a thought arises; this is an old withered tree stump. The description *"withered stump of tree"* has its origins in the poem of Ch'an Master Hsueh-tou.

> *"Stretched out across an old road lies a rabbit;*
> *The falcon sees and effortlessly captures it alive.*
> *Pitiful hunting dogs have not the intelligence;*
> *Noses down, they sniff around the withered stump of tree."*

It's hunting season and a rabbit just happens to rest in the middle of a road. The falcon flying above looks down, "Wow, there's a rabbit lying there!" It doesn't hesitate even for a second, swooping down and seizing the rabbit. The hunting dogs, still a long way off—you can picture the scene with all the dogs and horses and bugles—pick up the scent of the rabbit. "The pitiful hunting dogs have not the intelligence." They keep sniffing and circling but no rabbit is there to be found, *"Noses down, they sniff around the withered stump of tree."* Nothing left to do but sniff around the old empty stump in desperation. Master Hsueh-tou was one of the Grand Masters of Ch'an . He was criticizing all the people who practice Ch'an by looking into a *koan* or *hua tou*. They're all like the hunting dogs sniffing around the old tree stump. If one has great wisdom, they are like the falcon. Up in the bright sky, in the middle of emptiness it becomes bright and in one fell swoop they take the rabbit. This is the alambana of emptiness. We hunting hounds run around and around in circles, looking for an alambana, looking for an emptiness.

SECTION 21

EXPOUNDING BY NOT EXPOUNDING

"Subhuti, do not say that the Tathagata ever thinks, I must expound a Dharma. Never have such a thought. Why? Because one who says so will slander the Buddha, as he does not understand what I have said. Subhuti, when the Tathagata expounds a Dharma, there is no Dharma that could possibly be expounded. This is called expounding the Dharma."

Thereupon, Living Wisdom Subhuti addressed the Buddha saying, "World-Honored One, in future ages might there be sentient beings in whom, will arise faith upon hearing this teaching?"

The Buddha said, "Subhuti, those referred are neither living beings nor not-living beings. Why is this? Because the so-called sentient beings, the Tathagata says, are not sentient beings and so are merely called sentient beings."

Not a Thing

> *"Subhuti, do not say that the Tathagata ever thinks, I must expound a Dharma. Never have such a thought. Why? Because one who says so will slander the Buddha, as he does not understand what I have said."*

Here again it is the Buddha who raises this discussion starting with an admonition to Subhuti against falling into the wrong idea that while the Buddha was in this world he expounded a Dharma. Actually, the World-Honored One started his teaching after his enlightenment at age 31 and continued up until he passed into nirvana at age 80. His 49 years of teaching have all been negated in this statement. *"Never have such a thought."* To say that the Buddha propagated a Dharma is to slander him. He taught samatha and samapatti, discipline, samadhi and wisdom, the thirty-seven steps to bodhi, prajna, wisdom, dharmalaskana, consciousness only and so forth. These were all taught by the Buddha himself but now here it is saying that if we say the Buddha taught any Dharma, we are slandering him. It seems to make no sense. Why is this slander? "They do not understand what I have said." Even though such a person has heard the Dharma, he didn't or couldn't understand. If they say that I taught a Dharma, this is incorrect.

We can approach this from the general subject of education. One who is really and truly an educator has had an experience of these words and can verify them. In my opinion, someone who has been a teacher all his life has been paying off some serious karmic debts. Teaching in many ways is a form of suffering. Why do I say this? Because one hundred people hear the same class and all of them have different understanding and explanations of what they've heard. Also there is always a small percentage who will say that the teacher was saying gray when he was clearly saying white. Those who've been in the field of education for a long time will agree that teaching is a form of suffering.

Another facet of this is that the greatest obstacle to human beings is language. Language can never fully express what is in our hearts. Take for example the question commonly asked by Chinese as a greeting, "Have you eaten yet?" Simply asking this question could result in a number of reactions. One person may feel that his friend really cares, cares about him enough to ask if he's eaten. Another person may hear this and get really angry. This person may think the question is implying that he can't provide for himself. A third person may feel really annoyed at having to go through this whole polite charade. From this simple example we can see that good communication is extremely difficult. Meaning and interpretations go off in all different directions. Sometimes it's better not to say anything. One speaks and misinterpretations follow. Other beings communicate differently. Fish, for example, do so with their eyes. Bats have their own special ways of communicating. We humans actually communicate a lot non-verbally, for even our skin will convey messages. If two people stand close to each other and feel too hot, they will naturally move away a little so that each has the space necessary to dissipate the heat. There is physical communication going on. This is the nature of communication. Verbal expression is too often misunderstood. The original meaning of the Buddha's words are for us to not grasp onto appearances, forms or words.

Enlightenment is understanding anuttara-samyak sambodhi. The Dharma spoken by the Buddha is like a raft, a boat for crossing the river. After getting across, you don't lug the boat along with you. If you say that you don't need the Buddha's boat to get across because you can swim, then bravo for you. The Buddha never said that his boat was the only way to cross. Ch'an masters have used many kinds of methods including that of not giving you any boat. That master wants you to get yourself over by whatever method you can.

This is what the Buddha wishes us to understand. Still most will hear this and not awaken to their mind and original nature. Rather, they will once again grasp onto these words. "They do not understand my words." They don't understand the meaning behind the words.

Mahakasyapa Smiles

"Subhuti, when the Tathagata expounds a Dharma, there is no Dharma that could possibly be expounded. This is called expounding the Dharma."

The Buddha used one word to sum up the real Dharma, inconceivable. One day at Rajagriha, Shakyamuni Buddha sat down in the place from which he usually spoke. The disciples and other students sat waiting in anticipation of a teaching. For the longest time, the Buddha sat there without saying a word. Then out of the blue, he picked up one of the flowers that was in front of him, held it up and twirled it back and forth in his fingers. No one could quite understand what was meant by this whole thing, except Mahakasyapa who "broke the solemnity with a gentle smile." This description is just wonderful. You can just picture everyone sitting there waiting. The mood is thick and serious. Everyone is very uptight and finally Kasyapa can't hold it any longer and he just starts grinning. The Buddha seeing this says, *"I have the treasury of the true Dharma eye, the ineffable mind of nirvana; the form of reality is formless, true form has no form, the wonderfully subtle Dharma door does not rely on words, is not established by words and is transmitted outside of the teaching. This I entrust to Mahakasyapa."* Because Mahakasyapa understood, thus began the Ch'an Sect.

We can stop for a moment and think about all this. The Buddha held up a flower for everyone to see. What does this mean? It is saying that in expounding the Dharma there is no dharma to expound. There is no set model which can be expressed. In the end, the Dharma is unspeakable, inexpressible, inconceivable...any state is not the first meaning. The wondrous Dharma is inexpressible. This is why when the Buddha became enlightened under the Bodhi tree, he wanted to enter nirvana right then and there. He never wished to expound a Diamond Sutra. He didn't wish to say anything. In the sutras, it tells how at that time, celestial beings from the Sakra or Indra Heaven knelt down begging him not to do so. They reminded him of all the great vows he'd made time and time again to save all sentient beings after his own enlightenment. Now, finally he has achieved his Great Awakening, Great Enlightenment and he wants out. He wants to forget about all of you, but this is not all right. The Buddha then said to them, "Stop, stop. My Dharma is wondrous and difficult to conceive." It is recorded in both the Flower Adornment Sutra and the Avatamsaka Sutra that this is what the Buddha said.

This brief statement captures the essence of the *Diamond Sutra*. He repeated twice the word *stop*, meaning stop right there, just stop. If he explained in words his realization, no one could understand. So, in saying, stop, he is telling you to just stop, "not a thought arises, the whole body appears." STOP! No mental understanding, no rumination, all phenomena are empty. If you can do this, you will understand the Buddha Dharma. "Stop, stop. My Dharma is wondrous and difficult to conceive." This says it all, no need to expound a *Diamond Sutra*.

Actually, even just the single word *stop* would have sufficed. It is very difficult to get our minds to come to a stop. If we could just stop, sila, samadhi, prajna and the six paramitas are at that moment consummated. Stopping gives rise to them. This is why all expounded teachings are merely expediencies. To put it another way, the twelve categories within the Tripitaka are all different teaching methods. Teaching methods are only that, methods to get you to understand something. If you hold onto the teaching methods as being the education, this is wrong.

There is a famous saying about this by a Ch'an master which goes, *"Perception equal to the master, still lacks half the master's merit. Perception surpassing that of the master, makes one worthy of transmission."* If the student's level of understanding is equal to the master's, *he "still lacks half the Master's merit".* For instance, if the master is eighty years old and the student is thirty when she has her awakening, still the master has an additional fifty years of practice and cultivation. This is what is meant by *"half the master's merit."* As to, *"perception surpassing that of the master, makes one worthy of transmission,"* it's only when the student's awakening surpasses the master's that this disciple is worthy of receiving transmission of the bowl and robe (i.e., the lineage). Many great masters of the past have lamented that there is no one onto whom to pass the bowl. The teaching of the Buddha is a means of transmission. The Dharma He spoke was in hopes that you would awaken and become a Buddha. If the student's perception surpasses the master's, there is no need for expedient means or words. It is already real and true for the student. This is what is meant by this part of the sutra.

The next line of the sutra brings a twist, so pay attention. Everything up to now has been, *"Subhuti...."*, *"Subhuti...."*, now an epithet has been added to his name.

The Dialogue of Subhuti and the Buddha

"Thereupon, Living Wisdom Subhuti addressed the Buddha saying, 'World-Honored One, in future ages might there be sentient beings in whom, will arise faith upon hearing this teaching'?"

Here there suddenly appears two words in front of Subhuti's name, "Living Wisdom" Subhuti. It's as if Kumarajiva put them there on purpose.

The Buddha didn't actually teach any Dharma. All He told us was: 1) not to take the physical body as the Buddha; 2) not to grasp form or appearance; 3) that He did not expound any Dharma. Aside from these three points, the Buddha didn't teach any Dharma door and yet, there seemed to be someone who understood. This someone was our Elder Brother Subhuti. To understand is to take on, to carry the Tathagata's living wisdom. This is why here he is called Living Wisdom Subhuti. Among the Buddha's disciples he was foremost in discussing the nature of emptiness. If there is someone among us here today who instantly awakens to the self nature of emptiness, this person has also achieved living wisdom. He or she is the extension of living wisdom. Dipankara means the right light, which is also the instantaneous perception/understanding of the nature of emptiness. When a person has living wisdom, he or she extends the life of wisdom and can pass on the inextinguishable light of wisdom.

Subhuti heard what was said and just understood. The Buddha Dharma is ineffable and inexpressible because there is nothing to be said. Because he understood, Subhuti took it upon himself to ask on behalf of future sentient beings, might there be sentient beings in the future who, hearing you speak like this, would believe what you said? *"The Buddha said, 'Subhuti, those referred to are neither living beings nor not-living beings'."* Wow! The Buddha's answer is really subtle. The question is not even considered a question. What sentient beings? There never were any sentient beings to begin with. These are really intense words. The Buddha has negated all future beings. What then are called sentient beings? There never were any to begin with. Just what is going on? The Confucianists would say that it is the old trick of the water being poured back and forth from one bucket to another. The Dharma is not the Dharma, but is called the Dharma; the nirmanakaya is not the nirmanakaya, but is called the nirmanakaya... It's all this kind of talk.

If you look at the surface only, it certainly seems this way. Subhuti asks if anyone in the future will hear what you've said and believe it. The Buddha didn't even address this issue and retorted with, "What sentient beings?" Upon hearing this we might as well end class. Not being sentient beings, we might as well not even listen to the *Diamond Sutra* at all!

Why Did the Playful Rocks Nod?

So, if we are not sentient beings, then what are we? Each is a Buddha. Each and every sentient being is originally a Buddha. This is the Buddha's way of revealing this. There is no reason to worry about everyone because all will become Buddhas. This is the theory behind these words. The Buddha also spoke of this in the *Lotus Sutra* and the *Parinirvana Sutra*. In Chinese literature there are two lines which read, *"Honorable Sheng spoke the Dharma; the playful rocks nodded in agreement."* These lines have to do with an argument about this issue as it was spoken of in the *Parinirvana Sutra*. The story is as follows:

During the Northern and Southern Period of Chinese history, there was a young monk named Tao-sheng who later became known for his many abilities and charm. At that time, only half of the *Parinirvana Sutra* had been translated. A question was raised but not answered in this first half as to whether an *icchantika* could become a Buddha. An icchantika is someone who is extremely evil, evil through and through. They would kill their mother and father, an arhat and even a Buddha. Their evil habits are so strong and deep that they will fall into the avici hell, a never ending "life sentence." Is it the case that such beings cannot become Buddhas?

Tao-sheng wrote an argument that all beings, even icchantikas, will become Buddhas. This piece brought down a rain of criticism so harsh that he was banished from the North where

465

Buddhism had made its stronghold. This young monk was very well educated and wrote very well. Other monks of the time collectively rejected his theory and forced him to go south. Tao-sheng went to Suzhou where he lived in isolation in a small hut on Gold Mountain. One day, he was in the woods speaking on the question he had addressed in his famous piece of writing. Impassioned, he suddenly asked the rocks, Icchantikas will eventually become Buddhas, do you agree? The rocks then all nodded their heads. This is why it is said, *"Honorable Sheng spoke the Dharma; the playful rocks nodded in agreement."*

Before leaving the North, Tao-sheng made a public declaration that his explanation of the Dharma was absolutely in accord with the Buddha Dharma, and that he would leave this world with his body in the lotus position as proof. It came to pass, when the other half of the *Parinirvana Sutra* was translated, it concurred with what he had written: All beings will become Buddhas. Here in the *Diamond Sutra*, it also concurs as the Buddha tells "Living Wisdom" Subhuti, *"all sentient beings are not beings"* and so we mustn't underestimate people as each one is a Buddha.

Sentient Beings and Buddhas

> *"Why is this? Because the so-called sentient beings, the Tathagata says, are not sentient beings and so are merely called sentient beings."*

The meaning behind this is that the existence of the life of each sentient being is an illusion. All the beings of the three realms and the twelve categories are not fixed entities but rather arise from causes and conditions. This is why it is said that sentient beings are not sentient beings. The original nature of all beings is the Buddha nature. If one can turn back and through introspection perceive one's mind and original nature, then this person is not a sentient being. Each and every one is a Buddha. As we were just mentioning, the Venerable Tao-sheng argued that icchantikas finally come to be Buddhas. Not only in the *Parinirvana Sutra* was this mentioned, but also in the *Lotus Sutra* as well. Shakyamuni Buddha is the fourth Buddha of this aeon. This aeon is called the aeon of sages, throughout which one thousand Buddhas will appear. The last of these thousand will be Rucika, whom we know as Wei-tuo Bodhisattva. His vow is to support all one thousand Buddhas of the aeon of sages, making sure that each one achieves his full realization of enlightenment and then he himself will enter Buddhahood. This is one of the things written about this particular aeon.

It is also said that all forms of life in the world, anything with spirit and consciousness can become a Buddha. All beings are equal. If you really wish to understand this theory, you must study the Dharmalaksana or Consciousness Only school. This school proposes a scale of different levels of perspective. People have the idea of a self and so there are people. There are opposing views and so there is frustration and in turn, pain and suffering. All these things are interlinked. Everyone has a body but the body is not the self. The body is the coming together of the four elements under certain causes and conditions. When these causes and conditions no longer exist, the body will break down to its elements and disperse. The real self nature is beyond birth and death. This self nature is the nature of emptiness. To get to this nature, one must let go of the idea of self. The state of having let go of the self is also one kind of wisdom. In the Consciousness Only school, this wisdom is called the wisdom of equality; no self, no others, no sentient beings, no frustrations and so forth. When all is empty, there is no idea of sentient beings. The Consciousness Only school spells things out for you while the *Diamond Sutra* tells through implication.

Gatha of Section Twenty-one

For whom is the bodhisattva path so painstakingly taught?
Lying weary in the empty mountain, the sun again goes west.
Point to the distance, a new moon rises over the eastern sea.
The night is deep but eventually the cock crows if but far away.

"For whom is the bodhisattva path so painstakingly taught?" Didn't the Buddha say that he didn't expound any Dharma? In other sutras, he has said the same thing, that for 49 years he hasn't spoken a word. The Buddha Dharma is inexpressible. Since the dharmakaya is within the realm of the inexpressible, the Buddha painstakingly taught the path of the Bodhisattva. For whose benefit is he explaining all this? For the benefit of sentient beings. It's like the T'ang poet, Luo-yin wrote in his famous lines, *"Having collected from the flowers and turned it into honey; For whom is this toil, for whom is made this nectar?"* Human existence is also as such. We are like the bees who gather pollen from the flowers and make it into honey. In the end, the bees themselves don't eat all that honey. For whom is this toil, for whom is this nectar? This line is bemoaning the life of humans.

The Buddha couldn't possibly be in this same situation of not knowing for whom he toils. He works to save all sentient beings, to help all sentient beings see their original nature and become Buddhas. But originally there is no self, so for whom is this toil?

"Lying weary in the empty mountain, the sun again goes west." Many of the Buddha's disciples as well as many later enlightened masters go up into the mountains and lie low. Some don't even say one word. One example is Ch'an Master Hui-ssu, the founder of the T'ien T'ai sect, who never left the mountain after his enlightenment. People would ask why such an enlightened master would not come down and help save other beings. His response to such talk was that, sitting on his peak, he had already saved all the sentient beings in one swallow so why should he come down?

People have asked me about this, and I told them that of course he can speak like this and not come down from the mountain because Master Chih-che, also known as Little Shakyamuni, was his disciple. Producing one such disciple is enough. He need not come down from the mountain and can speak the way he did. If a person doesn't have great wisdom achievement and merit, he could never have such a disciple and should not speak in the same manner as Master Hui-ssu. One who has such a level of enlightenment might never say a word for the rest of his life and yet still save countless numbers of beings.

There is an example of a Ch'an master like this whose image we frequently see, the Cloth Bag Monk. This monk was from Wenzhou, and it is said that he was an emanation of Maitreya Buddha. He expounded the Dharma by carrying a cloth bag. He always had this bag with him. If someone asked him what is the Dharma or the Buddha, he would put his bag down and just stand there without saying a word. If he saw that you understood, he would smile and laugh; if you didn't understand, he would pick up his bag and leave. We somehow just can't put down this "cloth bag" that our parents gave us. Dropping a cloth bag and standing there is the Buddha Dharma. He looks and sees that you don't understand, the bag gets shouldered once again, and the monk leaves. If you can't let it go, then pick it up. It's all the same. Buddhism is that simple. He didn't say a word, and that is the Buddha Dharma. Can sentient beings be saved by not expounding the Dharma? Not necessarily. Sentient beings still need many methods of teaching to be saved.

Pointing to the distance, a new moon rises over the eastern sea." Later generations compiled the stories of the enlightened Ch'an Masters in a large volume called *The Record of Pointing to the Moon.* This name comes from the *Surangama Sutra* wherein someone asks where the moon is and another person points and says, the moon is here. You don't want to look at the person's finger, you want to look at the moon. In looking at the person's finger, the finger then becomes useless since the finger is not the moon. The Buddha's teaching of the Dharma is the finger pointing. However, all of us who've been studying Buddhism for a long time still take the finger to be the moon.There is a story of the Taoist Lu Ch'un-yang which illustrates this whole thing very well. Lu Ch'un-yang eventually became enlightened through Ch'an Master Huang-lung, became his disciple and vowed to be a protector of the Buddha Dharma. There are two famous lines of his which say, *"Sentient beings are easy to save; but humans are most difficult."* "Sentient beings" here means all beings other than humans. *"I'd rather the sentient beings and not the humans save."*

One day Lu Ch'un-yang went to Nanjing and disguised himself as a pitifully poor old man. He went up to a street vendor selling sticky rice snacks and she gave him one. He ate it and went away without giving any money. The vendor didn't say anything. This old man would often come to the vendor who would always give him food without any questions asked.

After some years, he finally spoke to her one day. He asked, "Old woman why is it you've never asked me for money?"

"Because you are a poor old man with no money!" Lu Ch'un-yang said, "There are no other good people on this earth. You're the only one. Would you like to become an Immortal?" The old woman replied that she was quite comfortable just selling her snacks. "Would you like to become rich?" Lu asked, "I have a method I can teach you and in three years you would be able to turn things into gold with the touch of your finger." The old woman retorted, "How is it that you can turn things into gold but you don't even have enough money to buy my snacks? I don't believe you." He touched her wok, which immediately turned into gold, saying, "I don't pay money but I do have this. Do you want to learn?" She was taken aback but still declined. "What do you want then?" Lu asked, thinking to himself that finally he had found a truly virtuous person. She thought for a moment and said, "Learning is too much trouble, just give me that finger of yours." Lu Ch'un-yang just shook his head saying, *Sentient beings are easy to save, but humans are most difficult. I'd rather the sentient beings and not the humans save.*

The sutras tell us not to grasp the finger but to look at the moon. But most Buddhists are like the old lady that Lu Ch'un-yang met. This is what is meant by "pointing to the distance, a new moon rises over the eastern sea."

"The night is deep but eventually the cock crows if but far away." Don't give up hope! If but far, far away, the cock will crow. There will be someone who makes it through the night. Don't just

look at the night's thick darkness; the light will eventually come to shine.

SECTION 22

NO DHARMA TO ATTAIN

Subhuti said to the Buddha, "World-Honored One, when you attained anuttara-samyak sambodhi, was it that you did not attain anything whatsoever?"
The Buddha said, "Just so, just so, Subhuti! In the attainment of anuttara-samyak sambodhi, I did not gain even the least Dharma, and this is called anuttara-samyak sambodhi."

One Finger Ch'an

> *Subhuti said to the Buddha, "World-Honored One, when you attained anuttara-samyak sambodhi, was it that you did not attain anything whatsoever?"*
> *The Buddha said, "Just so, just so, Subhuti!"*

In Section 21 of the *Diamond Sutra*, the Buddha said that there is no Dharma to be expounded. In this section, he goes a step further in saying that there is no Dharma which can be attained. Subhuti asks the Buddha if at the time when he had his Great Awakening and enlightenment under the bodhi tree, he attained nothing at all. *"Just so, just so."* That's exactly right, just like that or rather, just like this.

In the Sung Dynasty, there was a Ch'an master, a monk called Chu-chi from Jin Hua (Gold Flower) Mountain. He never went around to other temples looking for other teachers. One day, he finally decided to set out the next morning on a journey to seek teachings. That night, he heard a voice from the void telling him not to leave because a living Bodhisattva would soon come to personally teach him the Dharma. A living Bodhisattva is a living, breathing person just like us who happens to be a Bodhisattva. That very next day a monk called T'ien-lung came to visit him. Chu-chi asked T'ien-lung, what is the Buddha Dharma. T'ien-lung was in fact a Ch'an master and he simply held up one finger. Chu-chi had a great awakening quite effortlessly.

Having been awakened by one finger, from then on if someone asked him what is the Buddha Dharma, he would hold up his finger. If you understood, it was just this; if you didn't understand, it was still just this, no further explanation. Because of this finger of his, many people awakened to the Dharma. Some of his young disciples who had been with him for some time, knew exactly what would happen when people would come to ask the Dharma. There would be much prostrating, laudatory oration, gifts and money. When the question finally came, "What is the Buddha Dharma?" the master would say, "It's this," and hold up his finger.

One day, while the master was away a lay person came to ask the Dharma. One young monk told him that his master was out, but that he knew his master's Dharma method. The person knelt

475

down respectfully and asked to be taught. Like the master, the young monk waited for his head to be just coming up from bowing and said, "It's this!" holding up his finger. This person also had an awakening. The little monk was thrilled. He knew now exactly what the Dharma was. When Master Chu-chi returned, the little monk said to him, "A lay person came today and I helped enlighten him," and proceeded to tell the whole story to which the master simply responded, "Oh." Chu-chi went inside for a moment and then came back out asking the monk to tell him again how to enlighten someone. The little monk said, "It's this!" and stuck out his finger, which the master promptly chopped off. There was blood everywhere, and the monk kept screaming, "Ow! Ow!" Master Chu-chi loudly asked him, "What is the Dharma?" The monk stopped and said, "It's this!" As soon as he motioned as before, he awakened. His finger was short one segment, but he had awakened. It's this! "Just so, just so," is the "this" of Ch'an. And what is "this"? You have to figure that out for yourself.

There are five or six Chinese translations of the *Diamond Sutra*. Looking at all of them, Kumarajiva's version is still the most wonderfully subtle. Master Hsuan-tsang's version is more clear in its words but loses some of the meaning of the Buddha Dharma. Kumarajiva's translation has the Ch'an flavor to it. It's "like pearls rolling in a pan"; they don't fall to the sides nor stick to any one point. This is why the later Ch'an masters always used the *Diamond Sutra* to help people awaken.

"In the attainment of anuttara-samyak sambodhi, I did not gain even the least Dharma and this is called anuttara-samyak sambodhi."

The Buddha said, I tell you, when I attained supreme enlightenment at the foot of the bodhi tree, don't think that I attained anything. It can be understood, but not had. This is the same as the lines of the Sixth Patriarch's poem of awakening, *"Originally, there is not a thing, on what then can dust gather?"* It can be understood, but not had. If there were some little bit of Dharma which could be attained—an emptiness, a light, a samaya, something round, something bright —it's not it. These are all phenomena. *"I did not gain even the least Dharma."* This is what is called anuttara-samyak sambodhi, Supreme Enlightenment.

This section is very simple. It's called "No Dharma to Attain." Let's look at the gatha.

Gatha of Section Twenty-two

Many years of wandering, searching for the place you belong;
Entering the place, you realize that the Path had you fooled.
Rummaging, one finds the old robe and bowl, still good as new.
Understand, there is not a thing to hold nor to lean upon.

"Many years of wandering, searching for the place you belong." People study Buddhism for many years, practicing different methods, taking vows and so forth, all in search of the road that will lead them back. All are searching for the road back home, home being the root source of life.

"Entering the place, you realize that the Path had you fooled." It's only when you have truly awakened that you realize how foolish your search has been. You've been fooled by the Path and fooled by the methods. The 84,000 Dharma doors deceived you. We mentioned before a Ch'an master who followed many different masters using all kinds of methods. Upon his great awakening, he realized that he had wasted a lot of time and wrote the following lines, *"My eyes were originally clear, but I was blinded by the teachers."* Running around trying this, trying that and as a result, blinding oneself. It's not one's physical eyes which get blinded, but rather it's one's perception and understanding that is blocked. Entering the place, you see that the path had you fooled.

"Rummaging, one finds the old robe and bowl still good as new." To those enlightened to the Tao, I am still myself and all is empty. It can be understood, but not had. The robe and bowl (the symbols of a lineage which are passed from master to disciple) are still the same old robe and bowl. You stored them away many, many years ago, but had forgotten where. Now you've recovered them again and they're still those same things of yours, still as good as new.

"Understand, there is not a thing to hold or lean upon." Originally there is not a thing, not an alambana, nor a Dharma to be had.

In these five or six sections, the Buddha is telling us not to grasp onto appearances, not to grasp onto Dharma. Next, even though we don't want to grasp form, the Buddha tells us there *is* one thing we must grasp, virtuous conduct. This next section called "The Pure Mind's Virtuous Conduct" explains this.

SECTION 23

THE PURE MIND'S VIRTUOUS CONDUCT

"Furthermore, Subhuti, this Dharma is without differentiation or degree, and is therefore called anuttara-samyak sambodhi. The practice of all virtues, free from the concepts of self, person, being, and life will result in the attainment of Supreme Enlightenment. Subhuti, these so-called virtues, the Tathagata says are not really virtues, but are nevertheless called virtues."

Cultivate All Virtues

> *"Furthermore, Subhuti, this Dharma is without differentiation or degree, and is therefore called anuttara-samyak sambodhi. The practice of all good virtues, free from the concepts of self, person, being, and life will result in the attainment of Supreme Enlightenment."*

In the sections before this one, everything was being negated; it's not the Buddha, it's not form, it's not phenomena, it's not Dharma...everything isn't it! Here, on the other hand, it is saying very clearly that if one wishes to become a Buddha, one must cultivate all virtues. Do not the least evil and work for the benefit of all beings. Cultivating all virtuous merits is absolutely necessary. It's not by just reading some Buddhist books, talking about Ch'an and *koans*, crossing the legs and meditating that one becomes a Buddha. If you have a lifetime of non-virtuous conduct behind you, go to a temple, meditate, eat vegetarian for two days and expect to attain Bodhi; this Bodhi is too cheap. You've paid only two cents for it. Do you really think it's that easy? Young people in particular have this problem. They read a book and practice meditation, then think that they've got it. They think they've taken to Buddhism like a fish to water. You think it's that easy? Jump in the water and see! Better yet, go buy a real fish.

The practice of all good virtues will result in the attainment of Supreme Enlightenment. We have trouble doing one virtuous deed each day. On the other hand, we have no trouble doing at least one non-virtuous act each day. Can you do one virtuous act each day? If you don't cultivate all good virtues, you cannot reach "no form." To think you can is cheating yourself. The Buddha told Subhuti that *"this Dharma is without differentiation or degree"*. The 84,000 Dharma doors, whether it be reciting the Buddha's name, doing esoteric practices, Ch'an , samatha and samapatti or even methods taught by those who've gone down a side path, can all lead to success according to the *Avatamsaka Sutra*. The real Dharma is without differentiation or degree. Earlier the Buddha also said that the saints and sages of all ages and places differ in their mastery of the effortless Dharma. This is to say, there is no differentiation.

The South Peak Is High, the North Peak Low

There is a *koan*("public case") in Ch'an which tells of a master known for teaching the *Diamond Sutra*. One day, he met a Ch'an master who asked him a question: Since the Dharma is without differentiation or degree, why is it that the South Peak is high while the North Peak is low? The other master couldn't answer this. He thought out loud to himself. "That's right! The *Diamond Sutra* says there is no differentiation or degree. Why is the South Peak high and the North Peak low? A myriad of things have differentiation; how can it be said that they don't?' This is something to think about.

We all know the term "undifferentiated wisdom." This comes when we've reached the eighth bhumi, or ground. The sixth consciousness, when empty, is the "subtle discerning wisdom." When one is empty of the grasping of a self, then the seventh consciousness transforms into "undifferentiated wisdom." At this point, self and others, all sentient beings, are equal. We feel everything from annoyance to suffering due to our distinguishing of self and others. If we can empty ourselves of these concepts, then our undifferentiated wisdom will arise and all beings will appear equal. Is this anuttara-samyak sambodhi? One must still cultivate all virtues in order to realize real emptiness. The practice of all good virtues will result in the attainment of Supreme Enlightenment.

"Subhuti, these so-called virtues, the Tathagata says are not really virtues, but are nevertheless called virtues."

If it is the case that you see the fruit of Buddhahood and practice all virtues so as to attain fortune and merit for yourself, this will only result in the fruit of human or celestial fortune. If one practices with an ordinary motivation and mind, this is only ordinary virtue. Virtue is practiced to attain the fruit of bodhi. This is the practice of virtue without holding onto any notion of practicing virtue whatsoever. *"These so-called virtues, the Tathagata says are not really virtues, but are nevertheless called virtues."* Not seeking merit and fortune for oneself is the real practice of virtue.

Gatha of Section Twenty-three

A flower in a mirror, the moon on the water and the stuff of dreams;
Not grasping, one realizes such stuff is the treasure as well;
But a painted peony in the end is still an illusion;
Can the springtime come without tendrils, roots or soil?

"A flower in a mirror, the moon on the water and the stuff of dreams." All things of this world are illusory, like a flower reflected in a mirror, the moon's reflection and the stuff of dreams. The Buddha uses this comparison a lot. All of the phenomena of

this world are like the reflection of a flower in a mirror. You can't say that there is no flower. There is a flower, but you can't grab it or touch it. The moon on the water also isn't not there. The water didn't produce its own moon. Behind that reflection there is a real moon the same as there is a real flower. The "stuff of dreams" is also this way. If it weren't for you, there would be no dream. Our minds and bodies produce dreams and the things in dreams exist like holographs. Those people who are studying Buddhism should pay attention to the fact that *"a flower in a mirror, the moon on the water"* doesn't mean non-existent. Rather, it is pointing to an illusory, unreal, temporary existence which cannot be held onto because of its impermanence.

"Not grasping, one finally realizes such stuff is the treasure as well." Understanding the theory of flowers in mirrors, moons in waters and the stuff of dreams, one can understand that the relationship between existence and emptiness is without differentiation or degree. Emptiness is Buddhism; existence is Buddhism. In the *Diamond Sutra*, the Buddha told us the most important points for cultivation, those being, don't dwell and don't grasp. Do not fool yourself by thinking, emptiness is due to not grasping. As well, if you grasp emptiness, then emptiness becomes an object. Emptiness is also stuff. In really not grasping, not even emptiness is grasped. When one doesn't grasp emptiness, one dares to enter the world and practice in the world. Sentient beings don't dare to enter the world because they are scared of getting caught up in existence. When one really doesn't grasp, one finally

realizes that the dust, the stuff, the illusion is also the treasure. One dares to enter the world because it is both empty and existent.

There is an old Chinese adage, *"Even though the peonies are lovely, they still need the green of the leaves as a complement."* Practicing Buddhism, cultivating the Tao, meditating or reciting the Buddha's name are in hopes of being able to completely let go of everything. But unless you've cultivated all good virtues, you won't be able to let go! Many of my retired friends say that now with all this free time on their hands, they will get down to business and start practicing Buddhism, tomorrow. Tomorrow, something else comes up, or they catch a cold, or this or that... Ha! Don't think that letting go is an easy thing to do. To really let go, clean and pure, it takes great merit and fortune.

"But a painted peony in the end is still an illusion." Even though the peonies are lovely, they still need the green of the leaves as a complement. One must cultivate all good virtues in order to cultivate anuttara-samyak sambodhi.

"Can the springtime come without tendrils, roots or soil?" A peony is the flower which represents wealth and power, but it needs the leaves to bring out its beauty. As well, it needs its roots. Without roots, there would be no flower. What is the root of the Buddhist practice? It is the same as every religion—commit not the least evil and work for the betterment of all. This is the first step. If you don't cultivate virtue and wish to become enlightened, you are like a frog leaping into a well, *pu-tong*! Besides being a very foolish thing for a frog to do, this action creates a noise very

much like the sound of the words which mean "ordinary" in Chinese.

SECTION 24

FORTUNE AND WISDOM BEYOND COMPARE

"Subhuti, if a person bestows in charity an amount of the seven treasures as great as all the Mount Sumerus in all the worlds of the galaxies of the Great Universe put together, and if another person receives, retains, reads and recites even a single stanza of this Prajnaparamita Sutra and expounds it to others, the merit of the former could not be reckoned as one-hundredth, one-thousandth or even one-hundred-thousandth part of that obtained by the latter; indeed, no conceivable comparison can be made between the two."

This chapter is a summary of the last few chapters. The title, "Fortune and Wisdom Beyond Compare," is referring to equal amounts of fortune and wisdom, sufficient to incur the realization of Bodhi, of Buddhahood. In this chapter, the Buddha puts forth this same kind of question for the third time. Why does it appear again here? In the last chapter, the Buddha tells us that we must cultivate all good virtues in order to achieve Supreme Enlightenment. Meditating, thinking of a *koan*, prostrating or any other such practices are not enough. "Commit not the least evil, and work for the benefit of all." Commit not the least evil is stopping, letting go, inactive; work for the benefit of all is doing, taking up, active. One needs to act and to do in order to become enlightened.

The end of Section 23 brings us back to true form prajna with the lines, *"the so-called virtues are not really so but are called good virtues."* Simply put, you do all these virtuous things but don't grasp onto them. Grasping is the alambana of ordinary beings; no grasping is the alambana of a Bodhisattva. There is nothing special about aiding others, saving the world and performing all good virtues. That's just the way it should be.

Cultivating Sufficient Amounts

> *"Subhuti, if a person bestows in charity an amount of the seven treasures as great as all the Mount Sumerus in all the worlds of the galaxies of the Great Universe put together"*

The Buddha talks about Mount Sumeru and the four continents surrounding it. Whether or not this is referring to the Himalayas and surrounding continents of the ancient world is not clear. This question has been debated for centuries. In recent years, there has been a movement in Buddhist circles to take this supposition as a certainty and not argue. I feel there is a big problem with such a movement. Here we will look upon the Buddha's words as a comparison. In that respect, *the "Mount Sumerus in all the worlds"* refers to the highest mountains of each world. Such a mountain is the size of the "measuring cup," so to speak, for the seven treasures.

> *"And if another person receives, retains, reads and recites even a single stanza of this Prajnaparamita Sutra and expounds it to others, the merit of the former could not be reckoned as one-hundredth, one-thousandth or even one-hundred-thousandth part of that obtained by the latter; indeed, no conceivable comparison can be made between the two."*

To give away such a great volume of things in charity will result in great merit and fortune. We discussed this before in section 13. Here, the Buddha once again stresses the importance of the giving of Dharma. Most religious-minded people think in terms of gaining power and privilege. If one wants real power and privilege, if one wants to really be able to get big results with only a minimum of effort, one must cultivate all good virtues. Someone who gives away that much in charity, whether or not they are looking to gain merit and fortune, naturally there will be great fortune to follow. We've talked about this before.

The *Prajnaparamita sutra* mentioned here is referring specifically to the *Diamond Sutra.* (There are many prajnaparamita sutras, most notably the 60-volume *Maha Prajnaparamita Sutra*.) If a person receives, retains, reads or recites and expounds to others, not necessarily this whole sutra but even just four lines of it, their merit is greater than that of having given away all that treasure.

Receive, Retain, Read and Recite

"Receives, retains, reads and recites," I would like to elaborate a little on these four. Receiving isn't just hearing or buying a copy of the sutra. It is receiving it into your heart and mind. A lot of Buddhists study the *Diamond Sutra* and think that they understand "emptiness" because they usually feel so comfortable and at peace. This is because they haven't encountered any situations like having insults hurled at them, getting cheated out of all their money, or going into the hospital with their life hanging by a thread. In these situations is the "emptiness" still there? If so, if it's there for you, then you have received it.

Receiving is just the first step. You must retain it, integrate it into your conduct. Use it like an artificial limb until it becomes part of you. If you were walking into a life-threatening situation and your mind was still at ease, this would be receiving and retaining. "Reading" is using your eyes and as with some people, quietly murmuring the words as you read. "Reciting" is reading it out loud at a normal speaking level or even singing it. The students of today aren't taught to recite their lessons, and it is difficult to memorize or even remember what you've read if you don't recite it out loud. Also, the students nowadays just put it in short term memory and never really digest the material. By singing and reciting, however, it will go into your long-term memory, into your alaya-consciousness and without too much mental effort, will always be there to access. So it is important to read and recite the *Diamond Sutra*. This is what is meant by "receive, retain, read and recite".

The Merit of Real Education

The Buddha said that if in addition to receiving, retaining, reading and reciting even four lines of this sutra, one uses one's understanding to teach others how to escape their frustration and suffering, such a person has greater merit than the giver of treasures. By teaching, the Buddha doesn't necessarily mean becoming a formal teacher. The most noble of beings will by any means available, empower others to alleviate their own suffering. The giving of material goods can in no way be compared with the giving of Dharma. The giving of Dharma could be equated with the work of educating others, helping others to understand, and heal themselves so they have a better chance in life. This kind of giving, the giving of wisdom, in no way can compare to the giving of material goods. Giving material goods doesn't merit a hundredth or even a billionth part.

In writing a sutra, it would lack refinement if this were stated in our everyday vernacular, such as, "It's beyond compare!" This sounds like a commercial. The language of a sutra needs to be more refined, so we have, *"no conceivable comparison can be made between the two"*. Numerical figures are not sufficient for expressing the comparison. What does it mean to talk about something which cannot be calculated? When talking about something enormous, like the heavens, for example, the only way to sufficiently communicate the size is through comparisons. Elsewhere the Buddha used the number of grains of sand in the Ganges River as a multiplier to express the infinite. Using such comparisons is easier for the mind to grasp than is using numbers.

This section is relatively straightforward and easy to understand. It's talking about the power of culture and education. The power of the Buddha's teaching is far greater than material charity. It affects people's spirit by opening their wisdom, education for one's "wisdom life" so to speak. This section is basically stressing the importance of wisdom and of helping oneself.

Gatha of Section Twenty-four

Wealthy but forlorn, grumbling a thousand is too few;
Poor men live deplorably, fettered by their bodies.
Why did Chuang-tzu say then, that all things are equal?
The bell sounds, rousing one from all things.

"Wealthy but forlorn, grumbling a thousand is too few." A Ch'an master once said, *"One thousand people for a rich man's home, he complains are not enough; one despised body to a man*

who's poor seems too much." In times of old a wealthy man may have had one hundred sons, daughters, cousins, aunts...as well as their children all living on one estate. Each household had their own servants, in addition to those who cared for the estate. One estate could easily have a thousand people working on it and still, the help could seem to not be enough. A man who is so poor that he cannot even provide himself with a bowl of noodles despises the fact that he has this body to keep alive. One thousand people for a rich man's home, he complains are not enough; one despised body to a man who's poor, often seems too much. I took these lines as inspiration and wrote two portraits representing greater and lesser fortune. "Wealthy but forlorn, grumbling a thousand is too few." A wealthy man with a large estate providing for a thousand people still feels lonely and forlorn, as if the thousand weren't enough.

"Poor men live deplorably, fettered by their bodies." Being poor, it's easy to feel like one has been given this body, this life as punishment. It's just endless suffering. These are two ends of the spectrum. One is having wealth, power and fame with never a moment to rest. One is so busy every day without even five minutes of peace. If you've never been there, you don't realize it's only those who've never had such experience that wish for it. Once you've been there, you don't want to return. Every day is lived for other people. Even if you don't feel like it, you have to smile. This so-called worldly fortune is not actually fortune but a form of suffering.

There was a monk of the Ch'an school who lived in a simple hut in the mountains. Someone asked him what his experience was like. He told them, *"Last year I was somewhat poor, having only the ground upon which I stand. This year I'm really poor, not even having the ground upon which to stand."* Not even having the ground on which to stand, can you imagine someone so poor! Actually he is talking about his realization of emptiness. Last year, he still had an alambana of emptiness; this year, there's not even an emptiness.

What does it mean to not even have an emptiness? Completely empty. To have the feeling of a body is a kind of punishment; it is always there. Rich and poor represent those with and without worldly fortune, the opposite ends of the spectrum. Beautiful and ugly, fat and thin, long and short, they're all opposites. We live in the world of opposites. There is a time for each person to also be poor and rich. When does a poor person become rich? One didn't have a cent yesterday and suddenly today one comes across fifty dollars. This feels even better than winning at the races. Rich and poor are all relative. All are relative—dialects, birth and death—nothing final.

"Why did Chuang-tzu say then, that all things are equal?" Chuang-tzu proposed the theory of "all things being equal," in which he related his famous experience of dreaming he was a yellow butterfly who knew nothing of Chuang-tzu and upon awakening, knowing he was Chuang-tzu, wondered if he was now actually the yellow butterfly's dream. From the perspective of

original nature, all things are equal. Rich and poor alike all have to die. It's the same for everyone, death. We sit here with our seeming differences; lighter, darker, thinner, fatter, male, female, and so forth. This is something in which we are all equal. Tonight from about three or four until about five or six a.m., we will all be in the same state of deep, dreamless sleep. This state is exactly the same for everyone regardless of one's financial situation, age or gender. Whether or not one has wisdom, dreamless sleep is still dreamless sleep. In this, all can be said to be equal. All the things of the natural world are also not equal in their appearance. The five fingers individually are all different but relative to the hand, they are all the same, fingers. Hands and feet are different but when there is no more "I" these too will eventually become one and the same thing. This is Chuang-tzu's "All Things Being Equal" theory. Understanding this, it no longer matters whether one's fortune is great or small.

"The bell sounds, rousing one from all things." What is the real fortune? Immaculate fortune, the pure fortune of this world. Someone who has been under a lot of stress or has really been suffering will sometimes go off into the mountains or the countryside. If this person comes across an old monastery and happens to hear the sound of the bell being struck, "bong," at this moment, the head clears and all the worries slip away. That very moment, one has absolutely nothing. It's an awakening from a big dream. This is great fortune, and so the *Diamond Sutra* tells us

that the greatest merit is in understanding the truly liberating prajna wisdom of the *Diamond Sutra*.

SECTION 25

TRANSFORMING WITHOUT TRANSFORMING

"Subhuti, consider this. Do not say the Tathagata has the thought, I must save sentient beings. Subhuti, you should never think so. Why? Because there are actually no sentient beings which the Tathagata can save. If there were, the Tathagata would be holding the concept of a self, a person, a being and a life. Subhuti, when the Tathagata speaks of Himself, there is really no existent self, although the ordinary person thinks so. Subhuti, 'ordinary person', the Tathagata says, is not but merely called 'ordinary person'."

Have Teaching, No Students

The word *transforming* in the title means the same thing as saving. Before the T'ang Dynasty, the word *transforming* was used in all the Chinese translations of Buddhist works. But you can't really save or transform someone else. During the Yuan and Ming periods, they started combining the older and newer translations together, "saving transformation." Actually, it's all a matter of educating someone. *"Subhuti, consider this. Do not say that the Tathagata has the thought, "I must save sentient beings."*

Here the Buddha Himself brings up the subject, telling them that they must absolutely not go around saying that the Buddha ever said, *"I must save sentient beings"*. The Buddha is really quite mysterious. If you look carefully at the *Diamond Sutra*, he has refuted many things he did throughout his life. Forty-nine years of teaching and he says that he never said a word. He said it himself, I've got the book right in front of me! Earlier on he had said that we must vow to save all beings, and here again this is overturned. You absolutely must not say that I want to save sentient beings. This is what the words look like on the surface.

> *"Subhuti, you should never think so. Why? Because there are actually no sentient beings which the Tathagata can save. If there were, the Tathagata would be holding the concept of a self, a person, a being and a life."*

"Subhuti, you should never think so." Get the idea out of your head! The Buddha again emphasizes not holding onto this idea. This is pretty clear to us now, so don't go cowering in fear begging to be saved by the Buddha. He's very busy in nirvana. Why shouldn't we think like this? "Because there are actually no sentient beings which to save." This is quite serious. Just now we were joking about the Buddha refuting everything, but when he gives this as an explanation, it's almost bewildering. There is not one sentient being that the Buddha should save. Pay careful attention! There is not one person the Buddha needs to save.

"If there were, the Tathagata would be holding the concept of a self, a person, a being and a life." In the Ch'an school, they have another way of expressing this, "two people in one coffin; one said, 'I saved you', the other said, 'I needed to be saved'." Neither of these two is enlightened. The Buddha said Himself, number one, I never saved a single being, because there are no sentient beings that I need to save. Number two, if there were someone who became a "Buddha" because of my having saved him, this person isn't a Buddha. He is just an ordinary person. A Buddha has no concepts of a self, a person, a being and a life.

This is why I always tell people not to bow or prostrate to me. This whole thing really scares me. I start to get nervous and sweat when someone even joins their palms together to greet me. The modern way is much better. When your eyes meet, just smile and nod to one another. If you prostrate to me, thinking that I am your teacher and that I ought to accept your prostration, the eighteen levels of hell aren't enough—but don't worry, I've heard they've added a basement under the last level. I'll be going straight down to that basement if I accept this. If a person thinks he or she has Tao and must teach and save everyone, the Tao isn't worth a cent.

One who is truly worthy of being a teacher of people has realized emptiness. Would such a person hold to concepts of higher and lower? Most certainly not. To such a person, all beings are equal; self and others are equal. And so the Buddha says, one who has such ideas of saving others is not a Buddha. This person is grasping at all kinds of notions—I am Buddha, I'm a teacher, you are all my students, my disciples... This kind of talk is not that of a Buddha. Somewhere in mainland China, there was a monk who saw all beings as equal. If he saw a monkey, he would address it as "respected monkey." If he saw a snake, he would call it "respected snake." This is really the spirit of Buddhism. It's not thinking that I've taught and transformed these disciples of mine. Because of me, they've realized the Tao. They should show me respect and honor. Anyone with this kind of thinking is done for; they are "holding the concept of a self, a person, a being and a life."

Buddha! Buddha! We understand, really. You are so incredibly modest, you don't even want to take credit for helping others. We actually have been transformed and liberated by you. From your side, you act in modesty; from our side, we are respectful. In this, there is no contradiction. Still, there is one question left unanswered. You said that there are no sentient beings who need you to liberate them. This is a big question.

Self-Liberation

> "Subhuti, when the Tathagata speaks of Himself, there is really no existent self, although the ordinary person thinks so. Subhuti, ordinary person', the Tathagata says, is not but merely called ordinary person'."

The Buddha here talks about people, the humans among the sentient beings. The real Buddha Dharma teaches us just one thing and all 84,000 Dharma doors are for one purpose, to understand that there is no actual self. It's very simple; cultivation is the path to understanding selflessness. Since there is no self, "I" obviously don't need the Buddha to save or liberate me. I am a Buddha to begin with! If there is another to be saved, this Buddha has notions of self, person, being and life. If I am really enlightened, I don't have a self, nothing to be liberated. So, of course, the Buddha says there are no sentient beings he should save. Another way to look at this is that the Buddha taught 84,000 Dharma doors, methods by which one can become enlightened, and if you apply them, you, too, can become enlightened. He cannot become a Buddha on your behalf. You must liberate your own "self." If you work on your cultivation, you will achieve success and liberation of your own accord. This is why the Buddha said, there are no sentient beings which I should liberate, nor could I possibly liberate them.

There are no mistakes in what the Buddha said, but the ways in which he chooses to express these ideas can sometimes sound quite shocking. As well, each line seems difficult to explain, but the theory behind these is very straightforward. All beings must seek liberation for themselves. If you don't save yourself, there is no one who can save you.

If one looks to heaven, to the Bodhisattvas and so forth for salvation, this is blind faith. If you wish for anyone's help, you must first make the effort to help yourself. How do you help yourself? By cultivating all good virtues. If you do this, then heaven and the Bodhisattvas can help you because, in cultivating virtues, you've opened up a connection of energy with them. If you spend your days and energy killing people and starting fires and still hope to receive the help of the Buddhas and Bodhisattvas, you'd better think again. The Buddha told us, there are no sentient beings which to save; they must save themselves.

What is the self? All beings originally have no self. This is the Buddha Dharma. All teachings of the twelve categories of sutras within the Tripitaka all boil down to this one sentence—there is originally no self. It's just that we haven't realized this. If we do, then we have become Buddhas. The Buddha also said, *"When the Tathagata speaks of Himself, there is really no existent self, although the ordinary person thinks so."* The ordinary person is exactly as the name suggests, your average person. This term here carries with it no connotations of social status, looks or income. Still, if you refer to your friend as an ordinary person, she would probably feel bad, thinking "I know I am just average, but why do you have to go pointing it out." She feels that you look down on her. The ordinary person, if told there was no self, would be afraid because people grasp onto a self. What is this thing to which we grasp then? In one of the sutras, it outlines 36 things into which it can be broken down, none of which could be said to be the self. Buddhism is actually quite scientific in its approach. This gets quite serious here as we look at it from today's scientific perspective. All of the millions of cells in the body are "me" but they are also not "me." So where then am I? If my body isn't me, am I what I am after death? Am I the soul? Have you ever seen your soul?

"The bell sounds, rousing one from all things." It is this alambana. The bell sounds and there is no self. Originally nothing has a self; there is not one thing which is the self. Still, all the Buddha can do is to break it down in different ways for us to consider. Thus, we study and meditate looking to verify this for ourselves. If we can verify it, then we've become Buddhas. The trouble is that during meditation, most people are just playing with the "self."   Thinking, breathing, counting...the breathing doesn't stop. Playing with the "self" one can never get to no-self or the Buddha Dharma.

After No-Self

The ordinary person grasps onto a self existence; the existence of a self during life and the existence of a soul upon death. Actually, that which is labeled as a soul is just a certain alambana of consciousness, which occasionally exists. This is not the real self. The common person always comes around to grasping something with appearance as the self. They're grasping the wrong thing. When the four notions—self, person, being, life—are empty, one can finally find the original nature of life. This you cannot call self, nor Buddha, nor bodhi—it cannot be named.

"Subhuti, the "ordinary person" the Tathagata says, is not so but is merely called "ordinary person." Why did the Buddha tack this onto the end? To prevent further grasping. There are many Buddhists who actually don't dare to be a Buddha but aren't satisfied with just being a "ordinary person." Most Buddhists are very pitiful, diddling around somewhere between a Buddha and a person, like children playing in the park.

So, the Buddha tells us that "ordinary person" is just a name. There is nothing real to it. It's just an illusory name. Strictly speaking, all sentient beings are Buddhas, but they just can't find their own original nature; not finding is called "ordinary person," all are Buddhas, all are equal. In later writings of the Ch'an sect, "mind," "Buddha" and "sentient beings" are without distinction. This mind is Buddha. Upon enlightenment, the mind is Buddha. While still unenlightened, the Buddha is a common person. "Mind," "Buddha" and "sentient beings" are all without distinction, all equal.

So is this section over? No, there is still a big question that we haven't yet addressed. We need to go back and look at the opening line of this section. *"Do not say that the Tathagata has the thought, I should save sentient beings."* The thing we need to look at here is the "I" in the Buddha's statement. "I" haven't saved any sentient beings. This is how it appears on the page. Why did the Buddha phrase it this way? The main point of this whole section is to tell us that a person who awakens to no-self, who verifies for him or herself the truth of no-self is a Buddha. This Buddha has no notion of self and thus will naturally have no notions of sentient beings.

To be without these notions is the alambana of a Buddha; to have the notions of self, person, being and life is that of the common person. From the grasping of the self, all other notions arise. No-self is the state of a Buddha, but after no-self, then what? Listen carefully! Most people hear the term *no-self* and automatically flip to empty. This is not the Buddha's explanation. All he said was no-self; the "empty" was your addition. If you completely drop, completely let go of all the notions of self and so forth that the common person holds, the original state of life will reveal itself. Stretching the term, that can be called the real self, the state of a Buddha. In the sutras, the Buddha never speaks in terms of a real self.

The Buddha taught for 49 years, but there are only a few main points which he emphasized. Impermanence—nothing is reliable, everything changes, nothing is "mine." Suffering—there is no lasting happiness or fortune. Emptiness—there is no way to hold onto anything. Things are constantly transforming and we can't hold onto them. Impermanence, suffering, emptiness and no-self. These are the basic teachings of the Buddha. During his time in the world, many of the Buddha's disciples attained the state of no-self, liberating themselves from suffering. However, they tended to fall into the alambana of emptiness, the Hinayana or lesser state of emptiness.

At the age of 81, before taking his big vacation into nirvana, the Buddha taught four things which seemed to completely overturn all the previous teachings. Those four are permanence, bliss, self and purity. He told his disciples that if they really reach the state of no notions of self, person, being and life where they've dropped everything even emptiness, this is the never changing origin of all life. Don't make the mistake of thinking that there is some "thing" which is unchanging. This is the theory of the Mind Only School, one of the outside paths. The permanence taught by the Buddha is not a permanence standing opposite to impermanence. This will be explained later on in the sutra.

Bliss is not suffering. Enlightened people move beyond suffering. Most people would imagine them to be happy and laughing the whole day, every day. This would certainly kill almost anyone. If such a person has a headache, of course it will still hurt and feel miserable. However, thinking you're not supposed to feel this and act happy and giddy in spite of the pain, might put you in a nuthouse. A few days of a headache usually doesn't kill anyone! Joy and suffering are opposite phenomena and seizing onto one or the other brings with it mental illness.

What then is the "bliss" talked of by the Buddha? No suffering, clean and pure joy. There is no mental state which accompanies clean purity. It is not like any of the states of bliss experienced in worldly alambanas. Permanent bliss is at the same time the true self beyond birth and death. This self which is beyond birth and death has none of the concepts or ideas onto which we normally hold, no idea of an existent self, and so it is absolutely pure and clean. The "pureland" has no alambana of purity. It's not sparkling clean floors or outer space; these things aren't really "clean" if you look closely at them. The space of clean purity has no good or evil, no suffering or joy and so it is the state of real bliss, the state of the Buddha. This is what is meant by the title of "Transforming Without Transforming." Now, let's look at the gatha which expresses this transforming without transforming, the no-self of enlightenment and the true nature of emptiness.

Gatha of Section Twenty-five

> *All in the Sahaloka are but transformation,*
> *Happy and sad without reason; just release your song!*
> *Bells and drums come to rest, wild dancing ends;*
> *The tune of "Wind and Waves Stop" plays leisurely.*

"All in the Sahaloka are but transformations." We are all physical transformations. In Chuang-tzu's words, the universe is a big chemical mixing pot. The leaves, trees, ants, animals and us are all just chemical bits in this big mixing pot. In ancient times in China, they didn't speak in terms of people dying, it was referred to as "transforming." The process of death is a transformation and the body is left behind, then, transforms, bones into dust, flesh into water. Things of the physical world will continually transform, as this is the property of its basic energy make up. Both coming to and being in this Sahaloka are states of transformation called sentient beings, actors in life's dramas, musicals and operas.

"Happy and sad without reason; just release your song!" Everyone has forgotten that they are in a stage play and don't appreciate their own performances. All that wonderful acting, singing, crying, laughing and so forth, everyone's got themselves fooled. All of the sadnesses, sufferings, frustrations, happinesses and joys are for no clear reason. The deeper the understanding and clarity people have, the more truly liberated they are in their expression; really singing and dancing when they do so.

In the temples, they sound the drums and bells and chant the sutras. Here on the 11th floor, we study the *Diamond Sutra*, so clean and pure. On another floor, they are dancing to music, boom, boom, cha, cha, cha! All are equal, each in their own alambana. After we've finished our sutra and they their dancing, all will go home and enter the dark cave of sleep. *"Bells and drums come to rest, wild dancing ends."* In the end, pure and impure, good and evil can all be understood but not had.

"The tune of "Wind and Waves Stop" plays leisurely." When you understand that there is nothing you can keep when you have achieved truly letting go, you are home. "Wind and Waves Stop" is the name of an ancient song. We don't need to bother with the contents of the lyrics, just the title will do. The wind and waves have stopped. The drum and bell no longer sound. The dancing has stopped, and the song is finished.

SECTION 26

DHARMAKAYA WITHOUT FORM

"Subhuti, what do you think? Can the Tathagata be observed through the thirty-two marks of physical excellence?"

Subhuti replied, "It is so, it is so. The Tathagata can be observed through the thirty-two marks."

Then Buddha said, "Subhuti, if that were so, then a Chakravartin would also be a Tathagata."

Subhuti then said to the Buddha, "World-Honored One, as I understand the meaning of your teaching, the Tathagata cannot be observed by his thirty-two marks of physical excellence."

Thereupon, the World-Honored One recited the following verse:

"One who looks for me in appearance
Or pursues me in sound,
Follows paths leading astray,
And cannot perceive the Tathagata."

Perceive

"Subhuti, what do you think? Can the Tathagata be observed through the thirty-two marks of physical excellence?"

*Subhuti replied, "It is so, it is so. The Tathagata can be
observed through the thirty-two marks."*

Here we have come to the heart of the main point of the
Diamond Sutra. The Buddha once again asks this question which
has already been discussed. Previously, Subhuti gave a different
answer, but by now, Subhuti's head was probably swimming. If
we just study the teaching methods employed by the Buddha, you
will see what an incredible educator he was. Earlier, Subhuti very
clearly gave the right answer. Then, the Buddha twirled him
around in circles with all those different questions and when he
asked again this question, Subhuti's self-confidence was shaken
and he answered incorrectly. The Buddha's disciples at the time
weren't called disciples, they were called "hearers." They were
educated by the Buddha through his voice. However, the Ch'an
masters would instead describe Subhuti's situation here as being
led around by the nose like a water buffalo!

The teaching method employed in the *Diamond Sutra* is really
quite interesting. Previously, the Buddha asked Subhuti if the
Tathagata could be perceived through form and he answered, "No,
World-Honored One." Isn't that so? The discussion continues on
very well for some time and here again the question, *"Can the
Tathagata be observed through the thirty-two marks of physical
excellence?"* Notice here the words Subhuti then replied, *"It is so,
it is so."* This is right, the Buddha, being a Buddha after all, has

thirty-two marks of excellence, and so Subhuti's answer isn't wrong.

"The Buddha said , 'Subhuti, if that were so then a chakravartin would also be a Tathagata'."

The Buddha gives Subhuti's rope a quick tug. Subhuti smarten up! If the thirty-two marks were used to recognize the Buddha, then a Chakravartin, the Wheel Turning King who has merited the thirty-two marks of excellence, would also be a Buddha. At this prompting, Subhuti shakes his head clear. Buddha, I was wrong! He starts again from the beginning. *"Subhuti then said to the Buddha, 'World-Honored One, as I understand the meaning of your teaching, the Tathagata cannot be observed by his thirty-two marks of physical excellence'."* Ignore the first answer. If I understand your meaning correctly, one should not look to the thirty-two marks to see the Buddha. Subhuti is really in the hot seat now! The more you study the *Diamond Sutra*, the more interesting it becomes.

Sound, Form and the False Path

"Thereupon, the World Honored One recited the following verse:" Subhuti barely finishes his sentence and the Buddha follows on his heels with these most important words:

"One who looks for me in appearance
Or pursues me in sound,
Follows paths leading astray,
And cannot perceive the Tathagata."

This moment was more powerful than the explosion of an atomic bomb. The Buddha knew that Subhuti was very close to a big awakening, so he turned him around and around until Subhuti wasn't sure which end was up. "Thereupon," Subhuti had yet to catch his breath when—"It's this!" —Subhuti had his awakening. This isn't spelled out in the sutra but then again, it wouldn't be the *Diamond Sutra* if it were.

Now let's take a look at the contents of these four lines. Most people look for the Buddha in appearance, "look for me in appearance." The Buddha includes both his "self" as well as our "selves" in this "me." Two levels of meaning are inherent within this word. Most people who are Buddhists wish to see a real Buddha standing in front of them. They work hard visualizing, prostrating or whatever and get fed up if it doesn't result in a Buddha appearing to them. In the event that a Buddha does appear, it is most likely one of two situations; either it is a problem with the nervous system or a problem related to blood circulation, both of which could cause hallucinations. How could the Buddha be perceived in form or appearance? Didn't the *Heart Sutra* also say that form is emptiness and emptiness is form? What you saw came from your own agitated mind and not from the Buddha. In many sutras, the Buddha says do not grasp onto form. To look for the Buddha in form is wrong.

There are also many people who "pursue me in sound." People meditate and recite mantras. Some people pay a lot of money to learn even one mantra. I know of about 1,400 of them. At five thousand dollars a mantra, I'd be set for the rest of my life. Some people recite mantras and attain different states of samadhi. Others will start to hear other sounds or voices. If you think this is Tao then, go see a doctor quickly! The sutras tell you not to seek "me" in sound. These "sounds" you hear are imagined. Our physical bodies produce a lot of internal sounds, just cover your ears and you'll hear some. Your heart beating, blood coursing through the veins, these things all make sounds. If you add to this a little imagination, it all sounds like mantras OM-AH, HUNG-AH, OM-AH, HUNG-AH.... These are all illusory phenomena. Many people aren't informed, however, and believe this is Tao. This is simply grasping onto phenomena. If people grasp onto these sounds and voices, thinking they've improved or even thinking they've attained Tao, the Buddha says such people have gone down a path leading them astray and cannot perceive the Tathagata. Going down such a path, one will never be able to achieve the state of a Buddha. This isn't even mentioning the practice of channeling spirits, which is another path leading far astray.

We've just been talking about seeing the "self" of the Buddha. In trying to perceive our own self nature, many search for "me" in form. During meditation, one is sitting very well. Suddenly one sees one's body sitting there. It's as if "I" am another "me" looking down at "me" there. Many people have this experience and think they can send out a spirit body (yin body). You absolutely must not fool yourself. This body is a false self to begin with and that which has come out is yet another false self. In the *Surangama Sutra*, it talks about this phenomenon. If you've been meditating for some time, your mental state quiets and your heart beat, breathing and other physical functions will slow down to an imperceptible rate; but are still functioning. This functioning of the physical body is enough to cause a subtle irritation to the quieted mind. This irritation manifests as mental phenomena. For example, the above mentioned yin body is one such phenomenon of a mental projection. This mental projection is still the "I" to which we've always grasped. This kind of experience is very enthralling to people in its novelty. Seeing your "self" sitting there or sleeping there seems so interesting. No sooner is there any grasping of the self than "you" and your body are again one. If you think this is Tao, you are seeking "me" in form and are sadly mistaken.

Another kind of common experience is when one is reciting mantras in a loud voice or with many voices from the void reciting along with you. Hearing this, some people think that they have some special power, or Tao. This is "pursuing 'me' in sound." What does the Buddha say about this? It is a path leading astray. Be aware of this. It leads to getting caught up in one's own mind.

It is very popular nowadays to play around with such things and it can seem very enticing, but it is actually extremely dangerous. If we weren't studying Buddhism, I might not put forth an opinion on such matters if questioned. People need to have a way to feed themselves. If my opinions result in cutting off people's food money, then it's better to not say anything.

Now, let's turn to another important question that comes up in this section. Going back to the opening line, *"Subhuti, what do you think? Can the Tathagata be observed through the thirty-two marks of physical excellence?"* I'd first like to apologize for passing over this important point previously. The most crucial word in this entire section is "observed." This "observing" includes introspection, as in samatha and vipassana (stopping and introspection); as well as visualization, which is the essential practice of the esoteric school. These are the foundations of Buddhist practice. One needs to first be able to attain samatha or to hold a visualization before one can reach samadhi. Once you achieve this, you've got your foot in the door.

This is easy to say but how many people can actually hold a visualization or a state of mental quiet? This is not even mentioning achieving a level of dhyana! Can you maintain concentration on a single object, a state of emptiness or a state of peace and quiet? Very few people can actually do this. You may work very hard at your practice but for the most part are just spinning your wheels. Samatha must first be achieved before you can really "observe." To maintain both samatha and vipassana simultaneously is samapatti. The Buddha taught the method of samatha and vipassana and if you examine carefully, all of the 84,000 Dharma doors are methods of samatha and vipassana. Take, for example, the method of reciting the Buddha's name, the pureland method. Whether it be reciting out loud or in one's mind if there is *only* NAMO AMITOFO, this is samatha. Samatha is not death nor is it oblivion. It is perfect clarity, the opening of great wisdom, "vipassana," understanding the Buddha's teachings.

Another kind of observing is through visualization. For example, in the sutras, the Buddha tells us to visualize a moon or a sun. Everyone has seen these before and so has an immediate impression. The trick is to maintain this image either at your heart center or in front of you, with or without your eyes closed. Can you keep it there clearly without it moving? When you can do this, you'll look as if you're spaced-out. It's not the kind of spaced-out look that someone with mental illness has; this would indicate a problem. The look that you'll see young people get when thinking of their girlfriend or boyfriend is more like it. It is the alambana of "I drink my tea but think about him. I eat my food but think about him." To have your visualization in mind to that extent is samatha, is observing.

The esoteric school has many methods to get to samatha and vipassana. They are just methods and are not the Buddha Dharma. Methods are for your convenience. They are there to help get our monkeying mind wrapped firmly around something. This is just the preliminary step. If you say, "then we don't need to use

Buddhist images, right?" Of course! You don't need anything. After this thought leaves, before the next thought arises, this is emptiness. Just stop right here forever. You're aware of everything going on around you, aware of the sounds or the quiet but they have nothing to do with you. Pure and clean, this is samatha and vipassana. Think about it. Can you do this? No! Well of course, the so-called common people are not ordinary people but are merely called ordinary people. Of course you can't do this and of course you're called ordinary people. If you could, then you'd almost be a Buddha.

The Buddha took us one step beyond this. In the end, you're observing an object of awareness, and so the Tathagata cannot be observed through the 32 marks of physical excellence. Earlier in the sutra, the Buddha asked Subhuti if the "Tathagata could be perceived through his perfect nirmanakaya." "Perceiving," perceiving one's mind and original nature has to do with the level of one's realization and wisdom. "Observing" refers to the time and effort one applies to one's cultivation. If you are doing scholarly work, studying the sutras, you need to remain very astute. I also was leading you in circles just now. Subhuti's answer to the Buddha was actually correct, and I will slowly explain why. You must look deeply into every word when you read or study a sutra. If you're wrong about one word, you will misunderstand the entire thing.

The Buddha has 32 special physical characteristics. In between his eyebrows is a small fleshy protuberance which gives off light. This is why in India it is the custom for females to wear a small jewel or mark a red dot between the eyebrows which represents wisdom and fortune. The Buddha's special characteristics aren't limited to this, as we've previously discussed. The *Diamond Sutra* says again and again not to grasp onto appearances but if one is practicing visualization of a Buddha, one must grasp onto this most auspicious physical appearance. The Buddha asked Subhuti if one could use this method of observing the Buddha with all 32 characteristics. Subhuti said, Of course! This is the way one who practices visualization should observe the Tathagata. His answer wasn't wrong! The Buddha himself taught visualizing Amitabha this way.

Lots of people recite Namo Amitofo (the Chinese pronunciation of Amitabha) but don't know that they ought to recite Namo Shakyamuni Buddha beforehand. Shakyamuni Buddha was the one who introduced Amitabha in the first place. People have forgotten the root teacher. This isn't right. The Western Paradise was introduced by the Buddha. If you wish to be successful at the pureland method, you mustn't neglect paying homage to Shakyamuni Buddha. People shouldn't forget their roots; this is true for Buddhism as well. Why, then, did the Buddha introduce the method of reciting Amitabha's name alone? Because, the Buddhas of the three times and the ten directions are of the same original nature. If you understand this, then reciting Namo Amitabha is the same as reciting Namo Shakyamuni Buddha or

Namo Kuan-shih-yin Pu-sa (Homage to Avalokiteshvara); if you don't understand this, then it is blind faith.

I take responsibility for what I say. If you speak on behalf of the Buddha Dharma and say such things carelessly, you will go straight to hell, straight to the basement of hell! I'm prepared to go at any time. (It's okay, I know they have an elevator going back up.) Now we will enter into a discussion on the central issue of observing the Tathagata. Please listen carefully.

A Chakravartin

"Subhuti, if the Tathagata could be observed through the thirty-two marks then a chakravartin would also be a Tathagata." Everyone listen carefully. There is a big question here. Many Buddhist scholars pass right over it. I want to take the opportunity to point it out now for everyone. The question has to do with "a chakravartin."

In the sutras it describes a chakravartin as an emperor, a sovereign, a supreme ruler during a time of total world peace, the wheels of whose chariot roll everywhere without obstruction. There are four kinds of chakravartin: those with wheels of gold, of silver, of copper and of iron. Each possesses seven precious things, for example, morality, a heavenly queen, great wealth, the best kind of transportation available, (today it would be a Lear jet perhaps) and so forth. Emperor Mo of the Chou Dynasty was an iron wheel chakravartin. The historians write of Emperor Mo going to the Jade Lake in the Western land of Immortals and meeting the Golden Queen as well as the Grandmother Queen (Wang-mu Niang-niang—the highest of the Taoist deities). How did he get to the Western land of the Immortals? He had eight mystical horses. This is why it is traditional to have paintings of eight fine horses. *"The eight fine horses cover thirty thousand li in one day, where could Emperor Mo possibly not have been?"* This is a line from a T'ang Dynasty poem describing the situation.

During the reign of a chakravartin, the world is at peace and the citizens live in peace, prosperity and propitiousness. These kinds of kings only appear at the Golden Age of a civilization. They have the dignified appearance of a Buddha with the same thirty-two auspicious signs. This is why when Gautama Shakyamuni Buddha was born, a seer came to witness the child and told his parents that he would either be the greatest king of this age or the teacher of a thousand worlds, a Buddha.

In many sutras, the Buddha himself praised chakravartins saying that their fortunes of merit were the same as a Buddha's. Buddhism doesn't ignore worldly dharma but how does one become a chakravartin through worldly dharma? How does a peaceful world come about? All people practicing good virtues will result in a peaceful world and a peaceful world will give rise to a great sovereign. In Chinese history, Confucius always referred to the consecutive reigns of Kings Yao, Shun and Yu as being the age of the chakravartins. In the *Avatamsaka Sutra* as well as other great sutras, the Buddha says that only one who is already a tenth level Bodhisattva can reincarnate as a chakravartin.

In other words, many chakravartins are living Buddhas who decide to live a worldly rather than a "holy" lifestyle. One needs great fortune of merit to be born into such a position. As well, it is only with the power of such fortune of merit that one in this position could bring about and maintain a generation of peace and prosperity in the world benefiting hundreds of thousands of people. *"This body won't sit on the Tathagata seat; The rivers and mountains still need tidying."* This world is quite dirty. It still needs people to sweep, mop and clean. I wrote this poem to answer people as to why I chose not to be a monk. The main point the Buddha stresses in the sutras is to teach people to cultivate virtue. If you point to the Sixth Patriarch saying that he awakened without having read a single sutra, so why should I study sutras? Well, yes, he was illiterate and got enlightened but there was only one such Sixth Patriarch. Before him and after him were there any like him? Do not compare yourself to him.

Tenth Bhumi Bodhisattvas and Chakravartins

The *Diamond Sutra* became the main sutra of the Ch'an sect by the T'ang Dynasty. The relationship between Ch'an and the *Diamond Sutra* is the teaching method they use, especially apparent in this section. This teaching method is simply leading another to the point of self discovery using the obverse and reverse sides one after another. Here in Section 26, the Buddha asks if the Tathagata could be observed through the thirty-two marks of excellence, and Subhuti answers that, yes, one could thus observe the Tathagata. The Buddha rebuts his answer by saying that if so, if the Buddha could be seen by means of his physical form, then a chakravartin, whose physical appearance also indicates the same power of merit that a Buddha has, would also figure to be a Buddha. This is still a question, but Subhuti in response to this says, Oh, I get it, one shouldn't observe the Tathagata through these thirty-two marks, through the physical form.

We've discussed this question of form and appearance before. Most people who put effort into cultivation easily get caught up grasping onto appearance. Today my ch'i feels full, my face looks good, I must be regaining my youth....these are all ideas which are actually just grasping onto appearances. Form and appearance aren't real. They are impermanent, temporary, the functioning of the dharmakaya of original nature not having any real, independent existence of their own. The Buddha doesn't just leave it at this, He recites the gatha to both summarize and emphasize the message. *"One who looks for me in appearance, or pursues me in sound follows paths leading astray and cannot perceive the Tathagata."* We've gone over this gatha before. The layers of meaning are many and deep. Anyone who calls himself a Buddhist should think very deeply about these words.

The next question we will discuss is about chakravartins. During the last lecture we started to talk about this. Most people explain Buddhism in terms of the supramundane. The Buddha spoke many times of a chakravartin's merits as well as the fact that only tenth level bodhisattvas can become chakravartins. It takes one such as this to bring peace below the heavens. Such an unparalleled leader only comes once in a thousand years, or as Mencius says, each five hundred years must have its great king. For human society to be at peace is not easy. The great merit of a chakravartin is to create a generation of peace. This is why the Buddha praises their merit. To become a Buddha is not easy and neither is becoming a chakravartin. One needs to have done a lot of virtuous deeds and accumulated a lot of merit. The merit gained through such worldly dharmas is different than the Buddha's merit in that the fortune of the Buddha's merit is prajna wisdom. There is a difference, and a chakravartin is not a Buddha. A chakravartin has not perceived the mind's original nature, but if he had, he would be a layman Buddha.

The *Avatamsaka Sutra* speaks of many kings who are already Buddhas; who've had their Great Awakening. The Buddha will also occasionally refer to the "merit of the Ten Kings." These are the Ten Kings of the Underworld, and even though they are Underworld Kings, you or I are nowhere near qualified to be one. It takes great merit to remain in the nether worlds and guide the beings there. Theirs is truly the alambana of a Bodhisattva. The Kings of the heavens, the four direction of the desire realm and so forth all have great merit to be able to occupy such a position. To be a leader who brings peace to society in the human real is just as difficult as becoming a Buddha. The difference between the two lies in the perception of the Tao.

The Buddha in this section says that seeking in form or sound will not result in perceiving the Tao. This is the same meaning as do not grasp. As the *Diamond Sutra* repeatedly tells us, if you practice the Buddha Dharma with grasping, you will never perceive the dharmakaya. This includes grasping to self, person, being, life or any other phenomenon. One who looks for me in appearance, or pursues me in sound has gone astray.

Why didn't the Buddha say, one who looks for the Tathagata in appearance or pursues the Tathagata in sound.... instead of "me"? This wasn't a question of the translator's discretion. In discerning the original nature of mind, the universe and the myriad of things are perceived to be of the same nature. One finds the "self" which is the origin of all life. Beyond all sound and appearance, not grasping, not dwelling is the mind seal of the Mahayana, "no dwelling, no form, no vow." Most of the *Diamond Sutra* is talking about these three things. It is this alambana which is perceiving the Tao, the Buddha and the "self" or "me." This "perceiving" is the "root wisdom," the body of the true form of prajna, the dharmakaya. Not grasping and not dwelling is the root wisdom perceiving the dharmakaya. It is still not the Great Awakening and Great Enlightenment. At this stage one still does not have mature wisdom. Ch'an speaks in terms of three passageways. At this stage one has gotten through the first passageway which has been described as "seeing that the mountains are not mountains and water is not water." Being here, of course, people are not people and spirits are not spirits. Not a thing is and so there is not a thing to grasp.

Gatha of Section Twenty-six

Powder, make-up, and panpipes, thick action on stage.
Who knew outside the window bars, snow fell so densely?
Push open the window to glance at the cool, clean world.
The bright moon, the reed flowers and no certain tracks.

"Powder, make-up, and panpipes, thick action on stage." The universe is a grand stage and people, all living beings, are the players, all with insignificant roles. Powdered and painted we go onstage to wave flags and shout. It's all action and noise onstage, but backstage is quiet. Returning backstage, with no costume, make-up or role, I am just me. At the same time, outside the theater, *"Who knew outside the window bars, snow fell so densely?"*

This was the feeling of winter during my retreat at Mount O'Mei. Everything was a haze of white, the drama of a world of snow. To feel as though acting out this play of human life is meaningless and run off to sit quietly contemplating the Tao, is still acting out a role. You may feel as if you are above the rest, that you are enlightened, but you are just playing the role of a monk, acting out the life of an ascetic. All is empty and this is the best there is! It's just a play, but the difference is that all around outside is a world of snow. Don't get enchanted by this scene! If you do, you'll never know the Tao.

This is why Master Han-shan of the Ming Dynasty wrote, *"Walking barefoot amidst the brambles is easy; difficult is turning away from the moonlit scene."* There are difficulties and obstacles at every turn for one who practices Buddhism, like thorny brambles underfoot. Most people would say that walking barefoot in brambles is a difficult thing, but one who is determined to walk the path of Tao doesn't feel this way. The worst that can happen is that one's body gets all scratched up. The most difficult thing is "turning away from the moonlit scene." To one who has reached the alambana of no-self, no body, all is empty, clean and pure. If you tell this person not to stay in this samadhi but to instead do what others aren't willing to do and endure what others aren't able to endure, this is the most difficult. Entering the sea of suffering to save the world and people is most difficult. In the Hinayana school, when one reaches this stage of purity, this pureland, then one has succeeded and has become an Arhat. According to the Vinaya of the Mahayana, this is breaking one's vows. It is clinging to a dhyana which results in incomplete merit. Master Han-shan wrote these lines as a warning because when you get to that point, it is very difficult to turn around. Not turning around, there is the danger of falling into the great arhat samadhi which could last 84,000 aeons.

"Push open the window to glance at the cool, clean world." One who is unwilling to give up this samadhi has not even a shadow of

mature wisdom. They have only perceived the clean, pure face of the dharmakaya but not the side of function. If we linger in the side of purity but poke around in there, if we open the window and look out, we'll see *"the bright moon, the reed flowers and no certain tracks."* Nowhere in this world isn't cool and clean. The pureland is everywhere; even the hells are the pureland. When one truly understands the dharmakaya, when there is absolutely no self, no form and no vow, there is bodhi within the suffering. If one grasps to the clean, pure side, bodhi becomes suffering. It's that simple.

At the Precipice Release Your Grip

Section 26, "The Dharmakaya Without Form," talks about the principle of not grasping and mentions that the *Diamond Sutra* is the "official" sutra of the Ch'an sect because of the teaching method employed in it. If you say "this," it's wrong; if you say "that," it's wrong. If you say, "it's wrong," it's wrong. If you say, "it's right," it's still wrong! When it finally comes down to it what is right? Yours is right, not the Buddha's. What the *Diamond Sutra* is trying to teach can be summed up in the words of one patriarch, "self-enlightenment, verify it for yourself." If you really wish to awaken to the true form of prajna, you must verify it for yourself. This is why the Ch'an masters said, *"At the precipice, dare to let go. Having gone completely beyond, one is reborn and can no longer be fooled."*

Those people who study Ch'an nowadays should be aware. Why is the Ch'an school called Ch'an? The word Ch'an (Zen) is derived from dhyana meaning meditative concentration. Without a firm base of meditative concentration, one can't even begin to talk about Ch'an. One needs to go to the pinnacle of sila, samadhi and prajna, the metaphor for this being "at the precipice," and jump off in a swan dive. If you jump, will you live? You have to take this risk, going from the highest point down to common ground. How does one come to be in such a position? It doesn't come of mere intellectual understanding. *"Having gone completely beyond,"* one must go through a big "Death." Of course, this doesn't mean swallowing a handful of sleeping pills! It means to completely throw yourself into your practice to the point where it's like dying and coming back to life again. To reach Great Awakening and Great Enlightenment *"one is reborn and can no longer be fooled,"* isn't empty talk. You can't cheat others saying you're enlightened. Cheating yourself and others is not final liberation. You must really work very hard.

The teaching method employed in the *Diamond Sutra* is this path. The Buddha drove Subhuti into a position where he was surrounded on all sides. No matter which way he moved, he would get hit. He spun Subhuti around until he was dizzy in the hopes that Subhuti would go completely beyond, be reborn and no longer be fooled. You cannot depend on outside help in becoming a Buddha and perceiving the Tao. You need to take matters into your own hands by really going beyond and being reborn a

Buddha. Of course, you must first get to the precipice. You do this by letting go of everything, all of the worldly dharma as well as the Buddha Dharma. It is at this point when one is empty of everything that one must jump, and then one will perceive the dharmakaya.

SECTION 27

NO NIHILITY

"Subhuti, if you have the thought that the Tathagata did not attain anuttara-samyak sambodhi because of His perfect nirmanakaya, Subhuti, do not have such a thought that the Tathagata did not attain anuttara-samyak sambodhi because of his perfect nirmanakaya.

"Subhuti, if in seeking the mind of anuttara-samyak sambodhi you think this way, you would be advocating the nihility of all dharma. Do not think this way. Why is this? Because one who attains anuttara-samyak sambodhi will not speak of the nihility of all dharma."

Outside of the Three Realms

"Subhuti, if you have the thought that the Tathagata did not attain anuttara-samyak sambodhi because of His perfect nirmanakaya, Subhuti, do not have such a thought that the Tathagata did not attain anuttara-samyak sambodhi because of his perfect nirmanakaya."

The Buddha called on Subhuti to check if he had the idea that the Tathagata didn't attain anuttara-samyak sambodhi because of

His perfect nirmanakaya, or in other words, thinking that just by not grasping one could perceive the Buddha, could become enlightened. He warned Subhuti not to make the mistake of thinking this way. Not to make the mistake of thinking one could awaken without accumulating merits. Just in the last section, we all saw very clearly what Subhuti was told—the Tathagata could not be observed through the thirty-two marks of physical excellence. The Buddha went on to emphasize this by saying, one who looks for me in form or pursues me in sound follows a path leading astray and cannot perceive the Tathagata. Now, here the Buddha is saying, Don't fool yourself thinking that you can become enlightened without complete and perfect merit.

"Subhuti, if in seeking the mind of anuttara-samyak sambodhi you think this way, you would be advocating the nihility of all dharma. Do not think this way."

If you think that after enlightenment everything is wonderful and empty, you are sorely mistaken. The Buddha is telling Subhuti this very clearly. I used to ask a lot of people about this particular point. There was one Ch'an master in Kunming with whom I spoke. I'd heard that he held the idea that after achieving nirvana and unlocking the mystery of life and death, one doesn't return. Under direct questioning, he admitted to holding this idea. I asked him why then does the *Lankavatara Sutra* say, *"There is no nirvana of the Buddha and there is no Buddha in nirvana."* If you don't come back then where do you go? If you leave the three realms, where are you? The Buddha never spoke of the fourth realm. To understand the mystery of life and death and then not return is not the Buddha Dharma. We argued about this question for a long time. There are many Buddhists that hold this same idea. They think that one practices, gets enlightenment, sits in the lotus position and then leaves, never to have to suffer through life again. This idea is absolutely wrong.

There are a lot of stories from people who work in the morgue about strange occurrences. Some of these can be used to verify certain things. One such story is of a girl who was in her early teens. Her parents forced her into marriage. She sat in lotus position and left this world. Her body stiffened after death. Locked in this lotus pose, she couldn't be placed in an ordinary coffin and so the morgue made a special one for her. This girl was certainly an achieved cultivator who'd returned to the world.

Nihilist Perspective

Let's go back to our question of the belief that once enlightened, one need not return, as if there were a place where they all go to hide. This is a wrong idea which has to do with one's perspective and understanding. Whether one is ordained or is a lay person, in order to truly verify the teachings, one must break the entanglements of perspective and states of mind. In Section 9, we went over these. If one's perspective is unclear, one will go astray. The five kinds of entangling perspective are: body, parameters, ideology grasping, heterodox and rule grasping. These five are obstacles to one's cultivation, and are the reason one cannot awaken.

People of today tend to be atheist and so they fall into thinking that death is annihilation. They don't believe in the three realms, the laws of karma or cyclic existence. Without solid proof of these, they can only believe that death is the end. This is a belief in nihilism which is one kind of heterodox perspective. The Buddha warns Subhuti against falling into such a view. He tells Subhuti twice not to grasp form or appearance and now he warns him about falling into not grasping form. Grasping is wrong, not grasping is also wrong. In "not grasping," everything is void and empty. The Buddha is empty, virtue is empty, everything is empty and killing doesn't matter because killing and all other evil is empty. This perspective repudiates the laws of cause and effect. It is the belief in void emptiness which is no different than atheism. You must be very clear on this point. This perspective of emptiness is what differentiates the Mahayana from the Hinayana. The Hinayana grasps emptiness. This view of emptiness, which says that even karma doesn't exist, is an extreme heterodox perspective of nihility. The Buddha, having told Subhuti not to seek the Buddha in appearance, was afraid he might fall into the side of "not grasping" which might lead to the perspective of nihility and so warned against this repeatedly.

Do Not Speak of Nihilism

"Why is this? Because one who attains anuttara-samyak sambodhi will not speak of the nihility of all dharma."

The *Diamond Sutra* is almost finished. Have we seen once in the original text the word emptiness? Many later explanations of the *Diamond Sutra* say that it is talking about emptiness. This is their opinion and not the Buddha's words. The Buddha did say, the past, present and future mind are ungraspable and one who looks for me in appearance or pursues me in sound follows paths leading astray and cannot perceive the Tathagata. In this method of teaching, the Buddha just blocks off the wrong paths. He only says what "it" isn't, but never what "it" is. In the beginning of the *Heart Sutra*, the Buddha says to perceive the five skandhas as empty but ends by saying that prajna paramita is real and not illusory. He may have said that the five skandhas are empty but not so prajna paramita! These are things not to be overlooked when studying sutras or practicing Buddhism. When overlooked, it is very easy to fall into heterodox views.

Empty is not the same as annihilation. A lot of people who study Buddhism will come to a point when they feel like everything is empty. This is not emptiness. A psychologist would call it a mild state of depression. It could be brought on by age, environment, misfortune and so forth. Everything may seem so "empty" but the state of depression is still there. Philosophers will also run around saying how they've seen through everything and it's all "empty." This just goes to show how un-empty they really are. Would there really be a need to go around saying "I see through everything and it's all empty" if you actually did? To go around huffing, "Oh, it's all so empty!" is just a sign of your own frustration, which is not in the least empty. To say "empty" or "emptiness" is just a convenient use of language. If you take "empty" as meaning non-existent, you fall into a perspective of nihility. The Buddha states clearly, "one who attains Supreme Enlightenment" will not say Dharmas are nihility. These words are extremely important! There is no nihility nor is there emptiness. "No Nihility" is the title of this section. Prince Chaoming picked the most important point. Even science has verified this with Einstein's theory saying energy transforms and cannot be created or destroyed.

Gatha of Section Twenty-seven

> *Once cloud and again water, water again becomes cloud.*
> *The silky chaos of drips and drops are not separate,*
> *Freezing begets glaciers and ice melts into water.*
> *In projections, slowly glimpse the oblique twilight rays.*

"*Once cloud and again water, water again becomes cloud.*" Observe the changes of nature; today it's rainy and tomorrow sunny. The rain becomes a cloud and a cloud becomes the rain.

No matter what, it's still the same water molecules involved in this transformation. *"The silky chaos of drips and drops are not separate."* As water reacts to temperature it changes. The rain comes tumbling down like threads of silk but in these each droplet has its own parameters. Similarly, all beings have the same original nature but once we become people and have our physical boundaries, you are you and I am I, distinctly different. Water molecules meet with cold and heat and alternately become rain and clouds. *"Freezing begets glaciers and ice melts into water."* Water freezes into ice which melts into water. These are the myriad transformations of the physical world. The transformations are the transformations and the original nature is the original nature. The original nature has no appearance, nothing to grasp. Is it empty? Is it permanent? Is it non-existent? All of these are not so.

"In projections slowly glimpse the oblique twilight rays." All things are light projections as ungraspable as holograms. The sun is setting and the light rays are slanted. The light of the setting sun is oblique like our minds. The sun itself is just an illusory projection of the universe. Why do we grasp onto projections of light? Where can we perceive the functioning of the original nature, the dharmakaya? All functioning, all appearances are its functioning and appearance. The original nature can be observed in form, appearance and function. With no grasping, one can perceive the original nature.

This is just about the last method which is taught within the *Diamond Sutra*. The Buddha has revealed everything to us.

SECTION 28

NO RECEIVING, NO LONGING

"Subhuti, if a Bodhisattva bestowed in charity quantities of the seven treasures sufficient enough to fill as many worlds as there are grains of sand in the Ganges, and if another person perceived that all dharmas are selfless thereby achieving the Perfection of Patient Endurance, the latter's merit would far surpass that of the former. Why is this? Subhuti, Bodhisattvas do not obtain fortune and merit."

Subhuti then asked the Buddha, "World-Honored One, why do Bodhisattvas not obtain fortune and merit?"

" Bodhisattvas should not have any longing for fortune and merit which they have created, and so do not obtain fortune and merit."

The Bodhisattva Who Loves to Do Charity

"Subhuti, if a Bodhisattva bestowed in charity quantities of the seven treasures sufficient enough to fill as many worlds as there are grains of sand in the Ganges and if another person perceived that all dharma are selfless thereby achieving the Perfection of Patient Endurance, the latter's merit would far surpass that of the former."

In addition to its educational method, the *Diamond Sutra* has another speciality—sales and marketing! Years ago in Shanghai, Hangzhou, Shandong and places around there, you would see people selling soft candy made from pears and honey. They would sing as they pushed their cart, "Children who eat my candy will pass all their tests. Old people who eat my candy will live forever, aging never more. Women who eat my candy become as fresh and beautiful as spring flowers..." Reading the *Diamond Sutra*, you might get the feeling that the Buddha is selling pear and honey candy. Every few lines you get told how wonderful this merit is or how great that merit is. But as soon as you start believing him, he overturns what he's just said. This is his teaching method.

It's at these places that we need to pay more attention. Each time the Buddha tells Subhuti how much or how great the merit of this sutra is, he will be saying something very important. Earlier on, the Buddha spoke of the merit of receiving, retaining, reading and reciting this sutra being very great. In this part, the Buddha starts off talking about a Bodhisattva doing charity, while earlier on the examples were of ordinary people doing acts of charity. Actually, everyone here today as well as all the other beings in this world are all Bodhisattvas, causal ground Bodhisattvas. It's similar to the situation where not until age 18 does one legally become an adult having all the rights and responsibilities of a citizen. These rights and responsibilities were always inherent within each person but just not activated until a certain age. If one is a sentient living being, then one is a causal ground Bodhisattva. Having cultivated all the necessary conditions one then becomes a fruition ground Bodhisattva. Everyone can boldly admit that they are a Bodhisattva. Being a Bodhisattva, one cannot commit suicide or otherwise knowingly harm one's body. These would be breaking the Bodhisattva vows just as drawing blood from a Buddha would be. This body being the body of a Bodhisattva is not to be intentionally harmed. In this lifetime you might succeed in becoming a fruition ground Bodhisattva, thus how can you harm the body of a living Bodhisattva?

How is it that a Bodhisattva should still be practicing charity? Actually, even the Buddha practices charity. In the teachings on the vinaya you will see this very often. For example, there was one of his students who was blind and the Buddha would often do things to help him out. Other students asked the Buddha why he would still take time to do these kinds of things. He told them that he still must cultivate merit. This is not something which has an end to it; furthermore, it has nothing to do with one's position. Don't fool yourself in thinking that when you reach the highest position, you've fulfilled your obligation for cultivating merit. This kind of "Buddha" can be pulled off his high horse. The real Buddha is forever the living example of his teachings. In practicing virtues, every Bodhisattva must also have this same spirit.

When I was in Tibet and other places studying with different masters, I saw a few great living Buddhas who would support a large number of disciples. They underwent a lot of hardship to get enough contributions to support these disciples. The disciples themselves were able to study, practice and do retreats with no worries.

If we look at the records of the Ch'an masters, we can see that before Master Cowhead (Niu T'ou-jung) was enlightened, he would sit in samadhi on Cowhead Mountain. During that time, birds would bring offerings of flowers and celestial beings would bring offerings of food. He didn't need to worry about food. When it was time to take sustenance, it would appear. This was before his enlightenment. After enlightenment, he didn't sit in samadhi in the mountains anymore. He taught and led people in Buddhist practice, but this is not to say he wasn't in samadhi while doing this. Usually his students numbered about 500 and every day, he would walk a few miles to buy rice and supplies, carrying them back on a shoulder pole.

We need to look at these stories carefully and consider the kind of behavior and conduct to which they point. Many Buddhists have the wrong idea that being Buddhist gives them the okay to be lazy or to run away from the world and responsibilities. This thinking and attitude is absolutely wrong. Not only is it not up to the level of the Hinayana path but also it is not even up to the level of being a good person! I brought all this up because here in the *Diamond Sutra* it talks about a Bodhisattva's charitable conduct of giving away large quantities of treasure.

All Dharmas Are Selfless

What merit could be greater than that of a Bodhisattva's merit of charitable conduct? *"If another person perceived that all dharmas are selfless, thereby achieving the Perfection of Patient Endurance, the latter's merit would far surpass that of the former."* In perceiving that all dharmas are selfless, this person has achieved the fruition ground of a Bodhisattva.

We were just speaking of the rain a while ago. The rain drops have no "self." As soon as they hit the ground, they seep into the earth. Thousands and thousands of raindrops fall down onto the earth or sea and become again a body of water. You might say then, "Oh, I understand, the raindrops don't exist individually and will eventually return to their original nature of water." This isn't right either because the elements—earth, water, fire and wind— have no self nature; not empty nor existent, and not temporary nor permanent. Buddhism's philosophical zenith is here. Many who research the Buddhist teaching methods and principles very easily go astray at this point.

The Consciousness Only school uses the words, "all dharma has no self nature" to describe what is called all dharma being selfless in the *Diamond Sutra*. It is the same principle. "All dharma includes all worldly dharma as well as all supramundane dharma, even the alambanas of arhats, bodhisattvas, Buddhas and perfect nirvana are included. All means *all*. Also, note that the Buddha spoke of understanding that all dharma is selfless but didn't go on to say that all things are therefore empty. He just said "selfless." Is there a real self outside of selfless? That's your problem.

We have seen in the *Diamond Sutra* from the beginning until now, only a blocking method has been used, blocking your moves, refuting everything. There hasn't been any affirmation or verification. So where does one go for affirmation or verification ? When you come to the point of all dharmas are selfless, at this precipice, dare to release your grasp. You must dare to awaken and verify for yourself.

When Master Hsuan-tsang made his journey to India, India at that time was divided into many kingdoms and, in addition, there were many spiritual and religious philosophies. Great debates were held among these many philosophies. The stakes of such debates were that the losing sides must convert to the winning school of thought or religious order. In spite of his age, Master Hsuan-tsang was already famed for his wisdom and so was invited to participate. The Buddhist monks had had difficulty holding their own until Hsuan-tsang ascended to the podium. He fielded all their questions and it finally came down to this most crucial point. There is no self, no phenomena, nor wisdom. How then is Buddhism verified? How is enlightenment verified? Master Hsuan-tsang answered, "only the one drinking the water knows if it is cold or warm." That was the final word. It was the statement which saved Buddhism from being vanquished.

Verifying for oneself is like drinking the water to know if it is warm or cold. Only you yourself will know for sure. Even if I tell you, you still won't really know. This answer was so deftly put. If we put this answer to a scientific debate it may fare differently, but we won't have one now. We should affix the words "empty" or "true self" to the state of knowing that all dharmas are selfless. Prajna wisdom is culminated by one's own efforts.

Samadhi and Patient Endurance

Perceiving that all dharmas are selfless, one thereby achieves the Perfection of Patience. This statement is very important because in Buddhism, the state of patience is quite significant. Everyone knows about achieving samadhi. Samadhi is within the sphere of the Hinayana but is a basic building block of both the Hinayana and the Mahayana. Without it, one's cultivation has no foundation and, whether one be an ordained member or a lay person, one is still at the stage of an ordinary student. Samadhi is not exclusive to Buddhism. In Mahayana Buddhism, one must strive to achieve the Perfection of Patience. Patience and samadhi are different. It is the achievement of the non-arising Dharma of Patience which demarks a Mahayana Bodhisattva. Non-arising Dharma of Patient Endurance cannot be explained as samadhi, otherwise it would be called the non-arising samadhi of patient endurance.

Of the six paramitas, the *Diamond Sutra* spoke directly of the paramita of charity but not of discipline. Although, within the achievement of the Perfection of Charity is the essence of discipline. Likewise, throughout the whole of the *Diamond Sutra* is discussed the Perfection of Wisdom, but never is there mentioned the Perfection of Dhyana. The achievement of dhyana will naturally be with the achievement of prajna. So it goes with the six paramitas, the culmination of charity, patience and prajna incorporates the achievement of discipline, enthusiasm and dhyana. In order to really understand this, you need to read or recite the *Diamond Sutra* again and again. The understanding will slowly come forth.

In the middle of the sutra, the Buddha spoke of the cultivation of his patience and the experience of having his body torn asunder by the Raja of Kalinga. During this experience, not a thought of anger or hatred stirred. He maintained a mind of compassion and therefore didn't experience any pain or suffering. What kind of alambana is this? It is the samadhi, the non-arising dharma of patience and the prajna of an enlightened alambana. People who study Ch'an nowadays read a poem, see a frog jump, or hear a dog bark and then, "Wow!" they think they're enlightened. If we applied a cleaver to such a person the same way the Raja of Kalinga did to the Buddha, we would immediately know if that person had achieved the Perfection of Patience or the perfection of terrified anger. If you are enlightened, you should have some level of achievement in the six paramitas! The word *enlightenment* is not to be thrown around lightly. The *Diamond Sutra* in its teaching shows us this.

When one truly understands that all dharmas are selfless, naturally one will have the non-arising Dharma of Patient

Endurance. This is still just the very first step of a Mahayana Bodhisattva, but it supersedes the other Bodhisattvas who gave away immeasurable amounts of jewels. This charity is within the notion of form and cannot be compared to even one millionth of the merit of charity without any notion of form.

Here in Section 28, the Buddha is preparing to bring up the main theme of this sutra. This part is very important. The state of non-arising Dharma of Patience is brought up first for theoretical discussion. There is no mention yet of verifying this state, nor is there a description of this state. Let's not forget what the Buddha said at the start of this teaching. *"Be skillfully mindful."* Within non-dwelling arises the mind; everything is ungraspable and without form. Through these, one can come to know that all dharma have no self, thereby achieving patient endurance. Right at the beginning, the Buddha told us all this. He was directly teaching the Dharma and not just talking about a sutra or a teaching.

There is a difference between lecturing on sutras and expounding the Dharma. The Buddha here is expounding the Dharma through a question and answer dialogue. It is much different than lecturing on the sutras, which is talking about what the Buddha and Bodhisattvas taught. In prior times, the temples in Mainland China had separate halls for expounding the Dharma and expounding the sutras. In the Dharma expounding hall, the master would not bring any materials from which to lecture, but rather would speak from his experience of cultivation, wisdom and enlightenment.

Right at the start, the Buddha told us the cultivation methods of being skillfully mindful and non-dwelling. From these will develop patient endurance and the Non-arising Dharma of Patient Endurance. Here, I'd like to talk about one of the *koans* in the Ch'an sect to illustrate this.

The Story of Muddlehead Chang

During the end of the T'ang Dynasty, Ch'an was at its peak. There was a lay person called Muddlehead Chang who went to see a master to ask about the Tao. The Ch'an master asked his name and he replied that he was called Muddlehead Chang. The master said that there is not a "cleverhead" to be found, so how then could there possibly be a "muddlehead"? He awakened right then and there. Upon hearing that one sentence he had an instant awakening. Look for yourself right now, to what did he awaken? He awakened to all dharma being selfless and achieved patience, right? According to the theory of what was taught by the Buddha you can understand this, can't you? Muddlehead Chang wrote this poem after his awakening:

Luminous, serenely shining across all the Ganges.
The ordinary, saintly and sentient are all of one family.
Not a thought arises, the whole body appears.

> *Cutting the root of affliction gives rise to great illness.*
> *The direction going toward truth is also astray.*
> *Nirvana, birth and death are but empty glitter.*

"Luminous, serenely shining across all the Ganges." This is talking about the substance, the original nature of all beings. The original nature's luminosity is pure and formless. "Serenely shining," shining isn't in the way we normally understand it to be. This is just a descriptive phrase here. "Across all the Ganges," without dwelling. *"The ordinary, saintly and sentient are all of one family."* All beings and Buddhas are equal. The mind, the Buddha and all beings are commensurate. *"Not a thought arises, the whole body appears."* Not a thought arises is the very beginning stage of the Non-arising Dharma of Patience. Why is it only just the beginning stage? In the true Non-arising Dharma of Patience, even in the midst of a myriad of thoughts, it is still the Non-arising Dharma of Patience. That is the fruit of a Bodhisattva's merit and the first harvest is "not a thought arises." We Buddhist cultivators should also be careful not to make the mistake of thinking that "not a thought arises" is the state of where all thoughts and thinking processes stop moving. This isn't "not a thought arises"; this is called dead asleep. So then, what is the state of not a thought arises? Keeping well the moment of mind, not dwelling, the past, present and future mind being unobtainable and the unobtainable being unobtainable are "not a thought arises," arising without arising.

This is also still the primary state of Non-arising Dharma of Patientcebecause one will finally come to a place where the six senses can all be active and don't form a shroud of clouds. This is what is called by the Buddha, "no form" and "not dwelling."

Don't forget that there are two levels of wisdom—one being the root of wisdom and the other being the fruition of wisdom. These two levels are different. One cannot become enlightened through sound or form. If one throws away sound and form, not a thought arises, but a movement of the six senses forms a shroud of clouds. This experience of "not a thought arises" is still just the seed of wisdom. The wisdom hasn't yet matured into fruition.

"Cutting the root of affliction gives rise to great illness." Why doesn't the root of affliction need to be cut? Why don't wandering thoughts need to be stopped? Sitting in meditation all day empty of thoughts and afflictions is really just a huge thought gone astray! That is an affliction! Rather than developing samadhi, one has developed a mental illness. This is why the line says cutting the root of affliction gives rise to great illness.

"The direction going toward truth is also astray." If in your mind you are grasping onto the idea of an alambana of Tao, this perspective is already astray. If you think all dharmas have no self existence and so there is alambana of suchness onto which can be grasped, such a thought itself is truly the alambana of an idea leading astray and the cause of affliction. It is not a state of understanding all dharma being selfless. It was because of this understanding that Muddlehead Chang didn't become a monk.

"Following the flow of worldly affairs, there are no obstacles." One who is truly enlightened and is living in this world following the flow of worldly affairs is described by one ancient Ch'an master as *"Engage in affairs whittling away ancient obstacles and moreover, not engendering new destruction."* This is talking about clearing up things, engaging in affairs whittling away ancient obstacles, and not adding to the power of destructive habits. Needless to say, such persons continually foster virtuosity. This is the meaning behind the line, "following the flow of worldly affairs, there are no obstacles."

The last line has the most panache and shows a thorough understanding of the *Diamond Sutra*. *"Nirvana, birth and death are but empty glitter."* Not only are birth and death empty glitter, but also the achievement of nirvana is nothing particularly special. Nirvana is also empty glitter, dreams, and illusions; it's nothing real.

We can look at Muddlehead Chang's *koan* to understand the meaning of "perceiving that all dharmas are selfless thereby achieving the perfection of patience."

Does Seeking Necessitate Dwelling?

"Why is this? Subhuti, Bodhisattvas do not obtain fortune and merit."
Subhuti then asked the Buddha, "World-Honored One, why do Bodhisattvas not obtain fortune and merit? Bodhisattvas

should not have any longing for fortune and merit which they have created, and so do not obtain fortune and merit."

"Bodhisattvas do not obtain fortune and merit." This is yet another important point. A person who is really practicing the Way of a Mahayana Bodhisattva does not cultivate virtuosity in hopes of obtaining the fortune of this merit. Rather this person performs such virtuous deeds simply because he feels this is what should be done. If such acts were performed in hopes of saving the world or saving people, these hopes are the alambana of an ordinary person and not a Bodhisattva. This is why a Bodhisattva does not seek or obtain fortune and merit.

Subhuti heard this and had some doubts. He asked, why wouldn't they obtain fortune and merit? Bodhisattvas don't perform meritorious virtues with a longing mind. These deeds are what they feel should be done and they do them with no question asked, no dwelling on them and no attainment to them. This is pretty easy to understand! Could it be that Subhuti was more obtuse than we are and had to ask why Bodhisattvas don't obtain fortune and merit? This question was actually very astute. Bodhisattvas aren't seeking fortune and since they don't dwell on anything, then why *not* seek to obtain something? In other words, seeking can also be done without dwelling. Don't you think Bodhisattvas have enough "chutzpah" to do such a thing? Subhuti's question really had a point to it and shouldn't be underestimated. It was a very serious question! Since

Bodhisattvas' minds don't dwell when they practice meritorious virtues and have no longing to obtain anything, would seeking necessitate dwelling? Is such a Bodhisattva not completely enlightened? This was what was behind the question, and so the Buddha was hard pressed for an answer.

"Subhuti, Bodhisattvas should not have any longing for fortune and merit which they have created and so do not obtain fortune and merit." Bodhisattvas are cultivating virtue and of course, should not have longing. Therefore, even though they have the merit of fortune, they won't covet it for their own. They aren't out to benefit themselves and so don't have a longing to obtain self-benefit. Rather, they dedicate or reciprocate all merits back to the world, to sentient beings in hopes that the world will be a better place. This is the great Dharma door of charity, the paramita of dana or generosity.

To sum it up, a Bodhisattva is not selfish and does not walk the path of the small vehicle, the Hinayana. Generosity is first and foremost. Bodhisattvas are always giving Dharma, material goods, safety and so forth.

Gatha of Section Twenty-eight

Wordless silence is real listening and understanding;
No mind sentiments mean no more than wisps of smoke.
Release the great universe, there is not a thing;
Don't argue the worth of merit and service in worldly terms.

"Wordless silence is real listening and understanding." This is speaking about Buddhism, wisdom and merit. All dharma has no individual nature, no self, and so all the Dharma taught by the Buddha was just convenient means. The real Buddha Dharma is inexpressible. There was a time period of three months when the Buddha was in silent retreat in the Kingdom of Magadha. The Buddha was completely silent in order to teach that there are no words which can express the Dharma. You must verify it for yourself. Wordless silence, having no words, is real listening and understanding.

"No mind sentiments mean no more than wisps of smoke." To be at the ground of "no mind," in all actions, all places there is "no mind." The sentiments and emotions of our consciousness are pure and clean, in the end they disperse like the smoke of incense. Just what is "no mind"? It is simply that the past, present and future mind are unobtainable. Arriving at the ground of no mind, the entire sixth consciousness has been transformed into the subtle discerning wisdom. It is the alambana of prajna wisdom.

"Release the great universe, there is not a thing." How can one cultivate so as to achieve the ground of no mind? To "release your grip at the precipice" is not enough. Take the great universe of worlds and give it away in charity, let go of everything for, as the Sixth Patriarch said, originally there is not a thing. There are two skills necessary in practicing Buddhism. The first is taking action, accumulating the merit of virtue by not committing the least evil

and practicing every virtue for the benefit of all beings. The second is letting go, letting go of everything in order that prajna wisdom be achieved. If one is able to take action and let go then one has what it takes to practice Buddhism and become a Buddha. The alambana of prajna is to let go of all that happens, commit not the least evil and practice all virtues for the benefit of sentient beings. The fortune of such meritorious action is not worldly fortune. To become a Buddha and achieve true wisdom, what is needed is not world fortune.

"Don't argue the worth of merit and service in worldly terms." People will often be impressed by some person who has spent years cultivating the Tao. There isn't a speck of Tao! Don't waste your time discussing and comparing whose practice is better, whose Tao is higher. Setting standards and creating a mystique is all worldly business. To say that this Buddha has more merit or that Buddha is more powerful is just poppycock!

SECTION 29

NEITHER COMING NOR GOING

"Subhuti, if someone should say it's as if the Tathagata comes and goes, sits and lies, this person does not understand the meaning of what I say. The reason is that having not whence to come nor whither to go is called the Tathagata."

This sutra is talking about the culmination of prajna paramita wisdom and the way to become a Buddha. Subhuti opened the dialogue with a question and the Buddha pointed out the way in— skillful mindfulness. This is the key point of the *Diamond Sutra*. Whether one is a lay practitioner or clergy, to truly cultivate you only need these few words, *"Be skillfully mindful."*

Be skillfully mindful? The Buddha doesn't say, keep well a moment of empty mind or a moment of an engaged mind. To specify empty or functioning shows a lack of understanding of the Buddha Dharma. This thinking is dialectical and polarized. We must also remember that the Buddha also said to not dwell and not grasp onto form or appearance. Thinking that to be skillfully mindful is to dwell in emptiness or to grasp onto an appearance of emptiness is one-sided. The middle part of the sutra is a discussion on how to cultivate not dwelling and not grasping. Furthermore, it talks about what is awakening and enlightenment.

Throughout the sutra, the term *Tathagata* is used. Anyone who becomes a Buddha will have ten titles in addition to his own name, for instance, World-Honored One, Tathagata, Sugata, Supreme Teacher, and so forth. *Tathagata* is a universal title shared by all Buddhas. Why is the Buddha called Tathagata? Broken down, *Tatha* means "as if" and *gata* means "to come".[3] Actually, the Buddha neither comes nor goes. The worldly phenomena of coming and going are used to show the functioning of original nature. It's as if to come but not coming. If you switch on a lamp or fan for example the electricity comes, but you don't see the electricity. You just see the light or feel the air moving. Has the electricity come? It has come but it's almost as if it hasn't come. It gets used up and then has it gone? It's not as if it has gone. As it is generated, more comes. It neither comes nor goes and is neither created nor destroyed. The Tathagata is the original nature of all sentient beings. Sentient beings are appearances of the body of Tao.

We all have happiness, anger, sorrow and joy, wandering thoughts and penetrating insights. There are those here who have twenty years at most, all the way up to those with seventy years of life experience. In all these lifetimes added together, who knows how much sadness, happiness, suffering, and joy, how many

---

[3] It can also be broken down into *tath*, "as if", and *agata* meaning "not to come."

successes and failures have transpired. However, sitting here, all that is gone. Not even a shadow of last year is here, even the events of yesterday are gone. But are they really all gone? Are the things of ten years ago gone? It's as if they had been here. "It's as if the Tathagata comes and goes." If you say they've never been here, it's not true. It's as if the things of ten years ago had occurred but nothing is left of them now. Yesterday's occurrences are like a dream gone by. Are they really gone though? It's as if they're gone but thinking about them, it's as if they are occurring yet again before your eyes.

The name Tathagata also describes the original nature and appearance of mind. In Buddhist sutras, one will often see the words *phenomenon* and *appearance*. These refer to the functioning of the original nature of mind. We'll bring the focus in a little closer to talk about what this means. Someone speaks and everyone hears. It's as if the sound came because we all heard the words and now it's finished. It's as if they're gone. The person speaks again and again the words seem to come. Notice throughout all this, it's as if the original nature doesn't move. This is a common description used in sutras. When in one's cultivation one is very near to the alambana of clean and pure emptiness, it's "as if to not be moving." It's as if there is no movement but there is not really "no movement." Really not moving would be annihilation. The original nature, the absolute, the *bhutatatha* is very, very lively and the only way to describe it is, "it's as if to not be moving." In the sutras the words *like* or *as if* are used often as in "like a dream, like an illusion," "real as" and so forth. "Real as" is the upside down version of "as" or "like real." If you grasp onto something as real, this is grasping onto an idea astray. "Real as" is as if to be real; Tathagata is as if to come.

All sentient beings as well as the Buddha all have three kayas, the dharmakaya, the sambogakaya and the kaya. The dharmakaya is the body of the original nature. We were just talking about the example of electricity. There is electric charge in the air. It is just one manifestation of energy transformation. This doesn't mean that if we wave our hands about in the air we will get an electric shock. It's only under certain causes and conditions such as with friction that it will manifest in a perceptible form. This electricity is something which always exists in the air but it is as if it comes and goes. The dharmakaya is neither created nor destroyed. "Neither created nor destroyed" is "neither comes nor goes," not dying nor born. It is eternal; it's as if it is always there. This describes the dharmakaya.

The nirmanakaya is the body given to us by our parents. Among those who study Buddhism and cultivate, some will awaken, some will achieve samadhi, some will leave *sarira* (relics). This, however, is only an indication of the achievement of the dharmakaya; the nirmanakaya has yet to be transformed. Upon completely transforming, the nirmanakaya becomes the perfect nirmanakaya. This is merely a state in which one doesn't experience illness or pain. Such a person has the physical experience of a heavenly being. This cannot be achieved by spending one's time meditating and holding ceremonies. It comes of the cultivation that one does after one has had an awakening. The perfect nirmanakaya can have hundreds of thousands of emanation bodies and actually, these bodies we have right now can have many emanation bodies. The three kayas are not separate but are in reality one body. When Bodhisattvas send out emanation bodies, they are not all in human form. For example, a Bodhisattvas might become a cow to teach other cows. The beef you ate may have come from a Bodhisattva cow!

The Alambana of the Tathagata

Out of what does the dharmakaya arise? Observe the thoughts. From where do they arise? To where do they go? *"Having not whence to come nor whither to go is called the Tathagata."* Why do you worry about your thoughts? They pop up suddenly and just as suddenly, disappear. Everyone sits there meditating, working as hard as they can, trying to "empty" their thoughts. This is stupid. It is no smarter than a diamond would be. Why do you want to get rid of thoughts? The thoughts are empty, having not whence to come nor whither to go and so are called the Tathagata. You can't keep them, either. Who can hold onto their thoughts forever? Even the pain and suffering of yesterday is gone without a trace. You're sitting here and there is none of it. If you are in pain and suffering now, later, after class perhaps, it will disappear. One cannot remain in pain and suffering forever. They don't stick around that long. The other side of the coin is that the clear, pure alambanas don't remain forever either. If you work hard at some practice, you may experience incredible peace and clarity but as soon as you uncross your legs, it's gone! How is it that it "goes"? "Having not whence to come nor whither to go is called the Tathagata." The peace and clarity haven't gone everywhere. It's your own wisdom and perspective which aren't clear enough. This is why you feel as though you've lost your accomplishment. Some people say, it neither comes nor goes so why should I practice. If this is really your understanding, you won't leave the state of peace and calm at any time.

To return to the subject of the three bodies, or kayas, the dharmakaya is the Tathagata, the nirmanakaya is the World-Honored One and the sambogakaya is the Buddha. Looking at it from theory, the dharmakaya is the basic material, the nirmanakaya is the form or appearance and the sambogakaya is the functioning. Everything has these three elements: substance, form and function. Now that we're clear on this let's turn to the question of cultivation. Many people go looking for famous teachers, special methods or secret teachings, but the Buddha held nothing back when he taught. If one who has Tao holds back teachings in hopes of money, or sells to the highest bidder, stay away. I would never involve myself with such a teacher. Such a one doesn't even have basic human integrity. The real Tao is the ordinary Tao which is to be found everywhere. It is nothing secret.

Tao is available to everyone. Some say that those who are bad should not be saved, only the good ones deserve a chance. The good ones don't need your help! They're already good. Why would Buddha come to save a Bodhisattva? The Buddha goes to the places of strife and difficulty to help the beings there. The Buddha taught the Tao to everyone. In the *Diamond Sutra*, He didn't hold back anything and on top of that, I've added a whole bunch of explanations; all this just to say, "Don't grasp onto appearances."

A lot of people who study Buddhism get caught up in religious rituals. Look at the first line in this section, it says, *"If someone should say it's as if the Tathagata comes and goes..."* This isn't to say that one won't dream about Buddhas. Some people will ask, "Teacher, was that real?" I say, Yes, that was real. Of course it was real, you dreamed it! At this moment you are also in a dream talking to me, right? It's the same as being awake and responding to someone talking in their sleep. In the Consciousness Only School, these realms of consciousness are studied in depth. No matter what dreams you have, they are not outside of the experiences of your lifetime, what you've heard, seen, thought about or experienced for the most part; dreams are all within these parameters. If they are beyond these...well, this topic should be discussed at another time. It is a very deep subject. Such images might have occasion to arise from the alaya-vijnana consciousness and show us glimpses of other worlds. If a person believes that the Buddha came to see them in a dream or that the

Buddha's light was shining down on them, or was sitting or was lying, *"this person does not understand the meaning of what I say."* Such a person absolutely does not understand the Buddha Dharma, nor the Buddha's teachings. The real Buddha, the substance of the dharmakaya, awakened the dharmakaya, has neither whence to come nor whither to go, is neither born nor dies and neither sits nor lies.

What is this alambana like? Don't get fooled by the words. It is a very ordinary state of being. It is the alambana in which you are right at this moment. It is neither sitting nor lying, coming nor going, without bad thoughts or good thoughts.   With a calm peaceful mind or no discrimination in this body, at this moment, one is in the alambana of the Tathagata. Don't create an idea of Buddhahood which is far away and unreachable when it is actually quite an ordinary state. We can use the Confucian theory of the Middle Way to explain this section of the *Diamond Sutra*, "At its zenith, the Tao is the middle way." What is the Tao like? At its zenith, the Tao is the Middle Way. It is the most common, neither coming nor going. It's right here. Understanding this theory, we will go on to look at the right way for a true Buddhist to practice. It is the practice of no practice. If you create a practice, you are grasping onto form and appearance.   We can observe our frustrations and mind movements as not coming or going, not sitting nor lying, and neither created nor destroyed. When a thought is no more, it is said to be dead and gone. The next arises and is said to be created. What is born must die and when it is dead is it all gone? It is not annihilation; it will arise again. Creation and destruction, birth and death, are like waves on the water's surface, one wave following another. Waves are made entirely of water. With or without moving, even if there are no waves to be seen, the water is not more or less. It just is.

People practice using many kinds of methods, trying to quell the mind's waves. They do anything they can to achieve this calmness, and so then when it's calm, then what? Or when it's not calm? It is still the water when it is not calm. So don't you think that applying all that effort to calm it is rather useless? Isn't that the point? I believe it is. If you look at it carefully, this is having neither whence to come nor whither to go. It is originally that state of the Tathagata. This is the prajna eye, the wisdom eye.

Gatha of Section Twenty-nine

> *Arranging and managing are all done for others*
> *No mind beyond the body, so don't grasp to friction*
> *It's like painting one's eyebrows to look darker or lighter*
> *Even more bewitching is a pile of coiled hair.*

"*Arranging and managing are all done for others.*" Those who practice Tao use all sorts of methods, meditation, reciting the Buddha's name and so forth, all kinds of arrangements. Thinking to practice Buddhism is to make an arrangement. As to those who do not practice? They just constantly manage and handle their pain and frustration. Arranging and managing thoughts and musings are all for the other.

"No mind beyond the body, so don't grasp to friction." This body is false; it is a temporary dwelling, a tool. We borrow it from our parents and use it for a few decades. What is no mind? Not paying attention to wandering thoughts is no mind. Thoughts are just waves on the surface, why pay attention to them? The more attention you give them, the more the illusory wandering mind becomes an obstacle. These are illusions. The real grandeur is in the quiet and still. If we don't understand the original nature of the mind, if we don't understand that thoughts and feelings are illusions, then we will continue to be fooled by the waves and be blind to the nature of water.

"It's like painting one's eyebrows to look darker or lighter." Most people get fooled by darker and lighter. Dark eyebrows, light eyebrows, and hair coiled in a bun can bewitch someone. This is from a T'ang Dynasty poem, a line of which goes something like, *"Eyebrows dark or eyebrows light, which ones are more stylish?"* A newly married bride is making herself up in the mirror and asks her husband if her eyebrows look nice. Should they be a little darker, a little longer, more arched or not? Do they suit the style of the times? Today people do all kinds of things to their eyebrows even dying them brownish or reddish. Some of it looks quite garish, like the bride of Frankenstein. During the T'ang Dynasty it was chic to color one's eyebrows yellow. Sometimes these T'ang Dynasty poems might seem a bit risqué, but I'd like to put my two

cents in about this. A scholar might go through his whole life without work because he doesn't fit in with the times. When he finally listens to someone's advice telling him to get in tune with the times and produces something modern, he might ask, "Do you think this is in style?" It's the same as painting one's eyebrows lighter or darker to be in style.

"Even more bewitching is a pile of coiled hair." People would grow their hair very long in the olden days. It was fashionable to coil up one's hair and arrange it in a large bun on top of one's head. It looked like a large conch shell, very pretty. Some women spend hours in the beauty shop to have their hair piled on their head in a certain way. Upon seeing such a pile of hair, many men have gone "gaga" and ended up bewitched. Actually, what is beauty? It's not only found in the physical attraction between male and female. We are completely taken by our entire existence and by all the different aspects of the physical realm. There isn't anything in this world which doesn't beguile us. How is it that we've all been cheated like this? It's because we don't recognize the Tathagata as our own self-nature. All we see are the waves on top of the water and still, every time, we get hoodwinked by those waves. If we can see clearly the nature of the waves, we will know that thoughts and feelings neither come nor go. This mind is originally pure and clean. If you can recognize this, you won't get fooled as much. You will be the Diamond Prajna Paramita.

SECTION 30

UNION OF FORM

"Subhuti, what do you think? If a good man or woman reduced to atoms of dust all the worlds in the great universe of galaxies, would the resulting particles of dust be many?

Subhuti replied, "Very many, World-Honored One." "The reason is that if they really existed, the Buddha would not say they were particles of dust. What the Buddha calls minute particles of dust, are not particles of dust but are merely called so." "World-Honored One, when the Tathagata calls the great universe of galaxies is not actually so but is merely called the great universe." "The reason is that if there really were worlds, they would be a union of form. The Tathagata says that a union of form is not so but is merely called a union of form."

"Subhuti, the union of form is inexpressible but common people have a longing for such things."

After Being Reduced to Atoms

"Subhuti, what do you think? If a good man or woman reduced to dust all the worlds in the great universe of galaxies, would the resulting particles of dust be many?"

Having spoken about the original nature of the Tathagata, I will now discuss an important issue about the dharmakaya and the Tathagata. The Buddha opens with a question about the physical universe. He proposes a situation in which someone, either male or female, pulverizes an entire Buddha world, an entire universe into dust. Think about it, would there be a lot of dust?

Subhuti replied, *"Very many, World-Honored One."* *"The reason is that if they really existed, the Buddha would not say they were particles of dust."* Subhuti answered that there would be a lot of particles. Then the Buddha spoke of the reason or theory behind this. If there really did exist this dust, if the atomic particles which make up the physical universe were eternally existent, I wouldn't tell you that the world had dust particles. These particles all put together make up the earth, the mountains, rivers and so forth of the physical world. The Buddha here is indirectly telling us that if you take the physical objects and keep breaking them down even past their atomic level, you will find that in the end they are empty. It is the fantastic power of emptiness out of which they are formed and in the end they return to this emptiness. Any good scientist would understand this. This emptiness isn't vacuous. It has great power, the kind of power released in the detonation of an atomic bomb. This is why the Buddha says, "If they really existed," if you really believed that there existed dust particles, then I won't discuss them. The reason being that they don't exist other than being formed from emptiness.

"What the Buddha calls minute particles of dust are not particles of dust but are merely called so." Once again we have one of these three section statements. Protons, neutrons and electrons are all just illusory names. It is through the function of naming that such things come into being. Even though we think of atomic or rather sub-atomic particles as being the smallest things, these can still be broken down. If you keep looking, in the end you'll find that there is not any "thing." All is empty. Beyond the parameters of the earth, the solar system, the universe and space is the power of emptiness. It is this power which is harnessed to form the physical world.

"World-Honored One, what the Tathagata calls the great universe of galaxies is not actually so but is merely called the great universe." What Subhuti is saying here is that he understands and that the great universe mentioned in the original question is also just an illusory name. There are no galaxies which exist forever and ever. They are just temporary phases of being. The physical world is constantly changing and eventually comes to an end.

One could use the metaphor of this floor that we're on. Paint, rug, some people, electric lights, seats and chairs all together can be called a lecture hall. The so-called lecture hall is not a lecture hall but is merely called a lecture hall. This is just a temporary arrangement or grouping. It is not final nor is it real and true. Tomorrow this could be turned into a small movie theater. And so it goes, the so-called movie theater is not a movie theater but is merely called a movie theater. All the things of the physical world have such an illusory composite existence. Don't get fooled by the troubles and sufferings of the world and one's family. The family is not a family but is merely called a family. Human existence is not human existence but is merely called human existence, as the same theory applies. The Buddha goes on to explain step by step.

What Is a Union of Form?

"The reason is that if there were really worlds, they would be a union of form." By simply going on to explain what the reasoning behind the statement was, the Buddha was verifying what Subhuti said. If there was an eternally unchanging world in existence, this would be a union of form. This would be like two things merging together and then staying like that forever. This is an enormous subject. The Buddha never said anything wrong, but when Kumarajiva translated the words "a union of form" a lot of misconceptions were created. Later Buddhists distorted the meaning and gave far-fetched interpretations, which had many ramifications. Some of the esoteric schools felt it necessary to practice "union." In China, people thought they needed to practice the "union of yin and yang" to succeed at cultivation. They believe that this is what was meant by these words in the *Diamond Sutra*. This translation incited many questions and arguments.

What exactly is this union of form? If you go to a seafood place and you get a clam whose two shells are clamped firmly together, resistant to any efforts to pry them apart, this is union!

Two kinds of metal smelted together is a union of form. Synthetic and cotton blend cloth is a kind of union. Blood, bones, muscle, etc. all come together to form a human and this is also a kind of union. These are unions of form which we see in the physical world. Actually, these are all constantly changing. Even mountains are constantly changing, growing or shrinking. It's just not apparent to our eyes. Even so, these supposed unions of form will all return to emptiness millions of years from now. From emptiness then, new forms will arise.

"The Tathagata says that a union of form is not so but is merely called a union of form." Union is a kind of illusory existence. Is there such a thing as eternal existence? Is there such thing as union of form? Is this physical world empty? This is just talk, sophism. The weather is hot today and so we feel hot. Turn on the air conditioner and we feel cool. The heat is empty and the air conditioning is also empty. It's dependent on the electricity coming through the wires, without electricity, it doesn't exist. Is it really "non-existent"? People are always saying life is like a dream, but in a way that implies that dreams don't exist. This is a mistaken idea. Dreams exist, but only in a temporary, random sort of way. Our dreams during sleep don't last any longer than a few minutes, but in this short time we may have experienced an entire lifetime in a dream. Time is a relative thing. Our sense of time in a dream, in regular life, when we are in love and so forth are all different. If we lived on the moon, there are only twelve long moon days during the time of one earth year. On other planets, a

day might be equivalent to one of our years. Taking a microscopic perspective, some forms of life go through thousands of generations being born and dying just during the course of one evening. Time is all relative.

"Subhuti, the union of form is inexpressible but common people have a longing for such things." So is the Buddha saying here that there isn't any union of form? No, there are such things, but they are inexpressible. There is no way to understand such concepts and there is no way to express them either. The Buddha finishes by saying that common people have a longing for such things. The esoteric sect, the Taoists and many individuals have distorted the meaning of these words and have created many practices which are off the Path on account of this.

What is the real meaning of the Buddha's words here? It is the successful cultivation of emptiness and the arisal of subtle, mysterious existence. This is what is behind the Buddha's words.

The Eighth Consciousness and the Nature of Seeds

At this point, we need to speak of prajna, but to be able to study prajna, we need to first study the Consciousness Only School; otherwise, it is easy to get confused when talking in depth about the nature of emptiness. If one is confused about the theory of the nature of emptiness, it is easy to fall into wrong perspectives such as nihilism. Believing that emptiness is equivalent to voidness is a perspective leading astray. Emptiness is an alambana and can be looked at in terms of studying the nature of mind. In the Prajna teachings such as the *Diamond Sutra*, the word *mind* includes everything. In the Consciousness Only and Dharmalaskana Schools, "mind" is broken down into smaller parts to be looked at. It is divided into eight consciousnesses.

Of the eight consciousnesses, the sixth consciousness is that which we all commonly understand as consciousness. The function of dreaming comes from the backside, or shadow side, of the sixth consciousness. This part of the sixth consciousness is what is referred to as the subconscious in modern terminology. The eighth consciousness or the alaya-vijnana includes past, present, and future time, space and all of the seeds of karma. It is the basis for being able to study the three realms and the functioning of karma.

The same parents may give birth to many children, but each child is different because only a little bit is passed on to each one from the parents. Each child also brings his or her own character, habits and behavior with him or her from their eighth consciousness. In terms its function, the eighth consciousness is called the sarvabijaka vijnana. In the *Sandhinirmocana Sutra*, the Buddha has a gatha about this:

> *"The sarvabijaka vijnana is deep and complex.*
> *Karmic seeds flow like a waterfall.*
> *To those ordinary or dull, I shan't expound it,*
> *For fear the discriminating mind grasps a self."*

The Buddhist sutras, especially the prajna sutras, often talk about emptiness. The Dharmalaskana and Consciousness Only teaching don't enter from this point; rather, they talk about phenomena. It's simply just another methodology of teaching. This is why in the *Sandhinirmocana Sutra*, the Buddha talks about the original nature of mind in terms of the eighth consciousness and the functioning of the sarvabijaka vijnana. He forewarned, though, if you wish to study it, know that it is very difficult to understand, deep and complex. The sarvabijaka vijnana is like a waterfall or a river that's been flowing for hundreds of thousands of years. The water and waves keep flowing onward never turning back. One wave follows another and passes by. The past mind is unobtainable, the present mind is unobtainable, and the future mind is unobtainable. The outer physical world is not unlike the inner world of our minds.

We look at the waves on the water as if they had a fixed existence. There is no fixed existence. A wave is made of water molecules. If you took away the part of the wave that is water molecules you'd be left without a wave. The same holds true for a waterfall. We piteous creatures don't see this; all we see are the waves. It's like an electric light. We turn it on, a wave of electricity goes through, which in turn creates a wave of light. This wave gone, another follows. All we see is a steady light. Actually, past, present and future electricity are unobtainable; the unobtainable is also unobtainable. There is electricity but this electricity is not electricity but is merely called electricity.

Waterfall of Thoughts

The situation in our mind is that one thought follows another without stopping from the moment we are born until the day we pass away. They're all water under the bridge, dead and gone. Just look at this lecture; we started at 8:00 and in each minute, each second since then, thoughts have gone by. They're unobtainable now. What will be said from now until the end? I myself don't even know! This is also unobtainable. Can you say these don't exist? There is a power behind them that does exist. The seeds of karma include past, present and future, intelligence and stupidity, virtue and evil. Virtuous people bring to fruition their seeds of virtue from the alaya and in so doing, slowly, slowly transform the evil seeds into virtuous ones. Through such cultivation, one becomes a person of superior virtuosity. This is performing all virtuous actions and attaining anuttara-samyak sambodhi.

On the other hand, if one nurtures bad habits or evil, the virtuous seeds will also become tainted. Karmic seeds flow like a waterfall. The waterfall is existent and flows on forever. This is why the Buddha said he won't expound this to those ordinary or dull. He didn't dare to teach this to those without wisdom.

You speak of no-self and of a real self, but on the real self there is no way to affix a name. If you add the words *permanent* and *unchanging* then you are caught by the idea of permanent and unchanging. Therefore, the Buddha wouldn't expound to those who were common or dull. He was afraid that if sentient beings didn't have enough wisdom, they would use their discriminating mind to look at this ever-flowing waterfall of karmic seeds and grasp onto a real self. This would be a grave mistake.

The theory of life being self-less is to break this small idea of self to which we grasp. This small idea of self is like an atom of water or a wind flower. If we can cultivate to the point where we awaken to purity and emptiness, we can find the origin of life that has neither whence to come nor whither to go. It is only after this that the union of form can function. What is the union of form? It is emptiness giving rise to subtle and mysterious existence.

How Real Emptiness Gives Rise to Subtle Existence

The physical body is a part of the sarvabijaka vijnana as well as the mind and so both must undergo a transformation. Cultivating only the "mind" is not good enough because the body is part of the larger mind. Through the practice of all virtues, the body will slowly transform and the union of form will manifest. This is when one really becomes a Bodhisattva. The three kayas are complete. The clean and pure dharmakaya, the perfect nirmanakaya and the ten-thousand manifestation sambogakaya. It is the union of the three forms, the union of substance, form and function. However, don't make the mistake of grasping onto this idea. That would be grasping onto form. The four elements are originally empty. There is nothing bad about them. They came about through the functioning of your original nature. To say that they are empty is to say that their existence is not permanent. If you awaken to the dharmakaya and succeed in cultivating the three kayas, you will be able to extend the existence of the illusory union of four elements.

It is for this reason that the Buddha said, *"The union of form is inexpressible but common people have a longing for such things."* It is also why he said, *"The sarvabijaka vijnana is deep and complex, and to those ordinary or dull, I shan't expound it, for fear the discriminating mind apprehends a self therein."* The "ordinary people" referred to are ordinary folks like us, we who have a habit of grasping onto things. We spend our whole lives trying to hold onto something, anything. Taoists have a saying that we enter into the world with clenched fists, go through life with hands half unfurled and leave the world with hands spread open. We can see from this that humans have a strong predisposition for grasping, grasping tightly. This is why the Buddha would not speak.

Gatha of Section Thirty

Dust and sand randomly gather into form;

Butterflies in bedlam, bees a'toiling—endless is sentimentality.
As well, guests come and go during this Age of Ashes,
Wronged by inaccurate figuring of winners and losers.

"Dust and sand randomly gather into form." This world is a random agglomeration of dust and sand. Our human lives—your parents, your husband, your wife, your children, your relatives and friends—are another kind of agglomeration.

"Butterflies in bedlam, bees a'toiling—endless is sentimentality." This random gathering of dust we call earth is really quite beautiful, with all the varieties of flowers and other kinds of natural beauty. *"Butterflies in bedlam, bees a'toiling,"* people are like butterflies and bees flying around madly, getting through things haphazardly and working insanely. Earlier on we mentioned a poem by the T'ang Dynasty poet, Luo-yin. It is a metaphor for the blindness with which we go through life, like the bees in the fields. *"Having collected from the flowers and turned it into honey; for whom is this toil, for whom is made this nectar?"* Bees spend their days busy collecting pollen from flowers but for whom do they toil? For whom is this sweetness? If you like honey, before you take a scoop you can recite those lines and then answer, "Why it must be me!" You have the right answer; the bees themselves don't even know the answer. After collecting pollen from the flowers, they are left with the question for whom do I toil, for whom is the sweet? It's the same with human life. We are busy

all of our days for our children, our families, busy right up to the very end. When we close our eyes, then the question arises, the one to which we have no answer, "What for, what for?" This is why I wrote the lines *"butterflies in bedlam, bees a'toiling."*

We all know that life is empty. Everyone sees this clearly at some point, but let's not fool ourselves, we still can't stand to concede. We are all quite sentimental about life, boundlessly sentimental. Sometimes I am quite amused by people. Some people are very opposed to gambling, but they don't realize that they themselves have been gamblers of another form all their lives. For example, some play at their computers with the same passion and intensity that others play mahjong. They are all bent over and focused on the screen. It's just another form of gambling. The whole world is one big gambling hall. Who are the winners? The losers? Even the winners are the losers in the end. This is basically the story of life. If we understand this, then the union of form is not the union of form.

"As well, guests come and go during this Age of Ashes." This world of ours now is in the Age of Ashes. It is built on the ashes of the previous age. Our lives in this world are like a stay in a hotel— the guests come and go. There is birth and death and birth and death; guests come and go during this Age of Ashes.

"Wronged by inaccurate figuring of winners and losers" Of human lives, whose are right and whose are wrong? Who are the winners and the losers? They're all about even. We leave this world and there is still no conclusion. Looking at things through a

Buddhist perspective, we come to the world for no apparent reason and leave without a conclusion. Having neither whither to go nor whence to come is called the Tathagata.

KNOWING AND PERCEIVING NOT ARISING

"Subhuti, if a person says the Buddha speaks of the perception of self, person, being and life, what do you think? Does this person understand the meaning of what I say?

"No, World-Honored One, this person does not understand the meaning of what the Tathagata says. The reason is that when the Tathagata speaks of the perception of a self, person, being and life, they are not the perception of a self, person, being and life but are merely called so."

"Subhuti, one who seeks anuttara-samyak sambodhi, in regard to all dharma, should thus know, thus perceive, thus believe and comprehend: do not give rise to notions of dharma. Subhuti, the notions of dharma of which I speak, the Tathagata says are not notions of dharma but are merely called so."

Perceiving Is Not Seeing

"Subhuti, if a person says the Buddha speaks of the perception of self, person, being and life, what do you think? Does this person understand the meaning of what I say?"

The Buddha starts off by asking Subhuti a supposition question. Is it correct to say that the Buddha speaks of perceptions of self, person, being and life. Up to now the Buddha had spoken in terms of the four "notions." Here there is a slight deviation in that the Buddha speaks of four perceptions. "Notion" has to do with phenomenal appearance; whereas, "perception" has to do with one's thoughts, perspectives and understanding. Perception is very much what we today would call one's perspective. In Ch'an, it is called one's ground of perception. It's not with one's eyes that one perceives the Tao. The *Surangama Sutra* has some famous lines about this:

> *When one sees the seer,*
> *This seeing is not seeing.*
> *Seeing must still go beyond seeing,*
> *For seeing cannot reach it.*

Sometimes the wording in these sutras is enough to make you crazy! The first level of "see" is that which we do with our eyes; it is our mind and eyes working together to see. The second level of "see" is perceiving the Tao. In other words, the act of seeing and that which is seen; the second is that which can see. When we engage in the act of seeing, this is in the realm of phenomena. If we turn this around to look inward, one can perceive one's mind and original nature. This is not engaging in the act of seeing. It is not a phenomenon which the eyes can see, nor is it an alambana. Those are not Tao. "When one sees the seer," one turns around and perceives the Tao. "This seeing is not seeing." This seeing is not the act of seeing phenomena. It is perceiving the Tao. So, of course, "this seeing is not seeing." Could it be, though, that the seeing which perceives the Tao has an alambana? "Seeing must still go beyond seeing." When one's eyes are not seeing, ears are not hearing and all is empty, if one says I have perceived the Tao, there is still an object which is perceived. This must be thrown out. The "emptiness" must still be emptied. "For seeing cannot reach it." The real perceiving of the mind and original nature is not that which can be seen with the eyes; nor is it that which the mind can perceive. It is *that which can perceive.* We've gone in a large circle with this "seeing." It is very difficult to understand. It is not as simple as seeing the mountains not as mountains, seeing the water not as water. That's like the sound a frog makes when it jumps into a well. When there is no seer nor seen, when the mountains, the earth, all the phenomena in the universe and even emptiness have been smashed to fine powder, when all is level and deep and when the four notions have nothing on which to stand, then we can talk about Ch'an. There is a shadow of a perception of the nature of mind. Mind you, only just a shadow.

The *Surangama Sutra* also has some other lines which are also very important when talking about this. *"Understanding and perceiving rely on knowing, this is originally ignorance. Understanding and perceiving without perception, this is nirvana."*

Understanding and *perceiving* are terms used a lot in the later periods of Buddhism in China. *Understanding* is knowing and it refers to knowing and understanding the theory of Buddhist sutras. *Perception* is having actual experiences through meditation and cultivation of the phenomena and alambana of which are spoken in the sutras. For example, if one is meditating and everything becomes empty but one is still aware of sitting there in total peace, this is understanding and perceiving. This peace and purity still isn't correct, "understanding and perceiving rely on knowing, this is originally ignorance." To have a peace and a purity implies that there is the strength of unpeaceful and impure hidden within. This is tantamount to affliction, and so it is said that "understanding and perceiving rely on knowing, this is originally ignorance." Only "understanding and perceiving without perception," is to finally really perceive emptiness. "This is nirvana." This is the edge of perception.

Knowing Is Originally Ignorance

In the past, there have been some great masters who have practiced Ch'an through reading sutras and have had awakenings. Practicing Ch'an doesn't necessarily mean one only meditates or holds a *koan* or *hua tou* in mind. During the Sung Dynasty at Rui Lu Temple in Wenzhou there was a famous Ch'an master named Yu-an. Every day he would read sutras and recite the name of the Buddha. Once, when he came upon the lines just mentioned, his heart started pounding. He suddenly saw it through different eyes and then changed the punctuation slightly so it read, *"Understanding and perceiving rely. Knowing, this is originally ignorance. Understanding and perceiving without meaning (are not). Perception, this is nirvana."* Upon doing this, he had a Great Awakening. From then on, he called himself the "Surangama Destroyer" because, by breaking apart the sutra's words, he suddenly became enlightened. "Understanding and perceiving rely." Having understanding, having perception, having calm purity are all feelings. "Knowing, this is originally ignorance." This "knowing" to begin with, is actually ignorance and affliction. "Understanding and perceiving without (are not)." All is empty: theory is empty, thoughts are empty, emptiness is empty. "Perception, this is nirvana." Once one perceives this, one has awakened. This is that to which the master awakened when he broke apart the original sentence.

Now, we've gone through all this explanation but let's not forget our starting point, perception of self, person, being and life. The *Diamond Sutra* in the beginning spoke of four notions. In the middle of the sutra, there was the gatha which said, *"If you look for me in form, seek me in sound, you are on a path leading astray and cannot perceive the Tathagata."* Here in the sutra no more of the four notions; suddenly it's the four perceptions. Forms are notions. Tea cups, towels, books, me, you, him, mountains, and rivers are notions. Even space, sleep, dreams, clear purity and wakefulness are all notions. All phenomenal notions, or forms, are transformations within the cycle of creation and destruction.

Some people meditate every day and if you ask them what their experience is they answer, "Oh, wonderful, so clear and peaceful." This is attachment to forms! Form is not Tao. Tao is not inside a form. Understanding and perceiving rely. Knowing, this is originally ignorance. Understanding and perceiving are not. Perception, this is nirvana. If you rely on clear purity to be Tao and on top of that open the front and back channels, left and right channels, more channels than pay T.V....well, this is not achieving the Tao. It is grasping onto form. Understanding and perceiving rely. Knowing, this is originally ignorance. When understanding and perceiving are not, then perception is nirvana.

Now that we've got an idea about understanding and perceiving, if someone said the Buddha speaks in terms of perceptions of self, person, being and life, would you say this person understands the meaning of what the Buddha says? Is this person someone who understands the Buddha dharma?

"No, World Honored-One. This person does not understand the meaning of what the Tathagata says." Subhuti said, even if this person is studying Buddhism, I beg your pardon but, they really don't have a clue as to the Buddha's meaning. *"The reason is that when the Tathagata speaks of the perception of a self, person, being and life, they are not the perception of a self, person, being and life but are merely called so."* The Buddha originally started this section with a question about the perception of a self, person,

being and life. This question was just a convenient means by which to speak of "perceiving," perceiving one's mind and original nature, perceiving the Tao. This question was the link to talking about the real issue, that there is nothing to understand or to perceive.

How to Understand and to Perceive

> "Subhuti, one who seeks anuttara-samyak sambodhi, in regard to all dharma, should thus know, thus perceive, thus believe and comprehend: do not give rise to notions of dharma."

This is the conclusion the Buddha wished to tell Subhuti. Those who wish to attain supreme enlightenment, to study the real Mahayana Buddha Dharma, and to attain Great Awakening, *"in regard to all dharma"*—this includes all worldly dharma as well as supramundane dharma—one should "thus know, thus perceive," each of the theories and teachings in the *Diamond Sutra* should be known and understood. Pay close attention here to this part. One must have this kind of knowing and perception.

I would like to give a little more explanation to knowing and perceiving. In both the Hinayana and the Mahayana teachings, but especially in the Hinayana teachings, there are five steps: discipline (sila), samadhi, wisdom, liberation and liberation from knowing and perceiving. One must first develop discipline, then cultivate samadhi, and then from this wisdom an awakening will spring. This awakening is liberation from suffering but the highest it can go is liberation from the bonds of the physical world. It can only free one from the frustration and sentimentality of the desire and the form realms. There is still the mental bondage of knowing and perceiving from which to be liberated. Only at that time will it be real emptiness. It is as we were saying earlier, knowing and perceiving rely. Knowing, this is originally ignorance. Knowing and perceiving are not. Perception, this is nirvana. So if you wish to be a true Mahayana Buddhist, if you wish to become a Buddha, in regards to all dharma, you should thus know and thus perceive.

How then should one know and how should one perceive? The Buddha Dharma is not the Buddha Dharma but is merely called the Buddha Dharma. The other paths are not so but are merely called the other paths. Demons are not demons and are merely called demons. I am not I, but am merely called I. All you need is this formula! If you put everything together, emptiness and existence do not dwell; therefore, do not dwell or grasp. All dharma should be thus known, thus perceived.

Now you understand and perceive, but how should one believe and comprehend. It is only when one is very clear on the theory and really comprehends it that the belief won't be superstitious. If a person isn't really clear on the Buddha's teachings and just practices due to some emotional factor, this is superstitious. Once one is clear on knowing and perceiving then one can "thus believe," correct faith. "Thus comprehend," after one has correct faith, one can in this way start to really comprehend it rationally. Studying Buddhism and cultivating the Tao is a rational endeavor, not an emotional one. It is not blind faith. Rationally, one should thus believe and comprehend.

Our Own Notions of Dharma

Why did the Buddha say *"Do not give rise to notions of dharma"*? Why not say "use," "dwell", or "grasp" or "fall into" notions of dharma? What is meant by "give rise to"?

Before we deal with this question, we need to understand the meaning of notions of dharma. All notions and images are phenomena. Our thoughts and ideas start to take shape and each person's internal condition and imaginings are different. The longer one holds onto one's imaginings, the stronger they become and the tighter one clings to them. This is basically what shapes the alambana of one's thoughts and ideas. In Buddhism, this is called dharma. Dharma includes all occurrences, theories, physical existence, thoughts and ideas. For example, many people think of the Great Awakening as an explosion of light and enlightenment as being forever in peaceful bright light. Most people have this idea firmly entrenched in their minds. They sit there meditating waiting for the light to envelop them. Some people have an image of a bright electric light, some the sunlight, others the moonlight, whatever, they are all notions of dharma.

Another example is the idea that after enlightenment, one doesn't need anything, that nothing matters after that, the world is of no concern and one would go live up in the mountains or in an old temple. People have this idea of a Buddha sitting there meditating all the time. If this is what a Buddha does, then the 1,000 Buddhas scheduled to come in the next aeon will really have no effect on the world. If you think in this way, the forests are already full of Buddhas in the form of rocks and boulders. They've been sitting there since time began, not concerned about anything. The mundane and the supramundane have nothing to do with them. It may seem very liberated, as if not grasping onto anything but actually it is completely selfish and self-serving. People get an image in their mind about what a Buddha is supposed to be and then strive to be the same way. This is a notion of dharma.

Many people think that Buddhism, meditation and samadhi are sitting there completely oblivious to everything. This is a notion of dharma. Another common notion is that Buddhism is everything being empty. Emptiness is a notion of dharma, a phenomenon. Still others strive for the channels and chakras to all open or to circulate a great cosmic circle of energy. Tell me how many rotations does one need? To what do the channel and chakras open? This is all grasping onto notions of dharma. People don't realize it but they have fallen into a self–centered notion of dharma. This is an idea or a shape of Tao formulated by the ego.

If you look at the different depictions of heaven in the different cultures, you will see that they are all different. In the

Chinese heaven, it looks like an old palace setting and everyone dresses like the emperor. The Western heavens have a Western look to them; the angels have blond curly hair and blue eyes. The heaven of the Arabs has yet another look to it. These images of heaven are ideas in the minds of people. Who has gone up there to actually see it and then returned? They are all subconscious images, notions of dharma which we hold. The Consciousness Only School is also called the Dharmalaskana sect. They investigate starting from the phenomenal world. In other words, they look at all dharma starting from the outer world and eventually looking at the internal working of the mind. Their studies cover all the phenomena in the universe. They start with the phenomena of this world, human life, then focus inward on the mind and then move to the spiritual essence. In other words, through the mind and body, they go beyond the mind and body into the essence of the original nature.

The *Avatamsaka Sutra* is also different in that it starts from the universal essence, from the infinite, and then makes the parameters smaller and smaller until finally concentrating on the mind. It is done this way so as to lead people to self-understanding through understanding original nature. Most of Buddhism is the other way around, getting people to understand original nature through understanding the self. They are simply two different teaching methods. This is what is called notions of dharma, all notions of dharma.

The *Diamond Sutra* is almost coming to a close and so here the Buddha is telling us something very important. He told Subhuti that if someone wishes to attain Supreme Enlightenment he or she ought to thus know, perceive, understand clearly and believe. How is this? *"Do not give rise to notions of dharma."* Don't go making any mental constructs; don't give rise to a notion of a Buddha from your subconscious. Everyone's understanding of Buddha, Tao, nirvana and so forth are all different simply because they are projections of your own self mind. They are something to which you gave rise. You don't want to be giving rise to notions of dharma. It's like a hundred people in a class, the depth and way of understanding will be different for each person simply because of the notions of dharma each carries with them. All of these are notions we have constructed are not final. It is like the metaphor of the blind men feeling an elephant and each describes the animal as the part which they felt. It's not that they are wrong, but each one only got a handle on a little bit. It's only when you put their stories together that you start to get an idea of the whole picture. To really understand the whole thing, we must not give rise to notions of dharma. Don't hold onto anything.

In the next breath, the Buddha completely overturns his words again.

I Want to Go By, You Come Over

> *"Subhuti, the notions of dharma of which I speak, the Tathagata says are not notions of dharma but are merely called so."*

What are called in the sutras, notions of dharma, are originally not notions of dharma and so are called notions of dharma. This kind of logic appears all over the *Diamond Sutra*. It is a method of teaching. Like the raft to get you across the river, once across you leave it at the shore. If you are carrying it with you, you'd better set it down and walk on, making your own way.

Throughout the different sutras in the Tripitaka, there are various ways of teaching; some speak of emptiness, some of existence, some say neither empty nor existent and still others say both empty and existent. In the end, which one has the right answer? Each is correct and also incorrect; they all don't want you to give rise to notions of dharma.

The Consciousness Only School, besides dividing the mind into eight consciousnesses, divides the functioning mind into 100 dharmas, or categories. These 100 are also further subdivided, ad infinitum. Most people who study the Consciousness Only School get lost in it and never find their way out. Just what is it in which they get lost? In existence, they get lost in the "higher meaning of existence," notions of dharma. Nagarjuna, on the other hand, took emptiness as a way of talking about prajna. These are just different approaches. Most people grasp onto the notion of dharma called emptiness, but one should not grasp onto any notion of dharma. The Buddha in the end even said that the notions of dharma were not notions of dharma. Speaking this way is a convenient means, a method of teaching to make use of an opportunity to help us gain understanding. If this way of speaking isn't helpful, He will try another method and another until we understand.

Those who came after the Buddha, however, took what was written about these different methods and grasped onto emptiness teachings or grasped onto the existence teachings, all believing them to be the final word. They never get it straight. Actually, the Buddha spoke quite clearly—don't fall into any notions of dharma. Still, people read this and say the Buddha is talking about emptiness. Very early on, I said that the *Diamond Sutra* doesn't talk about perceiving emptiness anywhere in it. The *Diamond Sutra* uses a blocking method; it just keeps blocking incorrect trains of thought. It doesn't point to any correct train of thought. You have to find that for yourself.

Do you remember at the beginning of our lectures we spoke about two Ch'an stories, one about a son who begs his father to teach him how to be a thief and the other story about a man in jail who finally escapes through the front door? I'd like to tell you now about another Ch'an story. A young man became a monk in hopes of becoming enlightened. He followed his master for more than ten years. The master was always particularly strict with him especially about this disciple's behavior. When the disciple would ask about cultivating Tao, the master would never say a word. This young man was just like the young people of today, wanting a famous teacher or a secret method. He thought that with these, he would sit down to meditate and instantly become a Buddha. In his mind, he was holding onto these notions of dharma. Every time he asked his master, though, the response was "You go search for yourself, go study for yourself!"

The young man was always thinking to himself, "Here I am a monk for more than ten years, I have the most famous Ch'an master in the world whom I've followed with great pain and suffering and he hasn't transmitted to me a dharma method." Finally, one day, he decided on a plan. He took a knife with him and lay in wait for the master to come up the mountain path as he usually did. It was raining and the master walked slowly up the slippery mud track. He knew what was in store for him but kept on steadily. Finally, the monk jumped out and said, "Master, I've followed you for ten years, and if you don't tell me, I'm willing to risk my life." Then, he pulled out the knife and said, "If you don't teach me the Dharma, I'll kill you!" The master was holding an umbrella in one hand. With his other hand, he grabbed hold of the disciple's hand holding the knife and said, "Whoa! The path is slippery. I want to go by, you come over." While saying that, he pulled the disciple toward him and then moved past him. The disciple was instantly enlightened upon hearing those words.

We all need to think about this carefully. "I want to go by, you come over." With these words, he awakened. Where is the logic in this? This is one of the koans of Ch'an. It is very difficult to come up with any conclusions about it. What I wish to say is not the "real answer" but is a metaphor to help you think about the meaning.

Studying Buddhism is very difficult. There are both mental afflictions and physical hardships. When we meditate, our bodies become quite uncomfortable. When not meditating, our minds are full of afflictions. Everyone is seeking peace and calm but can never attain them. There is no end to the afflictions. You ask yourself, what can I do? The master within you will say, "I want to go by, you come over!" The afflictions go by and are replaced by peace and calm but the past, present and future mind cannot be obtained. Do not give rise to notions of dharma. One should give rise to mind not dwelling. It's that simple. I want to go by, you come over. This path is open. Afflictions are bodhi. Where is there an affliction that stays in your mind forever? If I were to expend a lot of energy trying to empty my frustrations in hopes of finding peace and calm, wouldn't I be like the master and disciple forever stuck on that path not going past?

You see how simple these teaching methods are? I want to go by, you come over. He doesn't pay any attention to the knife or the disciple and the disciple not only understood but also had an awakening. We can see that this disciple was completely immersed in his notions of dharma, his ideas about Buddha and

Tao. People are so afraid of demons. Actually, if in studying Buddhism or Tao you get entangled in some notions, this is your demon. You've laid hold of the demon of Tao, the demon of cultivation or the demon of calm purity.

Yes, calm purity is also a demon! This is why the Ch'an masters would say, "The arisal of thoughts is the heavenly demon." What is this heavenly demon? Nothing but the activity of your mind, your giving rise to notions of dharma. "The non-arisal of thoughts is the demon of the skandhas." Pay attention here! A lot of people get caught by this demon alambana. The idea that one should sit in complete oblivion or that complete oblivion is samadhi is non-arisal of thoughts. One falls into the demon of the five skandhas in the non-arisal of thoughts "going back and forth from arising to non-arising is the demon of afflictions." Sometimes it's as if you are so calm and pure. Do you feel this way? Sometimes it feels as though there is a circus going on in your mind. It's nothing to worry about but, on the other hand, it's also pretty half-witted. This is going back and forth from arising to non-arising, the demon of ignorance. People always talk about falling into the demon's fire. From where do these demons come? They are completely creations of our own minds. They are not something outside. "The arisal of thoughts is the heavenly demon. The non-arisal of thoughts is the demon of the skandhas. Going back and forth from arising to non-arising is the demon of afflictions."

Buddhism categorizes the different demon alambanas quite clearly. The Ch'an masters also had a system of categorizing them. It was very simple. All these different mental situations, these alambanas are all the arisal of notions of dharma. The more one studies Buddhism, the Consciousness Only School, all the sutras and so on, the more tightly notions of dharma bind one.

We are almost to the final conclusion. The Buddha told us in this part not to give rise to notions of dharma.

Gatha of Section Thirty-one

From heaven's height, the crane sounds a traceless cry.
Weeping tears of blood, the cuckoo's spirit is exhausted;
The sound of music played on a lion-stringed guchin will cease.
For whom do you travail, singing to this deserted village?

"From heaven's height, the crane sounds a traceless cry." Most of you here have probably never heard the cry of a white crane. If you've been to the northwest of China or some of the central mountains, you may have heard it. When a white crane in flight cries out, it's like the striking of a gong which can be heard a long way off. The sound of a white crane is different than the sounds of other kinds of cranes. This is a metaphor of the Buddha teaching the Dharma. It's like the sound of the white cranes from the highest heavens resounding through the clouds. The cry is to

wake us from our hazy dream, but does the cry awaken us? There are many in this world who cannot be woken. It's really quite sad. Still there are others who hear it and travel great distances to study Buddhism.

"Weeping tears of blood, the cuckoo's spirit is exhausted." It is said that during ancient times there was an emperor whose nation (approximately where present day Sichuan is located) was conquered. He was so heartbroken that he cried every day. One day his spirit left his body and became a cuckoo bird. He continued to cry as he flew. He wept until he shed tears of blood which fell onto some white azaleas and stained them red. This is a metaphor for Shakyamuni Buddha who so painstakingly taught the Dharma until He was eighty-one. At that time, He decided to stop, to say no more. All those years, all for nothing. No one really understood. The tears are for Him and also for all of us. We all study Buddhism but haven't even glimpsed a shadow of Tao. We're waiting for a famous teacher, a special method. Actually, Buddhism is very ordinary, very simple. Everything is all here in the *Diamond Sutra*.

"The sound of music played on a lion-stringed guchin will cease." Usually, the strings of a gu*chin* (a Chinese instrument similar to a zither) are made with the sinews of cows or other animals, but this one is made from the sinews of a lion. Lions represent great teachers. The *Diamond Sutra* is the score of a piece played on the lion-stringed chin. This piece is about to end.

"For whom do you travail, singing to this deserted village?" Venerable One, why did You come? Who could understand Your teachings? Everyone is asleep. They can't hear. Why do You still labor? Why did You come here to sing? The song is wonderful but no one hears or understands. Reading the *Diamond Sutra*, I really feel for Shakyamuni Buddha.

Now, let's return briefly to the start of the sutra. The first important point was to be skillfully mindful. Whether one is an ordinary person or a Buddha, this is the one dharma door, be skillfully mindful. What mind? A mind that does not dwell. How does one not dwell? Do not give rise to notions of dharma. How about for those who have already become a Buddha? Also the same. He simply eats, puts on clothes, washes His feet and meditates as do we ordinary folk. There are no lights coming out of the crown of His head or from the heart chakra, no display of superpowers or anything of the sort, just eating, washing, meditating and the like. If you ask a question, He will give you an answer. It's that simple, that ordinary. The *Diamond Sutra* is the real and true within the ordinary, the supramundane within the ordinary.

SECTION 32

TRANSFORM THE REAL

"Subhuti, someone might fill the innumerable worlds throughout uncountable aeons with the seven treasures and give away all in alms, but if any good man or woman with bodhicitta practices this teaching, receives, retains, reads and recites even a four line stanza of this teaching and expounds it to others, the latter's merit would surpass that of the former."

"How should this teaching be expounded to others? Without attachment to form, at one with Suchness. Why is this? Because:

All phenomena are like

A dream, an illusion, a bubble and a shadow.

Like a dew drop and a flash of lightning,

Thus should you view them."

When the Buddha had finished expounding the sutra, the Venerable Subhuti, together with all the bhiksus, bhikshunis, upasakas, upasikas and the whole realm of devas, humans and asuras who had listened to His teaching were filled with joy and believed, received and observed it.

Transforming the Unreal

Prince Chao-ming named the last section, "Transforming the Unreal." The Buddha taught for forty-nine years, but in the *Diamond Sutra*, he said that he hadn't said a word. This Dharma is inexpressible. Anything said about it isn't it because this automatically falls into notions of dharma. You open your mouth and it's wrong. We all know about this. Close your eyes and imagine an object or a situation. Now, if you start to describe it, it will change with the description. Even something as simple as a watch, if you try to describe it or even draw it, somehow it's not exactly like the idea in your mind. This is the same reason why most people are not good writers. You may have some great scenes or plots in your mind but in putting the pen to paper, it just isn't what you've imagined, and the more you try, the worse it becomes. The words on paper are the words on paper, your imagination is your imagination and never the twain shall meet.

The speed of our thoughts is no match for the speed of our tongues. Our thoughts flow out at an incredible rate, and the more intelligent the person, the faster the speed. An incredible amount of information can be comprehended within the time span of one second. To write down all that information it would take at least five or six minutes, but while remembering so many more little thoughts have occurred that it is impossible to separate them. This is the reason that the Buddha said he never spoke words of the real and true Dharma. It is inexpressible; to speak isn't it. Still, how can we understand it if no words are spoken? The only thing to do is to pick up a flower and smile. This smile is much better than words.

Two friends have a private joke about someone else. When this other person appears on the scene, all the other two need to do is look at each other and there is that tacit understanding. Young people do this all the time. They also like to roll their eyes at things, but if their parents catch them, no words need to be said. The eyes become immediately fixed in their sockets. Eyes can pass a lot of information. We can see from this that there is much more to the world of thought than could ever be expressed in words. This is why the Buddha said he never spoke a word of Dharma his whole life. He went through the pain of being born into this world in order to expound the Dharma to the world, to educate this world. The sound of music played on a lion-stringed guchin will cease. He laboriously sang wondrous songs for 49 years but for whom did He travail, singing to this deserted village? Now, more than 2,000 years later, what is left? Here and there a lonely temple with a few old monks reciting as they hit the wooden fish in time. For whom did He travail? I really feel for Him. It's as the old saying goes, "The heroes of the ages all cry with the same anguish."

Inside Saint, Outside King "Bodhisattva"

> *"Subhuti, someone might fill the innumerable world throughout uncountable aeons with the seven treasures and*

give away all in alms, but if any good man or woman with bodhicitta practices this teaching, receives, retains, reads or recites even a four line stanza of this sutra and expounds it to others, the latter's merit would surpass that of the former."

The Buddha said, suppose there was someone who gave away an infinite amount of treasure. This person's merit and fortune would be immense. The *Diamond Sutra* is written in an archaic style, so it is not very detailed. Whether it be a piece of writing, a painting or a sculpture, the more slick and perfect it is, the worse it looks. It's like an antique—it may just be a pottery shard but if you display it, the more you look, the more interesting it becomes just because it's so old. You can imagine all kinds of stories about it and no matter what you dream up is fine. The things today are more and more refined but after three days, you're bored looking at it. It's like the clothing of today—in order to show off one's shape, clothing gets shorter and skimpier. At first you look, but then, after a while, you get used to it and don't even notice. Maybe it will come to the point where people walk around in only their skin, and then after that gets boring, they'll start with the clothing again. The writing style of the sutras is very broad and loose rather than being tight and detailed. Sometimes the terms are not specific, but you understand the meaning.

"... *A good man or woman with bodhicitta receives, retains, reads or recites even a four line stanza from this sutra and expounds it to others, the latter's merit is beyond comparison."* So, we all have a lot of merit and fortune! Actually, the merit is conditional on having the bodhicitta. This sounds quite heavy. Just what is bodhicitta? We talked about this very early on in the lectures, but I'll say it again just so the impression goes deeper. *Bodhi* means "awakened having sentiment." It means Great Awakening, enlightenment and prajna paramita. It means liberation from the three realms. *Citta* simply means mind. Awakening to the Tao is the substance of bodhicitta, and compassion is the form and function.

One who is awakened to the Tao doesn't need any encouragement to be compassionate. I sometimes hear people say that they believe everything about Buddhism, but they just can't be so compassionate. They all have this idea that being compassionate means crying about every little thing that's even remotely sad or touching. That is not compassion; that is some sort of imbalance of the nervous system or weak liver or kidney energy which causes one to easily feel moved or shed tears. One with real compassion and bodhicitta has hoary eyebrows and fiery eyes. Compassion and bodhicitta are the might and ire of a great king who brings peace to the land. In the language of those who worship the Immortals, it is called "inside saint, outside king." Such a one has the heart and wisdom of a saint but functions in the world as a king or great leader. In Buddhism, the heart or substance is Tao, anuttara-samyak sambodhi, prajna and so forth. Bodhicitta functions in the world as great compassion, loving all beings and helping to liberate all beings. It is not sitting all alone in a temple in the woods or being completely aloof from all others.

Receiving and retaining the *Diamond Sutra* should be in the context of this. Some people have been reciting the sutra daily for more than ten years but still don't know what mind to seek. They may only do it seeking the fortune of merit, and fortune does come to them but for other reasons. If none comes, you must examine carefully on what you base your seeking. The sutra itself says *"any good man or woman with bodhicitta practices this teaching."* This means we should practice and nurture what was taught. We must very diligently try to understand its meaning and cultivate it through and within our meditation, daily responsibilities and social interactions.

The Lazy Person's Buddhism

For a lot of people, the first problem that crops up when studying Buddhism is laziness. Those who study Buddhism or seek Tao look as though everything appears empty to them. Actually, if you know anything about behavior patterns, you would easily identify this as being lazy. It is absolutely just laziness. Emptiness is an illusion; laziness is real. They may say they are empty but I assure you that they sit there with their myriad of thoughts. They are quite happy to sit there with all their thoughts and states of mind, busy as a bee, but if you ask them to get up and do something, "No way man, like that's not the Buddhist deal." This is an excuse for being lazy. If you try to get such a person to practice compassion by helping others in this world, he or she says, "No way, man, that's for people doin' the Bodhisattva thing. I'm goin' straight to Buddha land." Not only lazy, but also having delusions of self-grandeur! In my experience, those who study Buddhism are more likely to be greedy and lazy. The Buddha taught us to be diligent, to not do anything harmful and to work for the benefit of all sentient beings. It's so simple but most people can't do it. Harmful behavior gets done, and of virtuous action, there is none. This is all because of laziness. We need to examine our own behavior very carefully because this really is quite a serious problem. In the last section of the sutra, we are reminded to "practice" the teaching. This is because people don't have the diligence, endurance or will to help others.

"... Receives, retains, reads and recites even a four line stanza of this sutra and expounds it to others..." Expounding here doesn't mean to lecture on it or to expound from a pulpit. It means to explain and to put into action this teaching, to allow others to gain an understanding. "The latter's merit will surpass that of the former." This is more powerful than giving away countless treasures because it is the giving of Dharma. In Buddhism, the giving of Dharma is more important than the giving of material goods. Just what is the giving of the Dharma? It is the gift of spirit. It is working to open the wisdom inherent in all beings and to improve culture for society in order that people gain merit for themselves. This is the giving of Dharma and this is why it surpasses the merit of giving of material goods.

All of us have been studying and talking about the *Diamond Sutra*, the merit of this must be pretty good right? Of course it is! We have the luxury of sitting in this air-conditioned room for two hours with no responsibilities. Shouldn't this be considered fortunate? What is fortune other than peace and security? Lu Chun-yang wrote a poem describing fortune:

"A clear day, nothing to do, free as celestial existence;
Spirit calm, body in balance, peaceful and secure.
Deep inside there is a jewel, at rest, no search for Tao;
The right place is no mind, don't ask about Ch'an !"

"A clear day, nothing to do, free as celestial existence." When a person has such a day it is like the alambana of a celestial being. *"Spirit calm, body in balance, peaceful and secure."* If also during this day, one has no physical or mental discomfort, this is fortune. *"Deep inside there is a jewel, at rest, no search for Tao.'* This is referring to the field of blessedness in our hearts and minds. If one is calm and clear, this is cultivation. There is no need to search for something else. *"The right place is no mind, don't ask about Ch'an!'* The right place is no mind; this is Ch'an! Why do you need to ask about Ch'an?

Peace and security are fortune. Spirit calm, body in balance, peaceful and secure is fortune. Don't think that fortune only comes from espousing the sutras or reciting them in temples. This is a notion of dharma. *"How should this teaching be expounded to others? Without attachment to form, at one with Suchness."* Don't hold onto phenomena or notions. If you are going to talk about the Buddha Dharma, you ought to have some of the spirit of the Buddha. Don't be dripping with religiousness. You should be very ordinary and calm. Expounding the *Diamond Sutra*, you also will need a little "diamondness", to be at one with Suchness. What does it mean, to be at one with Suchness? Not giving rise to notions of dharma, keeping well the moment of mind and not dwelling.

Four Line Stanza Beyond the Sutra

> *"All phenomena are like a dream, an illusion, a bubble and a shadow, like a dew drop and a flash of lightning, thus should you view them."*

This is the last gatha of the *Diamond Sutra*. In the Chinese translation, there are many four line stanzas and gathas, so people have always debated which "four lines" are referred to throughout the sutra. It refers to none of the four lines in it! The four lines are beyond the sutra—emptiness, existence, no emptiness or existence and both emptiness and existence. If you say that it has to be talking about a particular four lines and that a conclusion must be made, you have not paid attention to what was being said throughout the *Diamond Sutra*, namely: Do not give rise to notions of dharma and do not dwell. Saying that none of the four lines are in the sutra is to be without attachment to form, at one with Suchness. Suchness is the opposite of all phenomena. Suchness is the substance of nirvana, Tao, the essence, true form prajna and so forth. All phenomena are everything, that with form, to do, to act and to be. All phenomena are like dreams, like illusions and shadows, like bubbles on the water's surface. In the sutras, there are many such metaphors, for example, the moon's reflection in the water, a flower in the mirror, city on the ocean, banana tree, mirage...

When I was young, the metaphor of the banana tree really intrigued me. There was a story about a scholar in ancient times who was interested in a young woman. She planted a banana tree outside of her window. He wrote her a poem on one of the leaves of the banana tree. It said, *"Who was it so overzealous as to plant this banana tree; for it swooshes all night and it swooshes all day."* When wind blows through the big leaves of the banana, they swoosh and flap and make a lot of noise. The noise would keep the scholar awake at night, but actually he just used this as an excuse to make contact with her. She wrote back on another leaf, *"Is the gentleman's mind so unoccupied as to place so much importance and ire on a banana tree?"* In other words, it's all in your mind and you are obviously too bored. She was also implying that this was the end of the dialogue.

Could it be that the Buddha used the banana tree as a result of hearing this story? Obviously not, as this was a Chinese story. I took apart a banana tree once to find out just why the Buddha talked about them so much and found out that they are hollow in the middle. From the outside they look so well made but there is nothing in the middle. So all of these metaphors are talking about emptiness. Everything about this world is like a dream, an illusion, a shadow.

The Shadow in a Dream

If we think about things that happened twenty years ago, they are like dreams. Do dreams exist? They don't not exist, but they exist like, well, dreams. When you are dreaming, it's real to you, right? But when you awaken, you say, "Oh, it was just a dream". Right now we are all in the dream of the *Diamond Sutra*. It's true. If you close your eyes, whatever scene was there is gone. Is this a dream or not? Do you dare to say for sure? If so then you are grasping onto form.

An illusion also doesn't not exist. When there is the phenomenon of an illusion, is it real? If you watch a movie that makes you cry, is it real? This world is like that; all of the physical world is an illusion. Maybe the earth's existence lasts for some billions of years, but if you compare this with the lifespan of the universe, the earth's existence is just the snap of a finger. A long time? It's just an illusion. Is a bubble on the water's surface real or not? Some can last up to several days even! This earth is a bubble floating on a larger sea. This galaxy is another bubble. Real or not? Are shadows real or not? Movies are like shadows. Are they real? Bruce Lee is dead, but we can still see him on the screen just the same.

The *Diamond Sutra* does not say the world is empty, nor does it say that it is existent. Emptiness and existence are notions of dharma. If you study the *Diamond Sutra* and say that it talks about emptiness, you are quite wrong. There is not one place that it says "emptiness is." Rather, it says phenomena are like a dream, an illusion, a bubble.... This is to say don't grasp and don't dwell. It is not saying "empty." If you say emptiness is non- existence, the *Diamond Sutra* says, *"One who attains anuttara-samyak sambodhi will not speak of the nihilism of dharma."*

To say that emptiness is annihilation is to fall into the perspective of nihilism. It is an incorrect perspective because when there is a dream or an illusion, the dream and illusion are real. When gone, they don't exist. When they come again, again they're real. It's a matter of seeing clearly that this very moment is a dream and an illusion and that mind doesn't dwell. Within the dream, don't attach to form and be one with Suchness. This is the point. When you are in a dream, don't hold onto the notion of dreaming. When you hold a position, don't get bound by the notion of such a position. When you are doing business, don't get bound by money. When your children call you mommy or daddy, don't be fooled by these names. Don't dwell in notions; be one with Suchness. All are like dreams, illusions, bubbles and shadows. *"Like a dew drop and a flash of lightning."* The morning dew is ephemeral, a random composite of causes and conditions. It is a possibility which becomes manifest. The nature of all possibilities is emptiness and because their nature is emptiness, possibilities can arise. This is why they are also said to be like dew or lightning. Would you say that a flash of lightning doesn't exist? Would you want one to touch you? You'd be electrocuted if one did. In the sky, they just flash for a few seconds and then are gone.

A lot of people finish reciting the *Diamond Sutra*, put down the little wooden fish and breathe a sigh, "Oh, everything is empty!" I'm telling you phenomena exist, but like a dream, an illusion, a bubble and a shadow; like a drop of dew and a flash of lightning. Thus should you view them. This is a method. You should use it to recognize clearly and understand clearly. And then, after you recognize clearly, then what? Don't attach to form and be one with Suchness. This is really practicing Buddhism. Many people meditate and have different alambana arisen. They think they are going down the path of demons. There aren't any demons; demons are not demons! This is all in your mind; you're giving rise to notions of dharma. If you don't attach to phenomena, demons are also Buddhas. If you grasp phenomena, Buddhas are also demons. All phenomena are like a dream, an illusion, a bubble and a shadow; like a drop of dew and a flash of lightning; thus should you view them. These are the last of Buddha's words. The teaching is complete.

"When the Buddha had finished expounding the sutra, the Venerable Subhuti, together with all the bhiksus, bhiksunis, upasakas, upasikas and the whole realm of devas, humans and asuras who had listened to His teaching were filled with joy, and believed, received and observed it."

Within the *Diamond Sutra*, there are three different epithets for Subhuti, "Virtuous Manifestation, "Living Wisdom", and "Venerable." When you read sutras, you should take note of these. These three places are three levels of understanding for Subhuti. That to which he had awakened was different, hence, three different epithets.

Male and female members of the sangha and male and female lay people make up the four kinds of disciples. The Venerable Subhuti, the four kinds of disciples as well as other humans, celestial beings and asuras were all listening to the teaching and were filled with joy. They believed, accepted and received it and observed the teaching in their cultivation. The *Diamond Prajna-paramita Sutra* is complete.

Gatha of Section Thirty-two

The geese return to Heng Yang, sounding, sounding one sound.
Saints and immortals take turns at the border night watch.
Rain cloak, straw hat, bag on a pole; mists and rains have broken.

Clouds are water storehouses, take a slow leisurely stroll.

"The geese return to Heng Yang, sounding, sounding one sound." In the autumn, the geese migrate back south to Heng Yang after spending the summer up north. This is a metaphor for returning to the root of one's life, one's original nature. In other words, perceiving one's mind and original nature, that which you were before you were conceived.

"Saints and immortals take turns at the border night watch." A saint becomes a Buddha, and then becomes an ordinary person and realizes that being a human is also rather neutral. "I want to go by, you come over." You want to go by, I'll move over. Saints, humans, there's no difference among sentient beings. There have been a lot of people who read the *Diamond Sutra*, have some awakening to this and still go to get ordained and live an easy life.

"Rain cloak, straw hat, bag on a pole; mists and rains have broken." Really having awakened, one shaves one's head, puts on a monk's clothes, a straw hat and rain cloak; puts one's bag of things on the end of a pole and goes around free as a bird. Between heaven and earth there's nowhere one can't go. Rain cloak, straw hat, pole on the shoulder, bag on a pole; the mists and the rain have broken. After a rain, the weather is clear; understanding the Buddha Dharma is as such, one has also achieved the Tao. After achieving the Tao then what, become a Hinayana practitioner?

"Clouds are water storehouses, take a slow leisurely stroll." Come again to this world as a Bodhisattva. And? Play and act in

the human realm. Play around and then leave. That's all. Once you are liberated, it's all just like acting or playing. After enlightenment, the Buddha taught dharma for 49 years. He was just acting and playing. In the end, he just closed his eyes and left. This is what the *Diamond Sutra* is telling us. This is the whole thing.

CONCLUSION

I'd like to make a conclusion for everyone, reviewing all of the main points. I hope you'll all pay careful attention. "Virtuous Manifestation Opens the Question" is the title of section two. The main point is "skillful mindfulness". From ordinary existence all the way to becoming a Buddha, this is the one Dharma door, be skillfully mindful. What mind? The mind of not dwelling, not giving rise to notions of dharma, at one with Suchness, not attached to form. It is the state of inner peace and sanctuary.

Section Three, "True/Right Mahayana" explains more about being skillfully mindful. Practicing Buddhism is attaining the Tao, Supreme Enlightenment, that which Shakyamuni Buddha and all other Buddhas attained. That highest alambana is also called nirvana. Nirvana is not dying. It is perfection beyond birth and death, neither coming nor going, always clear and pure. Even in the midst of chaos, it is still clear and pure, at one with Suchness. Attaining the alambana of Tao is nirvana. Section three tells us that there is no method which will allow sentient beings to enter nirvana because one's own original nature will liberate one. The Buddha cannot save you. The saints and Buddhas are but those who have already liberated themselves. All a great teacher can do is share with you his experiences along the path. You still have to walk it yourself. All beings must liberate themselves and so there is no method to get to nirvana.

Knowing this, how then does one cultivate? Be skillfully mindful! Don't forget this, really be skillfully mindful, don't dwell on form and you will arrive at nirvana. Other than this there is no way.

Section Five, "Like Theory, the Truth Is Perceived," perceiving is perceiving the Tathagata. What perception? The Buddha told everyone not to hold onto a perception of a body. The most difficult thing in cultivation is letting go of our perception of a physical body. All meditation and cultivation kung fu (practice of transformational methods) are playing around in the physical realm, grasping onto form. All forms and phenomena are illusions. If one perceives that all phenomena are not phenomena, one will perceive the Tathagata. First one must rid himself of the notion of the body. Without getting rid of this, one cannot get rid of the notion of self; without getting rid of the notion of self, there are the notions of you and I and others. "Others" means the notions of people, beings and life. We who practice Buddhism need to check ourselves again and again so that we don't let this life go by without getting rid of even one of the form notions! Actually for most people the four become eight and the eight become sixty-four and so on ad infinitum. So if you wish to perceive the Tathagata, you must first rid yourself of your notion of your body.

Section Six follows this by telling how to rid oneself of the notion of mind. If one has a notion of mind, one also has notions of dharma. If one's perception is unclear, then, whether one is meditating or doing other kinds of cultivation, one is only just building on one's notions of dharma. In other words, you're deceiving yourself! You are going through the motions of cultivation but underneath you are building up a fortress of dharma notions. This is why the Buddha said, "Ye bhiksus, you should know that the Dharma I expound is likened to a raft which should be abandoned, how much more so the non-Dharma." All Dharma is not Dharma. The Dharma I expound is like a raft—used to ferry one across a river. After getting across, you leave the raft. So why would you hold onto a Dharma as true Dharma? This is simply not being able to let go.

Following this in section nine, "One Form, No Form." It tells us that the real Buddha Dharma is being able to let go of all notions of body and mind and to not create notions of Dharma. Don't be making up ideas in your head about what Dharma is. A lot of people adopt or enhance odd behavior patterns or appearances believing this to be the Tao or "Buddha like." Still others practice Taoist methods and try to grow an "immortal fetus." Ten months of "pregnancy," a round glowing egg inside of which is the immortal fetus. To give this a medical explanation, it is either a prolapsed stomach or a tumor. Do you really think there is a round glowing egg inside? These Taoist descriptions actually represent mental states of development. Don't grasp onto phenomena. Attaining the Tao, just what do you attain? There is nothing to attain! This is the most difficult thing to accept; there is nothing to attain. All are unobtainable. Don't dwell on notions of Dharma.

Section fourteen "Serenity Beyond Form and Appearance," the Buddha Dharma is the highest wisdom starting from the first paramita. What is the first paramita? Real wisdom has no wisdom. As Lao-tzu said, "Great wisdom looks foolish." To have a state of wisdom is wrong. Without thoughts, feelings, considerations, frustrations or afflictions, pure and clear awareness is the first paramita, the highest wisdom. Wisdom is the tool and the way to become a Buddha. The first paramita spoken of in the Diamond Sutra is the tool used to become a Buddha.

Next we go to section seventeen, "No Self in the End." The Buddha has explained to us what the tool for becoming a Buddha is. Actually, anything in the world can be used as a tool but to become a Buddha you need wisdom. The first paramita is not the first paramita but is merely called the first paramita. If you think that you have a lot of wisdom and that you're very smart, this is first-class stupidity. What is first-class wisdom?

At this alambana, there is no pondering or worrying. This is the first paramita. It is with this that one should seek enlightenment. Right from the very beginning, the Buddha told us not to dwell. Here in section seventeen, the Buddha presents another way of saying this, "no dwelling" and "no form." Emptiness, not dwelling and no form are the three seals of prajna; these are the same as emptiness, no form and no vow. The *Diamond Sutra* doesn't mention the word *emptiness* even once, but if there is no dwelling and no form, naturally you have emptiness. Empty and not empty fall into two ends of a spectrum and so aren't mentioned. Why can't we become Buddhas, become enlightened? First of all, we can't let go of our perception of a body. We always feel as if we have a self, a body and get very attached to these bodies. Let go of the notion of a body, a world, Buddha lands; let go of all notions of time and space, body and mind and then practice your cultivation.

In section eighteen, "One Substance, Same Perception," the Buddha tells us the second important method. Examine your own mind to see that the past mind is unobtainable, the present mind is unobtainable, the future mind is unobtainable and the unobtainable is unobtainable. This is what is called unobtainable. The past mind is already gone, the future is yet to arrive. The moment you say or think "present," it goes by, gone, like a dream or an illusion. Our afflictions come from not seeing clearly these three minds. It's like old men chatting in the barber shop about days gone by. They're gone, unobtainable. I fear having to chat with older people. Most of the time, I just nod my head as they reminisce about these or those days. The older one gets, the more one talks about the past. What's worse is that each time they assume you've never heard it before! I can really sympathize with young people who complain about talking to old people. Even I can't stand it. The biggest problem is that they are mired in a notion of dharma. They only want to think about the years gone by because they don't dare think about the future. The future is very unreliable.

Young people are only thinking about the future—what will I do tomorrow, this summer... So when you put old people and young people together, one thinking past, one thinking future, on what ground can they meet? Is it any wonder they don't mix well? Some advice to older people, think about the future. If there is no place to go, then start thinking of Amitabha's Western Paradise. Don't think of the past; the past is unobtainable.

Young people should also pay attention; the future mind is also unobtainable. Always dreaming about where and what you want to be in the future. I'll fill you in on the picture, you will become old like me in the future! What, you don't think you'll grow old? You want a short life? If you want a long life, you'll have to grow old. Still, that mind of the future is unobtainable, so, don't dwell on it!

The Buddha Dharma is the most practical; there's only the present moment. And the most realistic; the present mind is unobtainable. Understanding this one's mind is at peace, clear and pure. This is the Buddha Dharma. The three minds are unobtainable. At all times you should look into this carefully. The past is gone, the future yet to arrive; as soon as I say present, it's gone. Isn't that wonderful?

Everyone here meditates. That moment that you cross your legs goes by, now they're crossed. Don't pay attention to whether or not your ch'i is flowing. The future mind is unobtainable. Right now your legs are crossed. Relax, the present mind is unobtainable. Still, you soon feel fidgety, right? But you still keep sitting, cultivating Tao. This is so greedy! Even more so at this moment, you keep thinking about the unobtainable future. You imagine yourself looking like Amitabha with a lovely round face, light emitting from the crown, third eye, looking out over the Buddha land. Sitting there imagining things like this is calling trouble to yourself. I hope you young people will pay special attention to this. Sometimes when I hear you talk, it makes me very nervous. You must first learn how to be in the world. If you are successful at this, you will be successful at Buddhism. It's like building a house—you need a good foundation. You need the foundation of being a good person, acting in the world before you can become a Buddha.

The three minds being unobtainable is covered quite clearly up through section twenty two, "No Dharma to Attain." No Dharma to attain, the Buddha is very clearly stating this again. Do not dwell in notions of dharma. Having something which to attain is dwelling in a notion of form. It is not Tao, not the Dharma and not attaining.

In section twenty-six, "Dharmakaya Without Form," it talks about the emptiness of appearances. The Buddha recited a gatha, *"One who looks for me in appearance, or pursues me in sound, follows paths leading astray, and cannot perceive the Tathagata."* In this he points directly to one of the biggest mistakes that practitioners make, looking for Tao in appearance or sound. These notions, these paths are paths leading astray. If you follow them, you cannot perceive the Tathagata and will not succeed at cultivation.

Immediately following this in section twenty-seven, "No Annihilation," the Buddha did not speak of void emptiness nor of the perspective of annihilation. The Buddha Dharma is neither of these. In seeking Supreme Enlightenment, don't hold the view of annihilation. Following this, section thirty, "Union of Form," talks about the substance of the Tathagata; substance, appearance and function; the Path of Buddhahood; the theory of the dharmakaya, sambogakaya and nirmanakaya; and the theory of fusion of form. The Buddha did not talk about the nihilist view of emptiness nor did He speak of the common idea of existence. Existence is illusory and emptiness is true emptiness. True emptiness isn't voidness, it is that from which this illusory world arises. Existence is temporary serendipity.

At the start, the Buddha spoke about vowing to bring all sentient beings to liberation, to save all beings, but that actually, there are no sentient beings which are liberated. Why is this? One's original nature will liberate one. All phenomena are like a dream, an illusion, a bubble and a shadow; like a flash of lightning and a drop of dew. Thus, you should perceive them. At one with Suchness, do not attach to form. Why is it that no beings are liberated? Why does it depend on their self nature for them to be liberated? If you have taught before, you will understand. When you teach others, you will see that it is only the students who have a capacity and who help themselves, that really succeed in their studies. All you, as the teacher, do is stimulate their interest and facilitate the opening of their inherent wisdom. It's not as if the teacher uses mantras or incantations. Nor is it like a doctor performing acupuncture, whereby the right or wrong placement of a needle will make the difference in the cure. The wisdom is naturally there; the Buddha has not saved anyone. One's original nature will liberate one. Each being is a Buddha. One just needs to live a plain and simple life. What is a plain and simple life? Think back to the opening of the *Diamond Sutra*. Don't forget about the first section, wearing clothes, eating food, washing up and meditating. Be a sincere person and conduct your affairs honestly. Don't engage in the least harmful behavior and diligently work toward the benefit of all beings. No more needs to be said. At the beginning of the sutra, the Buddha has set an example for us. He put on his robes, went begging, ate, washed his feet, arranged his seat and sat down. He didn't wait for his disciples to prepare everything for him. He did it himself, fluffing up his meditation cushion and straightening it before he sat.

Just when he was comfortable, that student Subhuti asked a question, not letting him rest. With a full belly, he had no choice other than to speak. And finally, at this moment, the teaching is finished. One volume of the *Diamond Sutra* is complete.